THE BANKNOTE YEARBOOK

THE
BANKNOTE YEARBOOK

—FOURTH EDITION

Edited by
James Mackay, MA, DLitt
John W. Mussell, FRGS
and
the Editorial Team of BANKNOTE NEWS

Consultant Editors
Barry Boswell
Laurence Pope, LL.B Solicitor
Martin Mac Devitt

ISBN 1 870 192 69 9

Published by
TOKEN PUBLISHING LIMITED
Orchard House, Heathpark, Honiton, Devon EX14 1YD, UK
Telephone: 01404 46972   Fax: 01404 44788
e-mail: info@tokenpublishing.com   Website: www.tokenpublishing.com

Printed and Bound by J. H. Haynes & Co. Ltd., Sparkford

CONTENTS

PREFACE

THE fourth edition of the BANKNOTE YEARBOOK has been in gestation for almost two years, but we hope that it has been well worth the wait. The most important feature of this new volume is the addition of a comprehensive numbering system for all notes which we hope will be a great boon to collectors, whatever area they may specialise in. The system is simple to understand and is one which can be adjusted as new issues or extra entries are added. We are indebted to Martin Mac Devitt for permission to use his already well-established numbering system for the Irish section which fits neatly into our own, which simply uses the letters of the relevant country as a prefix. A further important enhancement this year is the full use of colour illustrations throughout the book which we hope will be a source of great pleasure to collectors. Apart from the annual survey of banknote design and a resume of the events over the period from the beginning of 2003 till the end of 2004, we have taken the opportunity to add several other features of permanent reference value.

Following the launch of the European single currency in 2002 the international monetary scene has been relatively quiet. Inflation continues to rock certain countries, mainly in Latin America, but on New Year's Day 2005 Turkey replaced the Turk lirasi (TL) which had sunk to such a low point that millions were required to purchase a postcard, far less send it. It has been replaced by the Yeni Turk lirasi (YTL) at the rate of a million to one. As a result the kurus makes a comeback, as the yeni kurus (new kurus) worth 10,000 old pounds.

Inflation is an economic headache for the countries affected, but from the notaphilic viewpoint it is a fertile source of relatively inexpensive material for the collector, as witness the prolific and colourful notes of Argentina, Brazil, Mexico, Peru, Bolivia, Venezuela and other countries which have seen the value of their money plummet in recent years.

The biggest problem facing the note-issuing banks and monetary authorities, however, lies in trying to keep one jump ahead of the counterfeiter. Not so many years ago the chief threat of forgery was posed by colour photocopiers, but now even personal computers, scanners and colour laser printers have become so powerful and sophisticated that they can often generate tolerable imitations of notes at a very low cost. The miracle is that counterfeiting has not been practised on an even larger scale.

It has forced many countries to take counter measures, embedding more and more complex security features into their notes to defeat the forger. Holograms, metal foil strips, watermarks, microprocessor printing, latent imaging all play their part, and now the era of the "smart" banknote, with a computer chip embedded in its surface, is just around the corner. The technology of note production has advanced by leaps and bounds in the past decade alone —all a far cry from the early 19th century when notes could be forged by any half competent engraver.

The most conservative country in the world, so far as its paper money is concerned, is the United States where the Federal Reserve Notes—the familiar "greenbacks"—had remained substantially unchanged for 70 years. During the period under review several denominations had subtly changed their appearance. Although the basic portraits had remained, they had been considerably re-engraved, and more recently colour was injected into the obverse in the $20 and $50 denominations in a bid to defeat the counterfeiters working overseas to undermine the almighty dollar.

The wonder is that the US Treasury has not adopted the measures applied elsewhere (especially holographic elements) to combat this rising menace. Even more remarkably, the humble dollar note portraying George Washington continues unchanged, even though you need more than two of them to purchase a gallon of gasoline or a hamburger. The life expectancy of a dollar bill these days must be only a matter of weeks, and until it is withdrawn and demonetised the attempts to introduce a circulating dollar coin will continue to be futile. The USA must be the only country in the western world that has such a low value note in everyday use. Interestingly, the European Central Bank gave some consideration to the issue of a 1 Euro note to compete with the Washington dollar note, but saner counsels eventually prevailed and no note below €5 is ever likely to appear.

The Euro notes have had their own share of problems from counterfeiting, and the time may now have come to make a radical overhaul of the designs in light of the latest technology. This will become imperative when the ten countries which were admitted to the European Union in May 2004 become eligible to enter the single currency zone.

The hobby of notaphily continues to grow steadily, not just as a sideline to a collection of coins and tokens but spreading farther afield as more and more philatelists become aware of the affinity between stamps and paper money—produced by the same security printers, designed and engraved by the same skilled artists and craftsmen, often deriving their motifs from the same images. Being two-dimensional they can be stored in albums. There is even a cross-over in the use of stamps as money in times of emergency or in the attachment of stamps to banknotes to revalidate them (as in the case of Austria, Hungary and Czechoslovakia).

Few coin dealers trade in stamps, but an increasing number of stamp dealers are branching out into paper money. At the grass roots level we note an increasing level of interest, year on year, at coin and stamp fairs, but at the upper end of the market auction records are continually being created and then surpassed. That confidence in the stability of paper money as a collectable is growing throughout the world is proven by the success of paper money auctions in Singapore and Hong Kong as well as in the UK and the USA. The tremendous growth of the collectables market in general in China, as economic conditions forge ahead, shows where the future of the hobby lies—singularly appropriate as the Chinese invented paper money in the first place.

Of course, another reason why paper money appears more and more attractive as an investment is the continuing poor performance of traditional stocks and shares, while low interest rates make savings less attractive. The steady growth of the notaphilic market inspires new confidence, and in turn, that confidence attracts more collectors to the hobby and then the laws of supply and demand ensure that growth will continue.

The IT Revolution which affects every aspect of our lives is having its effect on the paper money trade as well. Not so long ago it was quite remarkable to find a dealer who had a website; now this medium has become indispensable as more and more buying and selling is conducted on-line. A sign of the times, however, has been the disappearance of the InterCol shop in London's Camden Passage, a mecca for collectors for a quarter of a century. High overheads, rates and other running costs have led to the demise of many a collectors' shop in recent years.

E-shopping has become a buzzword of the 21st century, but it is not without its pitfalls, and the number of cases of material offered on the Internet turning out to be in a lower grade of condition than advertised—or, worse—cleaned, ironed or "reconditioned" as reported from time to time in COIN NEWS—gives fresh impetus to the old adage "let the buyer beware".

In producing a volume such as this we have had to call on a number of experts, all of whom have given freely of their knowledge and equally importantly, of their time. We are grateful to the Central Bank of Ireland for supplying the stunning illustrations of the notes of the Republic of Ireland. Barry Boswell has been the major contributor for the information and the illustrations in the other catalogue sections, whilst the English section has been supplied entirely by Laurence Pope. With his unerring knowledge of Irish paper money Martin Mac Devitt has kindly checked the Irish section and, in addition, amongst others John Harvey, Alan Kelly, Mark Ray and Noel Simpson have all been of immense help in the preparation of the book, which we hope will be received enthusiastically by the collecting fraternity.

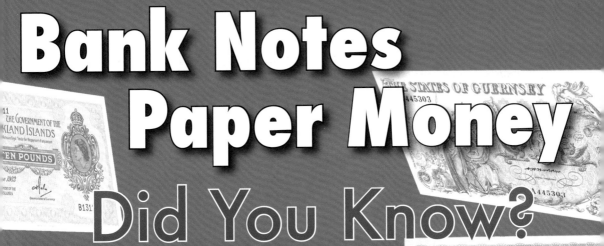

That was THE YEAR that was!

AN at-a-glance résumé of the main events and occurrences that affected banknotes and paper money during the past two years as reported in *Banknote News*, the note section of COIN NEWS.

January 2003

The death is intimated of Ernest Quarmby, the Isle of Man specialist who wrote the standard work on Manx paper money.

Kate Gibson takes over the business of her late father C. Gibson and begins trading as Kate's Paper Money, from Camberley, Surrey.

February 2003

Currency News, a periodical for paper money collectors, is launched at www.currencynews. info.

Rotographic Publications launch *Military Money*, a 56-page booklet on all forms of tokens and scrip used by armed forces in peace and war.

Problems arise with the new Elizabeth Fry £5 notes, as the serial numbers can be rubbed off. The Bank of England hastily remedies the problem, the new serials being lower down and very close to the £5 FIVE POUNDS inscription.

The ninth edition of *World Paper Money*, edited by Neil Shafer and George S. Cuhaj, is released by Krause Publications.

March 2003

A new record price is established at a Noble Numismatics auction in Sydney, when a Queensland Treasury £1 note (above right) estimated at $150,000 sells for $180,000 ($209,700 with buyer's premium). In the same sale, the John Pettit collection of promissory notes sells for $400,000 against a pre-sale estimate of $250,000.

The Bank of England mounts an exhibition tracing the history of the £5 note from 1793 to the present day.

The European Central Bank publishes a report on counterfeit Euro notes. Out of a total of 145,153 forgeries detected, no fewer than 121,826 were of the 50 Euro note.

A hitherto unrecorded note of the Coventry & Warwickshire Bank fetches £950 at a DNW sale on March 19.

April 2003

The Papermoney, Bond & Share 2003 show takes place at Valkenburg (Maastricht) on April 4-6, attracting dealers and collectors from all over the world.

In a bid to defeat counterfeiters using computer skills the United States Treasury introduced colour elements in its "greenback" notes, beginning with the $20 bill.

At the Spink sale on April 9 an extremely rare and possibly unique Palestinian £100 note of 1927 realises the record sum of £48,000 against a pre-sale estimate of £8,000–£10,000. A Palestinian £50 note of 1928 sold for £34,500.

At Bonham's sale on April 16 the rare Portsmouth Bank of England £5 sells for £20,700.

May 2003

The Pringle collection of Scottish banknotes is sold by Spink at an auction in the George Inter-Continental Hotel, Edinburgh on May 21, realising a grand total of £282,000.

The *Standard Price Guide of Malaysia Banknotes and Coins*, covering all issues from 1939 till 2002, is published by the Malaysian Numismatic Society.

De La Rue takes over the Bank of England printing works at Debden, paying £10 to secure a seven-year contract.

July 2003

With the release of the Bank of England £10 note portraying Charles Darwin, the obsolete note portraying Charles Dickens is withdrawn from circulation and ceases to be legal tender at the end of this month.

August 2003

A major sale of bank notes of the British Isles takes place at Carlisle on August 2.

De La Rue unveil plans to open a banknote printing plant in South Africa, the first contract being to produce cheques for the First National Bank of South Africa.

The Bank of England stages a summer exhibition introducing the characters on its banknotes to the general public. Actors in period costume re-create Darwin, Dickens, Faraday and Stephenson.

September 2003

Banknotes4U is launched by Roger and Liz Outing of Huddersfield.

The Bank of England authorises the Royal Mint to produce replicas of banknotes in .999 gold.

Following his promotion to Senior Deputy Governor of the Bank of Canada, Paul Jenkins becomes the latest signatory of Canadian notes.

October 2003

At the Spink auction on October 2, 1936 £500 and £1,000 Bank of England notes sell for £4,200 and £17,000 respectively. A Bristol £5 of 1894 realises £13,500 while a London £10 of 1869 fetches £13,000. The sale of British notes nets £260,948 while the sale of world notes the following day realises a total of £509,665.

Coinex takes place at the Marriott Hotel, London on October 10–11.

The second edition of *United States Paper Money Errors* by Dr Frederick Bart is published by Krause.

The Commonwealth Bank of Australia gives permission to Banknotes (a private company) to print replicas of the legendary £1,000 note of 1914. Only 1,000 notes are produced, mainly for museums and educational institutions.

November 2003

Almost 400 lots of world banknotes are included in the Ponterio mail bid sale on November 11.

December 2003

All 10 franc notes issued by France are demonetised at the end of the month, along with all old francs and the 50 and 100 new franc notes of the 1960s and 1970s.

The European Central Bank considers the inclusion of the radio microchip developed by Hitachi as a security feature of its notes. It also contemplates the issue of a 1 Euro note to compete with the ever-popular US dollar note.

Slovenia celebrates its imminent entry into the European Union by overprinting its high-value notes with the date "2004" in gold.

On December 15 Iraq replaces the notes portraying Saddam Hussein with a new series produced by De La Rue.

Dmitri Kharitonov publishes his *Jewish Paper Money in Russia*, detailing the issue of some 300 different notes in Jewish communities throughout the Tsarist empire.

The death of Ian R. Monins of Jersey is reported. He was widely regarded as a leading expert on the banknotes and coinage of the Channel Islands.

Following a serious stroke at her Texas home, Azie Taylor Morton, whose signature appears on the 1977 US Federal Reserve notes, dies at the age of 67.

January 2004

Merlyn Lowther retires as Head Cashier of the Bank of England and is replaced by Andrew Bailey whose signature appears on all notes printed after January 1.

The death of Stan Firmin is announced. An American by birth, he had been long established as a banknote dealer in Belgium.

February 2004

The De La Rue group's balance sheet for the six months ending September 30, 2003 reveals that the company made a profit of £19.6 million, mostly from the security printing division.

Canadian Currency Grading Service Inc of Calgary is launched, offering a service to dealers and collectors in the grading of Canadian banknotes.

March 2004

Banknotes4U produce an extensive list of cheques and banking memorabilia.

Adobe incorporates an anti-counterfeiting element in its Photoshop software programme, supplied by the international Central Bank Counterfeit Deterrence Group. This detects a complex geometric pattern that appears on most banknotes and warns the operator that it cannot proceed further.

April 2004

Top price at the Noble Numismatic auction on April 1 is $181,740 paid for a Queensland Treasury £1 note. It had been preserved in an envelope by Edward Drury, General Manager of Queensland's National Bank in 1893 and was the first number issued.

Milt Blackburn retires and disposes of his entire stock to Canadian dealers Olmstead Currency of St Stephen, New Brunswick.

The Bank of England mounts an exhibition entitled "From Quill Pen to Computer" which runs until October 27. The exhibition looks at the people behind the scenes at the Bank of England over the centuries.

Spink's sale of world banknotes on April 27 included about 150 lots of Scottish notes offered by the Royal Bank of Scotland, raising over £40,000 for the Autism charity. A 20 shilling note of the British Linen Company, dated October 1805, sells for £14,255.

May 2004

Trevor Wilkin takes over the new issues feature for COIN NEWS from the London Banknote and Monetary Research Centre. An Australian, he also writes a regular column for the *Australasian Coin & Banknote* magazine.

The death is announced of Gerald Bouey, Governor of the Bank of Canada in 1973–87, whose signature appears on the notes of that period.

Kate Gibson launches her website www. katespapermoney.com.

Baldwin holds a specialised sale of Islamic material, including a set of three Zanzibar uniface notes which sell for £15,173.

The Royal Bank of Scotland celebrates the 250th anniversary of the Open Golf Championship with a special £5 note depicting the Royal and Ancient Clubhouse at St Andrews on the reverse.

June 2004

Jerzy Koziczynski publishes the third volume of his mammoth survey of Polish notes, detailing the zloty notes from 1919 to 1938. Previous volumes have covered the earliest notes and the mark currency of 1916–23 respectively.

The banknote business of Bill Rosedale, who has retired, is taken over by Collectors Gallery of Shrewsbury.

July 2004

Bruce Goulborn of Rhyl launches a specialist list of English errors and oddities.

August 2004

Following the success of last summer's "live show", the Bank of England stages a second exhibition at which actors in costume re-enact the lives of the Duke of Wellington, Florence Nightingale, Charles Dickens and Sir Isaac Newton, featured on various banknotes.

September 2004

Yasha Beresiner of InterCol leaves Camden Passage after 25 years and concentrates on internet trading at www.intercol.co.uk.

The fifth Monexpo International Banknote Fair takes place at the Hotel Ibis, Paris on September 26.

The United States launches its new-look $50 note on September 28, incorporating many features as well as colour aimed at defeating counterfeiters.

Canada continues its scenic series entitled "Canadian Journey" with a new $20 on September 29, following the $5 (hockey players) and $10 (remembrance and peace-keeping).

October 2004

Spink's banknote sale on October 1 includes the first part of the Karouni collection of English notes. The sale of 1,400 lots also includes a fine selection of notes from the English provincial banks. Top price is £28,000 for the Peppiatt £1,000 note and the total realised is over £780,000.

The London World Paper Money Show takes place over the weekend of October 2–3.

The North-West Chapter of the International Banknote Society in Burnley celebrates its 30th anniversary.

November 2004

A comprehensive reconstruction of the note registers of the National Bank of Scotland covering the period from 1893 to 1959 is published, a mammoth operation which takes 20 years to complete. The original registers are believed to have been destroyed when the National Commercial Bank merged with the Royal Bank in 1969.

Spink's banknote sale in Hong Kong on November 20 nets over £300,000, indicating the recovery of the Far Eastern market after a quiet period.

The very first share certificate issued by Deutsche Bank in 1871 (above), is sold by Morton & Eden on November 23. The certificate number 00001 was found among the papers of Max Steinthal, a victim of the Holocaust, along with his Old Master paintings which the Nazis had stored in a Dresden museum and which were subsequently restored to his descendants.

Roger Outing publishes *Cheques of Barclays Bank,* believed to be the first detailed price guide to the cheques of one bank.

December 2004

The Governing Council of the ECB decides not to issue low denomination euro banknotes.

Milan Alusic retires from the position of General Secretary of the International Bank Note Society after 27 years.

The
Best and
worst
of recent banknote designs

UNLIKE the previous period reviewed (mid-2001 to the end of 2002) when the introduction of the Euro notes was arguably the single greatest event in the entire history of paper money, the only major political event reflected in the notes of 2003–4 was the toppling of Saddam Hussein which prompted a new issue of notes in Iraq.

Surveying the entire scene, as reflected in the new issues reported in COIN NEWS, one is left with the overall impression that portraiture now reigns supreme, as the vast majority of new notes regard a portrait on the obverse as almost *de rigueur*.

Of course, there were a few notable exceptions, although only one entire series was completely devoid of portraits. This was the set of six denominations introduced by the Central Bank of Qatar late in 2003, one of the few states in the Arab world that still clings to the Koranic ban on portraits. Previous notes had featured oil derricks, symbolic of the country's wealth, but the new series has provided a wide range of fauna and flora, as well as some of the extraordinary buildings that reflect Qatar's phenomenal development in quite recent years. These attractive images have been confined to the reverse, with text in English, but all notes have a common obverse inscribed in Arabic and featuring an arabesque motif with palm trees.

The other series which has largely, if not quite completely, dispensed with portraiture was released in Iraq in mid-October 2003, consequent on the fall of Saddam whose image had graced the previous notes. The

Iraqi notes prior to the invasion of Kuwait had portrayed the dictator in military uniform but after the first Gulf War notes portrayed him in western civilian clothes. Indeed, the last note prior to Saddam's downfall was a 10,000 dinar which portrayed him alongside a modern observatory (or perhaps advanced air defence system!) though the reverse clung to traditional values with a view of Al Mustansiryya School and an astrological medallion.

Now, however, the 1,000 and 10,000 dinar notes have replaced him with a turbaned and bearded portrait of Abulhasan ibn al Hisham, previously portrayed on the 10d notes of 1980-2 and one of the outstanding medieval Islamic scholars. The rest of the series features an interesting contrast between modern buildings and traditional Islamic art forms, designed and executed in the best De La Rue tradition.

In February 2003 the Bank of Tanzania introduced an entirely new series from 500 to 10,000 shillings which focused almost entirely on the rich wildlife of the country (obverse) and historic buildings (reverse). The only concession to portraiture was provided by the 1000 shilling note, the most

popular denomination, which bore a portrait of Dr Julius Nyerere, the first President of the Republic.

In April 2003 Cambodia adopted a new 500 riel note providing a fascinating example of the contrast between ancient and modern architecture. The front of the note bore a new image of the great Angkor Wat Temple, truly one of the wonders of the world, but the reverse featured the Kizuna Bridge spanning the Mekong in Kompong City, a nod at Japan whose money and technology had made it possible.

Hitherto the Faeroe Islands have flirted with portraits of the poet Nolosyar Pall and the linguist V. U. Hammarshaimb. Perhaps these were regarded as worthy but dull and it is significant that the series now in course of release has eschewed portraits of famous Faeroese in favour of a much more frankly pictorial approach. This began in 2003 with a 100 kronur and continued with the 200k in 2004. The first of these has a startlingly original motif, the tail of a cod symbolising the importance of the fishing industry. This is set against the background of an abstract watercolour by Zacharias Heinsen symbolising the sea. The reverse reproduces Heinsen's rather impressionistic view of Klaksvik, the country's second town (after Torshavn, the capital).

This off-beat approach is also apparent in the 200k whose obverse is dominated by a ghost moth, while the reverse depicts Heinsen's watercolour of the rocks of Tindholmur near Vagar. The watermark is a ram's head (an allusion to the name of the archipelago which translates as "sheep islands"). One of the security features on these notes is a holographic cruciform roundel in the top left-hand corner of the obverse, based on one of the carved pews from the medieval church at Kirkjubour.

The latest issue from Rwanda is also frankly pictorial, the front showing a ploughing scene while the back depicts an idyllic scene of a lake fringed by rugged mountains, clearly aimed at restoring the republic's hard-hit tourist industry.

The only other non-portrait note to come under notice in this period was released by Belarus, a 50,000 rouble which conformed to the existing series adopted in 2000 when the currency was reformed and 1000 old roubles became one new rouble. Judging by this high denomination, the new rouble has been rapidly following its predecessor into the maw of inflation. The obverse depicts the Mir Castle, a UNESCO World Heritage site while the reverse depicts a montage of architectural details from the castle. The watermark also features the castle, so the resulting note is an interesting example of a banknote in which all the design features are wholly integrated.

Busts Galore

Only two countries launched a complete portrait series during this period; in both cases these elements were placed on the right-hand side of the obverse which seems to be the preferred position in most cases. The series from Jordan is outstanding, not only in overall concept and layout but also in specific details. One has to regard this set in the context of the Middle East which has been undergoing considerable turmoil in very recent times. Jordan is perceived as a bastion of western-style democracy combined with Islamic traditional values, the best of both worlds, and these notes reflect this duality.

Thus we are treated to a veritable portrait gallery of the Hashemite dynasty from Abdullah I (1882–1951), founder of the kingdom to his namesake who succeeded Hussein in 1999. Interestingly, while Hussein II was previously portrayed bare-headed in western dress, he is almost unrecognisable in this line-up, bearded and clad in Arab dress.

The five kings of Jordan are joined by Hussein bin Ali (1853–1931), King of the Hejaz, on the 1 dinar note. In 1926 Hussein's kingdom was conquered by Ibn Saud, founder of Saudi Arabia, which explains why there is little love lost between the Jordanians and the Saudis to this day. Pictorial motifs on both sides of these notes present the colourful history and culture of Jordan from the overthrow of Turkish suzerainty in World War I to the present day. The layouts are well-balanced and the engraving is exquisite, making this series by far the most aesthetically attractive of all the issues under review.

By contrast, the only other all-portrait series in this line-up comes a pretty poor second. The facing portraits on the series adopted by Nicaragua in May 2003 merely reprise those from earlier series, but the layout and inscriptions have been "modernised", i.e. the cult of minimalism has been re-inforced . In fact, the dominant feature of the obverses is the denomination, rendered in very large numerals in the centre and then repeated in all four corners on back as well as front. The national arms occupy the centre of the reverse with a small pictorial vignette on the left to balance the watermark on the right. The use of a watermark (surely a redundant feature when a foil strip, hologram and latent imaging provide far greater security against counterfeiting) prevents a more panoramic treatment of the reverse as well as rendering the obverse insipid in general.

A much more imaginative use of portraiture combined with pictorialism is to be found on the 20 grivna of the Ukraine showing the scientist Ivan Franko and the façade of the Lvov Opera House. This was the first in a projected new series linking famous personalities to outstanding architectural landmarks.

Very few notes place the bust portrait centre stage although this tends to restrict the scope for the secondary images. In this category come the new 10,000 and 20,000 kip notes from Laos which carry a portrait of Kaysone Phomvihan (1920–92), the country's leading politician from 1975 till his death. The fronts of both notes also incorporate a tiny image of a temple that sits rather uneasily on Phomvihan's left shoulder, but the reverse motifs in both cases provide panoramic views of the lush countryside. Not quite central but well away from the right of the note is the portrait of Jose Maria Vargas on the new 50,000 bolivar note from Venezuela, the reverse featuring the Plaza of the Rectorado and the clock of the Central University—a nice one for collectors of notes with a horological theme.

Not many notes place the portrait on the left either, although an attractive example is provided by the last issue from the former Yugoslavia (now renamed Serbia and Montenegro). This was a 5,000 dinar note portraying Slobodan Jovanovic (1869–1957), lawyer, historian and leading figure of the Serbian Academy of Sciences and Fine Arts. This is one of those notes with a horizontal obverse but vertical reverse and shows Jovanovic standing in front of the Federal Assembly (an interior view being included for good measure).

The vast majority of note confine themselves to a single portrait but a noteworthy exception is the 10,000 cedi note from Ghana which has a group portrait of the men who came together in 1947 to found the United Gold Coast Convention, the precursor of Ghanaian independence. The six men are Kwame Nkrumah, Emanuel Obetsebi-Lamptey, Ebenezer Ako-Adjei, William Ofori-Atta, Dr Joseph Boakye Danquah and Edward Akuffo-Addo. Appropriately, the reverse depicts the Independence Monument in Accra.

Commemorative Notes

There were relatively few commemorative notes in this period. The Cayman Islands released a dollar note to celebrate their Quincentennial, the islands having been discovered by Columbus in 1503. In fact, this was only a modification of the existing note with double dates and a Quincentennial logo inserted in the centre of the obverse.

This is a ploy sometimes adopted by the Scottish banks (as, for example, the Clydesdale's £10 of 2000 with MM prefix and an inscription celebrating the Millennium). In the previous edition we noted the £5 note of the Royal Bank which celebrated Her Majesty's Golden Jubilee with an entirely redesigned reverse; in the period under review this bank produced a very attractive £5 note whose reverse celebrated the 250th anniversary of the Open Golf Championship with a splendid view of the Royal and Ancient Clubhouse at St Andrews.

After the terrible tragedy that overtook the Nepalese Royal Family when the crown prince went berserk with a machine gun and killed his nearest and dearest, The Nepal Rastra Bank produced a 10 rupeee note in

2003 to discreetly mark the first anniversary of the accession of King Gyanendra, portrayed on the left of the obverse, with the two antelopes reverse from previous notes of this value. Although intended primarily as a commemorative, it remains in general circulation. It is chiefly notable for the fact that it is the first polymer note from Nepal and also has a stylised Nepalese crown in an oval window below the watermark as a security feature. Gyanendra's portrait has now replaced that of his father on the other notes in the series.

Cuba has played a notable part in the development of the commemorative concept, and this is maintained in a new 200 peso, introduced in July 2003 to celebrate the 50th anniversary of the assault on the Moncada Fortress in Santiago, the opening round of the war waged by Fidel Castro on the dictatorship of General Batista. The obverse features a smiling portrait of the revolutionary hero Camilo Cienfuegos

while the reverse shows the dramatic scene of the guerrilla attack on the fortress.

Also from the Caribbean comes the 20 gourde note of Haiti celebrating the bicentenary of the world's first Negro republic, with double dates at the foot of the obverse. The front of the note has a bust of Toussaint L'Ouverture, the architect of independence from the French, while the reverse has the book of the Constitution opened at the middle. This note was subsequently retained in permanent circulation although this denomination was not previously in use.

Notaphily
the hobby

NOTAPHILY, the hobby of collecting paper money, is of relatively recent growth. The name for the hobby was invented as recently as 1969 and is not entirely satisfactory since it is partly from the Latin—*nota* (a note) and the Greek—*philos* (love), when it should preferably have been derived from the same language. That collectors should only have got around to coining an expression for their hobby within the past three decades or so is an indication of its very recent development. Yet there is evidence to suggest that paper money was being collected more than two centuries ago, for printed sheets of different *assignats* and *mandats* were produced as souvenirs and must have catered to people who were interested in them as historical documents of the French Revolution, rather than as actual spending money.

It is really only since World War I that paper money has been universally accepted in place of silver and gold and thus it is within the past three quarters of a century that notaphily has become popular. Many of the notes of the broken banks, or the paper money produced in times of economic upheaval, were only preserved by chance or by people who laid aside specimens as curiosities.

There was no market for obsolete paper money until fairly recently and notes were seldom acquired in large quantities for distribution to dealers and collectors. At the same time, apart from a few eccentric characters who collected paper money, collectors were few and far between, until after World War I. Some fantastically large collections of banknotes were formed in the nineteenth century and formed the nucleus of our present-day knowledge of the subject.

Ludwig Clericus of Magdeburg, for example, began collecting paper money in the 1870s. Clericus wrote several important books and many articles about paper money. After his death the German State Printing Works in Berlin purchased his collection but unfortunately it was destroyed in the bombing of Berlin in 1945. Most of the great nineteenth and early twentieth century collections were formed in Germany or Austria and many of them suffered great losses during the two world wars. The Pflumer collection, amounting to over 10,000 items, was purchased by the Marquess of Bute, who was also noted for his collection of airmail and war stamps, and these collections suffered heavy loss when the London home of the Marquess was destroyed during the London Blitz.

Notaphily received its first great stimulus during and after World War I with the appearance of the high-denomination German banknotes and the myriads of *Notgeld*. For the first time the hobby captured the imagination of the man in the street as well as the wealthy

Examples of Notgeld.

The introduction of the Euro notes has started many new collectors in the hobby..

scholar or historian. Interest waned in the 1930s, but rose again during and after World War II and a new generation of collectors was recruited to the hobby by the vast quantities of Japanese occupation currency which flooded Europe and America after the war. As coin and medal collecting boomed in popularity in the 1960s so also did paper money collecting. Hitherto collectors had little opportunity to purchase examples of paper money. Occasionally coin dealers would include a few banknotes in their stock but, generally speaking, they took little interest in this aspect of numismatics and knowledgeable collectors could often pick up rare items for a fraction of their true value. Now there are many important dealers who specialise in paper money and publish detailed catalogues and price lists.

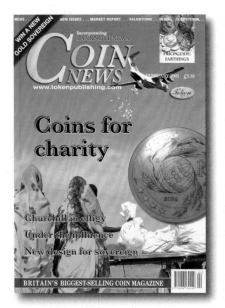

COIN NEWS, Britain's biggest selling coin magazine includes a BANKNOTE NEWS section every month. To subscribe call 01404 44166, fax 01404 44788 or visit: www.tokenpublishing.com for a free sample.

Numismatic magazines on both sides of the Atlantic now give a great deal of space to features on paper money and carry extensive advertising from dealers who specialise in this field. Collecting is made easier, especially for the beginner, by the attractive packets of mixed notes on offer. Packs of obsolete banknotes have also been given away as premium offers by manufacturers of many different commodities, from cigarettes to shampoo. By saving two or more packets or labels from the appropriate brand, the would-be collector could send off to the manufacturer and receive, in return, a bundle of attractive banknotes with which to start off his collection. In recent years there have also been several offers of a similar nature associated with newspaper or magazine promotions.

The traditional methods of acquiring new material should not be overlooked. Sixty years ago, before World War II, when there were no currency restrictions, banks and travel agents were a happy hunting ground for the banknote collector and attractive and unusual specimens of notes from all over the world could be obtained in this way, merely by paying the going exchange rates. There was a time when a friendly local bank manager, especially in a country like Scotland where many different notes were in circulation, might be prevailed upon to keep an eye out for rare or unusual specimens. I recall a bank manager in the Western Isles, during a wartime fund-raising campaign, receiving a bundle of notes of the City of Glasgow Bank which had crashed spectacularly in 1879. The notes had been lovingly hoarded for more than sixty years by some crofter, unaware that they had ceased to have any real monetary value, although their numismatic value must have been not inconsiderable.

Taxi-drivers, hoteliers and shopkeepers, especially those catering largely to tourists and foreign visitors, were another fertile source of collectable banknotes from far and wide. Even nowadays, when money has been largely superseded by credit cards, foreign notes are sometimes proffered in payment of relatively small amounts. Conversely, foreign travel by friends and family can often yield interesting examples of paper money. Servicemen in both world wars as well as a host of minor campaigns often had unrivalled opportunities to secure paper money in large quantities, especially in cases where the paper money has become worthless on account of the downfall of a government or the surrender of a country, as happened with Germany in 1918 and 1945.

Examples of old paper money turn up in the oddest places. Distrust of banks has led many a canny individual to salt away his or her money in the upholstery of furniture or a mattress and little caches of banknotes have often come to light when old bedding and furniture was being broken up. Banknotes have been used as bookmarks by absent-minded individuals, turning up many years later, perhaps when the books were cleared out and sold to a dealer. Antique dealers have sometimes found bundles of old banknotes secreted in the drawers of desks and bureaux and, if the original owner cannot be traced, these notes invariably come into the hands of collectors. Examples of the siege notes from Mafeking and the picturesque notes of the Confederate States have been known to turn up in contemporary correspondence, acquired as curiosities at the time but long-forgotten until brought to light many years after the event. Until the advent of banknote dealers, the search for old paper money added a great deal of zest and excitement to the hobby. Even now, part of the fun of collecting banknotes can lie in the unusual manner in which the prize specimens were obtained.

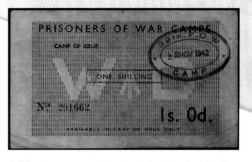

Top: A Prisoner of War note note. Below: A Confederate States of America $10 note.

A guide to
Condition

THE following introduction and Grading Guide is the result of work prepared under the guidance of the Grading Committee of the International Bank Note Society (IBNS) and is reproduced here with their kind permission. This grading guide has become the standard system used throughout the world.

Introduction

Grading is the most controversial component of paper money collecting today. Small differences in grade can mean significant differences in value. The process of grading is so subjective and dependent on external influences such as lighting, that even a very experienced individual may well grade the same note differently on separate occasions.

To facilitate communication between sellers and buyers it is essential that grading terms and their meanings be as standardised and as widely used as possible. This standardisation should reflect common usage as much as practicable. One difficulty with grading is that even the actual grade themselves are not used everywhere by everyone. For example, in Europe the grade "About Uncirculated" (AU) is not in general use, yet in North America it is widespread. The European term "Good VF" may roughly correspond to what individuals in North America call "Extremely fine" (EF).

The grades and definitions as set forth below cannot reconcile all the various systems and grading terminology variants. Rather, the attempt is made here to try and diminish the controversy with some common sense grades and definitions that aim to give more precise meaning to the grading language of paper money.

How to look at a banknote

In order to ascertain the grade of a note, it is essential to examine it out of a holder and under a good light. Move the note around so that the light bounces off at different angles. Try holding the note obliquely, so the note is even with your eye as you look up at the light. Hard to see folds or slight creases will show up under such examination. Some individuals also lightly feel along the surface of the note to detect creasing.

Cleaning, washing, pressing of banknotes

a. Cleaning, washing or pressing paper money is generally harmful and reduces both the grade and the value of the note. At the very least, a washed or pressed note may lose it original sheen and its surface may become lifeless and dull. The defects of a note had, such as folds and creases, may not necessarily be completely eliminated and their tell-tale marks can be detected under a good light. Carelessly washed notes may also have white streaks where the folds or creases where (or still are).

b. Processing of a note which started out as "Extremely Fine" will automatically reduce it at least one full grade.

Unnatural defects

Glue, tape or pencil marks may sometime be successfully removed. While such removal will leave a cleaned surface, it will improve the overall appearance of the note without concealing any of its defects. Under such circumstances, the grade of that note may also be improved.

The words "pinholes", "staple holes", "trimmed". "writing on face", tape marks" etc should always be added to the description of a note. It is realised that certain countries routinely staple their notes together in groups before issue. In such cases, the description can include a comment such as "usual staple holes" or something similar. After all, not everyone knows that certain notes cannot be found otherwise.

The major point of this section is that one cannot lower the overall grade of a note with defects simply because of the defects. The price will reflect the lowered worth of a defective note, but the description must *always* include the specific defects.

The term Uncirculated

The word *Uncirculated* is used in this grading guide only as a qualitative measurement of the appearance of a note. It has nothing at all to do with whether or not an issuer has actually released the note to circulation. Thus, the term "About Uncirculated" is justified and acceptable because so many notes that have never seen hand to hand use have been mishandled so that they are available at best in AU condition.

Either a note is uncirculated in condition or it is not; there can be no degrees of uncirculated. Highlights or defects in colour, centering and the like may be included in a description but the fact that a note is or is not in uncirculated condition should not be a disputable point.

GRADING GUIDE—Definitions of terms

UNCIRCULATED: A perfectly preserved note never mishandled by the issuing authority, a bank teller, the public or a collector. Paper is clean and firm without discoloration. Corners are sharp and square without any evidence of rounding (rounded corners are often a tell tale sign of a cleaned or "doctored" note). *Note: Some note issuers are most often available with slight evidence of very light counting folds which do not "break" the paper. Many collectors and dealers refer to such notes as AU–UNC.*

ABOUT UNCIRCULATED: A virtually perfect note, with some minor handling. May show very slight evidence of bank counting folds at a corner or one light fold through the centre, but not both. An "AU" note cannot be creased, a crease being a hard fold which has usually "broken" the surface of the note. Paper is clean and bright with original sheen. Corners are not rounded. *Note: Europeans will refer to an About Uncirculated or AU note as "EF–Unc" or as just "EF". The Extremely Fine note described below will often be referred to as "GVF" or "Good Very Fine".*

EXTREMELY FINE: A very attractive note with light handling. May have a maximum of three light folds or one strong crease. Paper is clean and firm without discoloration. Corners are sharp and square without evidence of rounding (rounded corners are often a tell tale sign of a cleaned or "doctored" note).

VERY FINE: An attractive note, but with more evidence of handling and wear. May have several folds both vertically and horizontally. Paper must have minimal dirt or possibly colour smudging. Paper itself is still relatively crisp and not floppy. There are no tears in the border area, although the edges do show slight wear. Corners also show wear but not full rounding.

FINE: A note that shows considerable circulation, with many folds, creases and wrinkling. Paper is not excessively dirty but may have some softness. Edges may show much handling with minor tears in the border area. Tears may not extend into the design. There will be no centre hole because of excessive folding. Colours are clear but not very bright. A staple hole or two would not be considered unusual wear in a Fine note. Overall appearance is still on the desirable side.

VERY GOOD: A well used note, abused but still intact. Corners may have much wear and rounding, tiny nicks, tears may extend in to the design, some discoloration may be present, staining may have occurred, and a small hole may sometimes be seen at centre excessive folding. Staple and pinholes are usually present and the note itself is quite limp but NO pieces of the note can be missing. A note in VG condition may still have an overall not unattractive appearance.

GOOD: A well worn and heavily used note. Normal damage from prolonged circulation will include strong multiple folds and creases, stains, pinholes and / or staple holes, dirt, discoloration, edge tears, centre hole, rounded corners and an overall unattractive appearance. No large pieces of the note may be missing. Graffiti is commonly seen on notes in G condition.

FAIR: A totally limp, dirty and very well used note. Larger pieces may be half torn off or missing besides the defects mentioned under the Good category. Tears will be large, obscured portions of the note will be bigger.

POOR: A "rag" with severe damage because of wear, staining, pieces missing, graffiti, larger holes. May have tape holding pieces of the note together. Trimming may have taken place to remove rough edges. A Poor note is desirable only as a "filler" or when such a note is the only one known of that particular issue.

Mounting and housing notes

CERTAIN museum collections and official bank archives are housed in cabinets with sliding frames in which banknotes are mounted on cards between glass panes. While this is a very attractive way of displaying a collection it is also very expensive and takes up a great deal of room. Until relatively recently most notaphilists were content to house their collections in conventional loose-leaf stamp albums, the notes being held in place by transparent mounting corners and the relevant data, such as date of issue, bank and country, could be written up on the page above each note. The disadvantage of this system is that only one side of the banknote could be examined without taking it out of its mounting corners.

An alternative to this, small transparent hinges, like those used by stamp collectors, were used to affix the notes to the album page. By this method the note could easily be turned over so that the back could be examined. This was considered more satisfactory, although many collectors felt uneasy about using stamp hinges which could leave an unsightly mark on the backs of notes and this would detract from their value. This method of mounting is certainly not recommended today.

The solution to these problems, widely disseminated in the 1970s, was the special album with plastic sleeves into which the notes could be inserted. These albums were actually produced initially for housing collections of postcards, but were found to be about the right size for banknotes. Unfortunately it was soon discovered that those sleeves made of polyvinyl chloride (PVC) reacted chemically with notes, either badly discolouring them or even depositing a viscous film on them. Subsequently better types

of plastic such as Mylar film or polyethylene were developed, and these seem to have obviated the risk of contamination.

Today there are many different systems available to the note collector. There are cards (punched with holes to be inserted in ring-binders or peg-fitting albums) with clear rigid plastic fronts, as well as the more conventional "postcard" sleeves. The latter often come with black card inserts, so that notes can be inserted back to back, on either side of the card, but that then brings us back to the original album pages, with only one side of the note readily visible. There are also stout cards with a plastic face, slightly larger than postcard size, which can be stacked in a box or case, with the salient details of the note on narrow cards inserted at the top of the mount and then held upright as if in a filing cabinet. The main thing to remember is that, which ever system you adopt, you preserve your notes in a dust-free atmosphere, at an even temperature and humidity.

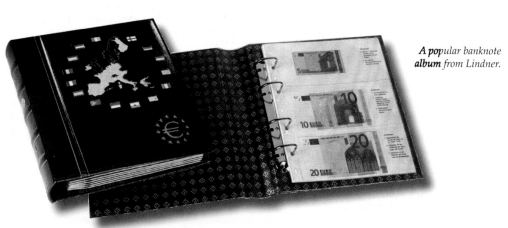

*A **popular** banknote **album** from Lindner.*

Around the world

Currency denominations of the world

Listed here are the names of all the currency units of the world found on banknotes or coins. Many of them have been around for a long time while others are no longer in use. Some of the denominations have been introduced only recently, whilst others are familiar household words, many have been superceded by the euro and other new names. A number of the names are shared by different countries and a few have even been used by different civilisations. We have included all that we know of, past and present.

Abbasi, Abbassi Afghanistan, Georgia, Persia
Afghani Afghanistan
Agora (ot) Israel
Ahmadi Mysore, Yemen
Amani Afghanistan
Anna Burma, India, Pakistan, Kenya, Muscat & Oman
Argentino Argentina
Ariary Malagasy Republic
Ashrafi Afghanistan, Awadh, Bahawalpur, Egypt, Hyderabad
At Laos
Atia Portuguese India
Att Cambodia, Laos, Siam (Thailand)
Aurar (plural **Eyrir**) Iceland
Austral Argentina
Avo Macau, Timor
Baht Thailand
Baiocco (plural **Baiocchi**) Papal States
Baisa Oman
Baiza Kuwait
Baizah Muscat & Oman
Balboa Panama
Ban (plural **Bani** or **Banu**) Roumania
Banica Croatia
Belga Belgium
Besa (plural **Bese**) Ethiopia, Somalia
Bipkwele Equatorial Guinea
Bir (r) Ethiopia
Bogach Yemen
Bolivar Venezuela
Boliviano Bolivia
Butut Gambia
Cache French Indian Settlements
Candareen China
Carbovanetz Ukraine
Cash China, Hong Kong, India, Mysore, Travancore, Turkestan, Vietnam
Cauri Guinea
Cent Australia, Bahamas, Barbados, Belize, Bermuda, Botswana, British East Caribbean Territories, British Honduras, British North Borneo, British Virgin Islands, Brunei, Canada, Cayman Island, Ceylon, China, Cochin China, Cocos (Keeling) Islands, Cook Islands, Curacao, Cyprus, Danish West Indies, East Africa, Ethiopia, Fiji, French Indochina, Gilbert and Ellice Islands, Guyana, Hawaii, Hong Kong, Indonesia, Jamaica, Kenya, Kiao Chau (Kiatschau), Kiribati, Laos, Liberia, Malaya, Malaysia, Malta, Mauritius, Netherlands, Netherlands Antilles, Netherlands Indies, New Zealand, Nova Scotia, Panama, Prince Edward Island, Sarawak, Seychelles, Sierra Leone, Singapore, Solomon Islands, South Africa, Sri Lanka, Straits Settlements, Suriname, Swaziland, Tanzania, Trinidad and Tobago, Tuvalu, Uganda, United States of America, Virgin Islands, Zanzibar, Zimbabwe
Centas (plural **Centa, Centu**) Lithuania
Centavo Angola, Argentina, Bolivia, Brazil, Cape Verde Islands, Chile, Colombia, Costa Rica, Cuba, Dominican Republic, Ecuador, El Salvador, Guatemala, Guinea-Bissau, Honduras, Mexico, Mozambique, Nicaragua, Paraguay, Peru, Philippines, Portugal, Portuguese Guinea, Portuguese India, Puerto Rico, St Thomas and Prince Islands, Timor, Venezuela
Centecimo Bolivia
Centesimo Bolivia, Chile, Dominican Republic, Ethiopia, Italian East Africa, Italy, Panama, Paraguay, San Marino, Somalia, Uruguay, Vatican
Centime Algeria, Antwerp, Belgian Congo, Belgium, Cambodia, Cameroon, Cochin China, Comoro Islands, Djibouti, France, French Equatorial Africa, French Guiana, French Indochina, French Oceania, French Polynesia, French Somali Coast, French West Africa, Guadeloupe, Guinea, Haiti, Laos, Monaco, Morocco, New Caledonia, Reunion, Senegal, Switzerland, Togo, Tunisia, Vietnam, Westphalia, Yugoslavia, Zaire
Centimo Costa Rica, Mozambique, Paraguay, Peru, Philippines, Puerto Rico, St Thomas and Prince Islands, Spain, Venezuela
Centu Lithuania

Chervonetz (plural **Chervontzy**)   Russia
Chetrum   Bhutan
Cheun   South Korea
Chiao   China, Formosa, Manchukuo
Chi'en   China
Chio   China
Chon   Korea
Chuckram   Travancore
Colon   Costa Rica, El Salvador
Condor   Chile, Colombia, Ecuador
Cordoba   Nicaragua
Corona   Austrian provinces of Italy, Naples
Cruzadinho   Brazil, Portugal
Cruzado   Brazil, Portugal
Cruzeiro   Brazil
Deutschemark   Germany
Dinar   Afghanistan, Algeria, Bahrain, Hejaz, Iraq, Kuwait, Morocco, Persia, Saudi Arabia, Serbia, Tunisia, Turkey, Yugoslavia
Diner   Andorra
Dinero   Peru, Spain
Dirham   Jordan, Libya, Morocco, United Arab Emirates
Dirhem   Dubai, Iraq, Morocco, Qatar
Dollar   Anguilla, Antigua and Barbuda, Australia, Bahamas, Belize, Bermuda, Canada, Cayman Islands, China, Cocos (Keeling) Islands, Cook Islands, East Caribbean Territories, Fiji, Great Britain, Grenada, Guyana, Hawaii, Hong Kong, Indonesia, Jamaica, Japan, Kiribati, Liberia, Malaysia, Mauritius, Montserrat, Newfoundland, New Zealand, Panama, St Kitts-Nevis, St Lucia, St Vincent, Scotland, Sierra Leone, Singapore, Solomin Islands, Straits Settlements, Trinidad and Tobago, Tuvalu, USA, Virgin Islands, Western Samoa, Zimbabwe
Dong   Annam, Vietnam
Drachma   Crete, Greece
Dram   Armenia
Ekuele   Equatorial Guinea
Emalangeni   Swaziland
Escudo   Angola, Argentina, Azores, Bolivia, Cape Verde Islands, Central American Republic, Chile, Colombia, Costa Rica, Ecuador, Guadeloupe, Guatemala, Guinea-Bissau, Madeira, Mexico, Mozambique, Peru, Portugal, Portuguese Guinea/India, St Thomas and Prince Islands, Spain, Timor
Forint   Hungary
Franc   Algeria, Belgian Congo, Belgium, Burundi, Cambodia, Cameroon, Central African Republic, Chad, Comoro Islands, Congo, Danish West Indies, Djibouti, Dominican Republic, Ecuador, France, French Colonies, Gabon, Guadeloupe, Guinea, Ivory Coast, Katanga, Luxembourg, Madagascar, Malagasy Republic, Mali, Martinique, Mauretania, Monaco, Morocco, New Caledonia, New Hebrides, Reunion, Ruanda-Urundi, Rwanda, St Pierre and Miquelon, Senegal, Switzerland, Togo, Tunisia, West African States
Franchi   Switzerland
Frang   Luxembourg
Frank(en)   Belgium, Liechtenstein, Saar, Switzerland
Franka Ara   Albania
Gersh   Ethiopia

Girsh   Hejaz, Nejd, Saudi Arabia, Sudan
Golde   Sierra Leone
Grivna (plural **Grivny**)   Ukraine
Grosz (plural **Grosze** or **Groszy**)   Poland
Grush   Albania
Guarani   Paraguay
Guerche   Egypt, Saudi Arabia
Gulden   Austria, Curacao, German States, Netherlands, Netherlands Indies, Swiss Cantons
Habibi   Afghanistan
Hryvnia   Ukraine
Hsien   China
Hwan   Korea
Imadi   Yemen
Jeon   Korea
Jiao   People's Republic of China
Kapeikas   Latvia, Belarus
Kina   Papua New Guinea
Kip   Laos
Korona   Bohemia and Moravia, Hungary, Slovakia
Korun(a) (plural **Koruny** or **Koruncic**)   Czechoslo-vakia
Krajczar   Hungary
Kran   Iran, Persia
Kreu(t)zer   Austria, Austrian States, Czechoslovakia, German States, Hungary, Liechtenstein, Poland, Roumania, Swiss Cantons
Krona (plural **Kronor** or **Kronur**)   Iceland, Sweden
Krona (plural **Kroner** or **Kronen**)   Austria, Denmark, German States, Greenland, Liechtenstein, Norway
Kroon(i)   Estonia
Kuna (plural **Kune**)   Croatia
Kurus   Turkey
Kuta   Congo-Kinshasa, Zaire
Kwacha   Malawi, Zambia
Kwanza   Angola
Kyat   Burma, Myanmar
Lati, Lats   Latvia
Lei   Roumania
Lek (plural **Leke** or **Leku**)   Albania
Lempira   Honduras
Leone   Sierra Leone
Leu (plural **Lei**)   Roumania
Lev(a)   Bulgaria
Li   Manchukuo
Licente   Lesotho
Likuta   Zaire
Lilangeni   Swaziland
Lion d'Or   Austrian Netherlands
Lira (plural **Lire**)   Eritrea, Italian East Africa, Italy, San Marino, Syria, Turkey, Vatican
Lira (plural **Lirot**)   Israel
Lisente   Lesotho
Litas (plural **Litai** or **Litu**)   Lithuania
Luhlanga   Swaziland
Lweis   Angola
Macuta   Angola
Makuta   Zaire
Maloti   Lesotho
Mark   Germany, German States, German New Guinea, Norway, Poland, Sweden
Marka   Estonia
Markka   Finland

Metical   Mozambique
Milreis   Brazil
Mon   Japan, Ryukyu Islands
Mongo   Mongolia
Mun   Korea
Mung   Mongolia
Naira   Nigeria
Ngultrum   Bhutan
Ngwee   Zambia
Omani   Oman
Pa'anga   Tonga
Pahlavi   Iran
Pataca   Macau
Pengo   Hungary
Penni(a)   Finland
Perper(a)   Montenegro
Pesa   German East Africa
Peseta   Andorra, Equatorial Guinea, Peru, Spain
Pesewa   Ghana
Peso   Argentina, Bolivia, Cambodia, Chile, Colombia, Costa Rica, Cuba, Dominican Republic, El Salvador, Guatemala, Guinea-Bissau, Honduras, Mexico, Netherlands Antilles, Nicaragua, Paraguay, Peru, Philippines, Puerto Rico, Uruguay, Venezuela
Piastre   Annam, Cambodia, Cochin China, Cyprus, Denmark, Egypt, French Indochina, Hejaz, Iraq, Khmer, Lebanon, Libya, Nejd, Saudi Arabia, Syria, Sudan, Tonkin, Tunisia, Turkey, Vietnam, Yemen
Piso   Philippines
Pond   Transvaal
Pound   Ascension, Australia, Biafra, Cyprus, Egypt, Falkland Islands, Ghana, Gibraltar, Great Britain, Guernsey, Iran, Ireland, Isle of Man, Israel, Jersey, Malta, Nigeria, Rhodesia, St Helena, South Arabia, South Africa, Sudan, Syria
Pruta(ot)   Israel
Pul   Afghanistan, China, Turkestan
Pula   Botswana
Pya(t)   Burma
Qindar(ka)   Albania
Quetzal   Guatemala
Real(es)   Argentina, Bolivia, Central American Republic, Chile, Colombia, Costa Rica, Dominican Republic, Ecuador, El Salvador, Venezuela
Reichsmark   Germany
Reis   Angola, Azores, Brazil, Madeira, Mozambique, Portugal, Portuguese India
Rentenmark   Germany
Rial   Iran, Morocco, Muscat and Oman, Oman, Persia, Yemen Arab Republic
Riel   Kampuchea
Ringgit   Malaysia
Riyal   Iran, Iraq, Saudi Arabia, United Arab Emirates, Yemen Arab Republic
Rouble   Russia, USSR
Rubel   German occupation of Russia
Ruble   Poland, Transnistria
Rublis   Latvia
Rufiyaa   Maldive Islands
Rupee   Afghanistan, Andaman Islands, Bhutan, Burma, China, Cocos Keeling Islands, India, Iran, Kenya, Mauritius, Nepal, Pakistan, Saudi

Arabia, Seychelles, Sri Lanka, Tanzania, Tibet, United Arab Emirates, Yemen
Rupia   Portuguese India, Somalia
Rupiah   Indonesia
Rupie   German East Africa
Ryal   England, Hejaz, Iran, Muscat and Oman, Nejd, Oman, Persia, Quaiti State, Saudi Arabia, Yemen, Zanzibar
Saidi   Oman
Satang   Siam (Thailand)
Scellino   Somalia
Schilling   Austria, German States, Poland, Swiss Cantons
Shahi   Afghanistan, Iran, Turkestan
Sheqal(im)   Israel
Shilingi   Tanzania
Shilling   Australia, Biafra, British West Africa, Canada, Cyprus, East Africa, Fiji, Gambia, Ghana, Great Britain, Grenada, Guernsey, Ireland, Isle of Man, Jamaica, Jersey, Kenya, Malawi, Malta, New Guinea, New Zealand, Nigeria, Scotland, Somalia, South Africa, Trinidad and Tobago, Uganda, Zambia
Sol(es)   Argentina, Haiti, Peru,
Soldo (plural **Soldi**)   Italian States, Swiss Cantons, Papal States,
Som   Kyrgyr Republic
Somalo   Somalia
Somoni   Tajikistan
Srang   Tibet
Sucre   Ecuador, Galapagos
Sueldo   Bolivia, Spain
Syli   Guinea
Tael   China, Laos
Taka   Bangladesh
Tala   Samoa, Tokelau
Talaro   Ethiopia
Taler   German States, Poland, Swiss Cantons
Tambala   Malawi
Tamlung   Siam
Tanga   Portuguese India
Tangka   Tibet
Tanka   Nepal
Thaler   Austria, Austrian States, Courland, Czechoslovakia, German States, Hungary, Liechtenstein, Poland, Roumania, Switzerland
Thebe   Botswana
Tical   Cambodia, Thailand
Toea   Papua New Guinea
Tola   India, Nepal
Tolar   Slovenia
Toman   Iran, Persia, Azerbaijan
Tughrik   Mongolia
Venezolano   Venezuela
Wan   Korea
Wark   Ethiopia
Warn   Korean
Wen   China
Whan   Korea
Won   South Korea
Xu   Vietnam
Yen   Japan
Yuan   China
Zaire Zaire
Zalat   Yemen Arab Republic
Zloty (plural **Zlote** or **Zlotych**)   Poland

Glossary of banknote terms

Allied Military Currency Notes produced by the British and American governments for the use of military personnel in territories occupied during the World War II.

Alteration A deliberate change in some feature of a note, usually of a fraudulent nature.

Assignat Type of paper money used in France, 1789–96, representing confiscated Church land assigned to the holders.

Asterisk Note Note issued in Canada and New Zealand since ther 1950s to replace a defective note and so-called on account of the asterisk in the serial number.

Authorised Circulation The amount of money in notes which Scottish banks were permitted to have in circulation, under the Bank Act of 1845, based on a twelve-month average for the period prior to the Act coming into force. Any amount above this had to be backed by gold and silver.

Auxiliary Payment Certificate Form of paper money intended for use by American military personnel in overseas countries. See also Baf, Behelfszahlungsmittel and Scrip.

Babel Note Nickname derived from the biblical Tower of Babel, given to the paper currency of the Russian Socialist Federated Republic (1919) because it bore the slogan "workers of the world unite" in seven languages.

Back The side of a note generally regarded as of lesser importance than the front, and otherwise known as the reverse or verso. In early notes the back was often left blank, but in more recent times it has been used for a florid representation of the national arms or vignettes of scenery and landmarks.

Baf Acronym from British Armed Forces, the popular name for the vouchers which could only be exchanged for goods in service canteens from 1945 onwards.

Banknote Form of paper money issued by banks and usually promising to pay the bearer on demand in coin of the realm.

Banknote Strictly speaking, this is a piece of paper money issued by a bank, although the term is often loosely applied to any form of paper in circulation as currency.

Bearer Cheque A piece of paper which looks like a cheque but actually payable for the stated sum to any person holding it (the bearer) without requiring endorsement. Some of the emergency money used in Italy in the late 1970s consisted of such cheques.

Behelfszahlungsmittel German term for auxiliary payment certificates used in occupied Europe from 1939 to 1945.

Bill of Credit An American term denoting the paper money of the Colonial and early Continental period, from which comes the common expression 'bill' meaning a paper note.

Bill of Exchange The law defines this as "an unconditional order in writing, addressed by one person to another, signed by the person giving it, requiring the person to whom it is addressed to pay on demand or at a fixed or determinable future time, a sum certain in money to or to the order of a specified person or to bearers". It is addressed to a person or company, rather than a bank. The earliest examples are entirely handwritten although examples from the 19th century onwards often had the stock formula printed, with the details inserted by hand.

Billet de Confiance French for "tickets of trust", signifying small-denomination notes of the French Revolution issued to meet a shortage of coin due to hoarding.

Block Number Tiny numerals often found in the corners of notes, denoting the block or plate from which the notes were printed.

Bogus A note which is entirely false, in that it purports to be the money of a non-existent bank or country.

Bon Pour French for "good for", inscribed on tokens, coupons and vouchers which circulated as cash during periods of shortage of coinage.

Bond A certificate of intention to pay the holder a specified sum, with or without interest, on a specified date.

Bradbury Popular name for the UK Treasury notes introduced in August 1914 when specie payments were suspended on the outbreak of World War I, from the Treasury official, Sir John Bradbury, who signed them.

Braille A system of reading by means of patterns of raised dots, invented by Louis Braille. In recent years such dots have been embossed on many banknotes to help identification by the blind and partially sighted, as well as provide an additional security feature.

Branch Banknote A note which includes in its inscription a reference to the particular branch of a bank which issued it. In the USA such notes even had quite distinctive designs, but in England the name of the town or city sufficed to distinguish such notes from those of the head office in London.

British Armed Forces Special Voucher Note issued from 1945 onwards for use in NAAFI canteens operated all over the world on behalf of the British armed services. Denominated in sterling, they could not be used outside the camp area and thus prevented black market operations between servicemen and the local population.

Broken Banknote Note issued by a bank which has failed, but often applied more generally to banknotes which have been demonetised.

Burele French term indicating a network of intersecting curved lines used as a security underprint.

Cancelled A note withdrawn from circulation and rendered worthless by means of an overprint or perforated inscription, generally the word CANCELLED or its equivalent in other languages, e.g. Annule (French), Annulado (Spanish) or Ausser Kurs (German). Such notes sometimes come on to the market at a fraction of their original face value.

Carton A form of soft card, much thicker than conventional paper, which has been used occasionally for emergency money, notably the small notes in Mexico, 1914–17.

Cartouche Oval or circular frame enclosing a portrait or armorial device, setting it apart from the rest of the design.

Changeling A note or cheque whose colour is altered from the norm as a result of exposure to humidity, sunlight or chemical action.

Chartered Bank A bank operating under charter from the government, as opposed to a private or commercial bank.

Cheque (American Check) A written order directing a bank to pay money.

Cheque Form A printed form issued by banks for the convenience of customers. Collectors use this term to denote an unused cheque (preferably with the counterfoil still intact).

Chop From the Hindi word chap, it means a stamp or seal used in India, China and other countries of Asia to make an official mark. The earliest paper money, for example, bore the chop of the Khan of Cathay, applied in vermilion, and

this tradition continues to this day in the paper money of China and Japan.

Clearing Bank A bank which is a member of a Clearing House.

Clearing House A banking institution where notes and cheques are exchanged between banks.

Clearing House Certificate A form of emergency money backed by coin or bullion deposited with the clearing house through which banks exchanged notes and cheques. Specifically the term is applied to American issues of 1907-8 and the early 1930s, during periods of economic crises and runs on banks.

Coin Note A note issued by the US Treasury in 1890–1, so-called because it was redeemable in coin. A special reserve of silver dollars was established to cope with the redemption of these notes.

College Currency Imitation money used in simulated transactions by business schools and colleges, mainly in the USA.

Colonial Currency Paper money issued by the thirteen American colonies in the period from 1690 to 1776 or even later in some cases, before the emergence of the United States.

Colour Shifting Ink Ink which appears to change colour as the note is tilted at a different angle.

Commemorative A note issued for the specific purpose of marking a current event or the anniversary of a historic event or personality. Apart from notes with distinctive designs, such notes may consist of an additional or overprinted inscription, or even cyphers and serial numbers arranged in the form of anniversary dates or initials.

Company Note A note issued by a commercial undertaking rather than a bank and redeemable in goods from the company store rather than actual cash. Such notes were common in Britain before they were rendered illegal by the Truck Acts of the 1840s.

Compound Interest Note Note issued during the American Civil War, so-called on account of the six per cent interest which was compounded every six months.

Concentration Camp Money Various forms of notes and vouchers produced immediately before and during the World War II in a number of Nazi concentration camps. These notes were intended to reward slave workers for their labour and were exchangeable for a limited range of goods, but more usually for such luxuries as the loan of library books or admission to camp concerts. Notes of this type are known to have been used in Oranienburg, Ravensbruck, Dachau, Sachsenhausen, Buchenwald, Mauthausen, Auschwitz, Westerburg, Gross-Rosen and Mittelbau-Dora as well as in the ghettoes of

Warsaw, Lodz (Litzmanstadt), Bielsk-Podlavsky and Theresienstadt. Notes denominated in US currency were also used in Deggendorf, Feldafing and Scheinfeld, former Nazi concentration camps which were used as displaced persons' camps, mainly for survivors of the Holocaust, prior to their immigration to Palestine in 1945–46. The British authorities also provided canteen money for Jews interned at camps in Cyprus in 1946–48, after being turned back from Palestine as illegal immigrants.

Continental Currency   Paper money authorised by the Continental Congress between 1775 and 1779 in the early stages of the American War of Independence.

Counterfeit   The forgery or imitation of a note intended for circulation to deceive the public and defraud the state or the issuing bank.

Counterfoil   The left-hand portion of a note or cheque, retained by the issuer as a record of the issue. It was usually divided from the main portion by some highly elaborate vertical design which, in the case of cheques especially, tended to become more pictorial in the 19th and early 20th centuries. From the 1840s the counterfoil was separated from the main part by some form of perforation, but earlier examples were cut apart by scissors, often in a serpentine or irregular line so that the two portions could be matched later on if required.

Coupon   Term from French couper, to cut, denoting a piece of paper which may be exchanged for goods or services, hence a detachable ticket or voucher entitling the holder to something. In the notaphilic context it denotes a detachable portion of a share certificate entitling the holder to a dividend, and has also been used to signify small notes used as emergency money.

Crossed Cheque   A cheque which bears parallel diagonal lines across the middle, either printed or handwritten, giving instructions to the paying bank to limit negotiability to the payee.

Crossing Stamp   A brass or rubber stamp applied by hand across the face of a cheque by the negotiating bank.

Currency   Notes intended to pass current in general circulation as money.

Current   Note still in circulation.

Cut Note   A note which has been officially cut into halves or quarters and re-issued, each part thereby serving as a note of appropriate value. As a rule, each portion bears an overprint signifying its new value.

Cypher   Term for the combination of letters which serve as a prefix in the serial number. In recent years such cyphers have often been deliberately contrived to serve a quasi-commemorative purpose, eg RLS (Robert Louis Stevenson), AGB (Alexander Graham Bell), SP (Scottish

Parliament) and G/AD Glasgow, City of Architecture and Design) on Scottish notes of the 1990s.

Darlehnskassen   German for 'state loan note', a form of paper money issued during the World War I in an abortive bid to fill the shortage of coinage in circulation. These low-denomination notes failed to meet demand and were superseded by local issues of Notgeld in 1916.

Date   In many cases the year, or even a full date, merely denotes the point in time at which a note was authorised or introduced, and may antedate the actual time or even the year of release. In other cases, however, the date signifies the actual time of issue.

Demand Notes   Name generally given to the first series of paper money authorised by the US federal government by Act of Congress in 1861 at the beginning of the American Civil War, and so-called because the United States promised to pay the bearer on demand. The formula, of course, is widely used on the notes of many other countries and is by no means confined to the USA.

Demonetisation   The withdrawal of notes from circulation and declaring them to be worthless.

Denomination   The face value of a note, expressed in words of figures or often a combination of both.

Depression Scrip   American term for temporary makeshifts issued in various parts of the USA during the Depression of the early 1930s.

Device   Heraldic term for the pattern or emblem on banknotes.

Devil's Head   Collectors' term for certain notes of Canada and the Seychelles in which an image of the Devil was fancifully detected in the hair of Queen Elizabeth.

Die   Hardened piece of metal, usually steel but sometimes copper, bearing a positive image of the device to be transferred to the printing plate.

Die Proof   An impression, usually pulled on soft carton or India paper, of an intaglio engraving of a banknote, usually taken during the progress of engraving in order to check the detail. Proofs of this nature usually consist of the portrait or some detail of the design, such as the border, rather than the complete motif.

Dividend Warrant   A cheque issued in payment of a dividend to a shareholder, often attached to a document setting out the details of the dividend.

Dix Note   Collectors' term for $10 notes of the Citizens' Bank of Louisiana in New Orleans, from the French word DIX (ten) inscribed on their backs. The widespread notion that this gave rise to the term 'Dixie' denoting the Southern States of the USA is utterly false. Apart from the fact that many Canadian notes are similarly inscribed, it should be stated that the term 'Dixie', first popularised by the patriotic song of 1859 by Daniel D. Emmett, comes from the Mason-Dixon Line which separated the states of the free North and slave-owning South, Charles Mason and Jeremiah Dixon being the surveyors who mapped the southern boundary of Pennsylvania in the late 18th century.

Double Note A note in which the front and back bear no relation to each other. This apparently first arose during the American Civil War when unfinished notes of a broken bank were pressed into service, with a new device on the blank side, by other banks as a result of a chronic shortage of paper.

Draft An alternative name for a cheque, sometimes used in the context of a bank draft.

Drawer The person drawing or issuing a cheque and whose signature appears on it.

Dual Currency Notes inscribed with values in two different currency systems. This situation sometimes arises during a period of transition from one currency to another, usually as a result of monetary reforms.

Educational Notes Name given to the US silver certificates of 1896 on account of the didactic nature of their designs.

Embossing A printing process which entails the use of male and female dies or matrices to raise a portion of the design above the normal surface. It is commonly found on old cheques and bills of exchange which bear an embossed device denoting the payment of stamp duty, but in many banknotes of recent vintage it is used as a security device and an aid to blind and partially sighted persons to identify the face value correctly.

Emergency Money Any form of money used in times of economic and political upheaval, when traditional kinds of currency are not available. In paper money this takes the form of all kinds of coupons, vouchers and scrip employed in military campaigns or in towns under siege, the Notgeld issued by many towns in Austria and Germany (1916–23), encased money, fractional currency, guerrilla notes, invasion, liberation and occupation money from the two world wars and minor campaigns. Among more recent examples may be cited the use of cheques in Italy (1976–77) and the issue of talons or coupons in many of the countries of the former Soviet Union pending the introduction of their own distinctive currencies.

Encased Money Postage and revenue stamps enclosed in small metal and mica-faced discs, circulated as small change in times of emergency. The device was invented by John Gault, a Boston sewing-machine salesman, during the American Civil War (1862). The face of the stamp was visible through the transparent window, while the back of the disc was embossed with firms'

advertisements. This practice was revived during and after the World War I when there was again a shortage of small coins. Encased stamps have also been recorded from Austria, France, Germany, Monaco and Norway. See also Stamp Money.

Endorsement The signature of the payee on the back of a cheque.

Endorsement Guarantee A statement indemnifying the paying bank in the case of an incorrect endorsement on a cheque, usually indicated by means of a rubber handstamp.

Engine Turning An intricate pattern of spiral and curved lines created by the Rose Engine, patented by Jacob Perkins between 1811 and 1819 as part of the process of steel engraving or siderography which established the fortunes of the security printing firm variously known as Perkins, Fairman & Heath, Perkins, Bacon & Heath or Perkins, Bacon. The French term guilloche is sometimes used.

Engraving The art of cutting lines or grooves into a die for recess-printing (intaglio) or cutting away parts of the surface leaving the portion to be printed standing out (letterpress). See these terms for further details.

Error Mistakes in paper money may be caused at the design or engraving stage, or as a result of a fault in the production processes. In the first category come misspellings in text or inscriptions, but more usually mistakes or inaccuracies in details of the design. In the second category the back of a note may be printed upside down in relation to the front, or a part of the design may be doubly printed or misplaced. Faulty registration of the printing plates may result in one colour being out of alignment. Other errors include serial numbers partially or wholly omitted or printed upside down. The commonest error consists of miscut notes.

Essay (From the French essai, a trial piece). In paper money this refers to any design, from the original artwork to a preliminary printing, for the purpose of examination by parliamentary or financial bodies, prior to the authorisation of an actual issue of notes, the counterpart of patterns in coinage or medals.

Face The surface of a banknote, more usually referred to as the front, the recto or obverse.

Face Value The value inscribed in words and/or figures at which the note passes current.

Facsimile An imitation, usually authorised officially, of a note, perhaps created long after the original has been withdrawn from circulation. Such notes, usually marked in some way to indicate their true nature, were sometimes produced for exhibition purposes or to complete gaps in the bank's official collection, often utilising the original plates or dies.

Fantasy A note purporting to be the currency of a country which does not exist. Recent examples include the notes of the Hutt River Province which declared its independence of Western Australia.

Federal Reserve Bank Note Type of note issued by the Federal Reserve Bank of the USA between 1915 and 1933 and thus inscribed.

Federal Reserve Note A note issued by the Federal Reserve of the USA from 1914 to the present day and thus inscribed. These notes are backed by the federal government and not by individual banks.

Fei-ch'ien Chinese for "flying money", denoting the earliest form of paper money in the world and dating from the 7th–9th centuries.

Fiat Money Notes issued by a government but not redeemable in coin or bullion.

Fiduciary Issue Notes issued purely on trust, without the backing of gold or other securities.

Flying Money See Fei-ch'ien.

Forced Issue Paper money imposed on a populace without any backing and usually issued by the authority of an occupying power in time of war.

Forgery An unauthorised copy or imitation of a note, made with the intention of deceiving collectors. Forgeries intended to pass current for real notes are more properly termed counterfeits.

Foxing Unsightly spots, ranging from yellow to brown or dark red, caused by iron impurities in old paper. It is, in fact, a form of fungus which can spread across the paper or attack other paper with which it comes in contact. It can often be checked, if not always entirely eliminated, by treating the affected part with a very weak solution of a bleaching agent such as Chloramine-T. It is exacerbated by lack of air circulation and for that reason it is important that notes should be examined periodically and allowed to breathe.

Fractional Currency Emergency issue of small-denomination notes by the USA in 1863-65, following a shortage of coins caused by the Civil War. This issue was superseded by the Postage Currency notes, but bore the inscription "Receivable for all US stamps", alluding to the most popular medium of small change at that time. Denominations ranged from 3c to 50c.

Frame That part of the design forming the border, prevalent in note design until the 1960s when a much lighter, open style of design came into fashion. In many older notes the frame was elaborately engraved and ornamented to defeat counterfeiters.

Front The main side of a note, otherwise the obverse or recto, on which appears the name of the bank and/or country, together with signatures of bank officials, the date and place of issue and usually some form of promise to pay the bearer in coin of the realm.

Fund Raising Note A note produced by an exiled organisation to raise money for the campaign to gain independence. Good examples are the notes issued mainly in the USA by Irish and Hungarian nationalists in the 19th century.

Funeral Money Imitations of banknotes, used in China and Latin America in funeral ceremonies. See also Hell notes.

Gold Bank Note A note issued in the 1870s by nine banks in California and one in Boston, so-called because they promised to pay the bearer in gold coin.

Gold Certificate A series of nine issues in the USA between 1863 and 1922, redeemable in gold coin.

Gold Note Term generally applied to any note specifically redeemable in gold.

Goodfor Popular name for emergency money made of paper or card, from the inscription "Good for" or its equivalent in other languages (e.g. French bon pour or Dutch goed voor) followed by a monetary value. Notes of this type have been recorded from Europe, Africa and America during times of economic crises or shortage of coinage.

Granite Paper Type of security paper which has tiny coloured threads enmeshed in it.

Greenback Popular name for the paper money issued under the authority of the US government, from the predominant colour of the verso.

Guerrilla Money Money issued in areas under the control of guerrillas and partisans during wartime range from the veld ponds of the Boer War (1899–1902) to the notes issued by the Garibaldi Brigade in Italy and the anti-fascist notes of Tito's partisans in Yugoslavia. The most prolific issues were those produced in Luzon, Mindanao and Negros Occidental by the Filipino resistance (1942–45).

Guilloche French term signifying the intricate pattern of curved lines produced by the rose engine and used as a security feature in the production of banknotes, cheques, stocks and share certificates. See also engine turning.

Gutschein German word for voucher or coupon, denoting the paper money used aboard ships of the Imperial Navy during the World War I. The last issue was made at Scapa Flow, Orkney, during the internment of the High Seas Fleet (1918–19). The term is also widely used in Germany nowadays for any giveaway, exchangeable for goods or services as part of a sales promotion.

Halved Note A note which has been cut in half as a precaution during transmission by post. On the safe arrival of the first half being notified, the other half is then sent by post. This practice was widespread in the early 19th century when highway robbery was prevalent. The two halves were subsequently re-united, often using specially printed strips of gummed paper.

Handsigned Notes which have been individually signed by hand, rather than by means of an engraved facsimile signature.

Hansatsu Japanese term denoting notes of purely local validity, usually printed by woodblocks on soft, thick handmade paper, hence the derisive trerm "blotter money".

Hell Notes Imitation paper money used in Chinese funeral ceremonies and buried with the dead to pay for services in the next world.

Holed Term denoting notes which have either been pierced with pins or staples to attach them to each other or to documents, thereby detracting from their collectable condition, or notes which have been deliberately punched with small holes as a security precaution. The latter device is sometimes applied to specimen notes or printers' samples to prevent them getting into general circulation. See also perforated.

Hologram A security device consisting of an image which changes colour or design depending on how it is tilted towards the light. It was first applied to credit cards in the early 1980s and to banknotes in 1988 (Australia), but has become much more widespread in very recent years.

Imitation Money Also known as play money or toy money, it consists of notes produced for games of chance (like Monopoly), children's toy shops and post offices, as tourist souvenirs or for political satire (e.g. the shrinking pound or dollar). See also funeral money, hell notes and skit notes.

Imprint Inscription on a note giving the name of the printer, usually found in the lower margin.

Indented Description of an irregular edge on the left-hand side of a note, matching a corresponding pattern in the counterfoil, used in the 19th century as a precaution against forgery.

Inflation Money Notes produced in Germany (1921–23), Austria (1923), Poland (1923), Hungary (1945–46), Greece (1946), China (1946–48) and many countries of Latin America and the former communist bloc since the 1980s and, most recently, by Angola and Turkey. Hungary holds the record for the highest value of any note ever issued—one thousand million adopengos equivalent to no less than 20,000,000,000,000,000,000,000,000,000 pengos.

Inscription Any kind of text printed on the back or front of a note.

Intaglio In the production of paper money, intaglio engraving is still commonly practised. In this process the engraver cuts the design into a steel die and the printing ink lies in the grooves. The paper is forced into the grooves under great pressure where it takes up the ink and results in the ridges which are characeristic of this process.

Interest Bearing Note A note whose promise to pay the bearer includes a reference to interest payable at the time of redemption.

Invasion Money Notes prepared in advance of a military invasion, either solely for the use of the invading forces, or also extended forcibly to the civil population and thus employed as means of controlling the local economy. *See also* liberation and occupation money.

Jugate (From Latin Jugum, a yoke). Heraldic term denoting the overlapping profiles of two or more persons portrayed on banknotes. A good recent example is provided by the notes of Thailand celebrating the Golden Wedding of the King and Queen, released in April 2000.

Kreditivsedlar (Swedish for "credit notes"). The name given to the first issue of paper money made in the western world. Paper money of this type was the invention of Johan Palmstruch at Riga in 1652 but nine years elapsed before it was implemented by the Stockholm Bank. The notes were issued up to 1666 and were mainly redeemable in copper platmynt though latterly in silver coin.

Labour Note A form of paper money devised by the industrialist and philanthropist Robert Owen and used to pay his employees at the textile mills in New Lanark, Scotland in the 1830s. The value was expressed in hours worked rather than any monetary terms. The concept spread briefly to England and America, but was generally frowned on as an abuse of the workers' rights to spend their money freely, rather than at the company store.

Latent Image A security device on a banknote which takes the form of an image that only becomes apparent when the surface of the note is tilted in a particular direction, and thus was a precursor of the hologram as a safeguard against forgery.

Leather Money Pieces of leather embossed with an official device have been used as money on several occasions, during the sieges of Faenza and Leiden and in the Isle of Man in the 15th and 16th centuries. Several towns in Austria and Germany produced lether tokens during and after the World War I.

Legal Tender Notes which are declared by law to be current money and which tradesmen and shopkeepers are obliged to accept in payment for goods or services. (*See* Banknotes and the Law).

Legend   The inscription on a banknote.

Letterpress   A printing process in which the ink is applied to the raised portions of a die or plate and then transferred to paper . It takes its name from the fact that this method was originally used in the printing of books and newspapers consisting mainly of lettering although from the outset it also included illustrations from woodblocks. This process is much cheaper and less secure than intaglio, and was used for many early banknotes. *See also* typeset.

Liberation Money   Paper money prepared for use in parts of Europe and Asia, formerly under Axis occupation. Liberation notes were used in France, Belgium and the Netherlands in 1944-45, while various Japanese and Chinese notes were overprinted for use in Hong Kong when it was liberated in 1945. Indian notes overprinted for use in Burma were issued in 1945-46 when that country was freed from Japanese occupation.

Lithography   A printing process patented by Alois Senefelder in 1795 and since widely used in the production of banknotes and cheques, mainly as an underprint, often in special fugitive inks. The name comes from the Greek lithos, a stone and graphein, to write, and alludes to the polished limestone slabs originally employed, although nowadays zinc or even paper plates are used instead. The image is laid down on the stone in greasy ink or by means of transfers. The printing ink adheres to the grease but is repelled by the blank areas of the plate.

Low Number   A note with a very low serial number, either one or two digits preceded by a string of noughts, is regarded by collectors as very desirable, indicating very early issue. Pandering to this, however, many banks now set aside the low-numbered notes for inclusion in presentation folders sold to collectors.

Mandat   Name given to a form of paper money issued in the period of the French Revolution. Like the assignat, which it replaced, the value of the mandat was theoretically backed by land confiscated from the Church and the aristocracy.

Margin   That portion of a note lying between the outer border of the design and the edge of the paper. Notes with regular margins on all four sides often command a premium, whereas notes with irregular margins are often discounted. Margins may be clean-cut (by guillotine), rough or even deckle-edged if produced from individual pieces of handmade paper instead of being printed in sheets.

Master Die   The original piece of steel or copper engraved by hand. It is then hardened chemically and an image taken by means of a transfer roller which, after hardening, transfers the image in reverse to the printing plate. Alterations to the master die, by means of punches or subsequent engraving, create secondary dies (often for the production of different denominations using the same basic design).

Metal Thread   A security device in the form of a thin strip of metal embedded in the paper pulp during manufacture.

Microprint   Printing in very tiny lettering, usually endlessly repeated, as a security precaution. It is often used in doubly fugitive ink on those parts of cheques where handwriting appears, to prevent attempts to alter or falsify details by washing, bleaching or chemical means.

Military Currency   Notes issued under military authority, mainly for the use of troops on active service.

Military Payment Certificate   A note produced by the US military authorities for the use of service personnel in PX (post exchange) canteens to prevent black market trading with local civilians.

Ming Note   A large-sized Chinese note issued during the Ming Dynasty (1368-1644), using paper made from mulberry bark. Now highly desirable as the earliest form of paper money available to the collector market.

Miscut   A note with very irregular margins, or even showing a portion of an adjoining note in the sheet, caused by misalignment of the blades cutting up the sheets of notes prior to issue. In some cases an additional piece of paper remains attached as a result of part of the wide sheet margin being accidentally folded over. Such errors in production are of curiosity interest rather than high monetary value, although they often command a premium.

Model   A mock-up of a banknote, produced at a preliminary stage of production, often incorporated the pasted-up portions of previously issued notes or a composite of different elements which may eventually form the complete design,

Moiré   French for "watering", denoting a security underprint of close wavy lines having the effect of watered silk.

Money Order   Certificate for a specific amount of money, which may be transmitted by post and encashed at a money order office or post office. This system was pioneered by Britain and the USA in the early 19th century and is now virtually worldwide. The term is now confined to certificates above a certain value, the terms postal order and postal note being used for similar certificates covering small amounts.

Moses Crowns   Popular name for the notes issued under the authority of the Jewish Council of Elders in Theresienstadt concentration camp during World War II, and so-called on account of the principal motif showing Moses holding up the Ten Commandments. *See also* concentration camp money.

Mule   A note whose back and front are printed from plates which were not originally intended to be paired together.

Multilingual   A note bearing inscriptions in many different languages. Apart from the so-called Babel notes of revolutionary Russia, good examples may be found in the issues of the Habsburg Empire, with values in up to eight languages and two scripts, or Indian notes with inscriptions in English and many different indigenous scripts. The Euro notes of the European Community bear the initials of the European Central Bank in the different languages and scripts of the member countries.

Multiple Denomination   A note with values expressed in two or more different currencies, generally to facilitate exchange. *See also* dual currency.

National Bank Note   American term applied specifically to the notes issued by banks, chartered by the federal government between 1863 and 1935, and backed by US Treasury bonds.

Negotiable   Term applied to a banknote or cheque which can be readily converted into coin.

Notaphily   Hybrid word from Latin nota (note) and Greek philos (love), coined in 1969 to denote the branch of numismatics devoted to the collection and study of paper money. *See also* syngraphics.

Note   A piece of paper money. In former times the term was also loosely applied to cheques or IOUs.

Notgeld   German word meaning "emergency money", applied to the various forms of currency, including notes, which circulated during the World War I when coinage disappeared from circulation, but rapidly overtaken by infinitely more prolific issues of paper money produced by shops, chambers of commerce, businesses and local authorities. Collectors distinguish between kleine Notgeld (small emergency money) in denominations from 10 to 50 pfennigs during and immediately after the war, and the large Notgeld whose denominations were in thousands, and later millions, of marks. Some 3,000 types appeared in 1922 and over 60,000 in 1923 alone. These quaint and colourful mementoes of the German hyperinflation ceased to circulate in 1924 when the currency was reformed.

Obsolete   Term denoting a note which is no longer issued and has been withdrawn from circulation. Notes which are no longer issued but which may still be current during a brief overlapping period are more properly described as obsolescent.

Obverse   The front of a note, equivalent to the "heads" side of a coin or medal, although the term recto is more appropriate for a piece of paper.

Occupation Money   Any form of money, but usually notes or vouchers, issued in wartime by enemy forces in the territory which they invade and occupy.

Order Cheque   A cheque payable to a specified person or to his or her order.

Out of Date Cheque   A cheque which is considered by the paying bank to have been in circulation for "an unreasonable period of time". This is usually regarded as at least six months, although there is apparently no statutory limit.

Overprint   Any form of printing added to a note or cheque after it was originally produced. Such a practice may be employed to alter the name of the issuing bank or authority or, in times of inflation and monetary reform, to convert the denomination to the reformed system. An overprint may also signify a change of government or regime, or even the name of the country.

Paid Cheque   A cheque which has been honoured by a bank and the amount debited to the drawer's account.

Paid Stamp   The handstamp applied to a cheque by the paying bank after debiting the sum to the drawer's account.

Paper Money   Any form of currency based on paper.

Partisan Note   A note produced by Tito's partisans operating in Serbia, Croatia and other parts of Yugoslavia after it was dismembered by the Axis during World War II, and used in those parts of the country which were effectively under their control.

Payee   The person to whom a cheque is made payable.

Perforation   A series of small holes punched out of paper. The earliest form, dating from the 1840s, was used to facilitate the separation of the cheque or banknote from its counterfoil, but later the punches were often arranged in the form of letters or numerals and could thus be applied to cheques to indicate the date on which they were presented for payment. In banknotes, perforation has sometimes been employed to mark them as Specimens intended for archival or publicity purposes and not valid for circulation. *See also* Cancelled.

Pilgrim Receipt   A form of paper money overprinted for the use of people going on a religious pilgrimage. Notes of Pakistan, for example, are specially overprinted for use by pilgrims from that country making the haj to the Moslem holy places of Mecca and Medina in Saudi Arabia.

Pinhole   A blemish on a banknote caused by it having been pinned or stapled to a document or another note. It should be noted, however, that certain notes only exist with this feature as they were put into circulation in batches stapled together for the sake of convenience.

Plain Back   A note which has no printing of any kind on the reverse. *See also* Uniface.

Plate Number A small number incorporated in the design of some notes to indicate the plate from which it was printed.

Play Money Imitations of banknotes produced for use in such games of chance as Monopoly or as part of children's toy outfits for shops and post offices. Of passing interest to notaphilists only in so far as the designs are often vaguely derived from actual notes.

Playing Card Money A form of emergency money created in French Canada from 1685 onwards during shortages of coin supplied from France. Governor Duplessis hit upon using playing cards, with his signature and the denomination added in handwriting.

Polymer A chemical compound containing repeating structural units and formed by chemical combination of many small molecules. In notaphily the term is applied to various plastic materials used in the manufacture of banknotes since the 1970s.

Postage Currency Small notes in denominations of 5, 10, 25 and 50 cents, issued by the US federal government in 1862–63, were thus inscribed and had reproductions of postage stamps engraved on them—five 5c stamps on the 25c and five 10c stamps on the 50c notes. The earliest issue even had perforations in the manner of stamps, but this unnecessary device was soon dispensed with. *See also* stamp money.

Postal Notes or Orders Low-value notes intended for transmission by post and encashable at post offices. Introduced by Britain in 1883, they were an extension of the earlier money order system and are now issued by virtually every country.

Post-dated A cheque bearing a date subsequent to that on which it is presented for payment. As banks are not obliged to honour such cheques they are invariably handed back to the payee or returned to the drawer for re-presentation on or after the due date.

Prisoner of War Money Under the terns of the Geneva Convention the belligerents on both sides during the world wars provided special issues of notes for use within prisoner of war camps. Similar provisions were also made for the camps in which civilian enemy aliens were interned.

Promissory Note A written promise to pay, either on demand or at some future time, a sum of money to a specified individual or to the bearer.

Proof A preliminary test printing of the back or front of a note, taken from the master die or the printing plate before actual production, in order to ensure that every detail is correct.

Propaganda Note A piece of paper money containing political slogans or a didactic element. During the World War II forgeries of German

and Japanese notes were produced by the Allies and additionally inscribed or overprinted with slogans such as "Co-Prosperity Sphere—What is it worth?" (a reference to the Japanese occupied areas of Southeast Asia). Forged dollars with Anti-American propaganda were airdropped over Sicily by the Germans in 1943 and counterfeit pounds with Arabic propaganda over Egypt in 1942-43. Various anti-communist organisations liberated propaganda forgeries of paper money by balloon over Eastern Europe during the Cold War period.

Provincial Note A note issued by a provincial bank or under the authority of a provincial government (as in Canada). Provincial banks in England were only permitted to issue notes so long as they did not have an office in London. The last of the English provincial banks was Fox, Fowler of Wellington Somerset, whose notes ceased in 1921 when the bank became part of the Lloyd's group.

Psywar Note A note produced as part of a campaign of psychological warfare. Effectively this means some kind of imitation paper money dropped as a leaflet by aircraft over enemy-held territory with the intention of demoralising the enemy and boosting the morale of the people enduring occupation.

Punched A note or cheque which bears the mark of a ticket punch to denote that it has been cancelled.

Rag Paper Paper made of linen rags, sometimes with an admixture of cotton or other textile substances, to produce a very tough, hard-wearing material for the production of banknotes.

Raised Note A note which has been revalued by means of an official overprint.

Reckoning Note A form of paper money issued to German troops on the eve of an invasion and exchangeable for local currency, usually at a considerable disadvantage to the economy of the occupied country.

Recto The proper term for the face or front of a note.

Refunding Certificate The official name for a $10 note issued by the US government in 1879 and made more acceptable to the general public on account of the 4 per cent interest per annum for an unspecified period. However, these notes were called in in 1907 by which time they were worth $21.30.

Reichskreditkassen German for State Credit Treasury, inscribed on certain notes intended for circulation in occupied territories of Europe during the World War II.

Re-issue A note issued again after an extended lapse of time.

Remainder A note from a bank or issuing

authority which has never been circulated, due to inflation, political changes or bank failure. Such notes, sometimes in partial or unfinished state (e.g. missing serial numbers or signatures) are generally unloaded on to the numismatic market at a nominal sum and provide a good source of inexpensive material for the beginner.

Repaired A note which has suffered damage, usually tears or splitting, and bearing the evidence of having been restored. Unless they are very rare, such specimens are usually heavily discounted.

Replacement Note A note issued to replace a defective note of the same serial number but generally identified as such by the inclusion of an asterisk of star alongside the number.

Reprint A note produced from the original plates but long after production has been generally discontinued. Such notes often differ subtly from the originals, either in the type of paper used or, more often, in the shade of inks employed.

Revalidation The process of bringing back into use notes which had previously been withdrawn from circulation and declared invalid. This has sometimes happened as a result of changes in political regime, such as in Austria where the notes of the early postwar period were similar to those immediately before the Nazi takeover in 1938, identifiable only by their dates.

Revalue An overprint which alters the face value of a note, usually as a result of currency reform.

Reverse The back of a note, more properly termed the verso.

Saddle Blanket Nickname for the very large notes of the United States in the 19th century.

Safe Conduct Pass A form of propaganda note airdropped behind enemy lines promising safe conduct to military personnel who decide to surrender.

Safety Paper A form of security paper which dramatically changes colour (usually deep blue) when exposed to water. It was formerly widely used in the production of cheques, in order to deter people from trying to alter signatures or other handwritten portions by washing off the ink.

Scrip Paper money of restricted validity or circulation, such as Bafs and other military notes used in service canteens and post exchanges.

Scripophily Term coined in the 1970s to denote the study and collection of stocks, bond and share certificates.

Seal A device, usually circular, which simulates the seal of a bank, a treasury or the state, formerly applied to documents in red sealing wax or embossed in metal foil, but now more generally applied by lithography or letterpress to the banknote design to enhance its official character. See also chop.

Sealskin Money Notes of 1818-30 issued by the Russian Company trading in Alaska, using a form of parchment derived from the skins of seals.

Secret Mark Any device concealed within the mass of engraving with the intention of tripping up the would-be counterfeiter. Such hidden marks, generally overlooked by forgers when fabricating notes, are known to the Secret Service (USA) and bank inspectors and are regarded as a test of genuineness.

Security Features Since 1820 various devices have been incorporated in the design and production of banknotes in order to obviate forgery. These include guilloche engraving, watermarks, metal threads, granite paper, latent images, images visible only under ultra-violet light, microprinting, colour shifting ink, embossing, lithographic underprinting and holograms.

Segmented Security Thread Security device in the form of a line of dashes running across the back of a note, either as a metallic thread or a minute holographic image.

Serial The sequence of figures in numerical order which identifies each individual note. As a rule, numbers are combined with prefix and / or suffix letters which considerably extend the range of serials. As well as very low serial numbers, indicating early issue, collectors also take note of different styles or colours of figures and the presence of symbols (asterisks or stars) denoting replacement notes.

Series A set of different denominations more or less issued within a clearly definable period if not always simultaneously, which possess common features in inscription, style or design. In some cases the word SERIES actually appears on the notes, followed by the date of its introduction.

Share Certificate A piece of paper, often highly ornate or intricately printed, which certifies that the holder possesses a certain specified number of shares in a company.

Shinplasters Derisory term originally applied to the Continental currency notes issued during the American War of Independence, the fractional currency of the Civil War period and also the low-denomination notes of Canada between 1870 and 1935, but often applied indiscriminately to any other low-denomination, small-format notes.

Shoshi Adhesive stamps affixed to Japanese banknotes in the immediate postwar period in order to revalidate them.

Siderography A printing process patented between 1811 and 1819 by Jacob Perkins and applied to the manufacture of printing plates for banknotes from 1820 onwards. From the Greek sideros, iron and graphein, to write.

Siege Note   A note produced by the defenders during the siege of a town, when supplies of normal currency are cut off. Notable examples include the notes issued at Venice during the Austrian siege of 1848 and by Mafeking in 1900 during the Boer War.

Sight Note   A type of promissory note, so-called on account of the formula "At . . . [number of days] after Sight, pay this to . . . Or Order, the Sum of . . ." Although in some cases the word "Sight" itself was inserted in manuscript, the period specified being usually 30 days.

Silk Thread   A security device patented in the 1830s by John Dickinson of Croxley Green and incorporated into some banknotes of the mid-19th century as a precursor of the metallic thread used nowadays.

Silver Certificate   Type of paper money introduced by the United States in 1878, redeemable by the Treasury in silver coin.

Signature   From the earliest times, bills, promissory notes, cheques and banknotes relied heavily on the signature of an individual or bank official. Handsigned notes survived in some instances until the late 19th century but from the 1820s onwards the vast majority of signatures have been engraved facsimiles. They are of importance to collectors as constituting a major variety in any series of notes, each change of signature constituting a collectable variant. One, two or even three signatures of different bank officials are the norm, although notes of the Austro-Hungarian Bank had three Austrian and three Hungarian signatures, on the front and back respectively.

Skit Note   A piece of paper masquerading as a banknote. It differs from a counterfeit in that its design parodies that of a genuine note, often for political, satirical or advertising reasons. Others were produced as April Fools' Day jokes or a form of Valentine (e.g. The Banks of Hearts or Lovers). In recent years they have been produced as advertising gimmicks or as coupons permitting a discount off the list price of goods. Also known as "Flash" notes.

Small Size Note   Collectors' term for the series of notes, in a reduced size from the preceding issues, which came into use in the USA in 1929 and are still in use.

Special Cheque   A cheque drawn on a form specially printed for the drawer and not of the standard design. Such cheques usually give far greater prominence to the names of the drawers (usually a company or institution) and may even be embellished with pictures of factories, premises or products. For this reason they are of immense interest to local historians.

Specie   Money in coin. Many issues of paper owe their existence to the suspension of specie payment in time of war or monetary crisis.

Specimen   Term generally used to denote a single item but more specifially applying to a note intended for circulation between banks or for press publicity and distinguished from the generally issued version by zero serial numbers, punch holes or a security overprint, usually the word SPECIMEN or its equivalent in other languages.

Stage Money   Notes specially printed for use in dramatic productions, on stage, screen or television, sometimes in vague imitation of real notes but often completely different to avoid any charge of counterfeiting.

Stamp Duty   A government tax on transactions involving money, and therefore applied in Britain to cheques between the beginning of the 19th century and 1962. The earliest duty was denoted by a colourless embossed stamp, followed in 1853-81 by various adhesive revenue stamps, then the small upright oval embossed stamps in red (1d) or blue (2d) and finally by the small circular crowned medallion stamps printed in black. Similar systems applied in many other countries. In the USA, for example, the duty could be denoted by a variety of adhesive stamps or by a device printed in orange-yellow across the middle of the cheque.

Stamped   Banknotes to which have been affixed adhesive stamps, either to denote the payment of a tax or to authenticate them. The latter practice has sometimes been used in lieu of an overprint to alter the validity of notes.

Stamp Money   Both postage and revenue stamps have circulated as money during shortages of coins, from the American Civil War onwards. Encased postage stamps were used in the USA (1861–62) before they were superseded by Postage Currency notes, but the same expedient was adopted by many other countries immediately after the World War I. Stamps affied to special cards have circulated as money in Rhodesia (now Zimbabwe) in 1900, the French colonies and Turkey during the World War I, in Spain during the Civil War (1936–39) and the Philippines during the Japanese occupation (1942–45). Stamps printed on thick card, with an inscription on the reverse signifying their parity with silver coins, were issued in Russia (1917–18) and also in Armenia, the Crimea and the Ukraine (1918–20). During World War II Ceylon (which is now Sri Lanka) and several Indian states issued small money cards with contemporary stamps printed on them.

Star Note   A replacement note issued in the USA, so-called on account of the five-pointed star before or after the serial number.

State Bank Note   A note issued by a bank chartered by one of the states in the USA, as opposed to the issues of the Treasury, Federal Reserve or other agencies of the federal government.

State Note   A note issued in the early 19th century by one of the states in the USA.

Stopped Cheque   A cheque on which payment has been countermanded by the drawer before it is presented at the paying bank.

Stub   Another term for the counterfoil, retained as a record of a bank transaction.

Subject   Term indicating an individual note which is part of a sheet. Thus a 20-subject sheet would contain 20 impressions of the note.

Surface Printing   An alternative name for letterpress, the printing process mainly employed in the production of banknotes before 1820.

Sutlers' Notes   A form of scrip issued by US army canteen-keepers for use on military posts and redeemable in merchandise. They were mainly issued during the late 19th century.

Syngraphics   Term coined in the 1970s, from the Greek syn (together) and graphein (to write) to denote the study and collection of cheques.

Travellers' Cheques   (American, Travelers' Checks)   Notes in various denominations issued by Thomas Cook, American Express and many banks which can be converted into cash by tourists and businessmen when travelling abroad. They are validated by the traveller who signs each note in the presence of the issuing agent and then signs them again at the point of encashment. They are issued in sterling, US dollars or some other widely recognised currency but can then be converted into the equivalent in local money. Since the advent of credit cards and bank cards, however, the use of travellers' cheques has dropped very dramatically.

Treasury Note   Paper money worth 10 shillings or one pound, issued by the British treasury on the outbreak of the World War I when specie payments were suspended, and continuing till 1928 when the Bank of England took over responsibility for note-issuing. They were popularly known as Bradburys, from the signature of the Treasury official, Sir John Bradbury, engraved on them.

Type   A major design.

Typeset   A note in which the design is entirely composed of lettering, ornament being confined to printer's rule and the use of conventional symbols, usually to create a border.

Uncirculated   A note which is in the most perfect condition, as received at the bank from the printer and never passed from hand to hand.

Uncut   A sheet or part of a sheet in which two or more notes are still unsevered.

Underprint   The background to the principal motif and inscriptions of a banknote, generally printed by a different process (e.g. lithography instead of intaglio) and in contrasting, lighter colours incorporating security features such as microprinting and latent images.

Uniface   A note which has printing on one side only.

Upham   A Philadelphia printer whose patriotism during the Civil War led him to produce facsimiles of Confederate notes. The reproduction was excellent and the imitations could only be readily distinguished by Upham's imprint and advertisement in the bottom margin. Unfortunately most of his notes had the advert trimmed off and swiftly found their way to the Confederacy where they were promptly circulated as genuine. As a result, Upham facsimiles with the imprint still intact are now relatively scarce, and certainly rarer than the notes they imitated.

Validating Stamp   A handstruck mark applied to notes either at the time of issue to render them valid or subsequently applied to extend their usage.

Varible Optical Ink   Ink which appears to change colour or density depending on the angle at which the note is viewed.

Variety   Variation in, or modification of type, effigy or inscription.

Verso   The proper term for the reverse or back of a note.

Victory Note   A banknote of the Philippines overprinted VICTORY from October 20, 1944 onwards to celebrate the liberation of the islands after almost three years of Japanese rule.

Vignette   Strictly speaking the pictorial element of a note, shading off into the surrounding unprinted paper rather than having a clearly defined border or frame, but nowadays applied generally to the picture portion of a banknote, as opposed to the portrait, armorial or numeral elements.

Voucher   A piece of paper exchangeable for goods or services of a specified value and therefore regarded as a form of paper money.

War Lord Note   A note issued by one of the many tuchuns or war lords who operated in various parts of China in the period between the fall of the Manchu Dynasty and the communist takeover in 1949. Seldom, if ever, backed by gold or collateral other than the barrel of the gun, these notes were often well designed and printed (employing the leading security printers of Europe and America to lend them respectability), but rendered worthless as the fortunes of civil war ebbed and flowed. They have left a rich legacy of relatively cheap but colourful material for the collector market.

Watermark   A security device, generally visible when the note is held up to the light, and ranging from an overall geometric or curvilinear pattern to state emblems and even portraits, the lastnamed often set within a circular or oval cartouche. The watermark derives its name from the fact that it is created at the wet pulp stage in the manufacture of the paper, in which the pressure from brass wires or "bits" of the required pattern causes a slight thinning in the paper. In some cases notes have been printed on paper bearing the papermaker's name or trademark, only a portion of which is visible on any one note.

White Note Collector's term for the early notes of the Bank of England which were printed in black ink on white paper, using a relatively large format. This tradition, dating from 1695, continued as late as 1957 when the "white fiver" was superseded by a £5 note of more conventional design. These white notes were deceptively simple, which may have encouraged the Germans, under Operation Bernhard, to forge them during the World War II, using skilled counterfeiters in prisons and concentration camps for the purpose. But in fact the secret of these notes lay in the quality of paper used, with its extremely intricate watermark pattern, and it was the failure to secure paper of the right quality which defeated the forgers in the long run.

Wildcat Notes Notes issued in the USA and Canada in the early 19th century by unscrupulous persons who purported to act on behalf of non-existent banks. Poor communications and lax banking laws enabled them to get away with these frauds for a short time before their notes were unmasked as false and worthless. Nevertheless they are not without considerable interest on account of their colourful designs and their role in the rather freewheeling commerce of the period.

Withdrawn Note A note which has been taken out of circulation. Sometimes, though by no means always, such notes are overprinted, perforated or punched in some way to indicate that they have no legal tender status or any actual worth.

The anatomy of a banknote

BELOW we illustrate typical banknotes in order to show the various elements which combine to make up the design. Modern banknotes generally involve two or more different printing processes, applied to specially prepared paper which may incorporate one or more security features. The notes reproduced here have been chosen to represent the various details which the collector is likely to encounter in notes in general, as well as demonstrate how the design is built up as a result of very considerable thought—even though most members of the public may never give it a second glance.

Bank of England £20

Front (Obverse)

1. Denomination, comprising the pound sign £ (from Latin Libra = pound) and numerals, both horizontally lined and in contrasting colours.
2. Numerals of value (upper right) cross-hatched.
3. Bank of England in Old English upper and lower case lettering.
4. Paraphs or flourishes for decorative effect.
5. Promise: I PROMISE TO PAY THE BEARER ON DEMAND THE SUM OF TWENTY Pounds in three different fonts.
6. Signature of Merlyn Lowther who personally makes the promise in her capacity as Chief Cashier.
7. Cypher or serial, consisting of a two-letter prefix followed by eight digits. The left-hand cypher is made up of numerals of varying sizes and colours, whereas that on the right is of uniform size and colour.
8. Three-quarter facing portrait of Her Majesty Queen Elizabeth.
9. Hologram, crowned and scrolled, containing the seated figure of Britannia, based on the original motif, with the numerals 20 in an overall background pattern. Tilt the note in another direction and the image appears as 20 on an engine-turned background. In both positions, microscopic numerals also appear across the foot.
10. Place of issue: "London, For the Govr. and Compa. of the BANK of ENGLAND" in antique copperplate script.
11. Watermark, showing a bareheaded portrait of Queen Elizabeth.
12. The Royal monogram E II R on a solid rectangular ground.
13. Copyright symbol followed by THE GOVERNOR AND COMPANY OF THE BANK OF ENGLAND, 1999.
14. Musical notes, symbolising the subject on the back of the note.
15. Continuous band inscribed £20 in microprint.
16. Value in words TWENTY POUNDS in microprint on a lithographed underprint.
17. Underprint consisting of a subtly changing pattern of ornament and wavy lines.
18. Anaglyphic pattern, creating the illusion of a three-dimensional motif.
19. Band containing word TWENTY and numerals 20 alternately.
Plus a solid vertical metal strip showing through when viewed from the front.

Back (Reverse)

1. Vertical metal strip showing as short dashes.
2. BANK OF ENGLAND in double-lined capitals.
3. Value £20 in different styles in the upper corners.
4. Portrait of the composer, Sir Edward Elgar (1857-1934).
5. View of the West Face of Worcester Cathedral.
6. St Cecilia, patron saint of music.
7. Angel blowing a trumpet.

8. Latin motto.
9. Underprint of musical notes and symbols, repeated in various colours.
10. Copyright symbol and text around the watermark portrait.

The bulk of the detail on the reverse is lithographed, but the inscriptions are intaglio, like most of the features on the front.

United States $1

Front (Obverse)

1. Border title: FEDERAL RESERVE NOTE
2. Country name: UNITED STATES OF AMERICA
3. Legal Tender statement.
4. Numerals of value: two different sizes and different frames
5. Green serial, upper right and lower left, consisting of a district letter (L), 8-digit number from 00000001 to 99999999, and a suffix letter. The serial is repeated in opposite corners in case of accidental damage to part of the note.
6. Check letter and quadrant number (upper left), denoting the position of the note on the printing plate.
7. Check letter and plate number (lower right), denoting the actual plate used for printing.
8. District number 8, appearing in four positions, and indicating Federal Reserve District of St Louis.
9. District letter H contained in the seal of the Federal Reserve Bank. The district numbers and letters are: A1 (Boston), 2B (New York), 3C (Philadelphia), 4D (Cleveland), 5E (Richmond),

6F (Atlanta), 7G (Chicago), 8H (St Louis), 9I (Minneapolis), 10J (Kansas City), 11K (Dallas) and 12L (San Francisco).
10. Treasury seal, in green.
11. Value expressed as the word ONE in double-lined shaded lettering.
12. Upright cartouche, framing a bust portrait of George Washington, first President (1789-97), after the painting by Gilbert Stuart.
13. Background of cross-hatching.
14. Signature of Mary Ellen Withrow, Treasurer of the United States.
15. Signature of Robert E. Rubin, Secretary of the Treasury.
16. Series 1995. The year indicates when the design was introduced in its present form, if a letter is also present this denotes modification to the design.
17. Border of guilloche or engine-turning, to defeat counterfeiting.
18. Value in words ONE DOLLAR in bottom border.

Back ((Reverse)

1. Country name in white on green engine-turned background.
2. Value as a word superimposed on a numeral, in all four corners.
3. Motto IN GOD WE TRUST, added in 1957.
4. Value in word ONE in ornamental shaded lettering.
5. Plate number.
6. Value in words ONE DOLLAR, in shaded capitals, across the foot.
7. Reverse of the Great Seal of the United States:
8. Latin motto ANNUIT COEPTIS (He has favoured our undertakings) made up of 13 letters representing the original states.
9. The eternal eye of God, symbolising the spiritual over the material.
10. Pyramid of 13 tiers representing solid foundations and strength, but top unfinished to symbolise perfection as the ultimate goal.
11. Roman numerals for 1876, centennial year of the United States.
12. Latin motto NOVUS ORDO SECLORUM (a new order of the ages).
13. Obverse of the Great Seal of the United States:

14. Glory, comprising 13 five-pointed stars in a sunburst.
15. Riband motto in Latin E PLURIBUS UNUM (out of many, one).
16. Eagle's head representing the Executive Branch of government.
17. Shield with 13 stripes symbolising Congress and national unity.
18. Talons holding an olive branch of 13 leaves, symbolising a desire for peace.
19. Talons holding 13 arrows. symbolising readiness for war.
20. Nine tail feathers, symbolising the Supreme Court and Judiciary.
21. Scrollwork ornament.
22. Reticulation.
23. Beading.

There is also an albino colourless impression round the outer edges of the design, from the engraving on the front. Most of the black (front) and green (back) printing is intaglio, but the Treasury seal is lithographed and the district numbers and serial are letterpress. The paper has a security watermark overall, as well as small coloured threads embedded in the surface.

A brief history
of paper money

THE late Enoch Powell, a politician who was also a well-known numismatist, once scathingly dismissed paper money as something "which does duty for money in our degenerate age". From this it would be reasonable to suppose that paper money is a tawdry substitute for the real thing—gold and silver—in an age when money has ceased to have real value. With mounting inflation and continual rises in prices, many people would be inclined to agree; but while it is true that paper money has been used to a very large extent in the past century, it is by no means a modern phenomenon. In Britain, America and many European countries, paper money was in use three centuries ago. In Asia, however, paper was being used as money while Europe was still in the Dark Ages.

Appropriately enough, paper money began in China where paper itself was invented. The earliest form of paper money was produced during the T'ang Dynasty, somewhere between 650 and 800 AD. At that time the coins used in China were made of bronze, and very large quantities of bronze *cash* were needed for even the smallest transactions. This was not only inconvenient because of its weight, but also rather insecure. The cumbersome wagons used to carry these coins from one part of the country to the other were likely to ambushed by bandits and it was in an attempt to foil highway robbers that the Chinese merchants invented *fei-ch'ien*, literally "flying money", consisting of paper drafts negotiable in bronze currency. These drafts were not authorised paper money in the modern sense, but they undoubtedly paved the way for the paper

An early Chinese printer.

money introduced by the Sung Dynasty about 1000 AD. These Sung notes were redeemable in coin and quickly gained acceptance.

Unfortunately, the number of banks grew rapidly (there were no fewer than sixteen in Szechuan province alone) and they were all too readily tempted into issuing more and more notes without the funds or assets to back them. These notes, known as *chiao-tzu* (exchangeable money) soon lost the confidence of the people whereupon the government began issuing *kuan-tzu* (citadel money) which, in turn, was over-issued and led to an inflation which contributed to the downfall of the Sung Dynasty in 1278.

Their successors, the Yuan Dynasty (1270–1368) also issued far too much paper money. Before the end of the Mongol occupation of China this paper money had been reduced to utter worthlessness. A few examples of these very large and impressive notes have survived to this day, but rather more plentiful are the notes produced by the Ming Dynasty (1368–1644). They were made from the bark of the mulberry tree and printed from wooden blocks. Marco Polo describes in some detail the paper money of Cathay, as China was then known:

"All these pieces of paper money are issued with as much solemnity and authority as if they were of pure gold or silver; and on every piece a variety of officials, whose duty it is, have to write their names, and to put their seals. And when all is prepared duly, the chief officer deputed by the Khan smears the seal entrusted to him with vermilion, and impresses it on the paper, so that the form of the seal remains printed upon it in red; the money is then authentic. And the Khan causes every year to be made such a vast quantity of this money which costs him nothing, that it must equal in amount all the treasure in the world. When any of those pieces of paper

are spoilt—not that they are so very flimsy either—the owner carries them to the mint, and by paying three per cent on the value he gets new pieces in exchange."

With the collapse of the Ming Dynasty in 1644 the use of paper money came to an end. Two centuries later, however, the economic crisis caused by the T'ai-ping Rebellion of 1853–64 led the imperial government to resurrect paper money as an easy way out of its financial difficulties. From then onwards China became one of the world's most enthusiastic issuers of paper currency, with disastrous results on the economy and political stability of the country, especially in the turbulent period between the world wars when large parts of the country were under the control of various warlords.

The designs of the early Chinese notes were often very elaborate, and usually had some religious significance. The *chops*, or seal marks, added in vermilion ink to make these notes authentic, were inscribed in Chinese characters and took the form of such phrases as "to circulate as cash" or "to circulate under the Heavens". Some notes even depicted a number of coins, of the equivalent value, so that no one would be in any doubt as to the value of the note.

Banking in Europe

There are numerous references in the Bible and the literature of ancient times to moneylenders and others who, in effect, were the world's first bankers. The Babylonians, Egyptians, Greeks and Romans all had elaborate banking systems whereby rich merchants and goldsmiths lent money to businessmen or stored money for others. In Mesopotamia, the Igibi Bank is known to have been lending money and taking deposits in the middle of the sixth century BC, if not earlier.

Banking transactions are referred to frequently in accounts of life in Roman times. In medieval Europe, the rich merchants of the Italian cities of Milan, Venice and Genoa, the Hanseatic ports of Hamburg and Lubeck, and the international towns of Antwerp, Bruges and Geneva were acting as bankers, lending and receiving vast sums of money.

Many of these transactions were done on paper or parchment and took the form of promissory notes. Merchant "A" would give a note to a banker

The introduction of weights and measures into Greece occurred alongside the introduction of coined money.

Rich merchants and traders of Antwerp.

"B" promising to pay him 100 marks when his ship returned with a cargo from the East. The banker "B" might then use the note to pay goldsmith "C" for a quantity of silver or gold. Goldsmith "C" might use the note to pay farmer "D" for a quantity of corn. Finally the farmer would present the note to the original merchant "A" when the date for payment fell due, and demand 100 marks in coin. In this way promissory notes came to be accepted in much the same way that we use paper money today. Sometimes these notes might pass from hand to hand for a considerable time before they were eventually presented to the original issuer for redemption.

The earliest promissory notes would have been made of vellum, parchment or some other kind of animal skin. Paper was virtually unknown outside China until the middle of the twelfth century and came to Europe via Arabia and North Africa. Herault in France claims to have had the first paper mill in Europe, established in 1189. For hundreds of years thereafter paper continued to be a scarce commodity in Europe. In England the earliest kind of paper money consisted of notes issued by goldsmiths as receipts for valuables deposited by merchants in their vaults. These receipts could be used as securities to get a loan and, like promissory notes, tended to circulate quite widely as a form of currency. These receipts and promissory notes were accepted as legal tender following an Exchequer Order made by the authority of King Charles II in 1665, but another thirty years elapsed before paper money, as we understand it today, was issued in Britain.

The first paper money to be issued in Europe made its appearance in 1661. The Stockholm Bank of Sweden issued credit notes (*kreditivsedlar*) in place of the very cumbersome copper currency which was rapidly losing its value. The idea of producing these notes originated with Johan Palmstruch, a Dutchman living in the Latvian city of Riga (which was then a part of Sweden). Palmstruch put forward this idea in 1652. His notes were the first banknotes in the modern sense and not like the previous receipts given by goldsmiths and merchant bankers for specific deposits. They were current in the hand of the bearer and did not earn interest, as the promissory notes often did.

None of the first issue of *kreditivsedlar* has survived and fewer than a dozen specimens of the issue of 1662 and 1663 are now in existence, all in various museum collections. The issue of 1666, however, is much more plentiful, though this was the last to appear. These notes seem to have been readily accepted by Swedish businessmen, being much more convenient to handle than the cumbersome copper plate-money, but the Stockholm Bank gave way to the temptation of over-issuing. As early as 1663, the Bank was unable to redeem its notes and two years later the Swedish government decided that they should be abolished. The last issue was redeemable in silver thalers, since copper went out of circulation in 1665–6.

Paper money became popular at the end of the seventeenth century in Britain and France, thanks

The founding of the Bank of England, 1694.

largely to the efforts of two Scotsmen. William Paterson founded the Bank of England in 1694 and the Bank of Scotland the following year. His fellow countryman, John Law, founded the first French bank, the *Banque Generale*, in 1716. Both men realised the convenience and advantages of paper money and were responsible for the first issues of banknotes on both sides of the English Channel.

The earliest notes of the Bank of England were issued in 1695 and were in denominations of £10, £20, £30, £40, £50 and £100. Altogether some 12,000 notes were issued in 1695–6. The notes were large in size and beautifully printed in black copperplate on white paper made of a mixture of linen rags and cotton. The date, bearer's name and cashier's

signature were entered in handwriting, while the rest was printed.

In the top centre was a little picture of Britannia seated and holding a spear and an olive branch. At her side was a shield bearing the cross of St George and at her feet was a pile of coins. At first the value of the note was printed, but later issues showed the amount in handwriting. The same basic design was retained for the higher-value Bank of England notes until 1956. Many people will recall the old-style "white fivers". Partly because of their high value and partly on account of fear of forgery, tradesmen and shopkeepers used to insist on their customers writing their names and addresses on these notes whenever they offered them in transactions, while examples passing through post offices often bore the office postmark as well.

After founding the *Banque Generale* John Law formed the French Mississippi Company of Louisiana in 1718 and speculation in its shares was equalled only by the British South Seas Company. Like the latter, the bubble burst in 1720 and Law (who by this time had been appointed Comptroller General of France) had to flee the country. Under John Law, the *Banque Generale* also issued its own notes, but these were quite ordinary in appearance. Apart from their serial number, which was written in by hand, the notes were printed in black on white paper and promised the bearer on demand various sums in livres Tournois coined in silver.

Examples of these notes, issued at Paris between 1716 and 1720, are now quite scarce. Law had several theories regarding economics and though he was discredited in 1720 his ideas survived him, to cause untold misery and financial chaos to his adopted country. He had proposed a land currency equal to the value of the land and to the value of actual coined money without being subject, as was coined money, to a fall in value. This system was adopted by the French government, when on the verge of bankruptcy, and this precipitated the Revolution of 1789–92.

Notes known as *Assignats* were issued issued in 1789, their value backed by the land confiscated from the Church at the outset of the Revolution. Each note had a nominal value of 100 livres bearing interest at 5 per cent. A total of 4,000 million livres was put into circulation in the first issue alone. Within a year the interest had been reduced to 3 per cent and a subsequent issue of 800 million livres bore no interest at all. The output of paper money grew faster and faster; by the middle of 1794, a total of 8,000 millions had been issued, but within two years the amount in circulation had spiralled to 45,500 millions. The value of the *assignat* fell rapidly. Even the earlier issues were reckoned to be worth only 20 livres in coin for every 100 livres in paper. By 1793 the depreciation had reached 97 per cent. The government body known as the Directory fixed the value of the *assignats* at a thirtieth of their original value and then reduced it to a hundredth.

When the *assignats* sank to utter worthlessness

the government had recourse to territorial money orders known as *Mandats* which were put into circulation at the rate of one for 30 *assignats*. These notes were no more trusted than the *assignats* and actually depreciated more rapidly. In many cases the *mandats* were worthless before they could even get into circulation. The Directory finally gave up its experiments with paper money in 1797 when *assignats* and *mandats* were called in and exchanged for coin in the ratio of one livre for every 3,000 livres paper money.

British Banks

Meanwhile, in England, the banking system developed along much sounder lines. By the 1680s there were about fifty merchants in London alone whose promissory notes were readily acceptable and these entrepreneurs were the founders of banks that bore their names, such as Martin's, Barclay's, Lloyd's, Glyn Mills, Coutts and Cox & King's. Regular denominations, from £20 to £1,000, were resumed by the Bank of England in 1725, notes for £10 and £15 being added in 1759. As the Bank of England did not issue notes of lower value it was left to the many private banks, which mushroomed in the eighteenth century, to remedy this deficiency. Some attempt to regulate this industry came by way of an Act of 1777 which forbade the private banks to issue notes under £5. Nevertheless small provincial banks came and went with alarming rapidity and in 1793 alone more than a hundred of them crashed. In that year the Bank of England issued its first £5 notes and four years later the 1777 Act was repealed in order that the Bank could issue £1 and £2 notes.

During the French Revolutionary and Napoleonic Wars, gold and silver coins were in short supply, and the private banks filled the gap with numerous issues

A Bank of England £1 note of 1797.

of notes. By 1810 there were more than 700 banks in operation in England and Wales alone, issuing more than £30 million each year. The wartime boom was followed by a slump in which many of the smaller banks disappeared or were taken over by their larger competitors. In November 1825 many companies went bankrupt and this precipitated a run on the banks. The position was exacerbated when many provincial banks could not get at the funds which they, in turn, had deposited with the major London

banks. When one of the major London banks failed early in December 1825 no fewer than 44 provincial banks crashed as a result. By December 17 four of the biggest London banks had ceased payment and the Bank of England's gold reserve was down to less than a million pounds.

To alleviate the situation the Bank hastily issued a large quantity of £1 notes which had been partially prepared for release in 1821 but had never been put into circulation. These notes bore the date 1821 at the top, but were dated 20 December 1825 at the foot. They circulated for a few months, until the Bank of England was able to replenish its stocks of gold with the assistance of Rothschilds, the French merchant bankers. From then until 1928 the Bank of England did not issue notes below £5 in face value.

In the economic crisis of 1825–26 hundreds of country banks went out of business and are remembered nowadays solely on account of their notes, many of which were attractively engraved with local landmarks and scenery. The notes of the broken banks are also of interest for the marks stamped on them indicating that they were produced in evidence in the bankruptcy courts. Many of them also have marks indicating how much was actually paid out to creditors in the end.

The Bank Charter Act of 1844 limited the number of note-issuing banks to 72 joint stock banks and 207 others, with a total note issue of £8,500,000. Thereafter the number of note-issuing banks dwindled. Under the terms of the 1844 Act no bank with offices in London could issue its own notes. As more and more of the provincial banks were taken over by London-based banks their privilege of issuing notes was curtailed. The last of the independent note-issuing banks was Fox, Fowler & Company of Wellington, Somerset which gave up this privilege in 1921 when it amalgamated with Lloyd's Bank.

Private banknotes continued to appear in the Isle of Man until 1961 when the Manx government took over the privilege hitherto enjoyed by the Isle of Man Bank, Lloyd's, Martin's and Barclay's. Since then, notes have been issued by the Isle of Man Bank under the authority of the Isle of Man government.

Scotland and Ireland have been issuing their own banknotes since 1696 and 1783 respectively and since the Bank Charter Act of 1844 did not apply to these countries, the private banks retained the right to issue their own notes. At the end of the World War II there were still about a dozen Scottish banks issuing distinctive notes in denominations from £1 upwards, but as a result of mergers and take-overs the number has now fallen to three. In Northern Ireland a number of banks continue to issue their own notes but in the Republic of Ireland notes are now confined to the issues of the Bank of Ireland. In the Channel Islands notes were issued by various private banks from 1797 onwards, while the States of Guernsey produced the first government notes in 1826. Of particular interest are the notes, ranging

Guernsey notes issued during the German occupation in World War II.

from sixpence to £5, issued by Guernsey and Jersey during the German occupation (1940–45). Attractive banknotes are produced to this day by the state banks in both bailiwicks.

In Britain, the gold sovereign and half-sovereign continued to be the preferred medium in circulation, but on the outbreak of the World War I in August 1914 specie payments were suspended and the government authorised the Treasury to issue notes of £1 and 10s, popularly known as Bradburies because they bore the signature of John Bradbury, Secretary to the Treasury. Treasury notes of various types continued until 1928 when their function was taken over by the Bank of England. Treasury notes lingered on in general circulation until July 1933 when they were called in and ceased to be legal tender.

The traditional white fivers were replaced by notes of a more conventional design in 1957. The subsequent history of Bank of England notes reflects the steady depreciation in the real value of money, through the reduction in the size of notes, the demise of the 10s note in 1970 and the pound note a decade later, as well as the greater prevalence of £10 and £20 notes at the present time. Pound notes survived longer in Scotland and the Isle of Man. Today, only the Royal Bank of Scotland persists with new issues of pound notes, although their average life is reduced to no more than a few months in circulation, and the cost of producing them must now outweigh the benefits of retaining them.

Banknotes in the Rest of the World

The pattern of note-issuing in the rest of the world follows similar lines. In North America,

for example, the earliest paper money in Canada consisted of playing cards with handwritten inscriptions, while Massachusetts had notes by December 1690. Although specie was generally preferred there was a rash of paper money in the rebellious colonies during the American Revolutionary War. This set a doubtful precedent for the prolific issues of state banks and countless private banks and even insurance companies in the nineteenth century. The American Civil War produced not only a profligate issue of notes in the Confederacy but various makeshifts on the Union side, ranging from encased postage stamps to fractional currency—small notes which reproduced postage stamps of the appropriate value.

After the Civil War the US government, through the Treasury, continued to release notes of various kinds: Demand Notes, Legal Tender Notes, Compound Interest treasury Notes, Interest Bearing Notes, Silver Certificates, Coin Notes and National Bank Notes. Under the terms of the Federal Reserve Act of 1913 new kinds of currency consisted of Federal Reserve Bank Notes and Federal Reserve Notes, redeemed by the banks and the US government respectively.

Generally speaking, most countries went through a period in which notes were issued by commercial and private banks, followed by legislation to limit or consolidate this practice. By the late-nineteenth century, however, note issues were more generally restricted to a national or state bank, sometimes augmented by lower denominations issued directly by the government, or one of its agencies such as the treasury or finance ministry. These latter issues were often produced in times of financial crisis or war, when there was a shortage of coinage.

In the course of the twentieth century, as people became much more confident in paper and appreciated its convenience over coinage, the range of denominations tended to expand, and notes of even quite low face value became more common. During both world wars paper largely superseded gold and silver coin, and in addition there were special issues by occupying powers for territories under their administration, or military notes prepared in connection with invasion or liberation of enemy-held territory. There were even distinctive notes for prisoner of war, internment and concentration camps. Emergency issues in time of economic crisis or rampant inflation have appeared in Germany, Austria and Poland in the early 1920s, in China, Greece and Hungary in the aftermath of World War II, and, more recently, in Turkey, Poland, Yugoslavia and many parts of Latin America an the former Communist bloc—all yielding an abundance of material for the natophilist to study and collect.

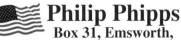 

The origin of
Pound notes

POUND NOTES are virtually a thing of the past; only the Royal Bank of Scotland continues to issue them, but for how much longer is doubtful, given their very limited life in general circulation. Although paper money of one sort or another had been in existence since the later 17th century pound notes were a relative latecomer, as the public preferred coins. Not surprisingly, it took a national crisis in the late 18th century to initiate pound notes, and significantly their revival in the early 20th century was also precipitated by an event of cataclysmic proportions…

In 1797, when Britain was at war with Revolutionary France, a rumour circulated that the enemy had landed an expeditionary force on the Welsh coast. As a matter of fact an American adventurer in the French service had led a flotilla of three warships which landed some 600 troops near St David's in Pembrokeshire. This was merely a diversionary tactic, intended to distract the British from the main thrust, which was an invasion of Ireland. The small contingent of French troops, stranded without support or supplies, was soon rounded up by the local militia.

Nevertheless, the invasion of Wales triggered off a nation-wide panic and this led to a run on the banks of such proportions that the gold reserves of the Bank of England were drastically depleted. Such was the shortage of specie that the government issued an Order in Council suspending bank payments in cash until Parliament could consider the situation. The Bank Restriction Act of 1797 gave legal sanction to this draconian measure, and it was not until 1821, long after the Napoleonic Wars, that specie payments were resumed.

In the intervening period, when silver was almost as scarce a commodity as gold, the Bank of England followed the example of the provincial banks and resorted to low-denomination notes for one or two pounds. At the same time, pound notes of the private banks proliferated and, as a consequence, forgery became very common, despite the severe penalties inflicted on those convicted of counterfeiting.

Bank of England one and two pound notes were withdrawn in 1821 when the Bank Restriction Act was repealed, but within a few years immense pressure on gold arose from another quarter. In November 1825 the eminent firm of Sir Peter Pole and Company, London agent for more than 40 provincial banks, failed

with a catastrophic knock-on effect. Once more, the public panicked and rushed to convert Bank of England paper into gold. As a result of the gold shortage, the Bank re-issued a stock of 1821 pound notes which, quite by chance, had not been destroyed and still reposed in the vaults. These notes were overprinted with the new date and are thus unique in having two dates, 1821 at the top and 20 December 1825 at the foot. These makeshifts were promptly withdrawn when the gold crisis evaporated a few months later.

It is a fallacy to suppose that there were no pound notes around at this period. In fact it was only the Bank of England which was prevented from issuing such low-denomination notes. The banks in Scotland and Ireland, as well as the country banks of England and Wales, had been issuing notes for a guinea or a pound for many years, but these notes tended to have very limited local circulation. As a result of numerous bank failures, however, the Bank Charter Act of 1844 limited the issue of notes in England and Wales to 72 joint-stock banks and 207 other banks in the provinces. As no bank with offices in London was permitted to issue notes, this regulation rapidly reduced the number, although it was not until 1921 that the last of the country banks to issue pound notes—Fox, Fowler & Company of Wellington, Somerset—gave up this privilege when it amalgamated with Lloyd's Bank.

In addition, there were various attempts, notably by the pioneer of industrial philanthropy, Robert Owen, to produce paper money as part of an experiment in industrial and social economy. In the 1830s Owen produced notes through his National Equitable Labour Exchange, whose headquarters were located in Charlotte Street, Rathbone Place, London, with branches in Birmingham and other industrial centres. Owen's notes were remarkably elaborate for the period, featuring two vignettes showing a beehive and

A selection of £1 Provincial notes.

a pair of scales to symbolise industry and justice or fair-dealing. These notes were unusual in being denominated not in any actual currency but in hours of labour. Thus workers were paid in notes according to the hours they worked, and the notes could then be spent in Exchange stores, goods being given of the requisite value. This was not so very different from the common practice of many factories and collieries in the early years of the Industrial Revolution, whereby workers were paid in vouchers or scrip which could only be redeemed in goods from the company store. This system was open to abuse and was eventually outlawed by the Truck Act of 1840.

In 1891 George Goschen, then Chancellor of the Exchequer, recommended that the Bank of England should resume the issue of pound notes in order to conserve the Bank's gold, but nothing came of the proposal, because the public preferred sovereigns. The general attitude was neatly summed up by a letter to the Referee, a periodical of the 1890s:

Mr Goschen has been considering the one pound notes from various points of view, but there is one aspect of the question he has overlooked, namely the sanitary, and I conclude from this he has never lived, as I have, in a one pound note country. The five pound Bank of England note is a clean crisp wholesome thing, the rustle of which is almost in itself a liberal education. This character the five pound note maintains because it passes through few hands before returning to the Bank, and enjoys what may be called a very select circulation. It is otherwise with the one pound note as known in Scotland and Ireland. Like Wellington's army it goes everywhere and does everything. It is fair to say that the five pound note is handled chiefly by ladies, gentlemen and professional cashiers, but when you produce paper money to the value of twenty shillings there is no hand so dirty but may grasp it. And that is not its worst fate. It is a common thing for Irish navvies and cattle drovers to carry one pound notes in their boots. At any wayside inn in Scotland or Ireland again you may see a dirty ruffian fish out of the lining of his clothes a something which he will carefully unfold and spread over the counter. When he has done this you see before

you a tattered one pound note—the same note that will tomorrow come into your possession. For the one pound note circulates until it falls to pieces, by which time it has absorbed nameless abominations. The people who coined the expression as to money having no smell knew nothing of the one pound note of commerce.

Until the outbreak of war in 1914 the people of Britain had considered themselves singularly exempt from the fears of invasion and the liability to personal military service, which plagued their Continental neighbours. While a professional soldier could be employed to do all the necessary fighting and dying for thirteen pence a day, all the ordinary citizen need do was to read the reports of his doings and supply the criticism, but the days preceding the fateful August 4 hung heavy with sinister portent and the refusal of post offices to change five pound notes brought a conviction of national crisis to the man in the street.

This conviction was emphasised when pound and ten-shilling notes, crudely printed in red and black, were issued by the Treasury. The makeshift nature of these notes has been offered in evidence that Britain was innocent of any premeditation of entering the war, and when one compares these early Treasury notes with the one-mark notes issued by the German government at this period, one can see that this argument carries considerable weight. Later issues were better in design and production, and were then replaced by a more colourful form of Treasury note which was certainly more like a banknote than a coupon cut from a newspaper.

After 1914 there was to be no reversion to gold coins in general circulation. Notes of relatively small denominations were here to stay. Only the relentless march of inflation since the 1960s would ensure the demise, first of the ten-shilling note, and then of the pound. And now it can only be a matter of time before the five pound note, the prerogative of the professional classes a century ago but now reduced in size, status and active life, goes the same way and becomes a thing of the past.

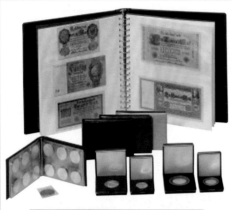

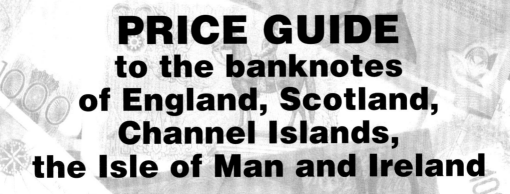

PRICE GUIDE
to the banknotes
of England, Scotland,
Channel Islands,
the Isle of Man and Ireland

The price one should pay for a banknote can vary depending on a whole variety of criteria. In this price guide the figures given are intended as a *guide only* to prices that one should expect to pay for notes in the condition noted at the top of each column—the grading is as explained in the grading table on page 25. Notes in lower grades would obviously cost far less and notes in exceptional condition can command higher prices than those given. The notes listed are ordinary circulating examples.
To comply with current legislation illustrations of all modern notes have been endorsed with the word SPECIMEN—this, of course, does not appear on the notes themselves. Proofs, specimen printings and other varieties are beyond the scope of this publication—for further information the reader is referred to the relevant specialist book as listed in the Bibliography in the Directory section at the end of this book.

EARLY BANK OF ENGLAND NOTES

By the close of the 17th century London was becoming one of the most important trading and commercial centres of the world. Its rich merchants and goldsmiths, many of whom are remembered to this day in the names of the banks such as Martins, Lloyds, Barclays and Glyn Mills, had been issuing promissory notes and receipts for valuables for many years and these pieces of paper were accepted as if they were actually money. By 1680 there were about fifty of these merchants whose promissory notes were readily acceptable. With the rapid development of England as a trading nation it became necessary to establish some sort of national bank. In 1694, the Bank of England was founded by William Paterson, a Scotsman whose proposals were readily endorsed by Charles Montagu, the Chancellor of the Exchequer at the time. In the year of its foundation the Bank issued only a few notes, for £20 and £50, and these were entirely hand-written like the merchants' notes.

The first printed notes were released on June 5, 1695 but had a very short life, being hurriedly withdrawn when a cunning forger obtained a quantity of paper from the same supplier as the Bank and then produced excellent counterfeits. The Bank got around this problem by using a different type of paper, with a marbled pattern. As a further precaution against fraud, these marbled notes were cut in half and only one half given to the customer. When the note came back to the bank it could be checked against the other half to prove that it was genuine. None of these marbled notes has survived, but the practice of cutting notes in half continued for some time. Later notes may be found with curved cuts between the two halves as well as a printed design.

A watermark was adopted as a security feature in 1697 and specially watermarked paper has been used for all Bank of England notes since then. The notes from 1696 to 1725 had the amounts written in by hand and could be issued for any odd amount from £10 upwards. Regular denominations were re-introduced in 1725 and were issued in values from £20 to £1000. In 1759 notes for £10 and £15 were added, and six years later a £25 was introduced. The Bank of England did not issue notes of lower value, and it was left to the many private banks to fill the gap. The first £5 notes appeared in 1793, a year when many private banks crashed as a result of the outbreak of war with Revolutionary France.

During a shortage of gold coin during the Napoleonic Wars, notes of £1 and £2 were added to the series and these continued until 1829, but thereafter the Bank reverted to notes from £5 to £1000 only. All of these 19th century notes are of the greatest rarity. They are generally grouped according to the signature of the Chief Cashier which appears on them. At various times from 1826 onwards branches of the Bank of England were opened in a number of provincial cities, resulting in notes specifically inscribed. Our listing of Bank of England notes is confined to the notes issued in London which are available in collectable condition. It has been decided to omit the higher values, including the £500 and £1000 (which ceased in 1943), which are of considerable rarity. Included are the notes issued by the Treasury following the outbreak of World War I. The Bank of England, at that time was only empowered to issue notes of £5 and over and due to the predicted restrictions on gold, Treasury notes were issued in denominations of ten shillings and one pound with the intention of replacing the sovereign and half sovereign.

BANK OF ENGLAND
Pre 1925

All of the black and white notes (commonly known as "White" notes) issued before 1913 are rare and only the £1 Hase is offered with any regularity by dealers and then only occasionally. All of the "White" notes were issued from London and most were also issued from branch offices in Birmingham, Bristol, Hull, Leeds, Liverpool, Manchester, Newcastle, Plymouth and Portsmouth. These branch notes are usually scarcer than the London issues and most are beyond the scope of this yearbook. Occasionally, however, a branch issue is either commoner than the corresponding London note or available in sufficient quantities to warrant a listing.

These notes were all printed in black on white paper in sheets of two notes (except for the smaller £1 and £2 values which were printed in sheets of four) which were then cut up to give one straight edge and three uncut (deckled) edges.

Later issues of the famous "White" notes are found under "Bank of England issues from 1928".

ONE POUND

BE1

		Fine
(1807-21)		
BE1	*Chief Cashier: H. Hase*	
	Printed date and serial numbers	£1000
(1825-26)		
BE2	*Chief Cashier: H. Hase*	
	Printed date and serial numbers, emergency issue	£1000

TWO POUNDS

BE3

(1807-21)   *Fine*
BE3   *Chief Cashier: H. Hase*
    Printed date and serial numbers £3500

BE4–BE9 [*Held in reserve*]

FIVE POUNDS

                                                      VF   *EF*
(1902-18)
BE10   *Signature: J. G. Nairne*
    London £375   £600

BE11

(1918-25)
BE11   *Signature: E. M. Harvey*
    London £200   £350

TEN POUNDS

BE12

		VF	EF
(1902-18)			
BE12	*Signature: J. G. Nairne*		
	London	£575	£950
(1918-25)			
BE13	*Signature: E. M. Harvey*		
	London	£300	£475

TWENTY POUNDS

		VF	EF
(1902-18)			
BE14	*Signature: J. G. Nairne*		
	Manchester	£1850	£3250
(1918-25)			
BE15	*Signature: E. M. Harvey*		
	London..	£850	£2000

FIFTY POUNDS

BE16

	VF	EF
(1902-18)		
BE16 *Signature: J. G. Nairne*		
Manchester	£1750	£3000
(1918-25)		
BE17 *Signature: E. M. Harvey*		
London	£1000	£2200

ONE HUNDRED POUNDS

BE18

(1902-18)		
BE18 *Signature: J. G. Nairne*		
Manchester...	£1500	£2750
(1918-25)		
BE19 *Signature: E. M. Harvey*		
London	£1100	£2300

Warwick & Warwick

Selling your Banknotes?

To satisfy overwhelming demand from our buyers Warwick and Warwick urgently require quality material of all types. We particularly need Great Britain, World and single country collections and accumulations of any size and in any condition from Fair to UNC.

The market for quality material has never been stronger and if you are considering the sale of your collection now is the time to act.

Free Valuations
We will provide a free professional and without obligation valuation of your collection. Either we will make you a fair, binding private treaty offer, or we will recommend inclusion of your property in our next public auction.

Free Transportation
We can arrange insured transportation of your collection to our Warwick offices completely free of charge. If you decline our offer we ask you to cover the return carriage costs only.

Free Visits
Visits by our valuers are possible anywhere in the country or abroad, usually within 48 hours, in order to value larger collections. Please phone for details.

Excellent Prices
Our ever expanding customer base means we are in a position to offer prices that we feel sure will exceed your expectations.

Act Now
Telephone Richard Beale today with details of your property, E-mail or fax us if you prefer.

Get the experts on your side.

TREASURY NOTES

Notes of one shilling (1/-), two shillings and sixpence (2/6) and five shillings (5/-) signed by John Bradbury and Norman Fenwick Warren Fisher, were produced between December 1917 and November 1919 but were never issued. However, a few notes survived destruction and, along with some examples of proof status, somehow escaped. They very occasionally come onto the market and command very high prices.

TEN SHILLINGS
FIRST (EMERGENCY) BRADBURY ISSUE (August 1914)
Red. 127 x 63mm. Blank reverse
Signature: John Bradbury   VF   EF

TR1a

TR1a   Prefix A. N<u>o</u> (*with dash*) followed by letter over
    number followed by 6 serial numbers £300   £550

TR1b

TR1b   Prefix S and T. Letter over number followed by *No.*
    (*with dot*) followed by 6 serial numbers £400   £850
TR1c   Prefix A-C. Letter over number followed by *No.* (*with dot*)
    followed by 5 serial numbers £500   £1000

SECOND BRADBURY ISSUE (January 1915)

Red. 136 x 76mm. Blank reverse. De La Rue printing
Signature: John Bradbury

TR2a

		VF	EF
TR2a	Prefix A-M. Letter over number followed by 5 serial numbers	£175	£325
TR2b	Prefix A1-M1. Letter and figure 1 over number followed by 5 serial numbers	£185	£350
TR2c	Prefix A2-C2. Letter and figure 2 over number followed by 5 serial numbers	£250	£425

Red. 136 x 76mm. Blank reverse. Waterlow printing
Signature: John Bradbury

TR3a

TR3a	Prefix N-Z. Letter over number followed by 6 serial numbers	£200	£375
TR3b	Prefix O1-Y1. Letter and figure 1 over number followed by 6 serial numbers	£200	£375

SECOND BRADBURY ISSUE DARDANELLES OVERPRINT
(May 1915)
Overprint in Arabic "Piastres silver 60" on TR3a above for the use of the British Expeditionary Forces in Turkey in 1915

TR4

		VF	EF
TR4	Prefix Y and Z. Letter over number followed by 6 serial numbers	£700	£1350

THIRD BRADBURY ISSUE
(October 1918)
Green, brown and purple. 138 x 78mm.
Signature: John Bradbury

TR5a

TR5a	Prefix A. Letter over number followed by *No.* (*with* **dot**) and serial numbers in black..	£225	£450

	VF	*EF*

TR5b

TR5b   Prefix A. Letter over number followed by *No* (*with* **dash**)
            and serial numbers in black...   £225   £450

(December 1918)
TR6a   Prefix B and C. Letter over number followed by *No.* (*with* **dot**)
            and serial numbers in red ....   £950   ---

TR6b

TR6b   Prefix B and C. Letter over number followed by *No* (*with* **dash**)
            and serial numbers in red £180   £375

FIRST FISHER ISSUE
(September 1919)
Green, brown and purple. 138 x 78mm.
Signature: N. F. Warren Fisher

TR7a   Prefix D-H. Letter over number followed by *No.* (*with* **dot**)
            and serial numbers in red £120   £250

VF   EF

TR7b

TR7b   Prefix D-H. Letter over number followed by *No* (*with **dash***)
and serial numbers in red £100   £225

SECOND FISHER ISSUE
(November 1922)
Green, brown and purple. 138 x 78mm.
Signature: N. F. Warren Fisher

TR8

TR8   Prefix J-S. Letter over number followed by serial numbers £90   £200

THIRD FISHER ISSUE ("NORTHERN" ADDED TO TITLE) (July 1927)

Green, brown and purple. 138 x 78mm.
Signature: N. F. Warren Fisher

TR9

	VF	EF
TR9 Prefix S-U, W. Letter over number followed by serial numbers...	£90	£200

ONE POUND

FIRST (EMERGENCY) BRADBURY ISSUE (August 1914)

Black. 127 x 63mm. Blank reverse
Signature: John Bradbury

TR10a

		VF	EF
TR10a	Prefix A., B. and C. (*with dot*) followed by 6 serial numbers..................	£750	£1500
TR10b	Prefix A, B and C (*without dot*) followed by 6 serial numbers..................	£1100	£2500
TR10c	Prefix A-T. Letter over number followed by No.(*with dot*) and 4 serial numbers..................	£950	£2300
TR10d	Prefix A-T. Letter over number followed by No.(*with dot*) and 5 serial numbers..................	£400	£850

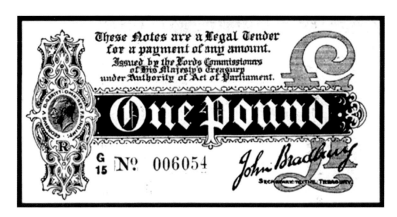

		VF	EF
TR10e	Prefix A-T. Letter over number followed by *No.(with **dot**)* and 6 serial numbers...	£350	£750
TR10f	Prefix A-T. Letter over number followed by *No.(with **dot**)* and 7 serial numbers...	£850	£1750
TR11a	Prefix K and L. Letter over number followed by *No* (*with **dash***) and 4 serial numbers	£950	£2300
TR11b	Prefix K and L. Letter over number followed by *No* (*with **dash***) and 5 serial numbers	£600	£1200
TR12a	Prefix B and D. Letter over number followed by *No* (*with **dash***) and 6 serial numbers in smaller type......................	£600	£1200
TR12b	Prefix B and D. Letter over number followed by *No.* (*with **dot***) and 7 serial numbers in smaller type	£850	£1750

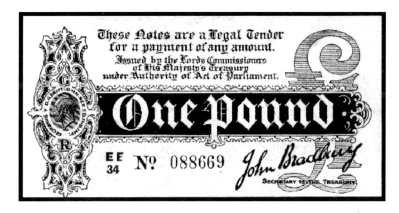

TR13

TR13	Prefix BB-LL. Double letter over number followed by *No.* (*with **dot***) and 6 serial numbers..	£600	£1200

SECOND BRADBURY ISSUE (October 1914)

Black. 149 x 85mm. Blank reverse
Signature: John Bradbury

TR14a	Prefix A-Z. Letter over number followed by 5 serial numbers..	£250	£400

TR14a

TR14b

	VF	EF
TR14b Prefix A1-L1. Letter and figure 1 over number followed by. 5 serial numbers	£250	£400

SECOND BRADBURY ISSUE DARDANELLES OVERPRINT (May 1915)

Overprint in Arabic "Piastres silver1200" on TR14a above for the use of the British Expeditionary Forces in Turkey in 1915

TR15

	F	VF
TR15 Prefix F, J, M, Y. Letter over number followed by 5 serial numbers	£1750	£3250

THIRD BRADBURY ISSUE
(January 1917)
Green, brown and purple.151 x 84mm.
Signature: John Bradbury

	VF	EF
TR16a Prefix A. Letter over number followed by serial numbers..........	£65	£160

TR16b

TR16b Prefix B-H. Letter over number followed by serial numbers	£60	£130
TR16c Prefix Z. Letter over number followed by serial numbers	£65	£150

FIRST FISHER ISSUE
(September 1919)
Green, brown and purple. 151 x 84mm.
Signature: N. F. Warren Fisher

TR17a Prefix K. Letter over number followed by serial numbers..........	£55	£110

TR17b

TR17b Prefix L-Y. Letter over number followed by serial numbers	£45	£90
TR17c Prefix Z. Letter over number followed by serial numbers	£55	£110

	VF	EF

SECOND FISHER ISSUE
(February 1923)
Green, brown and purple. 151 x 84mm.
Signature: N. F. Warren Fisher

TR18a Prefix A1. Letter and figure 1 over number followed
by *No.* and serial numbers £50 £100
TR18b Prefix B1-R1. Letter and figure 1 over number followed
by *No.* and serial numbers £40 £85

TR18c

TR18c Prefix Z1. Letter and figure 1 over number followed
by ° and serial numbers.. £50 £100

TR18d

TR18d Prefix H1, M1, N1, P1 and R1. As *TR18b* but with square
dot below.. £85 £185

	VF	EF

THIRD FISHER ISSUE
("NORTHERN" ADDED TO TITLE)
(July 1927)
Green, brown and purple. 151 x 84mm.
Signature: N. F. Warren Fisher

TR19a Prefix S1. Letter and figure 1 over number followed
by *No.* and serial numbers £60 £120

TR19b

TR19b Prefix T1-X1. Letter and figure 1 over number followed
by *No.* and serial numbers £45 £95
TR19c Prefix Z1. Letter and figure 1 over number followed
by *No.* and serial numbers £60 £120
TR19d Prefix S1 and X1. As *TR19b* but with square dot below £120 £200

TR19e

TR19e Prefix Z1. As *TR19c* but with square dot below £125 £225

BANK OF ENGLAND
From 1928

TEN SHILLINGS
SERIES "A" BRITANNIA ISSUE
(November 1928)

Red-brown. 138 x 78mm
Signature: C. P. Mahon   *VF*   *EF*
Prefix sequence: Letter/Number/Number

BE20a

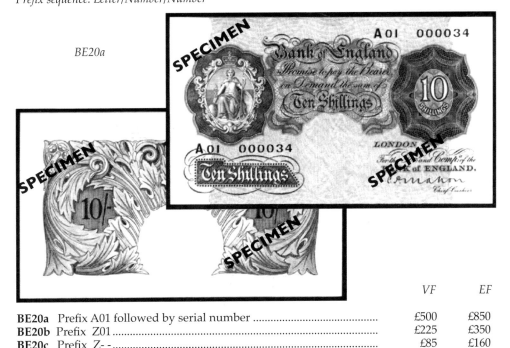

		VF	EF
BE20a	Prefix A01 followed by serial number	£500	£850
BE20b	Prefix Z01	£225	£350
BE20c	Prefix Z- -	£85	£160
BE20d	Prefix Y- -, X- -, W- -	£75	£150
BE20e	Prefix V- - (*traced to V12*)	£550	£950

(July 1930)
Red-brown. 138 x 78mm
Signature: B. G. Catterns
Prefix sequence: Letter/Number/Number

BE21a

		VF	EF
BE21a	Prefix V- - followed by serial number (*traced from V14*)	£65	£125
BE21b	Prefix U- - to L- -	£45	£80
BE21c	Prefix K- - (*traced to K99*)	£65	£125

(October 1934)

Red-brown. 138 x 78mm
Signature: K .O. Peppiatt

Prefix sequence: Letter/Number/Number

BE22b

BE22a	Prefix J01 followed by serial number	£250	£450
BE22b	Prefix J- -	£45	£100
BE22c	Prefix H- - to B- -...	£25	£60
BE22d	Prefix A- - (*traced to A99*)...	£45	£100

Prefix sequence: Number/Number/Letter

BE23b

BE23a	Prefix 01Z followed by serial number	£200	£400
BE23b	Prefix - -Z	£45	£100
BE23c	Prefix - -Y to - -R	£25	£60
BE23d	Prefix - -O (*traced to 42O*)...	£45	£100

VF   EF

(October 1940)
Mauve (shades). 138 x 78mm. With metal security thread
Signature: K .O. Peppiatt

Prefix sequence: Letter/Number/Number/Letter

BE24a

		VF	EF
BE24a	Prefix Z01D followed by serial number	£120	£200
BE24b	Prefix Z- -D	£25	£45
BE24c	Prefix Y- -D to B- -D	£20	£40
BE24d	Prefix A- -D (*traced toA99D*)	£30	£65
BE24e	Prefix Z- -E, Y- -E	£25	£50
BE24f	Prefix X- -E (*traced to X17E*)	£65	£135
BE24g	Prefix X21E	£200	£400

(June 1948)
Red-brown. 138 x 78mm. Without metal security thread
Signature: K .O. Peppiatt

Prefix sequence: Number/Number/Letter

BE25a

		VF	EF
BE25a	Prefix - -O (*traced from 42O-70O*) followed by serial number	£55	£120
BE25b	Prefix - -L (*traced from 05L-71L*)...	£50	£110

VF   EF

(October 1948)
Red-brown. 138 x 78mm. With metal security thread
Signature: K .O. Peppiatt

Prefix sequence: Number/Number/Letter

BE26a

		VF	EF
BE26a	Prefix - -L followed by serial number (*traced from 71L*)	£80	£175
BE26b	Prefix - -K, - -J, - -H..	£20	£45
BE26c	Prefix - -E (*traced to 91E*)	£25	£55

BE27c

		VF	EF
BE27a	Prefix 01A Replacement note..	£550	£1000
BE27b	Prefix 02A Replacement note..	£400	£700
BE27c	Prefix 03A Replacement note..	£450	£850

EF   UNC

(March 1950)
Red-brown. 138 x 78mm. With metal security thread
Signature: P. S. Beale

Prefix sequence: Number/Number/Letter

BE28a

		EF	UNC
BE28a	Prefix - -E followed by serial number (*traced from 92E*)	£125	£200
BE28b	Prefix - -D, - -C	£30	£50
BE28c	Prefix - -B (*traced to 99B*)	£40	£65
BE29a	Prefix 04A Replacement note	£750	—

BE29b

BE29b Prefix - -A Replacement note (*traced to 35A*) £125   £250

EF   UNC

Prefix sequence: Letter/Number/Number/Letter

BE30a

		EF	UNC
BE30a	Prefix Z- -Z followed by serial number..	£30	£50
BE30b	Prefix Y- -Z to E- -Z	£20	£45
BE30c	Prefix D- -Z *(traced to D85Z)*	£30	£55

(November 1955)

Red-brown. 138 x 78mm.
Signature: L. K. O'Brien

Prefix sequence: Letter/Number/Number/Letter

		EF	UNC
BE31a	Prefix D86Z followed by serial number....................................	£150	£275
BE31b	Prefix D- -Z...	£60	£100
BE31c	Prefix C- -Z, B- -Z...	£18	£35
BE31d	Prefix A- -Z	£30	£50
BE31e	Prefix Z- -Y...	£25	£40
BE31f	Prefix Y- -Y to B- - Y...	£15	£30
BE31g	Prefix A- -Y	£20	£40
BE31h	Prefix Z- -X...	£18	£35
BE31i	Prefix Y- -X..	£40	£75

BE31j

		EF	UNC
BE31j	Prefix Y25X *(last prefix of Britannia Series "A" 10/-)*..................	£100	£175

EF   UNC

Prefix sequence: Number/Number/Letter

BE32

BE32   Prefix - -A Replacement note (*traced from 35A-69A*)..................   £90   £180

SERIES "C" PORTRAIT ISSUE

(October 1961)

Red-brown. 140 x 66.7mm.
Signature: L. K. O'Brien

Prefix sequence: Letter/Number/Number

BE33a

		EF	UNC
BE33a	Prefix A01 followed by serial number...	£85	£160
BE33b	Prefix A- -..	£6	£12
BE33c	Prefix B- - to J- -...	£3	£6
BE33d	Prefix K- - (*traced to K64*)	£12	£20
BE34a	Prefix M01 Replacement note	£120	£200

EF   UNC

BE34b

BE34b Prefix M- - (*traced to M18*).. £50   £90

(April 1963)
Signature: J. Q. Hollom

Prefix sequence: Letter/Number/Number

BE35a

BE35a Prefix K65 followed by serial number... £150   £300
BE35b Prefix K- -... £15   £30
BE35c Prefix L- - to Y- -... £3   £6
BE35d Prefix Z- - (*traced to Z99*).. £12   £20

BE36

BE36 Prefix M- - Replacement note (traced from M19-M55).............. £25   £40

	EF	UNC

Prefix sequence: Number/Number/Letter

BE37a   Prefix 01A followed by serial number.. £120 £200

BE37b

BE37b Prefix - -A	£6	£12
BE37c Prefix - -B to - -N	£3	£6
BE37d Prefix - -R (*traced to 26R*)...	£12	£25

(February 1967)

Signature: J. S. Fforde

Prefix sequence: Number/Number/Letter

BE38a   Prefix 26R followed by serial number .... --- ---

BE38b

BE38b Prefix - -R	£12	£20
BE38c Prefix - -S to - -Y	£3	£6
BE38d Prefix - -Z (*traced to 99Z*)...	£7	£12

Prefix sequence: Letter/Number/Number/Letter

BE39a Prefix A01N followed by serial number....................................	£80	£130
BE39b Prefix A- - N.	£10	£18
BE39c Prefix B- -N, C- -N	£3	£6
BE39d Prefix D- -N	£6	£10

EF   UNC

BE39e

			EF	UNC
BE39e	Prefix D38N (*last prefix of Portrait Series "C" 10/-*)......................		£25	£45
BE40a	Prefix M56 Replacement note		£90	£160
BE40b	Prefix M- -		£8	£12

BE40c

			EF	UNC
BE40c	Prefix M80 (*last replacement prefix of Portrait Series "C" 10/-*) ...		£12	£25

ONE POUND
SERIES "A" BRITANNIA ISSUE
(November 1928)

Green. 150.7 x 84.4mm
Signature: C. P. Mahon

Prefix sequence: Letter/Number/Number

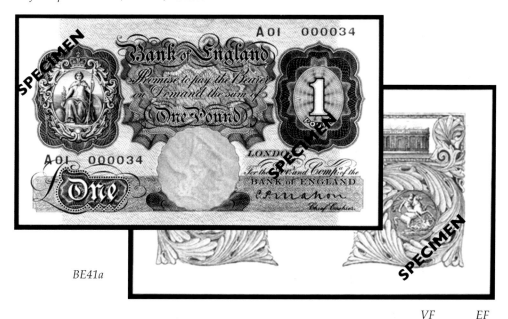

BE41a

		VF	EF
BE41a	Prefix A01 followed by serial number...	£500	£850
BE41b	Prefix A- -...	£60	£130
BE41c	Prefix B- - to G- -...	£45	£95
BE41d	Prefix H- - (*traced to H32*)	£85	£175

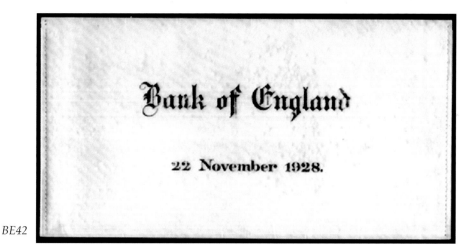

BE42

BE42 Presentation set of Ten Shillings and One Pound notes with matching A01 serial numbers in special Bank of England parchment envelope dated 22 November 1928. Only 125 sets were issued numbered A1 000001 to A01 000125.......................... *UNC* £5500

87

VF   EF

(July 1930)
Green. 150.7 x 84.4mm
Signature: B. G. Catterns

Prefix sequence: Letter/Number/Number

BE43a

BE43a	Prefix H- - followed by serial number (*traced from H33*)	£50	£100
BE43b	Prefix J- - to Y- -	£20	£40
BE43c	Prefix Z- -(*traced to Z99*)..	£25	£60

Prefix sequence Number/Number/Letter

BE44

BE44	Prefix - -A (*traced to 99A*)	£80	£160

(October 1934)
Green. 150.7 x 84.4mm
Signature: K .O. Peppiatt

Prefix sequence: Number/Number/Letter

BE45a	Prefix 01B followed by serial number	---	---
BE45b	Prefix - -B	£25	£50
BE45c	Prefix - -C to - -Y	£15	£30
BE45d	Prefix - -Z (*traced to 99Z*)...	£20	£45

	VF	EF

BE45d

Prefix sequence Letter/Number/Number/Letter

		VF	EF
BE46a	Prefix A01A followed by serial number …..................................	---	---
BE46b	Prefix A -A …...	£20	£45
BE46c	Prefix B- -A to K- -A	£12	£30

BE46d

BE46d	Prefix L- -A *(traced to L39A)* …	£20	£45

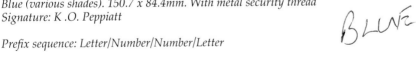

(March 1940)
Blue (various shades). 150.7 x 84.4mm. With metal security thread
Signature: K .O. Peppiatt

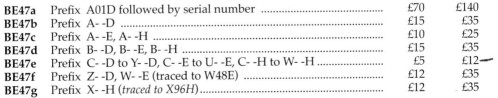

BLUE

Prefix sequence: Letter/Number/Number/Letter

		VF	EF
BE47a	Prefix A01D followed by serial number	£70	£140
BE47b	Prefix A- -D	£15	£35
BE47c	Prefix A- -E, A- -H	£10	£25
BE47d	Prefix B- -D, B- -E, B- -H	£15	£35
BE47e	Prefix C- -D to Y- -D, C- -E to U- -E, C- -H to W- -H	£5	£12
BE47f	Prefix Z- -D, W- -E (traced to W48E)	£12	£35
BE47g	Prefix X- -H *(traced to X96H)*..	£12	£35

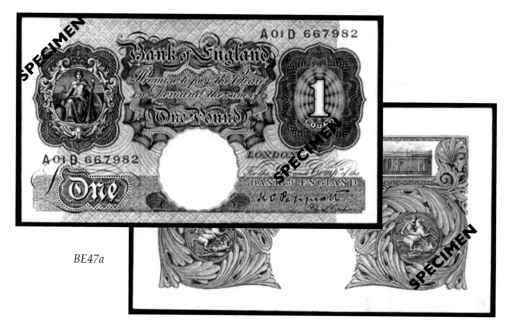

BE47a

THE STATES OF GUERNSEY OVERPRINTS
(September 18th 1941)

Green. 150.7 x 84.4mm. Without metal security thread
Signatures: C. P. Mahon, B. G. Catterns and K .O. Peppiatt
*Overprinted "Withdrawn from circulation September 18th, 1941." With stop after 1941 on front but
not on back*

		VF	EF
Prefix sequence: Various			
BE48a Signature Mahon. Prefix A- - to H- - (*48 known*)		£450	£800
BE48b Signature Catterns. Prefix H- - to Z- - (*69 known*)		£375	£650
BE48c Signature Catterns. Prefix - -A (*5 known*)		---	---
BE48d Signature Peppiatt. Prefix - -B to - -Z (*330 known*)		£325	£550

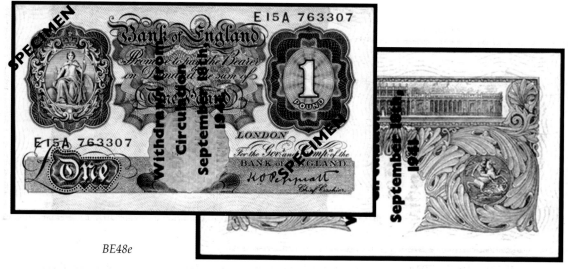

BE48e

BE48e Signature Peppiatt. Prefix A- -A to L- -A (*1,885 known*)...............		£200	£350

VF   EF

(September 18th 1941)

Blue (various shades). 150.7 x 84.4mm. With metal security thread
Signature: K .O. Peppiatt
Overprinted "Withdrawn from circulation September 18th, 1941." With stop after 1941 on front but not on back

Prefix sequence: Letter/Number/Number/Letter

BE49a

			VF	EF
BE49a	Prefix A- -D *(35 known)*		£550	£850
BE49b	Prefix C- -D *(85 known)*		£375	£600

(November 10th 1941)

Green. 150.7 x 84.4mm. Without metal security thread
Signature: K .O. Peppiatt
Overprinted "Withdrawn from circulation November 10th, 1941."

Prefix sequence: Letter/Number/Number/Letter

BE50a

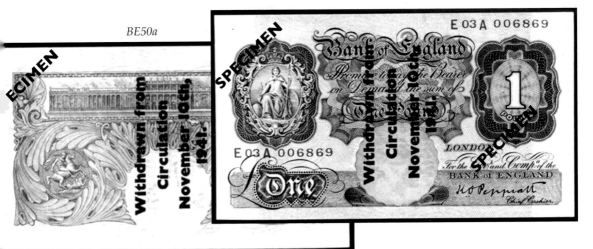

		VF	EF
BE50a	Prefix E03A. With stop after 1941 front and back *(75 known)* ..	£350	£600
BE50b	Prefix E15A. With stop after 1941 back only *(403 known)*	£250	£475

	VF	EF

(June 1948)
Green. 150.7 x 84.4mm. Without metal security thread
Signature: K .O. Peppiatt

Prefix sequence: Letter/Number/Number/Letter

		VF	EF
BE51a	Prefix R01A followed by serial number	£60	£130
BE51b	Prefix R- -A	£15	£35

BE51c

		VF	EF
BE51c	Prefix S- -A (*traced to S48A*)	£20	£40

(September 1948)
Green. 150.7 x 84.4mm. With metal security thread
Signature: K .O. Peppiatt

Prefix sequence: Letter/Number/Number/Letter

BE52a

		VF	EF
BE52a	Prefix S- -A (*traced from S40A*) followed by serial number.......	£20	£40
BE52b	Prefix T- -A to Y- -A...	£10	£18
BE52c	Prefix Z- -A (*traced to Z99A*)	£20	£35
BE52d	Prefix A- -B (*traced from A01B*)...	£20	£35
BE52e	Prefix B- -B to E- -B	£8	£15
BE52f	Prefix H- -B (*traced to H36B*)	£20	£40
BE53a	Prefix S01S Replacement note	£250	£375

	VF	EF

BE53b

BE53b Prefix S- -S Replacement note (*traced to S09S*) £125 £225

(March 1950)
Green. 150.7 x 84.4mm.
Signature: P .S. Beale

	EF	UNC

Prefix sequence: Letter/Number/Number/Letter

BE54a Prefix H37B followed by serial number...................................... £160 £300

BE54b

		VF	EF
BE54b	Prefix H- -B...	£15	£30
BE54c	Prefix J- -B to Y- -B	£6	£12
BE54d	Prefix Z- -B (*traced to Z99B*)	£12	£25
BE54e	Prefix A- -C (*traced from A01C*)	£12	£25
BE54f	Prefix B- -C to Y- -C	£6	£12
BE54g	Prefix Z- -C (*traced to Z99C*).................................	£12	£25
BE54h	Prefix A- -J (*traced from A01J*)	£12	£25
BE54i	Prefix B- -J to K- -J	£6	£12
BE54j	Prefix L- -J..	£15	£30
BE54j	Prefix L63J	£125	£225
BE55a	Prefix S10S Replacement note	£150	£275

EF   UNC

BE55b

BE55b   Prefix S- -S Replacement note *(traced to S70S)*.........................   £30   £50

(November 1955)
Green. 150.7 x 84.4mm.
Signature: L .K. O'Brien

Prefix sequence: Letter/Number/Number/Letter

BE56a	Prefix L64J followed by serial number....................................	£125	£225
BE56b	Prefix L- -J..	£18	£30
BE56c	Prefix M- -J to Y- -J...	£6	£12
BE56d	Prefix Z- -J *(traced to Z99J)*	£12	£25
BE56e	Prefix A- -K *(traced from A01K)*	£15	£30
BE56f	Prefix B- -K to Y- -K	£6	£12
BE56g	Prefix Z- -K *(traced to Z99K)*	£12	£25
BE56h	Prefix A- -L *(traced from A01L)*	£15	£30
BE56i	Prefix B- -L to J- -L	£6	£12
BE56j	Prefix K- -L	£40	£70

BE56k

BE56k	Prefix K13L *(last prefix of Britannia Series "A" £1)*	£250	£400
BE57a	Prefix S71S Replacement note	£130	£225
BE57b	Prefix S- -S Replacement note *(traced to S99S)*..........................	£30	£50
BE58a	Prefix S01T Replacement note.......................................	£150	£275

EF   UNC

BE58b

		EF	UNC
BE58b	Prefix S- -T Replacement note (*traced to S23T*)	£40	£75

SERIES "C" PORTRAIT ISSUE
(March 1960)
Green. 151 x 71.8mm.
Signature: L .K. O'Brien

Prefix sequence: Letter/Number/Number

BE59a

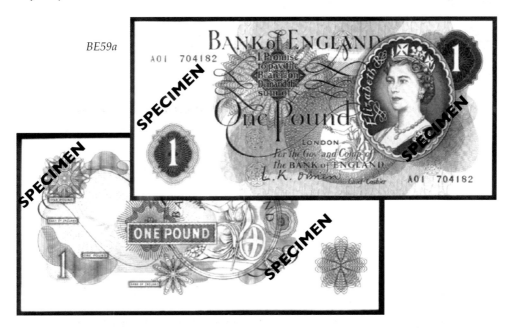

		EF	UNC
BE59a	Prefix A01 followed by serial number...	£120	£240
BE59b	Prefix A- -..	£10	£18
BE59c	Prefix B- - to Y- -..	£4	£7
BE59d	Prefix Z- - (*traced to Z99*)...	£10	£18

95

EF UNC

BE60a

		EF	UNC
BE60a	Prefix M01 Replacement note	£90	£160
BE60b	Prefix M- - Replacement note (*traced to M68*)	£15	£30

Prefix sequence: Number/Number/Letter

		EF	UNC
BE61a	Prefix 01A followed by serial number...	---	---
BE61b	Prefix - -A..	£10	£18
BE61c	Prefix - -B to - - Y..	£4	£7
BE61d	Prefix - -Z (traced to 99Z)	£10	£18

Experimental printing on a research machine
Prefix sequence: Letter/Number/Number/Letter

Long tail 'R' on reverse

BE62a

		VF	EF
BE62a	Prefix A01N (*small long tail 'R' on reverse for research*)................	£185	£350
BE62b	Prefix A05N and A06N (*small short tail 'R' on reverse*)...............	£225	£425

Prefix sequence: Letter/Number/Number/Letter

		EF	UNC
BE63a	Prefix B01N	£100	£200
BE63b	Prefix B- -N (*traced to B76N*)...	£15	£30

EF UNC

(February 1963)
Green. 151 x 71.8mm.
Signature: J .Q. Hollom

Prefix sequence: Letter/Number/Number/Letter

BE64a Prefix B77N followed by serial number. .... £125 ---

BE64b

BE64b Prefix B- -N £45 £75
BE64c Prefix C- -N to L- -N, A- -R to L- -R, A- -S to L- -S, A- -T to
L- -T, A- -U to L- -U, A- -W to L- -W, A- -X to K- -X, A- -Y......... £4 £6
BE64d Prefix B- -Y (*last series traced to B10Y*) £50 £95

Prefix sequence: Letter/Number/Number

BE65 Prefix M- - Replacement note (*traced from M68 to M99*) £25 £45

Prefix sequence: Number/Number/Letter

BE66a Prefix 01M Replacement note.. £95 £175

BE66b

BE66b Prefix - -M Replacement note (*traced to 99M*)..................... £18 £35

Prefix sequence: Letter/Number/Number/Letter

BE67a Prefix M01R Replacement note....................................... £100 £200

EF   UNC

BE67b

BE67b   Prefix M- -R Replacement note (*traced to M08R*) £55   £95

With small 'G' on reverse (indicating that note printed on a Goebel machine)

Prefix sequence: Letter/Number/Number/Letter

'G' on reverse

BE68a

		EF	UNC
BE68a	Prefix A- -N (*traced from A09N*)	£12	£20
BE68b	Prefix D- -T, C- -W.	£5	£8
BE68c	Prefix L- -X (*traced to L99X*)...	£6	£12
BE69a	Prefix M01N Replacement note.	£100	£200

BE69b

BE69b   Prefix M- -N Replacement note (*traced to M28N*)........................   £30   £50

EF   UNC

(February 1967)

Green. 151 x 71.8mm.
Signature: J .S. Fforde

Prefix sequence: Letter/Number/Number/Letter

BE70a

		EF	UNC
BE70a	Prefix B11Y followed by serial number..	£150	£275
BE70b	Prefix B- -Y	£15	£35
BE70c	Prefix C- -Y to L- -Y, A- -Z to J- -Z...	£4	£10
BE70d	Prefix L- -Z (*traced to L99Z*)..	£12	£30

BE71

		EF	UNC
BE71	Prefix M- -R Replacement note (*traced from M09R to M49R*)	£25	£50
BE72a	Prefix N01A...	---	---
BE72b	Prefix N- -A	£30	£60
BE72c	Prefix N- -B to N- -L, R- -A to R- -K, S- -L, T- -A to T- -L, U- -A to U- -H, W- -A to W- -D, X- -B.	£3	£6

BE72d

		EF	UNC
BE72d	Prefix X- -C (*traced to X42C*)...	£30	£45

		EF	UNC
BE73a	Prefix R- -M Replacement note (*traced to R53M*)	£15	£25
BE73b	Prefix S- -M Replacement note (*traced to S72M*).	£15	£25
BE73c	Prefix T- -M Replacement note (*traced to T04M*).	£160	£325

BE73d

BE73d	Prefix U01M Replacement note (*traced in U01M only*).................	£250	£500

With small 'G' on reverse (indicating that note printed on a Goebel machine)

BE74	Prefix E- -Y, K- -Z..	£6	£10

BE75a

BE75a	Prefix M29N Replacement note	£125	£225
BE75b	Prefix M- -N Replacement note..	£35	£55
BE75c	Prefix M42N Replacement note.	£100	£200
BE76a	Prefix R—B, R- -L	£5	£10
BE76b	Prefix U01E...	£65	£140
BE76c	Prefix U- -E (traced to U45E)	£7	£15
BE77a	Prefix N01M Replacement note	£350	£600
BE77b	Prefix N- -M Replacement note...	£50	£100
BE77c	Prefix N14M Replacement note	£95	£185
BE77d	Prefix T- -M Replacement note (traced from T29M to T32M).....	£95	£185

BE77d

(1970 – date unknown)

Green. 151 x 71.8mm.
Signature: J .B. Page

Prefix sequence: Letter/Number/Number/Letter

		VF	EF
BE78a	Prefix S87L followed by serial number	£450	£750
BE78b	Prefix S89L and S90L only	£350	£500

		EF	UNC
BE78c	Prefix T- -B to T- -L, U- -A to U- -H, W- -A to W- -H (*traced to W99H*)	£3	£5
BE78d	Prefix X- -A to X- -L, Y- -A to Y- -L, Z- -A to Z- -K	£3	£5
BE78e	Prefix Z- -L (*traced to Z84L*)	£10	£20
BE79a	Prefix R- -M Replacement note (*traced from R44M to R99M*)	£20	£50
BE79b	Prefix S- -M Replacement note (*traced from S32M to S99M*)	£10	£25
BE79c	Prefix W01M Replacement note	£60	£150
BE79d	Prefix W- -M Replacement note (*traced to W84M*)	£10	£25
BE79e	Prefix X01M Replacement note	£75	£175
BE79f	Prefix X- -M Replacement note (*traced to X60M*)	£10	£25

BE80

BE80	Pair of consecutively numbered notes with signatures of J. S. Fforde and J. B. Page (*traced in prefixes S- -L, T- -D, T- -H, T- -K, T- -L, U- -C, U- -D, W- -A, W- -B, W- -C, X- -B, X- -C, R- -M and S- -M*).	£275	£425

		EF	UNC
	Prefix sequence: Letter/Letter/Number/Number		
BE81a	Prefix AN01 followed by serial number	£100	£200
BE81b	Prefix AN- -	£6	£10
BE81c	Prefix AR- - to AZ- -, BN- - to BZ- -, CN- - to CZ- -, DN- - to DZ- -, EN- - to EZ- -, HN- - to HY- -	£2	£4
BE81d	Prefix HZ- -	£6	£10
BE81e	Prefix HZ63 *(last prefix of Portrait Series 'C' £1)*	---	---

BE82a

BE82a	Prefix MR01 Replacement note.	£120	£225
BE82b	Prefix MR- - Replacement note *(traced to MR48)*	£12	£30
BE82c	Prefix MS01 Replacement note.	£50	£110
BE82d	Prefix MS- - Replacement note *(traced to MS84)*	£4	£8
BE82e	Prefix MT01 Replacement note.	£50	£110
BE82f	Prefix MT- - Replacement note *(traced to MT23)*	£5	£10
BE82g	Prefix MU01 Replacement note..	£12	£25
BE82h	Prefix MU- - Replacement note *(traced to MU19)*.	£5	£10
BE82i	Prefix MW01 Replacement note..	£45	£90
BE82j	Prefix MW- - Replacement note.	£5	£10

BE82k

BE82k	Prefix MW19 Replacement note	£50	£120

EF UNC

SERIES "D" PICTORIAL ISSUE
(February 1978)
Green and multicoloured. 134.5 x 66.7mm.
Reverse depicting Isaac Newton
Signature: J .B. Page

Prefix sequence: Letter/Number/Number

BE83a

		EF	UNC
BE83a	Prefix A01 followed by serial number.	£6	£10
BE83b	Prefix A- -	£4	£6
BE83c	Prefix B- - to Y- -	£2	£4
BE83d	Prefix Z- -	£7	£15
BE83e	Prefix Z80	£100	£200

BE84

		EF	UNC
BE84	Prefix M01 Replacement note	£140	£250

		EF	UNC

Prefix sequence: Letter/Number/Number

		EF	UNC
BE85a	Prefix 01A followed by serial number..	£10	£30
BE85b	Prefix - -A	£4	£7
BE85c	Prefix - -B to - -X	£3	£5
BE85d	Prefix - -Y *(traced to 80Y)*...	£5	£12
BE85e	Prefix 81E, 81K, 81N, 81R, 81S, 81T, 81W, 81X, 81Y	£175	£300

BE85f

BE85f	Prefix 81Z	£275	£450

Prefix sequence: Letter/Number/Number/Letter

		EF	UNC
BE86a	Prefix A01N followed by serial number..	£18	£40
BE86b	Prefix A- -N	£7	£14
BE86c	Prefix B- -N to D- -N	£3	£5
BE86d	Prefix E- -N *(traced to E84N)*	£8	£16

(March 1981)

Green and multicoloured with enhanced background colours. 134.5 x 66.7mm.
Printed by web- offset with small "W" at lower left on reverse
Signature: D. H. F. Somerset

Prefix sequence: Letter/Letter/Number/Number

"W" on reverse

BE87a

		EF	UNC
BE87a	Prefix AN01 followed by serial number..	£15	£35
BE87b	Prefix AN- -.	£4	£8
BE87c	Prefix AR- - to D- -Y.	£3	£5
BE87d	Prefix DY21 *(last prefix of Pictorial Series "D" £1)*..	£18	£40
BE88	Prefix MN- - Experimental note *(traced from MN04 to MN18)* ...		Rare

FIVE POUNDS

BLACK AND WHITE SERIES (continued)

BE89

		VF	EF
(1925-29)			
BE89	*Signature: C. P. Mahon*		
	London...	£225	£375
(1929-34)			
BE90	*Signature: B. G. Catterns*		
	London...	£175	£325

BE91

(1934-44)			
BE91	*Signature: K. O. Peppiatt*		
	London	£100	£180

NB. There are deceptive German World War II forgeries of the White £5 note, almost all of these being forgeries of BE90 and BE91.

VF   EF

(1944-45—issued 1945)
Thicker paper. With metal security thread
Signature: K. O. Peppiatt
Prefix sequence: Letter/Number/Number

BE92a   Prefix E- - followed by serial number..   £80   £130

BE92b

BE92b   Prefix H- - to K- -...   £75   £125
BE92c   Prefix L- - *(traced to L02)* £125   £225

(1947issued 1948)
Thinner paper. With metal security thread
Signature: K. O. Peppiatt
Prefix sequence: Letter/Number/Number

BE93a   Prefix L- - followed by serial number (traced from L03).......... £75   £125

BE93b

BE93b   Prefix M- - *(traced to M71)*... £75   £125

	EF	UNC

(1949-52)
Thinner paper. With metal security thread
Signature: P. S. Beale
Prefix sequence: Letter/Number/Number

		EF	UNC
BE94a	Prefix M- - followed by serial number (*traced from M72*)	£100	£185
BE94b	Prefix N- - to X- -...	£90	£170

BE94c

		EF	UNC
BE94c	Prefix Y- - (*traced to Y70*)	£100	£185

(1955-56) ....
Thinner paper. With metal security thread
Signature: L. K. O'Brien
Prefix sequence: Letter/Number/Number

		EF	UNC
BE95a	Prefix Y- - followed by serial number (*traced from Y71*)	£100	£185
BE95b	Prefix Z- - (*traced to Z99*)...	£95	£175

Prefix sequence: Letter/Number/Number/Letter

BE96a

		EF	UNC
BE96a	Prefix A- -A followed by serial number	£100	£185
BE96b	Prefix B- -A and C- -A...	£95	£175
BE96c	Prefix D- -A (*traced to D99A*)..	£100	£185

SERIES "B" HELMETED BRITANNIA ISSUE
(February 1957)
Blue on multicoloured underprint. Shaded £5 symbols on reverse. 159 x 89mm
Signature: L. K. O'Brien

Prefix sequence: Letter/Number/Number

shaded £5 symbol

unshaded £5 symbol

BE97a

		EF	*UNC*
BE97a	Prefix A01 followed by serial number..	£150	£250
BE97b	Prefix A- -	£35	£75
BE97c	Prefix B- - to D- -	£30	£60
BE97d	Prefix E- - (*traced to E37*)	£35	£70

(July 1961)
Blue on multicoloured underprint. Unshaded £5 symbols on reverse. 159 x 89mm
Signature: L. K. O'Brien

Prefix sequence: Letter/Number/Number

BE98a	Prefix H01 followed by serial number	£500	£800
BE98b	Prefix H- -	£35	£75
BE98c	Prefix J- -	£30	£60

EF   UNC

BE98d

		EF	UNC
BE98d	Prefix K- -	£35	£70
BE98e	Prefix K45 (*last prefix of Helmeted Britannia Series "B" £5*)	£400	£600

SERIES "C" PORTRAIT ISSUE
(February 1963)
Blue 140 x 85mm.
Signature: J .Q. Hollom

Prefix sequence: Letter/Number/Number

BE99a

		EF	UNC
BE99a	Prefix A01 followed by serial number	£100	£175
BE99b	Prefix A- - …..	£25	£40
BE99c	Prefix B- - to N- -	£20	£35
BE99d	Prefix R- - (*traced to R19*)...	£40	£75

109

	EF	UNC
BE100a　Prefix M01 Replacement note..	£250	---

BE100b

| **BE100b**　Prefix M- - Replacement note (*traced to M12*)............................. | £120 | £225 |

(January 1967)
Blue 140 x 85mm.
Signature: J .S. Fforde
Prefix sequence: Letter/Number/Number

BE101a

BE101a　Prefix R20 followed by serial number	£90	£150
BE101b　Prefix R- -	£25	£50
BE101c　Prefix S- - to Y- -	£15	£30
BE101d　Prefix Z- - (*traced to Z99*)...	£20	£40
BE102　Prefix M- - Replacement note (*traced from M08 to M28*).............	£75	£140

Signature: J .S. Fforde
Prefix sequence: Number/Number/Letter

BE103a　Prefix 01A followed by serial number...	£120	---
BE103b　Prefix - -A	£18	£35
BE103c　Prefix - -B to - -K (*overlaps with Page BE105b, c, d below*)	£15	£30
BE103d　Prefix - -L (*traced to 40L*)	£70	£125

	EF	UNC
BE104a Prefix 01M Replacement note...	£130	---

BE104b

BE104b Prefix - -M Replacement note (*traced to 15M*)............................	£90	£175

Signature: J .B. Page
Prefix sequence: Number/Number/Letter

BE105a Prefix 03C followed by serial number...	£175	---
BE105b Prefix - -C (*overlaps with Fforde BE103c above*)............................	£30	£65
BE105c Prefix - -D and - -E (*overlaps with Fforde BE103c above*)...............	£15	£35

BE105d

BE105d Prefix - -H (*traced to 36H*) (*overlaps with Fforde BE 103c above*) .	£120	£200
BE106 Prefix - -M Replacement note (*traced from 04M to 18M*).............	£90	£175

BE107

		EF	UNC
BE107	Pair of consecutively numbered notes with signatures of J. S. Fforde and J. B. Page (*traced in prefixes - - C , - -D, and - -E*)......	£450	£700

SERIES "D" PICTORIAL ISSUE
(November 1971)

Blue and multicoloured. 145.5 x 78mm.
Reverse depicting the Duke of Wellington
Signature: J .B. Page

Prefix sequence: Letter/Number/Number

BE108a

BE108a	Prefix A01 followed by serial number	£90	£175

		EF	UNC
BE108b	Prefix A- -	£15	£30
BE108c	Prefix B- - to K- -	£12	£25
BE108d	Prefix L- - (*traced to L94*)	£35	£70

BE109

BE109	Prefix M- - Replacement note (*traced from M01-M05*)	£75	£150

(August 1973)
Blue and multicoloured. 145.5 x 78mm. Reverse printed by lithography. Small "L" on reverse
Signature: J. B. Page

Prefix sequence: Number/Number/Letter

BE110 – BE117 all have a small "L" for Litho on reverse

BE110a

BE110a	Prefix 01A followed by serial number	£100	£185
BE110b	Prefix - -A	£15	£30
BE110c	Prefix - -B to - -Y	£12	£25
BE110d	Prefix - -Z (*traced to 95Z*)...	£20	£40
BE111	Prefix - -M Replacement note (*traced from 01M to 08M*)	£85	£165

Prefix sequence: Letter/Letter/Number/Number

BE112a

		EF	UNC
BE112a	Prefix AN01 followed by serial number	£80	£160
BE112b	Prefix AN- -	£15	£25
BE112c	Prefix AR- - to CX- -	£10	£18
BE112d	Prefix EZ- - (*last series traced from EZ05-EZ56*)	£50	£85

(June 1980)

Blue and multicoloured. 145.5 x 78mm. Reverse printed by lithography. Small "L" on reverse
Signature: D. H. F. Somerset

Prefix sequence: Letter/Letter/Number/Number

BE113a

BE113a	Prefix DN01 followed by serial number	£70	£145
BE113b	Prefix DN- -...	£12	£22
BE113c	Prefix DR- - to LY- -	£8	£16
BE113d	Prefix LZ- - (*last series traced to LZ90*)	£25	£50
BE113e	Prefix NA- - (*not seen*)	---	---
BE113f	Prefix NB- - and NC- -	£10	£20
BE113g	Prefix NC90	£20	£40

	EF	UNC

BE114

BE114   Prefix DU55 to DU77 Error note missing signature £65   £130

Experimental notes for Optical Character Recognition (OCR)
Prefix sequence: Letter/Letter/Number/Number

BE115

	VF	EF
BE115 Prefix AN91, BR91, CS91, DT91, EU91, HW91, JX91, KY91 and LZ91	£600	£950

(July 1987)
Blue and multicoloured. 145.5 x 78mm. With 1mm wide security thread. Printed by web offset
Signature: D .H. F. Somerset
Prefix sequence: Letter/Letter/Number/Number

	EF	UNC
BE116a Prefix RA01 followed by serial number.....................................	£20	£45
BE116b Prefix RA- - to RC- -..	£10	£18
BE116c Prefix RC90..	£20	£40

(March 1988)
Blue and multicoloured. 145.5 x 78mm.
Signature: G .M. Gill
Prefix sequence: Letter/Letter/Number/Number

BE117a Prefix RD01 followed by serial number.....................................	£20	£45
BE117b Prefix RD- -	£15	£25
BE117c Prefix RE- - to RL- -, SA- - to SE- -...	£10	£18

EF   UNC

BE117d

BE117d Prefix SE90 (*last prefix of Pictorial Series "D" £5*) £40   £80

SERIES "E" HISTORICAL ISSUE
(June 1990)
Turquoise and multicoloured. With windowed security thread. 135 x 70mm.
Reverse depicting George Stephenson
Signature: G .M. Gill P
Prefix sequence: Letter/Number/Number

BE118a

		EF	UNC
BE118a	Prefix A01 followed by serial number	£12	£25
BE118b	Prefix A- -	£10	£20
BE118c	Prefix B- - to L- -..	£8	£16
BE118d	Prefix N- - (*traced to N54 official last run*)	£20	£40
BE118e	Prefix R- - to T- - (*overlaps with Kentfield BE119 below*)................	£15	£25
BE118f	Prefix U- - (*last series overlap traced to U17*)	---	---

	EF	UNC

(November 1991)

Turquoise and multicoloured. 135 x 70mm. Printed on web presses.
Signature: G .E. A. Kentfield
Prefix sequence: Letter/Number/Number

		EF	UNC
BE119a	Prefix R01 followed by serial number	£18	£35
BE119b	Prefix R- - (*overlaps with Gill BE118 above*)	£12	£25
BE119c	Prefix S- - to U- - (*overlaps with Gill BE118 above*)	£8	£16
BE119d	Prefix W- -	£20	£40

BE119e

		EF	UNC
BE119e	Prefix W18	£40	£80

(March 1993)

Turquoise and multicoloured. With darker £5 value tablet. 135 x 70mm.
Signature: G .E. A. Kentfield
Prefix sequence: Letter/Letter/Number/Number

		EF	UNC
BE120a	Prefix AA01 followed by serial number......................................	£10	£20
BE120b	Prefix AA- -, AB- -	£8	£16
BE120c	Prefix AB18..	£40	£80

Printed by sheet fed offset litho

BE121a

		EF	UNC
BE121a	Prefix AC01 followed by serial number.......................................	£60	£125
BE121b	Prefix AC- - to AL- -, BA- - to BL- -, CA- - to CK- -	£8	£14
BE121c	Prefix DA- -, DB- -	£8	£16
BE121d	Prefix DC- - (*traced to DC90*)	£10	£20
BE121e	Prefix DL99 (*special last run for collectors' packs*)	—	£40

		EF	UNC
BE122a	Prefix CL- - Column sort note	£15	£25
BE122b	Prefix LL- - Replacement note (*traced to LL45 and overlaps with Lowther BE124b below*)..	£25	£50

(January 1999)
Turquoise and multicoloured. 135 x 70mm.
Signature: Merlyn Lowther
Prefix sequence: Letter/Letter/Number/Number

		EF	UNC
BE123a	Prefix EA01 followed by serial number	£12	£25
BE123b	Prefix EA- - to EJ- - (*traced to EJ45 last official run*)	£6	£10

BE123c

		EF	UNC
BE123c	Prefix EJ90 (*special last run for collectors' packs and last prefix of Historical Series "E" £5*)	—	£50

BE124b

		EF	UNC
BE124a	Prefix CL- - Column sort note (*traced to CL45*)	£12	£20
BE124b	Prefix LL- - Replacement note (*traced to LL45 and overlaps with Kentfield BE122b above*)..	£18	£35

SERIES "E" NEW HISTORICAL ISSUE
(May 2002)

Turquoise and multicoloured. 135 x 70mm. Withdrawn issue with faulty varnish coating
Reverse depicting Elizabeth Fry
Signature: Merlyn Lowther
Prefix sequence: Letter/Letter/Number/Number

BE125a

		EF	UNC
BE125a	Prefix HA01 followed by serial number	£8	£18
BE125b	Prefix HA- -, HB- -, JA- -	FV	£12
BE125c	Prefix JA90 (*last prefix of withdrawn issue*)..................................	£18	£30
BE126a	Prefix DL- - Column sort note (*traced to DL45 and overlaps with BE128a below*)	£8	£18
BE126b	Prefix LL- - Replacement note (*traced from LL46-LL90 and overlaps with BE128c below*)	£8	£18

(August 2002)

Turquoise and multicoloured. 135 x 70mm. Reissue with improved varnish coating
Signature: Merlyn Lowther
Prefix sequence: Letter/Letter/Number/Number

BE127a	Prefix HC01 followed by serial number	---	---
BE127b	Prefix HC- - to HK- -	FV	£8
BE127c	Prefix JB- - (*traced to JB90 and overlaps with Bailey BE129 below*)	FV	£10

BE127d

BE127d	Prefix XA- - to XE- -, XH- - to XK- -	£25	£50

		EF	UNC

BE128a Prefix DL- - Column sort note (*traced to DL45 and overlaps with BE126a above*) £8 £18

BE128b Prefix EL- - Column sort note (*traced to EL45*) £8 £18

BE128c Prefix LL- - Replacement note (*traced from LL46-LL90 and overlaps with BE126b above*) £8 £18

(January 2004)
Turquoise and multicoloured. 135 x 70mm.
Signature: A. Bailey ....
Prefix sequence: Letter/Letter/Number/Number

BE129a

BE129a Prefix JB46 followed by serial number £30 £50

BE129b Prefix JB- - (*overlaps with Lowther BE127c above*) .... FV £10

BE129c Prefix JC- - (*continuing*) .... FV £8

BE130– BE149 [*Held in reserve*]

TEN POUNDS

BLACK AND WHITE SERIES (continued)

		VF	EF
(1925-29)			
BE150	*Signature: C. P. Mahon*		
	London	£350	£600

BE151

		VF	EF
(1929-34)			
BE151	*Signature: B. G. Catterns*		
	London	£250	£475

BE152

		VF	EF
(1934-44)			
BE152	*Signature: K. O. Peppiatt*		
	London	£175	£300

NB. There are deceptive German World War II forgeries of the White £10 note, almost all of these being forgeries of BE151 and BE152.

SERIES "C" PORTRAIT ISSUE
(February 1964)
Brown 150 x 93mm.
Signature: J .Q. Hollom
Prefix sequence: Letter/Number/Number

BE153a

		EF	*UNC*
BE153a	Prefix A01 followed by serial number	£70	£120
BE153b	Prefix A- -	£30	£45
BE153c	Prefix A40	£85	£140

(January 1967)
Brown 150 x 93mm.
Signature: J .S. Fforde
Prefix sequence: Letter/Number/Number

BE154a	Prefix A41 followed by serial number	£90	£170
BE154b	Prefix A- - *(overlaps with Page BE155a,b below)*	£30	£45
BE154c	Prefix A95	£120	£225

BE154a

	EF	UNC

(1971 – date unknown)

Brown 150 x 93mm.
Signature: J .B. Page
Prefix sequence: Letter/Number/Number

		EF	UNC
BE155a	Prefix A91 followed by serial number	£900	£1400
BE155b	Prefix A- - *(overlaps with Fforde BE154b, c above)*.......................	£600	£950
BE155c	Prefix B- -, C- -	£28	£40
BE155d	Prefix C90 *(last prefix of Portrait Series "C" £10)*	---	---
BE156a	Prefix M01 Replacement note...	£90	£175
BE156b	Prefix M- - Replacement note *(traced to M17)*.............................	£35	£50

BE157

BE157	Pair of consecutively numbered notes with signatures of J. S. Fforde and J. B. Page *(traced in prefixes A91 to A95 only)*..........	£1400	£2000

SERIES "D" PICTORIAL ISSUE
(February 1975)
Brown and multicoloured. 151 x 85mm.
Reverse depicting Florence Nightingale
Signature: J .B. Page
Prefix sequence: Letter/Number/Number

BE158a

		EF	UNC
BE158a	Prefix A01 followed by serial number	£85	£170
BE158b	Prefix A- -	£25	£45
BE158c	Prefix B- - to S- -..	£18	£35
BE158d	Prefix T- - (*traced to T20*)...	£45	£85

BE159a

BE159a	Prefix M01 Replacement note......................................	£140	£250
BE159b	Prefix M- - Replacement note (*traced to M50 but not inclusive*)	£75	£130

(December 1980)

Brown and multicoloured. 151 x 85mm.
Reverse depicting Florence Nightingale
Signature: D. H. F. Somerset

Prefix sequence: Letter/Number/Number

		EF	UNC
BE160a	Prefix U01 followed by serial number	£400	£600
BE160b	Prefix U- -	£45	£75
BE160c	Prefix W- - to Y- -...	£35	£55
BE160d	Prefix Z- - (traced to Z80)..	£45	£70

Prefix sequence: Number/Number/Letter

BE161a

BE161a	Prefix 01A followed by serial number...	£130	£250
BE161b	Prefix - -A	£30	£50
BE161c	Prefix - -B to - -K	£25	£40
BE161d	Prefix - -L (*traced to L40*)	£50	£80

(February 1984)

Brown and multicoloured. 151 x 85mm. With 0.5mm wide security thread. Reverse printed by lithography. Small 'L' on reverse (see extract of note below)
Signature: D. H. F. Somerset

Prefix sequence: Letter/Number/Number/Letter

BE162, BE163, BE164 and BE165 all have a small "L" for Litho at lower left on the reverse

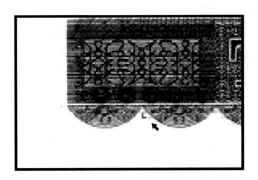

BE162a	Prefix AN01 followed by serial number	£90	£160
BE162b	Prefix AN- - to AZ- -, BN- - to BZ- -, CN- - to CR- -	£18	£30

BE162c

		EF	UNC
BE162c	Prefix CR90...	£100	£175

(July 1987)

Brown and multicoloured. 151 x 85mm. With 1mm wide windowed security thread.
Signature: D. H. F. Somerset
Prefix sequence: Letter/Letter/Number/Number

		EF	UNC
BE163a	Prefix CS01 followed by serial number	£45	£90
BE163b	Prefix CS- - to CZ- -	£18	£35
BE163c	Prefix DN (*traced to DN30*)...	£35	£60

(March 1988)

Brown and multicoloured. 151 x 85mm.
Signature: G. M. Gill
Prefix sequence: Letter/Letter/Number/Number

BE164a

		EF	UNC
BE164a	Prefix DR01 followed by serial number	£30	£50
BE164b	Prefix DR- - to DZ- -, EN- -, ER- - to EZ- -, HN- -, HR- - to HZ- -, JN- -	£18	£35
BE164c	Prefix JR (*traced to JR60*)	£40	£70

(November 1991)
Brown and multicoloured. 151 x 85mm.
Signature: G. E. A. Kentfield
Prefix sequence: Letter/Letter/Number/Number

		EF	UNC
BE165a	Prefix KN01 followed by serial number	£30	£50
BE165b	Prefix KN- -, KR- -	£18	£35

BE165c

BE165c	Prefix KR30 (*last prefix of Pictorial Series "D" £10*)	£60	£100

SERIES "E" HISTORICAL ISSUE
(April 1992)
Orange and multicoloured. With windowed security thread. 142 x 75mm.
Reverse depicting Charles Dickens
Signature: G .E. A. Kentfield
Prefix sequence: Letter/Number/Number

BE166a

		EF	UNC
BE166a	Prefix A01 followed by serial number	£20	£35
BE166b	Prefix A- - to E- -, H- - to L- -, N- -, R- - to X- -	£15	£25
BE166c	Prefix X40 (*last official run*)	£40	£80
BE166d	Prefix Y- - (*extra run using unenhanced design traced from*		
	Y41 to Y96)..	£35	£60
BE167a	Prefix M- - Experimental note (*traced from M01 to M40*)	£40	£70
BE167b	Prefix Z90 Experimental note..	£40	£70

(October 1993)

Orange and multicoloured but with enhanced and additional value tablets. 142 x 75mm.
Signature: G .E. A. Kentfield
Prefix sequence: Letter/Letter/Number/Number

BE168a

		EF	UNC
BE168a	Prefix AA00 followed by serial number (*Registration note*		
	issued in error)...	£650	£1000
BE168b	Prefix DA01 followed by serial number	£85	£150
BE168c	Prefix DA- - to KK- -..	£12	£20
BE168d	Prefix KK80 (*last official run*)	---	---
BE168e	Prefix KK99 (*special last run for collectors' packs*)	—	£45
BE169a	Prefix DL- -, EL- - Column sort note	£20	£35
BE169b	Prefix LL- - Replacement note (*traced to LL40 and overlaps*		
	with Lowther BE171b below)	£40	£85

(January 1999)

Orange and multicoloured. 142 x 75mm.
Signature: Merlyn Lowther
Prefix sequence: Letter/Letter/Number/Number

		EF	UNC
BE170a	Prefix KL01 followed by serial number	£20	£35
BE170b	Prefix KL- - and LA- -..	£12	£20

EF　　UNC

BE170c

		EF	UNC
BE170c	Prefix LA80 (*last prefix of Historical Series "E" £10*).................	£25	£45
BE171a	Prefix EL- - Column sort note......................................	£20	£35
BE171b	Prefix LL- - Replacement note (*traced to LL40 and overlaps with Kentfield BE169b above*)	£30	£70

SERIES "E" NEW HISTORICAL ISSUE
(November 2000)
Orange and multicoloured. 142 x 75mm.
Reverse depicting Charles Darwin
© 2000 wording incorrectly reads "The Governor and the Company of the Bank of England"
Signature: Merlyn Lowther
Prefix sequence: Letter/Letter/Number/Number

BE172a

		EF	UNC
BE172a	Prefix AA01 followed by serial number	£15	£25

		EF	UNC
BE172b	Prefix AA- - to AE- -, AH- - (*AD- - overlaps with BE174b below*)	FV	£15
BE172c	Prefix AH80...	---	---
BE173a	Prefix EL- - Column sort note (*overlaps with BE175a below*)	£18	£30
BE173b	Prefix LL- - Replacement note (*traced to LL40 and overlaps with BE175b below*)	£35	£75

(2000–date unknown)

Orange and multicoloured. 142 x 75mm.
© *2000 wording correctly reads "The Governor and Company of the Bank of England"*
Signature: Merlyn Lowther
Prefix sequence: Letter/Letter/Number/Number

Copyright 2000 wording on front and back reads, "The Governor and the Company..."   *Copyright 2000 wording on front and back reads, "The Governor and Company..."*

BE174a	Prefix AA01 (*special run for collectors' packs*)	—	£50
BE174b	Prefix AD- - (*overlaps with AD- - BE172b above*)........................	£25	£50
BE174c	Prefix AJ01 (*first official run*)	---	---
BE174d	Prefix AJ- -, AK- -, BA- - to BE- -, BH- - to BL- -, CA- - to CC- -	FV	£14

BE174e

BE174e	Prefix CC40	50	£85
BE175a	Prefix EL- - Column sort note (*overlaps with BE173a above and Bailey BE178a below*)	£12	£20

	EF	UNC

BE175b   Prefix LL- -   Replacement note (*traced to LL40 and overlaps with BE173b above and Bailey BE178b below*) £18   £30

BE176

BE176   Prefix MH- -, MJ- -, MK- -, MM- -   Experimental note £45   £80

(January 2004)

Orange and multicoloured. 142 x 75mm.
Signature: A. Bailey
Prefix sequence: Letter/Letter/Number/Number

BE177a

BE177a   Prefix CC41 .... £45   £80
BE177b   Prefix CC- -, CD- -, CE- - (*continuing*)... FV   £14
BE178a   Prefix EL- - Column sort note (*overlaps with BE175a above*)..... £12   £20
BE178b   Prefix LL- - Replacement note (*overlaps with BE175b above*)... £14   £25

BE179– BE199 [*Held in reserve*]

TWENTY POUNDS

BLACK AND WHITE SERIES (continued)
(1925-29)

	VF	EF
BE200 *Signature: C. P. Mahon*		
London	£1200	£2200

BE201

(1929-34)
BE201 *Signature: B. G. Catterns*		
London	£1000	£1850

(1934-42)
BE202 *Signature: K. O. Peppiatt*		
London	£600	£1100

NB. There are deceptive German World War II forgewries of the White £20 note, almost all of these being forgeries of BE201 and BE202.

SERIES "D" PICTORIAL ISSUE
(July 1970)
Purple and multicoloured. 160 x 90mm.
Reverse depicting William Shakespeare
Signature: J .S. Fforde
Prefix sequence: Letter/Number/Number

BE203a

		EF	UNC
BE203a	Prefix A01 followed by serial number	£160	£300
BE203b	Prefix A- -	£110	£225
BE203c	Prefix A05..	£185	£350

BE204

BE204	Prefix M01 Replacement note...	£225	£400

(1970–date unknown)
Purple and multicoloured. 160 x 90mm.
Signature: J .B. Page
Prefix sequence: Letter/Number/Number

BE205a

		EF	UNC
BE205a	Prefix A06 followed by serial number	£250	£450
BE205b	Prefix A- -	£50	£75
BE205c	Prefix B- - *(not seen)*	---	---
BE205d	Prefix C- -	£45	£65
BE205e	Prefix D- - *(traced to D80)*	£50	£75

BE206a

BE206a	Prefix M01 Replacement note	£175	£350
BE206b	Prefix M- - Replacement note	£125	£225
BE206c	Prefix M04 Replacement note	£225	£425

(March 1981)
Purple and multicoloured. 160 x 90mm.
Signature: D .H. F. Somerset
Prefix sequence: Letter/Number/Number

BE207a	Prefix E01 followed by serial number	£350	£550
BE207b	Prefix E- -	£50	£80
BE207c	Prefix H- -	£40	£70
BE207d	Prefix J- - *(traced to J40)*	£55	£95

(November 1984)

*Purple and multicoloured with enhanced green and brown colouring
and windowed security thread. Watermark is changed from H.M.
Queen Elizabeth II to Shakespeare. 160 x 90mm.*
Signature: D .H. F. Somerset
Prefix sequence: Number/Number/Letter

BE208a

		EF	UNC
BE208a	Prefix 01A followed by serial number	£70	£135
BE208b	Prefix - -A	£50	£80
BE208c	Prefix - -B to - -J	£40	£70
BE208d	Prefix - -K (*traced to 40K*)	£50	£95

(March 1988)

Purple and multicoloured. 160 x 90mm.
Signature: G. M. Gill
Prefix sequence: Number/Number/Letter

BE209a	Prefix 01L followed by serial number	£70	£135
BE209b	Prefix - -L	£50	£80
BE209c	Prefix - -M to - -W	£40	£70
BE209d	Prefix - -X	£50	£95

BE209e

	EF	UNC
BE209e Prefix 20X *(last prefix of Pictorial Series "D" £20)*	£90	£165

SERIES "E" HISTORICAL ISSUE
(June 1991)
Purple and multicoloured. With windowed security thread. 149 x 80mm.
Reverse depicting Michael Faraday
Signature: G. M. Gill
Prefix sequence: Letter/Number/Number

BE210a

		EF	UNC
BE210a	Prefix A01 followed by serial number	£35	£60
BE210b	Prefix A- - to D- -..	£28	£50
BE210c	Prefix D70 (last official run)	---	---

BE210d

		EF	UNC
BE210d	Prefix E- -, H- -, J- -, L- -, R- -, S- -, U- - (*overlaps with Kentfield BE212a, b below*)	£45	£80
BE210e	Prefix U19	---	---
BE210f	Prefix Z13 Experimental note	---	---
BE211	Prefix A- - to C- - Column sort note (*with control numbers above 70. Overlaps with Kentfield BE213a, b below*)	£40	£75

(November 1991)
Purple and multicoloured. 149 x 80mm.
Signature: G .E. A. Kentfield
Prefix sequence: Letter/Number/Number

BE212a

BE212a	Prefix E01 followed by serial number	£75	£140
BE212b	Prefix E- -, H- - to L- -, N- -, R- - to U- -, W- - (*overlaps with Gill BE210d above*)	£28	£50
BE212c	Prefix W35 (*last official run*)	£75	£135
BE213a	Prefix A- - Column sort note (*with control numbers above 70. Overlaps with Gill BE211 above*)	£50	£100
BE213b	Prefix B- - and C- - Column sort note (*with control numbers above 70. Overlaps with Gill BE211 above*)	£65	£120
BE214a	Prefix M- - Experimental note (*traced from M01 to M31*)	£50	£100
BE214b	Prefix Z- - Experimental note (*traced to Z90 but not inclusive*)	£50	£100

(September 1993)
Purple and multicoloured. With enhanced and additional value tablets. 149 x 80mm.
Signature: G .E. A. Kentfield
Prefix sequence: Letter/Number/Number

BE215a

		EF	UNC
BE215a	Prefix X01 followed by serial number	£40	£60
BE215b	Prefix X- - and Y- - (*traced to Y70*)	£25	£40
BE216	Prefix X- - and Y- - Column sort note (*with control numbers*		
	above 70)...	£70	£125

(1994 – date unknown)
Purple and multicoloured. 149 x 80mm.
Signature: G .E. A. Kentfield
Prefix sequence: Letter/Letter/Number/Number

BE217a

BE217a	Prefix AA01 followed by serial number	£85	£185

		EF	UNC
BE217b	Prefix AA- -	£28	£60
BE217c	Prefix AB- - to CJ- -	FV	£35
BE217d	Prefix CJ80 (*last official run*).	---	---
BE217e	Prefix CJ99 (*special last run for collectors' packs*)...........	—	£60
BE218a	Prefix CL- - Column sort note	£60	£125

BE218b

BE218b	Prefix LL01 Replacement note	£85	£175
BE218c	Prefix LL- - Replacement note (*traced to LL40*)	£50	£100

(January 1999)
Purple and multicoloured. 149 x 80mm.
Signature: Merlyn Lowther
Prefix sequence: Letter/Letter/Number/Number

BE219a	Prefix DA01 followed by serial number	£40	£75
BE219b	Prefix DA- -	£30	£60

BE219c

BE219c	Prefix DA80 (*last prefix Historical Series "E" £20*).	£50	£100

SERIES "E" NEW HISTORICAL ISSUE
(June 1999)
Purple and multicoloured. 149 x 80mm.
Reverse depicting Sir Edward Elgar
Signature: Merlyn Lowther ....
Prefix sequence: Letter/Letter/Number/Number

BE220a

		EF	UNC
BE220a	Prefix AA01 followed by serial number	£25	£40
BE220b	Prefix AA- -..	FV	£30
BE220c	Prefix AB- - to AE- -, AH- - to AK- -, BA- - to BE- -, BH- - to BK- -, CA- - to CE- -, CH- -, CJ- -, DB- - to DD- -	FV	£28
BE220d	Prefix DE- - (*overlaps with Bailey BE222a, b below*).......................	FV	£30

BE220e

BE220e	Prefix DE80 (*overlaps with Bailey BE222b below*)..........................	£60	£125
BE221a	Prefix AL- - Column sort note	FV	£35
BE221b	Prefix BL- - Column sort note (*overlaps with Bailey BE223a below*)	FV	£35
BE221c	Prefix LL- - Replacement note (*overlaps with Bailey BE223b below*)	£28	£50

(January 2004)

Purple and multicoloured. 149 x 80mm.
Signature: A. Bailey
Prefix sequence: Letter/Letter/Number/Number

BE222a

		EF	UNC
BE222a	Prefix DE41 followed by serial number	£60	£125
BE222b	Prefix DE- - (*overlaps with Lowther BE220d above*)........................	FV	£30
BE222c	Prefix DH- -, DJ- - (*continuing*)...	FV	£28
BE223a	Prefix BL- - Column sort note (*overlaps with Lowther BE221b above*)...	FV	£30
BE223b	Prefix LL- - Replacement note (*overlaps with Lowther BE221c above*)...	£25	£40

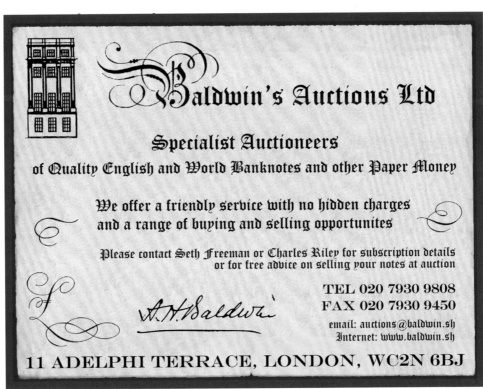

FIFTY POUNDS

BLACK AND WHITE SERIES (continued)

(1925-29)

		VF	EF
BE250	*Signature: C. P. Mahon*		
	London	£1100	£2000

(1929-34)

BE251	*Signature: B. G. Catterns*		
	London	£850	£1400

BE252

(1934-42)

BE252	*Signature: K. O. Peppiatt*		
	London	£550	£1000

NB. There are deceptive German World War II forgeries of the White £50 note, almost all of these being forgeries of BE251 and BE252.

SERIES "D" PICTORIAL ISSUE
(March 1981)
Deep green and multicoloured. 169 x 95mm.
Reverse depicting Sir Christopher Wren
Signature: D. H. F. Somerset
Prefix sequence: Letter/Number/Number

BE253a

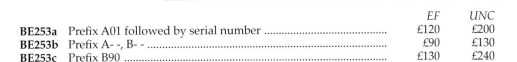

		EF	UNC
BE253a	Prefix A01 followed by serial number	£120	£200
BE253b	Prefix A- -, B- -	£90	£130
BE253c	Prefix B90	£130	£240

(July 1988)
Deep green and multicoloured with enhanced olive green colouring and windowed security thread.
169 x 95mm.
Signature: G. M. Gill
Prefix sequence: Letter/Number/Number

BE254a

BE254a	Prefix C01 followed by serial number	£175	£325

		EF	UNC
BE254b	Prefix C- -, D- -	£95	£140
BE254c	Prefix D90 (*last official run*)	£130	£250
BE254d	Prefix E- - (*overlaps with Kentfield BE256a, b below*)	£120	£225

BE254e

BE254e	Prefix E30 (*overlaps with Kentfield BE256c below*)	£150	£275
BE255	Prefix D- - Column sort note (*with control numbers above 90*)	£120	£225

(November 1991)
Deep green and multicoloured. 169 x 95mm.
Signature: G. E. A. Kentfield
Prefix sequence: Letter/Number/Number

BE256a	Prefix E01 followed by serial number	£100	£160
BE256b	Prefix E- - (*overlaps with Gill BE254d, e above*).	£90	£135

BE256c

BE256c	Prefix E30 (*last prefix of Pictorial Series "D" £50*)	£100	£170

SERIES "E" HISTORICAL ISSUE
(April 1994)
Red and multicoloured. 156 x 85mm.
Reverse depicting Sir John Houblon
Signature: G. E. A. Kentfield
Prefix sequence: Letter/Number/Number

BE257a

		EF	UNC
BE257a	Prefix A01 followed by serial number	£95	£150
BE257b	Prefix A- - to E- -, H- -	£60	£95
BE257c	Prefix H99 (*special last run for collectors' packs*)	—	£130
BE258a	Prefix A- -, B- -, H- - Column sort note (*with control numbers above 70*)	£80	£120
BE258b	Prefix L- - Column sort note (*traced to L35 and overlaps with Lowther BE 261 below*)	£80	£120

BE258c

BE258c	Prefix LL- - Replacement note (*traced to LL35*)	£100	£160
BE259	Prefix M- - Experimental note (*traced in M01 and M97 to M99*).	£175	£275

(January 1999)
Red and multicoloured. 156 x 85mm.
Signature: Merlyn Lowther
Prefix sequence: Letter/Number/Number

BE260a

		EF	UNC
BE260a	Prefix J01 followed by serial number	£95	£140
BE260b	Prefix K- -	FV	£75
BE260c	Prefix M- - *(traced from M01 to M35)*	£60	£90
BE261	Prefix L- - Column sort note *(overlaps with Kentfield*		
	BE258b above)..	£80	£120

BE262– BE274 *[Held in reserve]*

ONE HUNDRED POUNDS

BLACK AND WHITE SERIES (continued)

		VF	EF
(1925-29)			
BE275	*Signature: C. P. Mahon*		
	London	£1500	£2750
(1929-34)			
BE276	*Signature: B. G. Catterns*		
	London	£1000	£2000
(1934-42)			
BE277a	*Signature: K. O. Peppiatt*		
	London	£850	£1500

BE277b

BE277b	Liverpool..	£750	£1350

In addition to the notes listed there is also a series including £200, £500 and £1,000 white notes bearing various cashiers' signatures issued up to 1941. However as these are seldom seen on the market, it has been decided to omit them from this publication.

Isle of Man

The Isle of Man has a very long history of paper money with the first banknote issues appearing during the latter part of the 18th. Century. Over the next 150 years there were numerous mergers and acquisitions as the fortunes of the different banks rose and fell. By the early part of the 20th century the banknote issues were in the hands of five Commercial Banks—The Isle of Man Bank Limited, Westminster Bank Limited, Martins Bank Limited, Lloyds Bank Limited and Barclays Bank Limited.

In 1961 the Isle of Man Government Notes Act was passed and the note issuing licences of all of the commercial banks were revoked. The first Government note issues, comprising denominations of 10 Shillings, one Pound and five Pounds were put into circulation during July of this same year.

ISLE OF MAN BANK LIMITED

The Isle of Man Banking Company was established in Douglas in 1865 and subsequently set up branches in the other main towns in the Island. The name was changed to Isle of Man Bank Limited in 1925, and in 1961 the bank merged with the National Provincial Bank. Since 1969 the Isle of Man Bank has been part of the National Westminster Group.

ONE POUND NOTES

Size 168 mm x 120 mm approximately

Obverse – black with "ONE" in brown at the centre. Vignette of Douglas bay and harbour at the top
Reverse – blue. Triune and Isle of Man motto at the centre

	F	VF
IM1 *Signatories: Handsigned by Manager and Assistant Manager*		
Prefix P dated 9.6.1915 to prefix O/1 dated 1.3.1926..................		Rare

Size 158 mm x 90 mm approximately

 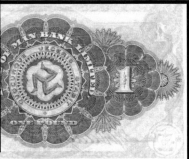

Obverse – black with "ONE" in pink geometric design at the centre. Vignette of Douglas bay and harbour at the top
Reverse – green panel. Triune and Isle of Man motto at the centre

			F	VF

IM2 *Signatories: Handsigned by Manager and Assistant Manager*
  Prefix O/1 dated 1.5.1926 to prefix L/2 dated 1.3.1926 ....   Rare

Size 150 mm x 84 mm approximately

Obverse – blue on a pale green underprint with brown geometric design at the centre. Vignette of Douglas bay and harbour at the top
Reverse – blue on a pale green underprint. Triune and Isle of Man motto at the centre

	F	VF

IM3a *Signatories: J. R. Quayle (Manager) and J. N. Ronan (Assistant Manager)*
  Prefix N/2 dated 1.10.1934 to prefix W/2 dated 5.5.1937 ....   Rare

IM3b *Signatories: J. N. Ronan (Manager) and C. M. Watterson (Assistant Manager)*, or
    J. N. Ronan (Manager) and Edw. Corteen (per pro Assistant Manager)
  Prefix X/2 dated 4.2.1938 to prefix L/3 dated 16.12.1942 .... £80   £130

IM3c *Signatories: J. N. Ronan (Manager) and W. E. Quirk (Assistant Manager)*
  Prefix L/3 dated 16.12.1942 to prefix P/3 dated 7.1.1948 .... £80   £130

IM3d *Signatories: J. N. Ronan (Manager) and R. H. Kelly (Assistant Manager)*
  Prefix P/3 dated 7.1.1948 to prefix B/4 dated 29.11.1954............ £70   £120

IM3e *Signatories: J. N. Ronan (Manager) and W. E. Quirk (Assistant Manager)*, or
    J. N. Ronan (Manager) and J. E. Cashin (Assistant Manager)
  Prefix B/4 dated 29.11.1954 ....   Rare

IM3f *Signatories: J. E. Cashin (Manager) and W. E. Quirk (Assistant Manager)*
  Prefix C/4 dated 5.1.1956 to prefix O/4 dated 24.10.1960 .... £70   £120

FIVE POUND NOTES

Size 176 mm x 92 mm approximately

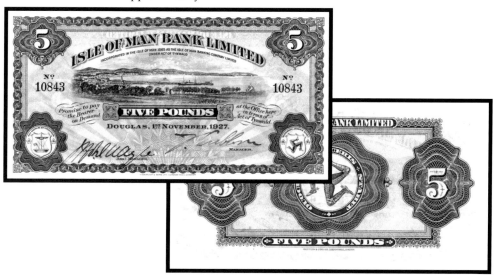

Obverse – blue on a pale green and pink underprint. Vignette of Douglas bay and harbour at the centre.
Reverse – blue on a pale green underprint. Triune and Isle of Man motto at the centre

		F	VF
IM4	Signatories: Handsigned by Manager and Assistant Manager		
	No prefix letters; dated 1.11.1927	£180	£300

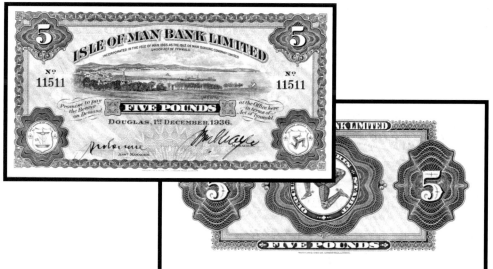

Obverse – brown on a pale pink and green underprint. Vignette of Douglas bay and harbour at the centre
Reverse – brown on a pale pink underprint. Triune and Isle of Man motto at the centre

		F	VF
IM5	Signatories: Handsigned by Manager and Assistant Manager		
	No prefix letters; dated 1.12.1936 to 7.4.1960	£250	£450

WESTMINSTER BANK LIMITED

ONE POUND NOTES

In 1918 the London County & Westminster Bank merged with Parr's Bank Limited to form the London County Westminster & Parr's Bank Limited. A few years later in 1923, the decision was taken to shorten the name to Westminster Bank Limited.

Size 176 mm x 92 mm approximately

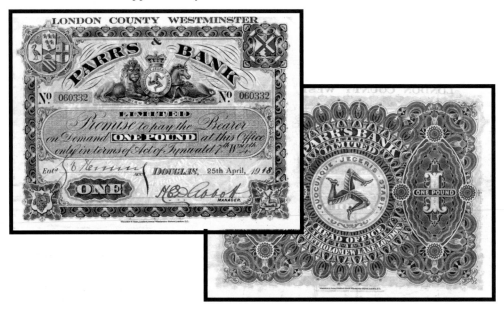

Overprint on banknote stock of Parr's Bank Limited
Obverse – black on a pale blue underprint. Triune flanked by a lion and unicorn at the top.
Overprinted in the top margin; "LONDON COUNTY WESTMINSTER"
Reverse –blue panel with the Isle of Man triune and motto at the centre

	F	*VF*
IM7 *Signatories: Handsigned by Manager and Accountant*		
No prefix letters; dated 28.3.1918 to 22.11.1918............................		Rare

From 1919 to 1921 there were issues of £1 notes with a similar design to the earlier Parr's Bank notes but with the new title of London County Westminster & Parr's Bank Limited. Only 5000 notes were printed and none are known to have survived. Following the adoption of the new Bank name in 1923, these notes were issued overprinted "WESTMINSTER BANK LIMITED" in the top margin.

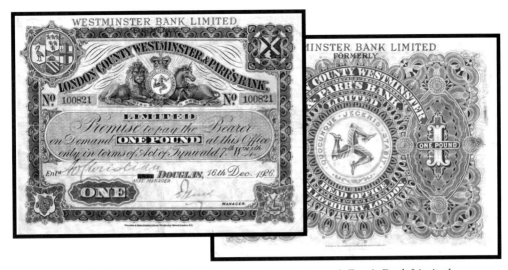

Overprint on banknote stock of London County Westminster & Parr's Bank Limited
Obverse – black on a pale blue/grey underprint. Triune flanked by a lion and unicorn at the top
Overprinted in the top margin; "WESTMINSTER BANK LIMITED - formerly"
Reverse –blue panel with the Isle of Man triune and motto at the centre

IM9   Signatories: Handsigned by Manager and Assistant Manager.
No prefix letters; dated 4.7.1923 to 4.4.1927 ....   Rare

Size 176 mm x 92 mm approximate

Obverse – black on a pale yellow underprint. Triune flanked by a lion and unicorn at the top
Reverse –blue panel with the Isle of Man triune and motto at the centre

		F	VF
IM10a	*Signatories: F. Proud (Manager) and A. O. Christian (Assistant Manager)* No prefix letters; dated 9.1.1929 to 14.11.1933		Rare
IM10b	*Signatories: A. O. Christian (Manager) and R. E. Callin (Chief Clerk)* No prefix letters; dated 22.1.1935 to 4.2.1943		from £150
IM10c	*Signatories: R. E. Callin (Manager) and W. G. Flinn (Chief Clerk)* No prefix letters; dated 11.2.1944 to 18.3.1949		Rare
IM10d	*Signatories: R. E. Callin (Manager) and G. D. Radcliffe (Chief Clerk)* No prefix letters; dated 7.11.1950 to 23.11.1955	£90	£160

		VF	EF
IM10e	*Signatories: P. F. Barlow (Manager) and G. D. Radcliffe (Chief Clerk)* No prefix letters; dated 4.4.1956 to 3.3.1959..............................	£120	£230
IM10e	*Signatories: P. F. Barlow (Manager) and T. D. Russell (Chief Clerk)* No prefix letters; dated 8.12.1959 to 10.3.1961.............................	£120	£230

MARTINS BANK LIMITED

ONE POUND NOTES

Martins Bank Limited acquired a foothold in the Isle of Man following a merger with the Lancashire & Yorkshire Bank Limited in 1928. This latter bank had already absorbed the Mercantile Bank of Lancashire Limited which previously had purchased the Manx Bank in 1900. Thus the Lancashire and Yorkshire Bank Limited had been issuing banknotes in the Isle of Man since 1920. The initial banknotes of Martins Bank Limited were overprints on existing stock of Lancashire & Yorkshire Bank.

Size 165 mm x 85 mm approximately

Overprint on notes of The Lancashire & Yorkshire Bank Limited
Obverse – black. Bank's Coat of Arms to the left and the Tower of Refuge to the right. Overprinted at the top: "MARTINS BANK LIMITED" in black, and "WITH WHICH IS INCORPORATED" in red.
Reverse – black. Isle of Man Triune at the centre with vignettes of Castle Rushen and the Laxey Wheel to the left and right

	F	VF
IM12 *Signatories: Handsigned by the Manager and Assistant Manager* No prefix letters; dated 9.10.1928 and 3.11.1928..........................		Rare

Size 150 mm x 84 mm approximately

Obverse – dark grey. Bank's Coat of Arms depicting a grasshopper and Liver bird to the left, and the Tower of Refuge to the right
Reverse – black. Isle of Man Triune at the centre with vignettes of Castle Rushen and the Laxey Wheel to the left and right

		F	VF
IM13a	*Signatories: R. H. Milner (Manager) and E. S. Oldham (Assistant Manager)* No prefix letters, dated 2.4.1929 no notes are known to have survived		
IM13b	*Signatories: A. F. Shawyer (General Manager) and E. S. Oldham (District Manager)* No prefix letters, dated 1.12.1931 and 31.12.1932....................... Rare		
IM13c	*Signatory: J. M. Furniss (General Manager)* No prefix letters, dated 1.8.1934 and 1.10.1938...........................	£80	£140
IM13d	*Signatory: Jas. McKendrick (Chief General Manager)* No prefix letters, dated 1.3.1946	£90	£150
IM13e	*Signatory: C. J. Verity (Chief General Manager)* No prefix letters, dated 1.6.1950 and 1.5.1953	£60	£100

		VF	EF
IM13f	*Signatory: M. Conacher (Chief General Manager)* No prefix letters, dated 1.2.1957	£80	£140

LLOYDS BANK LIMITED

Lloyds Bank Limited opened its first branch in the Isle of Man in Douglas in 1896 and acquired a licence to issue banknotes to a limit of £15,000 in about 1918. The first notes were issued in 1919, but the first known to have survived are dated 1921.

ONE POUND NOTES

Size 156 mm x 114 mm approximately

Obverse – black on a green and pale pink underprint. Black horse in panel towards top centre. Vignette of Viking ship at bottom centre
Reverse – blue. Isle of Man Triune and motto at centre

		F	VF
IM15	*Signatories: handsigned by the Manager and Accountant*		
	Prefix A dated 23.4.1919 to prefix B dated 21.1.1927.................		Rare

Size 150 mm x 84 mm approximately

Obverse – black on a pale green and pink underprint. Black horse in panel with vignette of Viking ship at bottom centre
Reverse – blue on a pink sunburst underprint. Isle of Man Triune and motto at centre

		F	VF
IM16a	*Signatories: H. Towler (Manager) and R. A. Hodder (Accountant)* Prefix C dated 1.8.1929 to 14.2.1934		Rare
IM16b	*Signatories: H. Towler (Manager) and J. Greenwood (Accountant)* Prefix C dated 28.1.1935 to prefix D dated 12.3.1941	£300	---
IM16c	*Signatories: J. Greenwood (Manager) and C. R. Collister (Accountant)* Prefix D dated 20.11.1942 to 6.3.1946		Rare
IM16d	*Signatories: J. Greenwood (Manager) and R. C. Sale (Accountant)* Prefix D dated 25.2.1948 and 27.4.1949		Rare
IM16e	*Signatories: J. Greenwood (Manager) and C. R. Collister (Accountant)* Prefix D dated 27.2.1951 to 25.2.1957...	£300	---
IM16e	*Signatories: D. Berry (Manager) and C. R. Collister (Accountant)* Prefix D dated 28.2.1958 to 14.3.1961...	£220	£350

BARCLAYS BANK LIMITED

Barclays Bank Limited established a presence in the Isle of Man when it opened a branch in Douglas in 1922. The one Pound notes which it issued from 1924 onwards were all of the same size and design.

Size 150 mm x 84 mm approximately

Obverse – brown on a yellow and green underprint
Reverse – brown. Vignette of Douglas Bay and harbour

		F	VF
IM18a	*Signatories: E. E. Swan (Manager) and J. E. Callister (Accountant)* No prefix letters; dated from 7.6.1924 to 7.4.1926		Rare
IM18b	*Signatories: E. E. Swan (Manager) and M. Pullman (Accountant)* No prefix letters; dated from 28.8.1926 to 19.4.1929		Rare
IM18c	*Signatories: E. E. Swan (Manager) and A. Tranter (Accountant)* No prefix letters; dated from 10.12.1929 to 7.4.1937		Rare
IM18d	*Signatories: T. H. Hall (Manager) and A. Tranter (Accountant)* No prefix letters; dated from 17.12.1937 to 20.3.1950		from £350
IM18e	*Signatories: T. H. Hall (Manager) and J. A. Butterworth (Accountant)* No prefix letters; dated from 13.11.1950 to 4.12.1953..................	£250	£450
IM18f	*Signatories: T. H. Hall (Manager) and J. A. Butterworth (Chief Clerk)* No prefix letters; dated from 10.4.1954 to 25.3.1958	£250	£450
IM18e	*Signatories: J. A. Butterworth (Manager) and A. Smith (Chief Clerk)* No prefix letters; dated from 25.3.1958 to 30.3.1960		Rare

ISLE OF MAN GOVERNMENT ISSUES

TEN SHILLING NOTES

Size 140 mm x 67 mm approximately

First issued in 1961.
Obverse – mainly red. Portrait of Queen Elizabeth II to the right; Triune and motto at the centre
Reverse – red. Picture of a Viking ship under sail

		EF	UNC
IM21a	*Signatory: R. H. Garvey (Lieutenant Governor)* No prefix letter (000001 to 1000000) and Prefix A (000001 to 250000)	£30	£45
IM21b	*Signatory: P. G. H. Stallard (Lieutenant Governor)* Prefix A (250001 to 517000)	£30	£45

FIFTY PENCE NOTES

Size 140 mm x 67 mm approximately

First issued in 1969
Obverse – mainly blue. Portrait of Queen Elizabeth II to the right; Triune and motto at the centre
Reverse – blue. Picture of a Viking ship under sail

		EF	UNC
IM22	*Signatory: P. G. H. Stallard (Lieutenant Governor)* No prefix letter (000001 to 679000)	£14	£18

Size 127 mm x 61 mm approximately

First issued in 1972
Obverse – mainly blue. Portrait of Queen Elizabeth II to the right; Triune and motto at the centre
Reverse – blue. Picture of a Viking ship under sail

		EF	UNC
IM23a	*Signatory: P. G. H. Stallard (Lieutenant Governor)* Prefix A (200001 to 800000)	£20	£30
IM23b	*Signatory: John Paul (Lieutenant Governor) – large signature* Prefix A (800001 to 1000000) and Prefix B (000001 to 370000)..	£14	£20
IM23c	*Signatory: John Paul (Lieutenant Governor) – small signature* Prefix B (370001 to 1000000) and Prefix C (000001 to 200000)	£9	£14

First issued in 1979. Similar to previous issue but for change of title of signatory
Obverse – mainly blue. Portrait of Queen Elizabeth II to the right; Triune and motto at the centre
Reverse – blue. Picture of a Viking ship under sail

		EF	UNC
IM24	Signatory: W. Dawson (Treasurer of the Isle of Man) Prefix C (200001 to 750000)	£4	£7

ONE POUND NOTES

Size 151 mm x 72 mm approximately

First issued in 1961
Obverse – mainly violet. Portrait of Queen Elizabeth II to the right; Triune and motto at the centre
Reverse – violet. View of Tynwald Hill and St. John's church

		EF	UNC
IM31a	*Signatory: R. H. Garvey (Lieutenant Governor)* No prefix letter (000001 to 1000000), Prefix A and prefix B (000001 to 200000)......................................	£35	£45
IM31b	*Signatory: P. G. H. Stallard (Lieutenant Governor)* Prefix B (200001 to 1000000) and prefix C (000001 to 745000)....	£35	£45

Size 135 mm x 67 mm approximately

First issued in 1972
Obverse – mainly violet. Portrait of Queen Elizabeth II to the right; Triune and motto at the centre
Reverse – violet. View of Tynwald Hill and St. John's church

		EF	UNC
IM32a	*Signatory: P. G. H. Stallard (Lieutenant Governor)* Prefix C (850001 to 1000000) and Prefix D (000001 to 970000)	£28	£40
IM32b	*Signatory: John Paul (Lieutenant Governor) – large signature* Prefix D (970001 to 1000000) and prefix E................................	£25	£35
IM32c	*Signatory: John Paul (Lieutenant Governor) – small signature* Prefix F, G and H (000001 to 440000)	£14	£20

First issued in 1979. Similar to previous issue but for change of title of signatory
Obverse – mainly violet. Portrait of Queen Elizabeth II to the right; Triune and motto at the centre
Reverse – violet. View of Tynwald Hill and St. John's church

		EF	UNC
IM33a	*Signatory: W. Dawson (Treasurer of the Isle of Man)*		
	Prefix H (440001 to 1000000) to prefix K....................................	£6	£10
	(issued before the Tyvek notes – ref. IM34)		
IM33b	*Signatory: W. Dawson (Treasurer of the Isle of Man)*		
	Prefix P (500001 to 1000000) to prefix R (000001 to 500000).......	£6	£10
	(issued after the Tyvek notes – ref. IM34, circa 1988)		

First issued in 1979 – manufactured from Tyvek polymer
Obverse – green on a light multicoloured underprint. Portrait of Queen Elizabeth II to the right;
Triune and motto at the centre
Reverse – green. View of Tynwald Hill and St. John's church

		EF	UNC
IM34	*Signatory: W. Dawson (Treasurer of the Isle of Man)*		
	Prefix M, N and P (000001 to 500000)...	£10	£15

Size 128 mm x 65 mm approximately

First issued in 1990
Obverse – mainly violet. Portrait of Queen Elizabeth II to the right; Triune and motto at the centre
Reverse – violet. View of Tynwald Hill and St. John's church

		EF	UNC
IM35a	*Signatory: W. Dawson (Chief Financial Officer)*		
	Prefix R (500001 to 1000000) and prefix S.....................................	£6	£9
	Prefix Z – replacement note..	£30	£45
IM35b	*Signatory: J. A. Cashen (Chief Financial Officer)*		
	Prefix T to prefix Y..	---	£2
	Prefix Z – replacement note..	£15	£22

FIVE POUND NOTES

Size 139 mm x 84 mm approximately

First issued in 1961
Obverse – blue and green on a multicoloured underprint. Portrait of Queen Elizabeth II to the right;
Triune and motto at the centre
Reverse – dark grey. View of Castle Rushen, 1775

		VF	EF
IM41a	*Signatory: R. H. Garvey (Lieutenant Governor)*		
	No prefix letter (000001 to 250000),.................................	£80	£160
IM41b	*Signatory: P. G. H. Stallard (Lieutenant Governor)*		
	No prefix letter (250001 to 500000).................................	£80	£160

Size 147 mm x 78 mm approximately

First issued in 1972
Obverse – blue and maroon on a multicoloured underprint. Portrait of Queen Elizabeth II to the right; Triune and motto at the centre
Reverse – dark grey. View of Castle Rushen, 1775

		EF	UNC
IM42a	*Signatory: P. G. H. Stallard (Lieutenant Governor)* No prefix letter (500001 to 950000)..	£130	£180
IM42b	*Signatory: John Paul (Lieutenant Governor)* No prefix letter (950001 to 1000000), prefix A and B (000001 to 600000)..	£65	£85

First issued in 1979. Similar to previous issue but for change of title of signatory
Obverse – blue and maroon on a multicoloured underprint. Portrait of Queen Elizabeth II to the right; Triune and motto at the centre
Reverse – dark grey. View of Castle Rushen, 1775

		EF	UNC
IM43a	*Signatory: W. Dawson (Treasurer of the Isle of Man)* Prefix B (600001 to 1000000), C and D (000001 to 100000 approx.) Prefix letters are in Serif script	£45	£60
IM43b	*Signatory: W. Dawson (Treasurer of the Isle of Man)* Prefix D (100000 approximately to 1000000) .... Prefix letters are in Sans Serif script	£45	£60

Size 135 mm x 69 mm approximately.

First issued in 1991
Obverse – blue and maroon on a multicoloured underprint. Portrait of Queen Elizabeth II to the right; Triune and motto at the centre
Reverse – dark grey on a multicoloured underprint. View of Castle Rushen, 1775

		EF	UNC
IM44a	*Signatory: W. Dawson (Chief Financial Officer)*		
	Prefix E and prefix F (000001 to 100000)	£15	£25
	Prefix Z – replacement note		Rare
IM44b	*Signatory: J. A. Cashen (Chief Financial Officer)*		
	Prefix F (100001 to prefix K and ongoing...................................	---	£10
	Prefix Z – replacement note	£15	£25

TEN POUND NOTES

Size 151 mm x 85 mm approximately

First issued in 1972
Obverse – brown and green on a multicoloured underprint. Portrait of Queen Elizabeth II to the right; Triune and motto at the centre
Reverse – shades of brown. View of Peel Castle, circa 1830

		EF	UNC
IM51a	*Signatory: P. G. H. Stallard (Lieutenant Governor)*		
	No prefix letter (000001 to 050000)		Rare
IM51b	*Signatory: John Paul (Lieutenant Governor)*		
	No prefix letter (050001 to 360000)	£100	£140

Size 150 mm x 85 mm approximately

First issued in 1972. Similar to previous issue but for change of title of signatory.
Obverse – brown and green on a multicoloured underprint. Portrait of Queen Elizabeth II to the right;
Triune and motto at the centre
Reverse – shades of brown. View of Peel Castle, circa 1830

		EF	UNC
IM52	*Signatory: W. Dawson (Treasurer of the Isle of Man)*		
	No prefix letter (360001 to 1000000) and prefix A	£80	£130

Size 142 mm x 75 mm approximately

First issued in 1991
Obverse – brown and green on a multicoloured underprint. Portrait of Queen Elizabeth II to the right;
Triune and motto at the centre. The clause under the title at the top of the note reads: "promise to pay
the bearer on demand at any office of Isle of Man Bank Limited"
Reverse – shades of brown. View of Peel Castle, circa 1830

		EF	UNC
IM53a	*Signatory: W. Dawson (Chief Financial Officer)*		
	Prefix B (000001 to 010000)		Rare
IM53b	*Signatory: J. A. Cashen (Chief Financial Officer)*		
	Prefix C to prefix G..	£14	£22
	Prefix Z – replacement note	£35	£50

First issued in 2002
Obverse – brown and green on a multicoloured underprint. Portrait of Queen Elizabeth II to the right; Triune and motto at the centre. The clause under the title at the top of the note reads: "promise to pay the bearer on demand at any office of Isle of Man Bank"
Reverse – shades of brown. View of Peel Castle, circa 1830

		EF	UNC
IM54	Signatory: J. A. Cashen (Chief Financial Officer)		
	Prefix H to prefix M...	---	£20
	Prefix Z – replacement note...	£25	£35

TWENTY POUND NOTES

Size 160 mm x 90 mm approximately

First issued 1979. Commemorating the millennium year of the Isle of Man
Obverse – red and brown on a multicoloured underprint. Portrait of Queen Elizabeth II to the right; Triune and motto at the centre. Clause below Queen's portrait reads: "ISSUED DURING MILLENNIUM YEAR 1979"
Reverse – red, yellow and multicoloured. View of the Laxey Wheel, 1854

		EF	UNC
IM61	Signatory: W. Dawson (Treasurer of the Isle of Man)		
	No prefix letter (000001 to 005000).	£160	£230

First issued 1979. Similar to above but without commemorative clause
*Obverse – red and brown on a multicoloured underprint. Portrait of Queen Elizabeth II to the right;
Triune and motto at the centre*
Reverse – red, yellow and multicoloured. View of the LaxeyWheel, 1854

		EF	UNC
IM62	*Signatory: W. Dawson (Treasurer of the Isle of Man)*		
	No prefix letter (005001 to 150000).	£150	£220

Size 150 mm x 80 mm approximately

First issued 1991
*Obverse – red and brown on a multicoloured underprint. Portrait of Queen Elizabeth II to the right;
Triune and motto at the centre. The clause under the title at the top of the note reads: "promise to pay
the bearer on demand at any office of Isle of Man Bank Limited"*
Reverse – lilac and orange brown. View of the Laxey Wheel, 1854

		EF	UNC
IM63a	*Signatory: W. Dawson (Chief Financial Officer)*		
	No prefix letter (150001 to 450000)	£60	£80
IM63b	*Signatory: J. A. Cashen (Chief Financial Officer)*		
	No prefix letter (450001 to 1000000) and prefix A to prefix D	£30	£45
	Prefix Z – replacement note	£60	£90

First issued 2002
Obverse – red and brown on a multicoloured underprint. Portrait of Queen Elizabeth II to the right; Triune and motto at the centre. The clause under the title at the top of the note reads: "promise to pay the bearer on demand at any office of Isle of Man Bank"
Reverse – lilac and orange brown. View of the Laxey Wheel, 1854

		EF	UNC
IM64	*Signatory: J. A. Cashen (Chief Financial Officer)*		
	Prefix E and F (ongoing)..	---	£40
	Prefix Z – replacement note	£50	£80

FIFTY POUND NOTES

Size 170 mm x 95 mm approximately

First issued 1983
Obverse – blue and green on a multicoloured underprint. Portrait of Queen Elizabeth II to the right; Triune and motto at the centre
Reverse – blue green and multicoloured. View of Douglas Bay 1841

		EF	UNC
IM62	*Signatory: W. Dawson (Treasurer of the Isle of Man)*		
	No prefix letter (000001 to 250000)...	---	£100

Guernsey

SOME EXAMPLES OF BANKNOTES IN CIRCULATION IN GUERNSEY PRIOR TO WWII

Guernsey banknotes issued before the outbreak of WWII are all scarce; quantities issued were small and relatively few have survived. Many note types are true rarities with just a handful being known in private collections. For this reason no attempt has been made to fully catalogue, or ascribe values to these issues, but a number of notes are illustrated below.

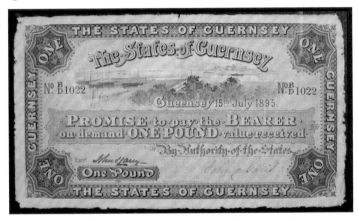

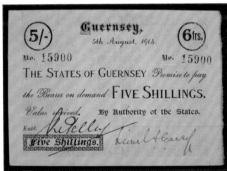

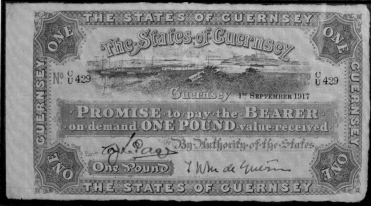

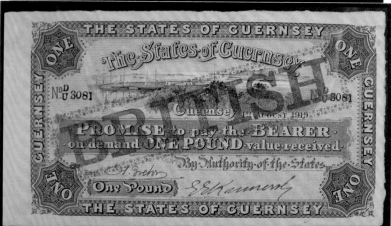

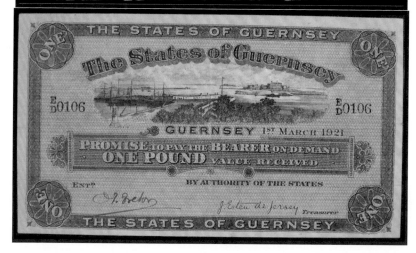

Size 140 mm x 85 mm approximately

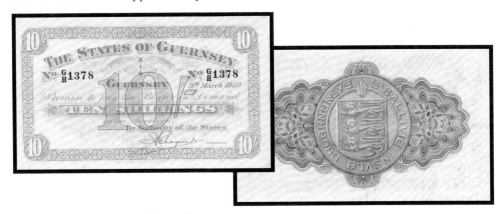

Obverse – pale blue with 10/- in red/orange at the centre
Reverse – red panel with the Guernsey seal at the centre

		F	VF
GU21	**Ten Shillings** - *Signatory: H. E. Marquand (Treasurer)*		
	Prefix B/R (circa 1932) to prefix G/H dated 9.3.1940 .... from £325		£600

Size 150 mm x 87 mm approximately

Obverse – black with £1 in a red panel at the centre.
Reverse – blue panel with the Guernsey seal at the centre.

GU22	**One Pound** - *Signatory: H. E. Marquand (Treasurer)*		
	Prefix K/G (circa 1933) to prefix S/L dated 9.3.1940 .... from £400		£650

GUERNSEY WORLD WAR II ISSUES

Following the occupation of the Channel Island by Germany during WWII there was an acute shortage of coinage in the Island and permission was given by the Germans for the printing and distribution of small denomination banknotes, subject to the withdrawal from circulation of an equivalent amount of Guernsey and Bank of England notes. These Bank of England notes were overstamped "Withdrawn from Circulation September 18th, 1941." and "Withdrawn from Circulation November 10th, 1941." Some 5,000 Bank of England £1 notes and a similar amount of Guernsey 10 shilling and £1 notes (there is some doubt about the exact figure) were withdrawn to balance the introduction of notes of 6 pence, 1 shilling, 1 shilling and 3 pence, 2 shillings and 6 pence, and 5 shillings.

During the occupation, notes of 10 shillings, 1 pound and 5 pounds (references GU29 to GU31) were also printed covertly on the island and issued immediately following the liberation on Wednesday, May 9, 1945. They were used to redeem the small denomination occupation notes and were quickly superceded by the post War issue dated 1.8.1945.

Bank of England notes (above) were withdrawn from circulation in Guernsey prior to the issue of the small denomination notes below. For full information and values on these notes, see catalogue references BE48 to BE50 in the Bank of England section.

Size 90 mm x 60 mm approximately

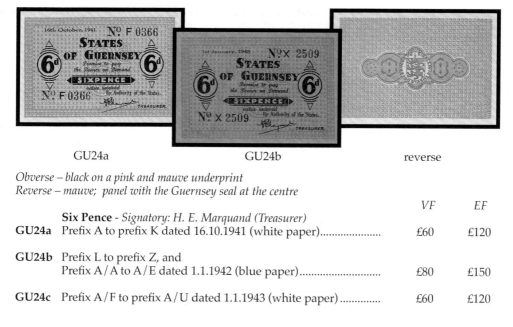

| GU24a | GU24b | reverse |

Obverse – black on a pink and mauve underprint
Reverse – mauve; panel with the Guernsey seal at the centre

		VF	EF
Six Pence - Signatory: H. E. Marquand (Treasurer)			
GU24a Prefix A to prefix K dated 16.10.1941 (white paper)		£60	£120
GU24b Prefix L to prefix Z, and Prefix A/A to A/E dated 1.1.1942 (blue paper)		£80	£150
GU24c Prefix A/F to prefix A/U dated 1.1.1943 (white paper)		£60	£120

Size 90 mm x 60 mm approximately

Obverse – 1 Shilling overprint in red/brown on a note for 1 Shilling and 3 Pence
Printed on white or blue paper; black on a yellow and brown underprint
Reverse - brown; panel with the Guernsey seal at the centre

		VF	EF
One Shilling - *Signatory: H. E. Marquand (Treasurer)*			
GU25a Prefix G to prefix M dated 18.7.1942 (blue paper)		£150	£260
GU25b Prefix N to prefix Z dated 1.1.1943 (white paper)		£80	£140

Size 90 mm x 60 mm approximately

GU26a   GU26b   reverse

Obverse – Printed on white or blue paper; black on a yellow and brown underprint
Reverse - brown; panel with the Guernsey seal at the centre

		VF	EF
One Shilling and Three Pence - *Signatory: H. E. Marquand (Treasurer)*			
GU26a Prefix A to prefix F dated 16.10.1941 (white paper)		£80	£180
GU26b Prefix G dated 18.7.1942 (blue paper – only 500 notes printed)			Rare

Size 90 mm x 60 mm approximately

GU27a   GU27c   reverse

Obverse – Printed on white or blue paper; blue, with "2/6" in brown at the centre
Reverse – blue; panel with the Guernsey seal at the centre

		VF	EF
Two Shillings and Six Pence - *Signatory: H. E. Marquand (Treasurer)*			
GU27a Prefix A/A to prefix A/E dated 25.3.1941 (white paper)		£90	£180
GU27b Prefix A/F to prefix A/K dated 17.5.1941 (white paper)		£90	£180
GU27c Prefix A/L to prefix B/A dated 1.1.1942 (blue paper)		£90	£180
GU27d Prefix B/B to prefix B/J dated 1.1.1943 (white paper)		£80	£170

Size 100 mm x 65 mm approximately

 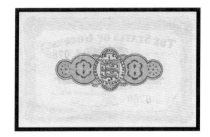

Obverse – Black with "5/-" in red at the centre
Reverse - red; panel with the Guernsey seal at the centre

		VF	EF
Five Shillings - *Signatory: H. E. Marquand (Treasurer)*			
GU28a	Prefix A/F to prefix A/H dated 25.3.1941	£100	£190
GU28b	Prefix A/H to prefix A/K dated 1.1.1942......................................	£190	£300
GU28c	Prefix A/L to prefix A/T dated 1.1.1943	£140	£220

Notes issued immediately following the liberation of Guernsey on May 9, 1945

Size 135 mm x 80 mm approximately

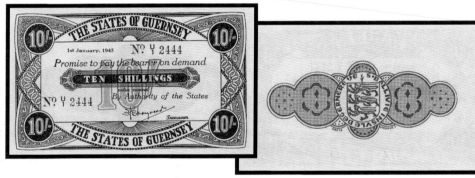

Obverse – Blue with "10/-" in red at the centre
Reverse - red; panel with the Guernsey seal at the centre

		VF	EF
Ten Shillings - *Signatory: H. E. Marquand (Treasurer)*			
GU29	Prefix A/1 to prefix W/1 dated 1.1.1943	£300	£450

Size 150 mm x 87 mm approximately

Obverse – Printed on white or blue paper; black, with "£1" in red at the centre
Reverse - blue; panel with the Guernsey seal at the centre

		VF	EF
	One Pound - *Signatory: H. E. Marquand (Treasurer)*		
GU30a	Prefix A/1 to prefix Z/1, and		
	Prefix A/2 to prefix N/2 dated 1.1.1943 (white paper)	£350	£550
GU30b	Prefix O/2 to prefix S/2 dated 1.1.1945 (blue paper)		Rare

Size 165 mm x 95 mm approximately

Obverse – Printed on blue paper; green with red date and serial numbers
Reverse - green; panel with the Guernsey seal at the centre

	Five Pounds - *Signatory: H. E. Marquand (Treasurer)*	
GU31	Prefix 1/A to prefix 1/H dated 1.1.1945	Rare
	(only 53 notes are outstanding)	

GUERNSEY POST WAR ISSUES

TEN SHILLING NOTES

Obverse – Lilac on a light green underprint.
Reverse – purple; panel with the Guernsey seal at the centre

	VF	EF
GU32a *Signatory: H. E. Marquand (Treasurer)*		
Prefix 1/A to prefix 2/Z dated 1.8.1945.	£60	£120
GU32b *Signatory: L. A. Guillemette (Treasurer)*		
Prefix 2/Z dated 1.1.1950 to prefix 24/G dated 1.7.1966 .... from £30		£50
(Some dates are scarce and worth considerably more)		

ONE POUND NOTES

Size 155 mm x 87 mm approximately

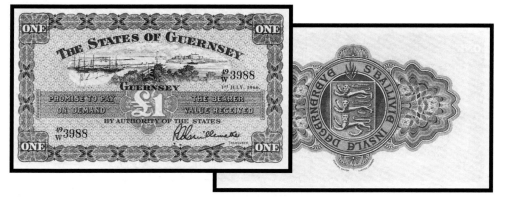

Obverse – purple on a green underprint. "£1" in a green panel at centre.
Reverse - green; panel with the Guernsey seal at the centre

	VF	EF
GU33a *Signatory: H. E. Marquand (Treasurer)*		
Prefix 1/A dated 1.8.1945 to prefix 5/X dated 1.4.1948	£70	£140
GU33b *Signatory: L. A. Guillemette (Treasurer)*		
Prefix 5/Y dated 1.1.1950 to prefix 49/W dated 1.7.1966 .... from £40		£90
(Some dates are scarce and worth considerably more)		

Size 135 mm x 75 mm approximately

First issued 1969
Obverse – olive on a pink and yellow underprint. Guernsey seal at the centre
Reverse - olive; illustration of Castle Cornet

		EF	UNC
GU34a	*Signatory: L. A. Guillemette (Treasurer)*		
	Prefix A to prefix C 100000	£30	£45
GU34b	*Signatory: C. H. Hodder (Treasurer)*		
	Prefix C 100001 to prefix G 630000	£14	£20
GU34c	*Signatory: W. C. Bull (Treasurer)*		
	Prefix G 630001 to prefix H 860000	£16	£22

Size 135 mm x 67 mm approximately

First issued 1980
Obverse – green on a multicoloured underprint. Guernsey seal at bottom left; picture of the old market square circa 1830 in underprint at the centre
Reverse - green; portrait of Daniel de Lisle Brock to the right with illustration of Royal Court, St. Peter Port 1840, in the background

		EF	UNC
GU35a	*Signatory: W. C. Bull (States Treasurer)*		
	Prefix A to prefix G..	£5	£9
	Prefix Z – replacement note.	£15	£25
GU35b	*Signatory: M. J. Brown (States Treasurer)*		
	Prefix H only	£7	£12
	Prefix Z – replacement note.		Rare

Size 129 mm x 65 mm approximately

Similar to previous issue, but reduced size. First issued 1991
Obverse – green on a multicoloured underprint. Guernsey seal at bottom left; picture of the old market square circa 1830 in underprint at the centre.
Reverse - green; portrait of Daniel de Lisle Brock to the right with illustration of Royal Court, St. Peter Port 1840, in the background.

		EF	*UNC*
GU36a	*Signatory: M. J. Brown (States Treasurer)*		
	Prefix J to prefix L	--	£4
	Prefix Z – replacement note.	£7	£12
GU36b	*Signatory: D. P. Trestain (States Treasurer)*		
	Prefix M to prefix S	--	£3
	Prefix Z – replacement note.	£6	£10
GU36c	*Signatory: D. M. Clark (States Treasurer)*		
	Prefix T and ongoing	--	£2
	Prefix Z – replacement note.	£6	£10

FIVE POUND NOTES

Size 155 mm x 90 mm approximately

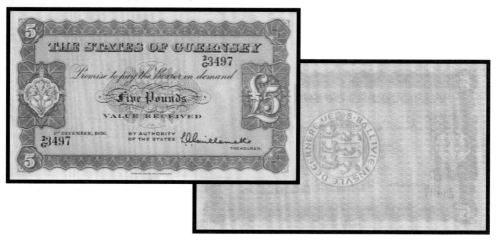

Obverse – green on a multicoloured underprint
Reverse – light green; Guernsey seal at the centre

		F	*VF*
GU41	*Signatory: L. A. Guillemette (Treasurer)*		
	Prefix 1/J dated 1.12.1956 to prefix 4/C dated 1.7.1966	£150	£250

Size 145 mm x 85 mm approximately

First issued 1969
Obverse – purple on a light brown underprint. Guernsey seal to the lower right
Reverse – mainly purple; town sea front and harbour scene

		EF	UNC
GU42a	*Signatory: L. A. Guillemette (Treasurer)*		
	Prefix A (to 400000)	£60	£90
GU42b	*Signatory: C. H. Hodder (Treasurer)*		
	Prefix A and prefix B (to 850000)......................................	£45	£65
GU42c	*Signatory: W. C. Bull (Treasurer)*		
	Prefix B (from B850001) and C	£45	£65

Size 145 mm x 78 mm approximately

First issued 1980
Obverse – brown and multicoloured. Guernsey seal at bottom left; Fort Grey in underprint at the centre
Reverse – mainly brown; portrait of Thomas de la Rue with illustrations of Fountain Street, St. Peter Port 1977, and an envelope making machine, 1851

		EF	UNC
GU43	*Signatory: W. C. Bull (States Treasurer)*		
	Prefix A to prefix F...	£16	£25
	Prefix Z – replacement note.	£40	£60

Size 135 mm x 70 mm approximately

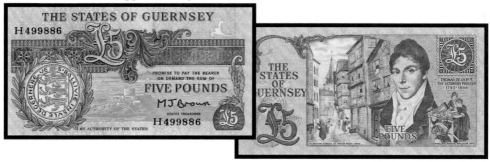

Similar to earlier issue but reduced size. First issued 1991
Obverse – brown and multicoloured. Guernsey seal at bottom left; Fort Grey in underprint at the centre
Reverse – mainly brown; portrait of Thomas de la Rue with illustrations of Fountain Street, St. Peter Port 1977, and an envelope making machine, 1851

		EF	UNC
GU44a	*Signatory: M. J. Brown (States Treasurer)*		
	Prefix G and prefix H (to 500000)	£12	£20
	Prefix Z – replacement note.	£25	£35
GU44b	*Signatory: D. P. Trestain (States Treasurer)*		
	Prefix H 500001 and prefix J	£10	£18
	Prefix Z – replacement note.	£25	£35

First issued 1996.
Obverse – brown and multicoloured. Portrait of Queen Elizabeth II to the right; Guernsey seal at bottom centre.
Reverse – multicoloured, illustrations of Fort Grey and Hanois Lighthouse, 1862

		EF	UNC
GU45a	*Signatory: D. P. Trestain (States Treasurer)*		
	Prefix A and prefix B	—	£12
	Prefix Z – replacement note.	£20	£30
GU45b	*Signatory: D. M. Clark (States Treasurer)*		
	Prefix C and ongoing	—	£10
	Prefix Z – replacement note.	probably exists	

Similar to previous issue. Issued in 2000 to commemorate the Millennium
*Obverse – multicoloured. Portrait of Queen Elizabeth II to the right; Guernsey seal at bottom centre
Commemorative overprint to the left*
Reverse – multicoloured, illustrations of Fort Grey and Hanois Lighthouse, 1862

	EF	UNC
GU46 Signatory: D. P. Trestain (States Treasurer)		
Prefix M only.	--	£12

TEN POUND NOTES

Size 150 mm x 90 mm approximately

First issued 1975
*Obverse – blue and multicoloured; Britannia at left centre holding a spear and the Guernsey seal
Reverse – blue; an illustration of the Battle of Queenston Heights 1812, with a portrait of Major
General Sir Isaac Brock KB, to the right*

	EF	UNC
GU51 Signatory: C. H. Hodder (States Treasurer)		
Prefix A (to 571400)	£150	£220

Size 150 mm x 85 mm approximately

First issued 1980.
Obverse – blue on a multicoloured underprint. Guernsey seal at bottom left; Castle Cornet in underprint at the centre
Reverse – blue; an illustration of the Battle of Queenston Heights 1812, with a portrait of Major General Sir Isaac Brock KB, to the right

	EF	UNC
GU52a *Signatory: W. C. Bull (States Treasurer)*		
Prefix A and prefix B	£35	£50
Prefix Z – replacement note.	£50	£80
GU52b *Signatory: M. J. Brown (States Treasurer)*		
Prefix C and prefix D...	£25	£35
Prefix Z – replacement note.	£40	£70

Size 143 mm x 75 mm approximately

Similar to above but smaller size. First issued 1990
Obverse – blue on a multicoloured underprint. Guernsey seal at bottom left; Castle Cornet in underprint at the centre.
Reverse – blue; an illustration of the Battle of Queenston Heights 1812, with a portrait of Major General Sir Isaac Brock KB, to the right

	EF	UNC
GU53 *Signatory: M. J. Brown (States Treasurer)*		
Prefix E and prefix F.	£18	£25
Prefix Z – replacement note.	£30	£50

First issued 1995

*Obverse – blue and multicoloured. Portrait of Queen Elizabeth II to the right; Picture of Elizabeth
College to the left of Guernsey seal, lower centre*
*Reverse – blue and multicoloured; illustrations of Saumarez Park, Le Trepied Dolman and Les Niaux
Waterwheel*

		EF	UNC
GU54a	Signatory: D. P. Trestain (States Treasurer)		
	Prefix A to prefix C	--	£20
	Prefix Z – replacement note.	£25	£40
GU54b	Signatory: D. M. Clark (States Treasurer)		
	Prefix D and ongoing	--	£18
	Prefix Z – replacement note.	£22	£35

TWENTY POUND NOTES

Size 160 mm x 90 mm approximately

First issued 1980
*Obverse – red on a multicoloured underprint. Guernsey seal at bottom left; Saumarez Park, 1815 in
underprint at the centre*
*Reverse – red on a multicoloured underprint; an illustration of British ships in Gibraltar Bay
1801with a portrait of Admiral Lord de Saumarez to the right*

		EF	UNC
GU61a	Signatory: W. C. Bull (States Treasurer).		
	Prefix A (to 500000)	£50	£80
	Prefix Z – replacement note.	£100	--
GU61b	Signatory: M. J. Brown (States Treasurer).		
	Prefix A (500001 - 813000).	£50	£80
	Prefix Z – replacement note.	£100	--

Size 150 mm x 80 mm approximately

Similar to above but smaller size. First issued 1990
Obverse – red on a multicoloured underprint. Guernsey seal at bottom left; Saumarez Park, 1815 in underprint at the centre
Reverse – red on a multicoloured underprint; an illustration of British ships in Gibraltar Bay 1801 with a portrait of Admiral Lord de Saumarez to the right

		EF	UNC
GU62a	*Signatory: M. J. Brown (States Treasurer)*		
	Prefix B (to 500000)...	£35	£50
	Prefix Z – replacement note.	£60	£80
GU62b	*Signatory: D. P. Trestain (States Treasurer)*		
	Prefix B (500001 upwards).	£35	£45
	Prefix Z – replacement note.	£60	£80

First issued 1995
Obverse – red and multicoloured. Portrait of Queen Elizabeth II to the right; Picture of St. James Concert Hall to the left of Guernsey seal, lower centre
Reverse – red and multicoloured; illustrations of St. Sampson's Church with Sailing dinghies in the foreground and Vale Castle in the background

		EF	UNC
GU63a	*Signatory: D. P. Trestain (States Treasurer)*		
	Prefix A and prefix B...	--	£40
	Prefix Z – replacement note.	£35	£50
GU63b	*Signatory: D. M. Clark (States Treasurer)*		
	Prefix C and ongoing..	--	£35
	Prefix Z – replacement note.	£35	£50

FIFTY POUND NOTES

Size 155 mm x 85 mm approximately

First issued 1994
Obverse – brown and multicoloured. Portrait of Queen Elizabeth II to the right; Picture of The Royal Court House to the left of Guernsey seal, lower centre
Reverse – multicoloured; illustrations of St. Andrew's Church, La Gran'mere, the Letter of Marque and the Pointe de la Moye

	EF	UNC
GU71a *Signatory: D. P. Trestain (States Treasurer)*		
Prefix A	--	£90
Prefix Z – replacement note	probably exists	

Jersey

Prior to the Jersey States banknote issues of 1963, Bank of England notes were used in Jersey. During the German occupation of the Channel Islands during WWII, permission was given for the printing and circulation of banknotes from six Pence to one Pound (reference JE1 to JE6 below). This was to alleviate a shortage of cash, particularly coinage, in the island.

JERSEY WORLD WAR II ISSUES

Size 110 mm x 70 mm approximately

Obverse—black on a red/brown underprint which has "six pence" in large script. Jersey Shield to the left
Reverse—red/brown with "six pence" in large script, exactly as the underprint on the obverse

		VF	EF
JE1	**Six Pence**—*Signatory: H. F. Ereaut (Treasurer of the States of Jersey)*		
	Prefix JN only, issued from April 1942 to February 1945...............	£25	£50

Size 110 mm x 70 mm approximately

Obverse—brown on a blue underprint of a silhouette of two old people chatting. Jersey Shield to the left
Reverse—brown; silhouette of two old people chatting—same as obverse underprint

		VF	EF
JE2	**One Shilling**—*Signatory: H. F. Ereaut (Treasurer of the States of Jersey)*		
	Prefix JN only, issued in April 1942 and June 1942........................	£25	£50

Size 108 mm x 70 mm approximately.

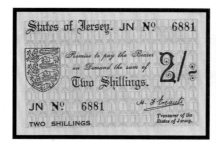 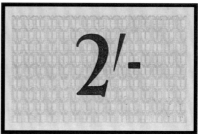

Obverse—blue on a salmon pink underprint; Jersey Shield to the left
Reverse—large "2/-" in blue on a salmon pink underprint

		VF	EF
JE3	**Two Shillings**—*Signatory: H. F. Ereaut (Treasurer of the States of Jersey)*		
	Prefix JN only, issued in June 1941..	£70	£130

Size 108 mm x 70 mm approximately

Obverse—blue on a light brown and blue underprint depicting a cart and two horses in silhouette Jersey Shield to the left
Reverse—blue; silhouette of a cart and horses, same as obverse underprint

		VF	EF
JE4	**Two Shillings**—*Signatory: H. F. Ereaut (Treasurer of the States of Jersey)*		
	Prefix JN only, issued in April 1942..	£35	£70

Size 130 mm x 85 mm approximately

Obverse—green on a pale green and brown underprint. Jersey Shield to the left
Reverse—green; picture of a milkmaid with three cows

		VF	EF
JE5	**Ten Shillings**—*Signatory: H. F. Ereaut (Treasurer of the States of Jersey)* Prefix JN only, issued in April 1942 and June 1942.........................	£90	£180

Size 130 mm x 85 mm approximately

Obverse—mauve on a pale mauve and green underprint. Jersey Shield to the left
Obverse—picture of a cart and horses on the sea shore

		VF	EF
JE6	**One Pound**—*Signatory: H. F. Ereaut (Treasurer of the States of Jersey)* Prefix JN only, issued in April 1942 and June 1942.........................	£125	£250

JERSEY STATES ISSUES FROM 1963

TEN SHILLING NOTES

Size 140 mm x 70 mm approximately

First issued 1963
Obverse—brown on a multicoloured underprint. Portrait of Queen Elizabeth II to the right
Reverse—brown on a pale blue underprint. Illustration of St. Ouen's Manor

	EF	UNC
JE10 Signatory: Pagham (Treasurer of the States)		
Prefix A, B and C first issued 1963	£12	£20

ONE POUND NOTES

Size 150 mm x 77 mm approximately

First issued 1963
Obverse – green on a multicoloured underprint. Portrait of Queen Elizabeth II to the right
Reverse – green. Illustration of Mont Orgueil Castle

	EF	UNC
JE11a Signatory: Pagham (Treasurer of the States)		
Prefix A to prefix E, first issued 1963	£30	£45
JE11b Signatory: Clennett (Treasurer of the States)		
Prefix F to prefix K, first issued 1972	£25	£40
Prefix Z - replacement note.	rare	

Size 135 mm x 67 mm approximately

First issued 1976
Obverse—blue on a pink and blue underprint. Portrait of Queen Elizabeth II to the right
Reverse—mainly blue. Picture of the death of Major Peirson at the Battle of Jersey

		EF	UNC
JE12a	Signatory: Clennett (Treasurer of the States)		
	Prefix AB to prefix LB, first issued 1976	£6	£9
	Prefix ZB - replacement note...	£15	£22
JE12b	Signatory: L. May (Treasurer of the States)		
	Prefix MB to prefix TB, first issued 1985	£5	£8
	Prefix ZB - replacement note...	£13	£20

Size 128 mm x 66 mm approximately

First issued 1989
Obverse—green on a multicoloured underprint. Portrait of Queen Elizabeth II to the right
"£1" at top right in outline print
Reverse—mainly green. Illustration of St. Helier Parish Church

		EF	UNC
JE13	Signatory: L. May (Treasurer of the States)		
	Prefix AC to prefix GC, first issued 1989...	£2	£4
	Prefix CZ - replacement note.	£12	£20

First issued 1993

Obverse—green on a multicoloured underprint. Portrait of Queen Elizabeth II to the right. "£1" at top right in solid print
Reverse—mainly green. Illustration of St. Helier Parish Church

		EF	UNC
JE14a	Signatory: G. Baird (Treasurer of the States)		
	Prefix GC to prefix RC, first issued 1993	--	£3
	Prefix CZ - replacement note	£8	£15
JE14b	Signatory: I. Black (Treasurer of the States)		
	Prefix SC and ongoing	--	£2
	Prefix CZ - replacement note	£8	£15

Issued to commemorate the 50th. Anniversary of the liberation of Jersey, 9th. May 1995
Obverse—green on a multicoloured underprint. Similar to regular issue notes , with a commemorative overprint to the left
Reverse—mauve, green and yellow with a reproduction of the front and back of the German occupation £1 note, ref. JE6

		EF	UNC
JE15	Signatory: G. Baird (Treasurer of the States)		
	Prefix LJ only, issued in 1995...	--	£4

Issued to commemorate the 800th anniversary of the States of Jersey, 1204–2004
Obverse—green on a multicoloured underprint. Similar to regular issue notes with
"Jersey 1204–2004" overprint to the left.
Reverse—green, brown and multicoloured. Illustration of Mont Orgueil Castle.

	EF	UNC
JE16 Signatory: I. Black (Treasurer of the States)		
Prefix J8C, issued in 2004..	--	£2

FIVE POUND NOTES

Size 140 mm x 91 mm approximately

First issued 1963
Obverse—red on a multicoloured underprint. Portrait of Queen Elizabeth II to the right
Reverse—red. Illustration of St. Aubin's Fort

	EF	UNC
JE21a Signatory: Pagham (Treasurer of the States)		
Prefix A only, first issued 1963	£80	£120
JE21b Signatory: Clennett (Treasurer of the States)		
Prefix B and prefix C, first issued 1972.	£30	£45
Prefix Z - replacement note.	£55	£85

Size 145 mm x 78 mm approximately

First issued 1976
Obverse—brown on a multicoloured underprint. Portrait of Queen Elizabeth II to the right
Reverse—brown and mauve. Beach scene with old ships and Elizabeth Castle in the background

		EF	UNC
JE22a	Signatory: Clennett (Treasurer of the States)		
	Prefix AB and prefix GB, first issued 1976	£20	£30
	Prefix ZB - replacement note..	£30	£45
JE22b	Signatory: L. May (Treasurer of the States)		
	Prefix GB to prefix KB, first issued 1983..	£20	£30
	Prefix ZB - replacement note..	£30	£45

Size 135 mm x 70 mm approximately

First issued 1989
*Obverse—maroon on a multicoloured underprint. Portrait of Queen Elizabeth II to the right. "£5" at
top right in outline print*
Reverse—mainly purple. Illustration of La Corbiere lighthouse

		EF	UNC
JE23	Signatory: L. May (Treasurer of the States)		
	Prefix AC and prefix BC, first issued 1989	£10	£15
	Prefix CZ - replacement note	£18	£25

First issued 1993
Obverse—maroon on a multicoloured underprint. Portrait of Queen Elizabeth II to the right. "£5" at
top right in solid print
Reverse—mainly purple. Illustration of La Corbiere lighthouse

		EF	UNC
JE24	Signatory: G. Baird (Treasurer of the States)		
	Prefix CC to prefix JC, first issued 1993..	--	£12
	Prefix CZ - replacement note	£15	£25

TEN POUND NOTES

Size 151 mm x 86 mm approximately

First issued 1963
Obverse—purple on a multicoloured underprint. Portrait of Queen Elizabeth II to the right
Reverse—purple. Illustration of St. Ouen's Manor

		EF	UNC
JE31	Signatory: Clennett (Treasurer of the States)		
	Prefix A only, first issued 1972	£45	£60
	Prefix Z - replacement note.	£80	£120

Size 150 mm x 85 mm approximately

First issued 1976
Obverse—green on a multicoloured underprint. Portrait of Queen Elizabeth II to the right
Reverse—mainly green. Picture of Victoria College

		EF	UNC
JE32a	Signatory: Clennett (Treasurer of the States)		
	Prefix AB and prefix DB, first issued 1976	£35	£50
	Prefix ZB - replacement note..	£55	£80
JE32b	Signatory: L. May (Treasurer of the States)		
	Prefix DB to prefix GB, first issued 1983..	£30	£45
	Prefix ZB - replacement note..	£50	£70

Size 143 mm x 75 mm approximately

First issued 1989
Obverse—orange and brown on a multicoloured underprint. Portrait of Queen Elizabeth II to the right
"£10" at top right in outline print
Reverse—mainly red/brown. Picture of the death of Major Peirson at the Battle of Jersey

		EF	UNC
JE33	Signatory: L. May (Treasurer of the States)		
	Prefix AC to prefix CC, first issued 1989	£15	£25
	Prefix CZ - replacement note	£30	£45

First issued 1993
Obverse—orange and brown on a multicoloured underprint. Portrait of Queen Elizabeth II to the right.
"£10" at top right in solid print
Reverse—mainly red/brown. Picture of the death of Major Peirson at the Battle of Jersey

		EF	UNC
JE34a Signatory: G. Baird (Treasurer of the States)			
Prefix DC to prefix MC, first issued 1993		--	£20
Prefix CZ - replacement note		£25	£40
JE34b Signatory: I. Black (Treasurer of the States)			
Prefix NC and ongoing		--	£18
Prefix CZ - replacement note		£25	£40

TWENTY POUND NOTES

Size 160 mm x 90 mm approximately

First issued 1976
Obverse—green on a multicoloured underprint. Portrait of Queen Elizabeth II to the right
Reverse—mainly green. Picture of Victoria College

		EF	UNC
JE41a Signatory: Clennett (Treasurer of the States)			
Prefix AB only, first issued 1976		£50	£75
Prefix ZB - replacement note		£80	£130
JE41b Signatory: L. May (Treasurer of the States)			
Prefix AB and prefix AC, first issued 1983		£45	£70
Prefix ZB - replacement note		£100	£150

Size 150 mm x 80 mm approximately

First issued 1989
Obverse—mainly blue on a multicoloured underprint. Portrait of Queen Elizabeth II to the right
"£20" at top right in outline print
Reverse—blue on a multicoloured underprint. Illustration of St. Ouen's Manor

		EF	UNC
JE42	Signatory: L. May (Treasurer of the States)		
	Prefix AC and prefix BC, first issued 1989	£35	£50
	Prefix CZ - replacement note	£50	£70

First issued 1993
Obverse—mainly blue on a multicoloured underprint. Portrait of Queen Elizabeth II to the right
"£20" at top right in solid print
Reverse – blue on a multicoloured underprint. Illustration of St. Ouen's Manor

		EF	UNC
JE43a	Signatory: G. Baird (Treasurer of the States)		
	Prefix BC to prefix JC, first issued 1993	--	£45
	Prefix CZ - replacement note	£40	£55
JE43b	Signatory: I. Black (Treasurer of the States)		
	Prefix KC and ongoing..	--	£35
	Prefix CZ - replacement note	£35	£50

FIFTY POUND NOTES

Size 155 mm x 85 mm approximately

Obverse dark grey on a multicoloured underprint. Portrait of Queen Elizabeth II to the right
"£50" at top right in outline print
Reverse – mainly dark grey. Picture of Government House with the Jersey flag to the left

		EF	UNC
JE51	Signatory: L. May (Treasurer of the States)		
	Prefix AC only, first issued 1989	£85	£120
	Prefix CZ - replacement note		rare

First issued 1993
Obverse—dark grey on a multicoloured underprint. Portrait of Queen Elizabeth II to the right
"£50" at top right in solid print
Reverse—mainly dark grey. Picture of Government House with the Jersey flag to the left

		EF	UNC
JE52a	Signatory: G. Baird (Treasurer of the States)		
	Prefix AC only, first issued 1993	--	£100
	Prefix CZ - replacement note	£110	£160
JE52b	Signatory: I. Black (Treasurer of the States)		
	Prefix AC and ongoing..	--	£85
	Prefix CZ - replacement note	£100	£150

Ireland

Ireland was a relative latecomer to banking, the first notes of the Bank of Ireland being introduced in 1783. Thereafter the history of banking paralleled that of Scotland, with a number of private banks in the early 19th century which, as a result of mergers and amalgamations, resulted in half a dozen major banks still producing distinctive notes at the turn of the century.

The situation was complicated by the political developments which led to the establishment of the Irish Free State and the province of Northern Ireland in 1921. The Belfast Banking Company, whose notes circulated through the whole of Ireland, confined its activities to Northern Ireland from 1922 onwards. On the other hand, the Bank of Ireland, which was traditionally based in Dublin, was obliged to produce separate issues from 1929 onwards for Northern Ireland and the Irish Free State, while both the Provincial Bank of Ireland and the Ulster Bank likewise had distinctive issues for the Free State and Northern Ireland in the same period.

In the Irish Free State, the government established a Currency Commission in 1927 under whose auspices notes, inscribed in English and Irish, were issued from 1928 onwards, notable on account of the portrait of Hazel, Lady Lavery in the guise of an Irish colleen. The inscriptions in these notes were altered in 1938 from Irish Free State (Saorstát Éireann) to Ireland (Eire), following the constitutional changes of that year. In addition the Currency Commission produced distinctive notes, showing a farmer ploughing, with the names of one or other of the eight "shareholder" banks inscribed at the foot: the Bank of Ireland, the Hibernian Bank, the Munster & Leinster Bank, the National Bank, the Northern Bank, the Provincial Bank, the Royal Bank and the Ulster Bank. These notes were replaced from 1943 onwards by the notes of the Central Bank of Ireland, which at first retained the Lady Lavery portrait, but since 1976 have used historic scenes and personalities.

Distinctive notes for circulation in Northern Ireland have been produced by the Bank of Ireland, the Belfast Banking Company and the National, Northern, Provincial and Ulster banks and it is interesting to note that the Bank of Ireland even produced a commemorative £20 in 1983 to celebrate its bicentenary. Generally speaking, the notes of Northern Ireland have always been much more varied in their designs and subject matter. Bank amalgamations led to the formation of the Allied Irish Banks Limited whose notes, similar to the last issue of the Provincial Bank, were introduced in January 1982.

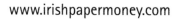

REPUBLIC OF IRELAND

CURRENCY COMMISSION
(Consolidated banknotes) (1929–41)

Designs for the notes issued by the eight Banks under the auspices of the Currency Commission are virtually identical except for the values, titles and signatures. Notes representative of the design, are illustrated below. (In keeping with the current regulations for the reproduction of banknote illustrations, the serial numbers have been obscured.)

ONE POUND
Size: 151 x 84mm

Obverse—Green on orange and mauve underprint; "Ploughman"
Reverse—The Customs House, Dublin

FIVE POUNDS
Size 165 x 92mm

Obverse—Brown on green and mauve underprint; "Ploughman"
Reverse—St Patrick's Bridge, Cork city

TEN POUNDS
Size 189 x 107mm

Obverse—Blue on green and mauve underprint; "Ploughman"
Reverse—Currency Commission Building, Foster Place, Dublin

TWENTY POUNDS
Size 203 x 114mm

Obverse—Red on yellow and mauve underprint; "Ploughman"
Reverse—Ruined Monastery on the Rock of Cashel, Co. Tipperary

FIFTY POUNDS
Size 203 x 114mm

Obverse—Mauve on yellow underprint; "Ploughman"
Reverse—View of Croagh Patrick Mountain, Co. Mayo

ONE HUNDRED POUNDS
Size 203 x 114mm

Obverse—Brown on mauve and yellow underprint; "Ploughman"
Reverse—View of Killiney Bay, Co. Dublin

> **NB. £20, £50 and £100 notes exist only as Bank of Ireland Specimens. No issued notes remain. We illustrate them here but have not included them in the listings that follow.**

The catalogue numbering used in this section is as the standard work on the subject: *Irish Banknotes—Irish Paper Money from 1928* by Mártan Mac Devitt.

THE BANK OF IRELAND

		VF	EF
ONE POUND			
E001	*Signatures: Joseph Brennan and J. A. Gargan*		
	1929–38. Prefix 01BA–89BA	£200	£250
E002	*Signatures:: Joseph Brennan and H. J. Johnston*		
	1939–40. Prefix 89BA–09BB	£170	£285
FIVE POUNDS			
E003	*Signatures: Joseph Brennan and J. A. Gargan*		
	1929–31. Prefix 01BK–02BK	£360	£500
E004	*Signatures: Joseph Brennan and H. J. Johnston*		
	1939. 02BK–03BK	£575	£725
TEN POUNDS			
E005	*Signatures: Joseph Brennan and J. A. Gargan*		
	1929. Prefix 01BT	£900	£1200

HIBERNIAN BANK LTD.

ONE POUND

		VF	EF
E009	*Signatures: Joseph Brennan and H. J. Campbell*		
	1929–39. Prefix 01HA–22HA	£225	£300
E010	*Joseph Brennan and A. K. Hodges*		
	1939–40. Prefix 23HA–24HA	£250	£400

FIVE POUNDS

		VF	EF
E011	*Signatures: Joseph Brennan and H. J. Campbell*		
	1929–May 1939. Prefix 01HK–03HK	£550	£725

TEN POUNDS

		VF	EF
E013	*Signatures: Joseph Brennan and H. J. Campbell*		
	1929–31. Prefix 01HT	£850	rare

MUNSTER & LEINSTER BANK LTD.

ONE POUND

		VF	EF
E016	*Signatures: Joseph Brennan and J. L. Gubbins*		
	1929–35. Prefix 01MA–24MA	£200	£275
E017	*Signatures: Joseph Brennan and A. E. Hosford*		
	1936–40. Prefix 26MA–50MA	£225	£300

FIVE POUNDS

		VF	EF
E018	*Signatures: Joseph Brennan and J. L. Gubbins*		
	1929–33. Prefix 01MK–03MK	£360	£550
E019	*Signatures: Joseph Brennan and A. E. Hosford*		
	1938–39. Prefix 03MK	£360	£550

TEN POUNDS

		VF	EF
E020	*Signatures: Joseph Brennan and J. L. Gubbins*		
	1929–31. Prefix 01MT	£900	rare
E021	*Signatures: Joseph Brennan and A. E. Hosford*		
	1938–39. Prefix 01MT	£900	rare

NATIONAL BANK LTD.

ONE POUND

E025 *Signatures: Joseph Brennan and H. A. Russell*
1929–39. Prefix 01NA–44NA.. £175   £250

FIVE POUNDS

E026 *Signatures: Joseph Brennan and H. A. Russell*
1929–May 1939. Prefix 01NK–04NK £360   £550

TEN POUNDS

E027 *Signatures: Joseph Brennan and J. L. Gubbins*
1929–39. Prefix 01NT ....   rare

NORTHERN BANK LTD.

ONE POUND

E028 *Signatures: Joseph Brennan and S. W. Knox*
1929. Prefix 01OA £750   £1150
E029 *Signatures: Joseph Brennan and H. H. Stewart*
1931–33. Prefix 03EA–04EA... £700   £900

FIVE POUNDS

E032 *Signatures: Joseph Brennan and S. W. Knox*
1929. Prefix 01OK... £1500   £1800
E033 *Signatures: Joseph Brennan and H. H. Stewart*
1931–33. Prefix 01EK £900   £1100

TEN POUNDS

E034 *Signatures: Joseph Brennan and S. W. Knox*
1929. Prefix 01OT ....   rare

PROVINCIAL BANK OF IRELAND LTD.

ONE POUND

E036 *Signatures: Joseph Brennan and Hume Robertson*
           1929. Prefix 01PA–06PA £250   £350
E037 *Signatures: Joseph Brennan and F. S. Forde*
           1931–36. Prefix 07PA–13PA £215   £270
E038 *Signatures: Joseph Brennan and G. A. Kennedy*
           1937–40. Prefix 13PA–23PA £215   £270

FIVE POUNDS

E039 *Signatures: Joseph Brennan and Hume Robertson*
           1929. Prefix 01PK... £800   £1000
E040 *Signatures: Joseph Brennan and F. S. Forde*
           1931–36. Prefix 01PK–02PK... £500   £650
E041 *Signatures: Joseph Brennan and G. A. Kennedy*
           1937–40. Prefix 02PK... £500   £650

TEN POUNDS

E042 *Signatures: Joseph Brennan and Hume Robertson*
           1929. Prefix 01PT £1000   £1285
E043 *Signatures: Joseph Brennan and F. S. Forde*
           1931–36. Prefix 01PT £1000   £1285
E044 *Signatures: Joseph Brennan and G. A. Kennedy*
           1937–40. Prefix 01PT £1000   £1285

ROYAL BANK OF IRELAND LTD.

ONE POUND

E046 *Signatures: Joseph Brennan and G. A. Stanley*
           1929. Prefix 01RA–08RA £350   £425
E047 *Signatures: Joseph Brennan and D. R. Mack*
           1931–39. Prefix 009RA–26RA £285   £350
E048 *Signatures: Joseph Brennan and J. Wilson*
           1939. Prefix 26RA–28RA £350   £425

FIVE POUNDS

E049 *Signatures: Joseph Brennan and G. A. Stanley*
           1929. Prefix 01RK.. £950   £1150
E050 *Signatures: Joseph Brennan and D. R. Mack*
           1931–39. Prefix 01RK £950   £1150

TEN POUNDS

E052 *Signatures: Joseph Brennan and G. A. Stanley*
           1929–31. Prefix 01RT ....   rare

ULSTER BANK LTD.

ONE POUND

E056 *Signatures: Joseph Brennan and C. W. Patton*
      1929–39. Prefix 01UA–07UA.. £300   £400
E057 *Signatures: Joseph Brennan and C. W. Lester*
      1939–40. Prefix 08UA–12UA.. £300   £400

FIVE POUNDS

E058 *Signatures: Joseph Brennan and C. W. Patton*
      1929–39. Prefix 01UK... £725   £1000
E059 *Signatures: Joseph Brennan and C. W. Lester*
      1939. Prefix 01UK–02UK.. £725   £1000

TEN POUNDS

E060 *Signatures: Joseph Brennan and C. W. Patton*
      1929–39. Prefix 01UT...   rare
E061 *Signatures: Joseph Brennan and C. W. Lester*
      1939. Prefix 01UT..   rare

For example illustrations of the "Ploughman" notes see pages 205–207.

SERIES A
"LADY LAVERY" NOTES (1928–77)

Designs for the notes issued under the auspices of the Currency Commission Irish Free State, the Currency Commission of Ireland and the Central Bank of Ireland are virtually identical except for the values, titles and signatures. Notes representative of the design, are illustrated below. (In keeping with the current regulations for the reproduction of banknote illustrations, the serial numbers have been obscured.)

TEN SHILLINGS
Size: 138 x 78mm

Orange on green and mauve underprint.

ONE POUND
Size: 151 x 84mm

Green on pink and yellow underprint.

FIVE POUNDS
Size: 166 x 92mm

Brown on yellow and mauve underprint.

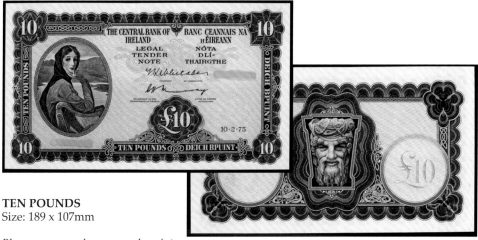

TEN POUNDS
Size: 189 x 107mm

Blue on green and mauve underprint.

TWENTY POUNDS
Size: 203 x 114mm

Red on orange and mauve underprint.

FIFTY POUNDS
Size: 203 x 114mm

Mauve on yellow underprint.

ONE HUNDRED POUNDS
Size: 203 x 114mm

Black on yellow and mauve underprint.

CURRENCY COMMISSION IRISH FREE STATE

TEN SHILLINGS

		VF	EF
	Signatures: Joseph Brennan and J. J. McElligott		
E065	Fractional prefix—Letter over Number (1928)	£250	£350
E066	Straight prefix—Number/Number/Letter (1929–37)	£85	£175

ONE POUND

	Signatures: Joseph Brennan and J. J. McElligott		
E075	Fractional prefix—Letter over Number (1928)	£175	£250
E076	Straight prefix—Number/Number/Letter (1930–37)	£85	£150

FIVE POUNDS

	Signatures: Joseph Brennan and J. J. McElligott		
E088	Fractional prefix—Letter over Number (1928)	£175	£275
E089	Straight prefix—Number/Number/Letter (1932–37)	£145	£275

Series A, "Lady Lavery". Currency Commission Irish Free State (continued)   VF   EF

TEN POUNDS

Signatures: Joseph Brennan and J. J. McElligott
E100 Fractional prefix—Letter over Number (1928).............................. £350   £725
E101 Straight prefix—Number/Number/Letter (1932–33)................... £275   £725

TWENTY POUNDS

Signatures: Joseph Brennan and J. J. McElligott
E113 Fractional prefix—Letter over Number (1928).............................. £950   £1400

FIFTY POUNDS

Signatures: Joseph Brennan and J. J. McElligott
E121 Fractional prefix—Letter over Number (1928).............................. £1250   £1650

ONE HUNDRED POUNDS

Signatures: Joseph Brennan and J. J. McElligott
E128 Fractional prefix—Letter over Number (1928).............................. £1350   £1650
E129 Straight prefix—Number/Number/Letter (1937)......................... £1250   £1650

CURRENCY COMMISSION IRELAND

TEN SHILLINGS

E067 *Signatures: Joseph Brennan and J. J. McElligott. With title of Secretary of the Department of Finance as "Rúnaidhe na Roinne Airgedais" (1938–39)* £100   £175
E068 *Signatures: Joseph Brennan and J. J. McElligott. With Emergency Tracer Overprint codes H, K, J in circles (1940–41)* £50   £75

ONE POUND

E077 *Signatures: Joseph Brennan and J. J. McElligott. "Rúnaidhe na Roinne Airgedais" (1939)* £45   £75
E078 *Signatures: Joseph Brennan and J. J. McElligott. With ETO codes T, B, P, V in circles (1941–42)* £45   £75

FIVE POUNDS

E090 *Signatures: Joseph Brennan and J. J. McElligott "Rúnaidhe na Roinne Airgedais" (1938–39)* £55   £125
E091 *Signatures: Joseph Brennan and J. J. McElligott. With ETO codes A, C, D in circles (1940–42)*.. £75   £125

Series Λ, "Lady Lavery". Currency Commission Ireland (continued)   VF   EF

TEN POUNDS

		VF	EF
E102	Signatures: Joseph Brennan and J. J. McElligott. "Rúnaidhe na Roinne Airgedais"(1938–40)	£150	£285
E103	Signatures: Joseph Brennan and J. J. McElligott. With ETO codes E, F in circles (1941–42)	£115	£175

CENTRAL BANK OF IRELAND

TEN SHILLINGS

		VF	EF
E069	Signatures: Joseph Brennan and J. J. McElligott. With ETO codes L, M, R, E in circles (1943–44).................................	£55	£75
E070	Signatures: Joseph Brennan and J. J. McElligott. ETO codes discontinued (1945–50)	£25	£40
E071	Signatures: Joseph Brennan and J. J. McElligott. Serial nos. extended (1951–52)..	£15	£30
E072	Signatures: J. J. McElligott and O. J. Redmond (1955)	£25	£65
E073	Signatures: J. J. McElligott and T. K. Whitaker (1957–59)	£10	£20
E074	Signatures: M. Ó Muimhneacháin and T. K. Whitaker (1962–68)	£5	£15

ONE POUND

		VF	EF
E079	Signatures: Joseph Brennan and J. J. McElligott. With ETO codes G, Y, E, F in circles (1943–44).................................	£50	£70
E080	Signatures: Joseph Brennan and J. J. McElligott. ETO codes discontinued (1945–50)	£15	£30
E081	Signatures: Joseph Brennan and J. J. McElligott. Serial nos. extended (1951–52)..	£5	£10
E082	Signatures: J. J. McElligott and O. J. Redmond (1954–55)	£5	£15
E083	Signatures: J. J. McElligott and T. K. Whitaker (1957–60)	£5	£10
E084	Signatures: M. Ó Muimhneacháin and T. K. Whitaker (1962–68)	£5	£10
E085	Signatures: T. K. Whitaker and C. H. Murray (1969–70)	£5	£10
E086	Signatures: T. K. Whitaker and C. H. Murray. Metallic security thread introduced (1971–75)..	FV	£10
E087	Signatures: C. H. Murray and M. O. Murchú (1976).........................	FV	£5

FIVE POUNDS

		VF	EF
E092	Signatures: Joseph Brennan and J. J. McElligott. With ETO codes N, R, M in circles (1943–44)	£80	£120
E093	Signatures: Joseph Brennan and J. J. McElligott. ETO codes discontinued (1945–51)	£35	£60
E094	Signatures: Joseph Brennan and J. J. McElligott. Serial nos. extended (1952–53)..	£20	£35
E095	Signatures: J. J. McElligott and O. J. Redmond (1954–55)	£20	£55
E096	Signatures: J. J. McElligott and T. K. Whitaker (1957–60)	£20	£35
E097	Signatures: M. Ó Muimhneacháin and T. K. Whitaker (1961–68)	£10	£20
E098	Signatures: T. K. Whitaker and C. H. Murray (1969–70)	£10	£20
E099	Signatures: T. K. Whitaker and C. H. Murray. Metallic security thread introduced (1971–75)..	£5	£20

Series A, "Lady Lavery". Central Bank of Ireland (continued) VF EF

TEN POUNDS

		VF	EF
E104	*Signatures: Joseph Brennan and J. J. McElligott. With ETO codes S, W, B, G in circles (1943–44)*	£80	£180
E105	*Signatures: Joseph Brennan and J. J. McElligott. ETO codes discontinued (1945–52)*	£30	£75
E106	*Signatures: J. J. McElligott and O. J. Redmond (1954–55)*	£50	£120
E107	*Signatures: J. J. McElligott and T. K. Whitaker (1957–1960)*	£30	£60
E108	*Signatures: J. J. McElligott and T. K. Whitaker. Serial numbers extended (1960)*	£30	£60
E109	*Signatures: M. Ó Muimhneacháin and T. K. Whitaker (1962–1968)* ..	£30	£60
E110	*Signatures: T. K. Whitaker and C. H. Murray (1969–1970)*	£30	£60
E111	*Signatures: T. K. Whitaker and C. H. Murray. Metallic security thread introduced (1971–1974)*	£45	£75
E112	*Signatures: C. H. Murray and M. O. Murchú (1976)*	£50	£75

TWENTY POUNDS

		VF	EF
E114	*Signatures: Joseph Brennan and J. J. McElligott. With ETO code A in circle (1943–44)*	£1000	£1500
E115	*Signatures: Joseph Brennan and J. J. McElligott. ETO codes discontinued (1945–52)*	£150	£225
E116	*Signatures: J. J. McElligott and O. J. Redmond (1954–55)*	£100	£180
E117	*Signatures: J. J. McElligott and T. K. Whitaker (1957)*	£100	£180
E118	*Signatures: M. Ó Muimhneacháin and T. K. Whitaker (1961–65)*	£30	£100
E119	*Signatures: T. K. Whitaker and C. H. Murray (1969–75)*	£30	£50
E120	*Signatures: T. K. Whitaker and M. O. Murchú (1976)*	£30	£50

FIFTY POUNDS

		VF	EF
E122	*Signatures: Joseph Brennan and J. J. McElligott (1943–51)*	£250	£350
E123	*Signatures: J. J. McElligott and O. J. Redmond (1954–55)*	£250	£350
E124	*Signatures: J. J. McElligott and T. K. Whitaker (1957–60)*	£175	£300
E125	*Signatures: M. Ó Muimhneacháin and T. K. Whitaker (1962–68)*	£100	£200
E126	*Signatures: T. K. Whitaker and C. H. Murray (1970–75)*	£90	£175
E127	*Signatures: C. H. Murray and M. O. Murchú (1977)*	£70	£130

ONE HUNDRED POUNDS

		VF	EF
E130	*Signatures: Joseph Brennan and J. J. McElligott (1943–49)*	£285	£425
E131	*Signatures: J. J. McElligott and O. J. Redmond (1954)*	£250	£380
E132	*Signatures: J. J. McElligott and T. K. Whitaker (1959)*	£200	£320
E133	*Signatures: M. Ó Muimhneacháin and T. K. Whitaker (1963–68)*	£150	£275
E134	*Signatures: T. K. Whitaker and C. H. Murray (1970–75)*	£130	£220
E135	*Signatures: C. H. Murray and M. O. Murchú (1977)*	£120	£200

For a concise and complete study of the notes of Ireland
visit the website
www.irishpapermoney.com

CENTRAL BANK OF IRELAND
SERIES B NOTES, 1976–93

ONE POUND

           EF   *UNC*

1976–93 ISSUE
Green on multicoloured underprint. Obverse—Portrait of Queen Medb, legendary Queen of Connaught. Next to portrait is an early Irish geometric design.
Reverse—Decorated excerpt from Lebor na hUidre.
Size 150 x 78mm

		EF	UNC
E136	*Signatures: C. H. Murray and M. O. Murchú (1977)*	£3	£8
E137	*Signatures: C. H. Murray and Tomás F. Ó Cofaigh (1978–81)*............	£3	£8
E138	*Signatures: Tomás F. Ó Cofaigh and Maurice F. Doyle (1982–87)*	£3	£8

FIVE POUNDS

1976–93 ISSUE
Brown on multicoloured underprint. Obverse—Portrait of philosopher John Scots Eriugena (c. 828–878).
Reverse—Extract from the Book of Kells.
Size 156 x 83mm

		EF	UNC
E140	*Signatures: T. K. Whitaker and C. H. Murray (1976)*	£15	£30
E141	*Signatures: C. H. Murray and M. O Murchú (1976–77)*....................	£8	£20
E142	*Signatures: C. H. Murray and Tomás F. Ó Cofaigh (1979–81)*	£8	£20
E143	*Signatures: Tomás F. Ó Cofaigh and Maurice F. Doyle (1983–87)*.......	£8	£20
E144	*Signatures: Maurice F. Doyle and S. P. Cromien (1988–93)*	£8	£20

Central Bank of Ireland. Series B (continued) EF UNC

TEN POUNDS

1976–93 ISSUE
Purple on multicoloured underprint. Obverse—Portrait of Jonathan Swift (1667–1745), Dean of St Patrick's Cathedral, Dublin.
Reverse—Famous map of Dublin by John Rocques, first published 1756.
Size 164 x 86mm

		EF	UNC
E145	*Signatures: C. H. Murray and Tomás F. Ó Cofaigh (1978–81)*............	£15	£40
E146	*Signatures: Tomás F. Ó Cofaigh and Maurice F. Doyle (1983–87)*	£15	£30
E147	*Signatures: Maurice F. Doyle and S. P. Cromien (1987–93)*...............	£15	£30

TWENTY POUNDS

1976–93 ISSUE
Blue on multicoloured underprint. Obverse—Portrait of poet and writer William Butler Yeats (1865–1939).
Reverse—Group of the Blasket Islands of the Kerry coast.
Size 172 x 90mm

		EF	UNC
E148	*Signatures: C. H. Murray and Tomás F. Ó Cofaigh (1980–81)*.............	£25	£70
E149	*Signatures: Tomás F. Ó Cofaigh and Maurice F. Doyle (1983–86)*	£25	£60
E150	*Signatures: Maurice F. Doyle and S. P. Cromien (1988–89)*................	£22	£45

FIFTY POUNDS

1976–93 ISSUE
Brown on multicoloured underprint. Obverse—Portrait of harpist and composer Turlough Ó Carolan
(1670–1738).
Reverse—Design based on the wood carving in the organ loft of St Michans Church, Dublin.
Size 180 x 94mm

E151 *Signatures: Tomás F. Ó Cofaigh and Maurice F. Doyle (1982)*............   £65   £130
E152 *Signatures: Maurice F. Doyle and S. P. Cromien (1991)* £60   £100

CENTRAL BANK OF IRELAND
SERIES C NOTES, 1992–2001

FIVE POUNDS

1992–2001 ISSUE

Brown and blue on multicoloured underprint. Obverse—Catherine Macauley (1778–1841), foundress of the Catholic Order of the Sisters of Mercy.
Reverse—A classroom scene.
Size 120 x 64mm

		EF	UNC
E153	*Signatures: Maurice F. Doyle and S. P. Cromien (1994)*	—	£20
E154	*Signatures: Muiris S. Ó Conaill and P. Mullarkey (Dec. 1994–97)*	—	£20
E155	*Signatures: Muiris S. Ó Conaill and P. Mullarkey (Dec. 1998)*	—	£10

TEN POUNDS

1992–2001 ISSUE

Brown, blue and green on multicoloured underprint. Obverse—James Joyce (1882–1941).
Reverse— River mask sculpture from the Dublin Custom House.
Size 128 x 68mm

		EF	UNC
E156	*Signatures: Maurice F. Doyle and S. P. Cromien (1993–94)*	—	£20
E157	*Signatures: Muiris S. Ó Conaill and P. Mullarkey (1995–97)*	—	£20
E158	*Signatures: Muiris S. Ó Conaill and P. Mullarkey (Dec. 1997–98)*	—	£15

Central Bank of Ireland. Series C (continued)   *EF*   *UNC*

TWENTY POUNDS

1992–2001 ISSUE
Mauve and brown on multicoloured underprint. Obverse—Daniel O'Connell (1775–1847).
Reverse—Four Courts Building, Dublin.
Size 136 x 72mm

E159	*Signatures: Maurice F. Doyle and S. P. Cromien (1992–94)*...............	—	£40
E160	*Signatures: Muiris S. Ó Conaill and P. Mullarkey (1995–97)*..............	—	£35
E161	*Signatures: Muiris S. Ó Conaill and P. Mullarkey. With prefix letters*		
	M–Z (O and Q not used) (1997–98)...	—	£30

FIFTY POUNDS

1992–2001 ISSUE
Blue and green on multicoloured underprint. Obverse—Douglas Hyde (1860–1949).
Reverse—An uillean piper.
Size 144 x 76mm

E162	*Signatures: Muiris S. Ó Conaill and P. Mullarkey (1995–96)*..............	—	£85
E164	*Signatures: Muiris S. Ó Conaill and P. Mullarkey. New design security*		
	thread introduced (1999)...	—	£85
E165	*Signatures: Muiris S. Ó Conaill and John A. Hurley (2001)*................	—	£85

Central Bank of Ireland. Series C (continued)   *EF*   *UNC*

ONE HUNDRED POUNDS

1992–2001 ISSUE
Purple, red and blue on multicoloured underprint. Obverse— Charles Stewart Parnell (1846–1891).
Reverse—Parnell Monument, O'Connell Street, Dublin.
Size 152 x 80mm

E163 *Signatures: Muiris S. Ó Conaill and P. Mullarkey (1996)*..................... £110   £160

NORTHERN IRELAND

ALLIED IRISH BANKS LIMITED

Formed in 1966 as a result of a merger of the Provincial Bank of Ireland Ltd. with the Munster & Leinster Bank and The Royal Bank of Ireland. The Banknotes share a common design with the last issues of the Provincial Bank. In the early 1990's the Allied Irish Banks plc merged with the Trustee Savings Bank to form the First Trust Bank.

ONE POUND

Size 134 mm x 67 mm approximately

Obverse—green and brown on a multicoloured underprint. Portrait of a teenage boy to the right
Reverse—mainly green. Illustration of the Spanish galleass "The Girona" at the centre

		EF	UNC
NI.101	*Signatory: P. O'Keiffe (Group Chief Executive).*		
	Prefix PN dated 1.1.1982..	£15	£20
	Prefix ZY—replacement note.......................................	£45	£60

FIVE POUNDS

Size 146 mm x 78 mm approximately

Obverse—blue and purple on a multicoloured underprint. Portrait of a young lady to the right
Reverse—mainly blue. Illustration of Dunluce Castle at the centre

NI.102	Signatory: P. O'Keiffe (Group Chief Executive).	EF	UNC
	Prefix QN dated 1.1.1982; 1.7.1983 and 1.12.1984	£25	£35
	Prefix ZY—replacement note...	£45	£70

TEN POUNDS

Size 150 mm x 84 mm approximately

Obverse—brown and purple on a multicoloured underprint. Portrait of a young man to the right
Reverse—mainly brown. Illustration of the sinking of the Spanish galleass The Girona at the centre

NI.103	Signatory: P. O'Keiffe (Group Chief Executive).	EF	UNC
	Prefix RN dated 1.1.1982; 1.7.1983 and 1.12.1984......................	£40	£60
	Prefix ZY—replacement note...	£75	£100

TWENTY POUNDS

Size 160 mm x 90 mm approximately

Obverse—mauve on a multicoloured underprint. Portrait of a mature lady to the right
Reverse—mauve on a multicoloured underprint. Illustration of rock chimney at Lacada Point at the centre

NI.104	*Signatory: P. O'Keiffe (Group Chief Executive).*	*EF*	*UNC*
	Prefix SN dated 1.1.1982; 1.7.1983 and 1.12.1984	£80	£110
	Prefix ZY—replacement note..		probably exists

ONE HUNDRED POUNDS

Size 160 mm x 90 mm approximately

Obverse—black green and olive on a multicoloured underprint. Portrait of an older man to the right
Reverse—black on a mainly green underprint. Illustration of the Spanish Armada at the centre

NI.105	*Signatory: P. O'Keiffe (Group Chief Executive).*	*EF*	*UNC*
	Prefix TN dated 1.1.1982...	£300	£400
	Prefix ZY—replacement note..		probably exists

ALLIED IRISH BANKS P.L.C.

FIVE POUNDS

Size 146 mm x 78 mm approximately

Obverse—blue and purple on a multicoloured underprint. Portrait of a young lady to the right
Reverse—mainly blue. Illustration of Dunluce Castle at the centre

		EF	UNC
NI.106	*Signatory: G. B. Scanlon (Group Chief Executive).*		
	Prefix QN and UN dated 1.1.1987 and 1.1.1990	£20	£30
	Prefix ZY—replacement note..	£40	£70

TEN POUNDS

Size 150 mm x 84 mm approximately

Obverse—brown and purple on a multicoloured underprint. Portrait of a young man to the right
Reverse—mainly brown. Illustration of the sinking of the Spanish galleon The Girona at the centre

NI.107	*Signatory: G. B. Scanlon (Group Chief Executive).*	*EF*	*UNC*
	Prefix RN dated 1.1.1986 to prefix WN dated 18.5.1993	£35	£45
	Prefix ZY—replacement note..	£65	£85

TWENTY POUNDS

Size 160 mm x 90 mm approximately

Obverse—red and maroon on a multicoloured underprint. Portrait of an older woman to the right
Reverse—maroon on a multicoloured underprint. Illustration of rock chimney at Lacada Point at the centre

NI.108	*Signatory: G. B. Scanlon (Group Chief Executive).*	*EF*	*UNC*
	Prefix SN dated 1.1.1987, 1.4.1987 and 1.1.1990	£55	£70
	Prefix ZY—replacement note..		probably exists

ONE HUNDRED POUNDS

Size 160 mm x 90 mm approximately

Obverse—black, green and olive on a multicoloured underprint. Portrait of an older man to the right
Reverse—black on a mainly green underprint. Illustration of the Spanish Armada at the centre

NI.109	*Signatory: G. B. Scanlon (Group Chief Executive).*	*EF*	*UNC*
	Prefix TN dated 1.12.1988...	£260	£350
	Prefix ZY—replacement note..		probably exists

BANK OF IRELAND

Established in Dublin by royal charter in 1783, the Bank of Ireland quickly became the dominant force in Irish banking despite having no branch offices. For many years no rival bank was permitted by law to have more than six partners or shareholders, which led to the setting up of a large number of small and inadequately capitalised banks throughout Ireland.

Around 1820 many of these banks failed, but still the Bank of Ireland refused to establish branches outside Dublin, leading to an amendment in the law to permit the establishment of joint stock banking companies in Ireland from 1824 onwards. This change persuaded the Bank of Ireland to immediately open branch offices in order to compete with its new rivals.

For a time the Bank of Ireland retained some privileges, in that prior to 1845 no note-issuing joint stock bank was permitted to carry on business anywhere within a 65 mile radius of Dublin. Even after it lost that advantage, the Bank of Ireland remained by far the largest Irish bank until recent years. It was the Government banker and acted in a similar capacity to the Bank of England, whilst at the same time offering a full range of clearing bank services through a widespread branch network. Until 1929 it had a dominant share of the Irish note issue.

The Bank of Ireland's position was further strengthened when it took over the Hibernian Bank in 1958, and seven years later acquired the Irish business of the National Bank. However, Allied Irish Banks has recently come to rival it in size and profitability.

ONE POUND

Size 150 mm x 83 mm approximately

Obverse — black and green on a blue underprint. Statues of Hibernia to the left and right
Reverse — blue and green; Hibernia seated in a round panel with sunburst effect

		F	VF
NI.201a	*Signatory: J. H. Craig.*		
	Prefix B/10 dated 6.5.1929 and prefix B/11 dated 8.5.1929.....	£45	£75
NI.201b	*Signatory: G. W. Frazer.*		
	Prefix B/12 dated 3.4.1933 and prefix B/13 dated 9.3.1936.....	£35	£65

Obverse—black and blue on a green underprint. Statues of Hibernia to the left and right
Reverse—Hibernia seated in a blue panel with green underprint

		VF	EF
NI.202a	*Signatory: G. W. Frazer.*		
	Prefix B/13 dated 9.3.1936 to prefix B17 dated 1.11.1940.........	£60	£100
NI.202b	*Signatory: H. J. Adams.*		
	Prefix B/18 dated 23.2.1942 to prefix B/21 dated 15.11.1943 ..	£30	£50

Size 150 mm x 70 mm approximately

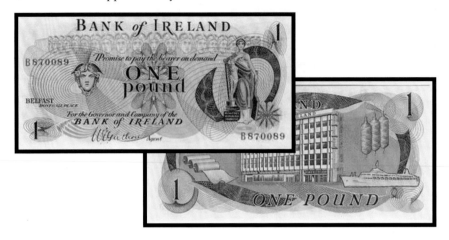

First issued in 1967
Obverse — blue grey on a multicoloured underprint. Hibernia to the right
Reverse — blue grey; Bank of Ireland building surrounded by images representing industry in Northern Ireland

		EF	UNC
NI.203	*Signatory: W. E. Guthrie (Agent)*		
	Prefix A to prefix C	£22	£30

Size 135 mm x 66mm approximately

Design similar to previous issue. First issued in 1972. Value sign at top right and bottom left is shown as "1".
Obverse – blue grey on a multicoloured underprint. Hibernia to the right
Reverse – blue grey; Bank of Ireland building surrounded by images representing industry in Northern Ireland

		EF	UNC
NI.204a	*Signatory: H. H. M. Chestnutt (Manager)*		
	Prefix D and E	£18	£25
	Prefix Z—replacement note		Rare
NI.204b	*Signatory: A. S. J. O'Neill (Manager)*		
	Prefix E and F	£10	£15
	Prefix Z—replacement note	£45	—

"Sterling" added at centre and value sign at top right and bottom left is now shown as "£1". (From 1984)

NI.205	*Signatory: A. S. J. O'Neill (Manager)*	*EF*	*UNC*
	Prefix G and H	£6	£10
	Prefix Z—replacement note	£8	£12

FIVE POUNDS

Size 178 mm x 97 mm approximately
Obverse—black and red on an orange/yellow underprint. Statues of Hibernia to the left and right
Reverse—red panel on an orange underprint. Hibernia seated at the centre

NI.211a	*Signatory: J. H. Craig.*	*F*	*VF*
	Prefix S/10 dated 5.5.1929 and 15.5.1929	£60	£110
	Prefix S/11 dated 7.5.1929	£60	£110
NI.211b	*Signatory: G. W. Frazer.*		
	Prefix S/12 dated 15.8.1935 to prefix S/15 dated 2.12.1940.....	£40	£75
NI.211c	*Signatory: H. J. Adams.*	*VF*	*EF*
	Prefix S/16 dated 16.2.1942 to prefix S/23 dated 20.12.1943...	£45	£80
NI.211d	*Signatory: S. G. Skuce.*		
	Prefix S/24 dated 1.9.1958 and prefix S/25 dated 1.10.1958 ...	£45	£80

Size 140 mm x 85 mm approximately

First issued in 1967
Obverse—blue grey on a brown/violet underprint. Hibernia to the right
Reverse—blue grey; Bank of Ireland building surrounded by images representing industry in Northern Ireland

		VF	EF
NI.212a	Signatory: W. E. Guthrie (Agent) Prefix M	£60	£110
NI.212b	Signatory: H. H. M. Chestnutt (Agent) Prefix M...	£50	£90

Size 146 mm x 77 mm approximately

Design similar to previous issue. First issued in 1972. Value sign at top right and bottom left is shown as "5".
Obverse—blue grey on a multicoloured underprint. Hibernia to the right
Reverse—blue grey; Bank of Ireland building surrounded by images representing industry in Northern Ireland

		EF	UNC
NI.213a	Signatory: H. H. M. Chestnutt (Manager) Prefix N and prefix P...	£50	£90
	Prefix Z—replacement note		Rare
NI.213b	Signatory: A. S. J. O'Neill (Manager) Prefix Q and prefix R..	£40	£80
	Prefix Z—replacement note		Rare

"Sterling" added at centre and value sign at top right and bottom left is now shown as "£5". (From 1984)

		EF	UNC
NI.214a	*Signatory: A. S. J. O'Neill (Manager)*		
	Prefix S..	£40	£80
	Prefix Z—replacement note	£90	----
NI.214b	*Signatory: D. J. Harrison (Manager)*		
	Prefix S to prefix V...	£22	£35
	Prefix Z—replacement note	£70	----

Size 136 mm x 70 mm approximately

Obverse—blue and violet on a multicoloured underprint. Hibernia to the left
Reverse—blue and multicoloured. Illustration of the Queen's University of Belfast

		EF	UNC
NI.215	*Signatory: D. J. Harrison (Manager)*		
	Prefix A dated 28.8.1990 to prefix U dated 1.7.1994..................	£14	£22
	Prefix Z—replacement note	£40	£60

Similar to previous issue with bolder colours.
Obverse—blue and purple on a multicoloured underprint. Hibernia to the left
Reverse—blue and multicoloured. Illustration of the Queen's University of Belfast

		EF	UNC
NI.216a	*Signatory: G. McGinn (Chief Executive N.I.)*		
	Prefix U dated 1.7.1997 to prefix Y dated 4.8.1998, and		
	Prefix AA dated 4.8.1998 to prefix AY dated 5.9.2000..............	------	£12
	Prefix Z—replacement note	£18	£25
NI.216b	*Signatory: M. S. Soden (Group Chief Executive).*		
	Prefix AY dated 1.3.2003 and ongoing.......................................	------	£10
	Prefix Z—replacement note	£18	£25

TEN POUNDS

Size 200 mm x 108 mm approximately

Obverse—black and blue on an green underprint. Statues of Hibernia to the left and right
Reverse—blue panel on a green underprint. Hibernia seated at the centre

		F	VF
NI.221a	*Signatory: J. H. Craig.*		
	Prefix U/10 dated 4.5.1929 and 14.5.1929.	£120	£240
NI.221b	*Signatory: H. J. Adams.*	VF	EF
	Prefix U/11 dated 26.1.1942 and prefix U/12 dated 19.1.1943	£70	£130

Size 150 mm x 93 mm approximately

First issued in 1967
Obverse—brown on a multicoloured underprint. Hibernia to the right
Reverse—brown and grey; Bank of Ireland building surrounded by images representing industry in Northern Ireland

		VF	EF
NI.222	Signatory: W. E. Guthrie (Agent)		
	Prefix T	£160	£300

Size 152 mm x 85 mm approximately

Design similar to previous issue. First issued in 1972. Value sign at top right and bottom left is shown as "10".
Obverse—brown on a multicoloured underprint. Hibernia to the right
Reverse—brown on a green underprint; Bank of Ireland building surrounded by images representing industry in Northern Ireland

		EF	UNC
NI.223a	Signatory: H. H. M. Chestnutt (Manager)		
	Prefix U..	£200	£300
NI.223b	Signatory: A. S. J. O'Neill (Manager)		
	Prefix U and prefix V...	£120	£180
	Prefix Z—replacement note		Rare

"Sterling" added at centre and value sign at top right and bottom left is now shown as "£10". (From 1984)

		EF	UNC
NI.224a	*Signatory: A. S. J. O'Neill (Manager)*		
	Prefix V and prefix W..	£55	£80
	Prefix Z—replacement		Rare
NI.224b	*Signatory: D. J. Harrison (Manager)*		
	Prefix X and prefix Y, and..	£40	£55
	Prefix AA to AF		
	Prefix Z—replacement note	£100	---

Size 142 mm x 75 mm approximately

Obverse—purple and maroon on a multicoloured underprint. Hibernia to the left
Reverse—maroon and multicoloured. Illustration of the Queen's University of Belfast

		EF	UNC
NI.225	*Signatory: D. J. Harrison (Manager)*		
	Prefix A dated 14.5.1991 to prefix P dated 28.5.1992.................	£18	£25
	Prefix Z—replacement note	£30	£50

Similar to previous design.
Obverse—blue and brown on a multicoloured underprint. Hibernia to the left
Reverse—maroon and multicoloured. Illustration of the Queen's University of Belfast

		EF	UNC
NI.226	Signatory: G. McGinn (Chief Executive N. I.).............................		
	Prefix R dated 1.7.1995 to prefix BB dated 5.9.2000 and ongoing. -------		£20
	Prefix Z—replacement note.		£40

TWENTY POUNDS

Size 200 mm x 108 mm approximately

Obverse – black on an orange/brown and pale green underprint. Statues of Hibernia to the left and right
Reverse – orange/brown panel on a pale green underprint. Hibernia seated at the centre

		F	VF
NI.231	Signatory: J. H. Craig.		
	Prefix X/10 dated 9.5.1929.		Rare

Size 160 mm x 90 mm approximately

Issued in 1983 to commemorate the bicentenary anniversary of the Bank of Ireland 1783–1983.
Obverse—green on a multicoloured underprint. Hibernia to the right
Reverse—mainly green; Bank of Ireland building surrounded by images representing industry in
Northern Ireland

NI.232	*Signatory: A. S. J. O'Neill (Manager)*	*VF*	*EF*
	Prefix A..	£220	£350
	Prefix Z—replacement note		Rare

Similar to the above note but without the commemorative text near the top. (From 1984)
Obverse—green on a multicoloured underprint. Hibernia to the right
Reverse—mainly green; Bank of Ireland building surrounded by images representing industry in
Northern Ireland

NI.233a	*Signatory: A. S. J. O'Neill (Manager)*	*EF*	*UNC*
	Prefix A and prefix B	£100	£140
	Prefix Z—replacement note		Rare
NI.233b	*Signatory: D. J. Harrison (Manager)*		
	Prefix B to prefix F..	£70	£100
	Prefix Z—replacement note.	£130	£160

Size 150 mm x 80 mm approximately

Obverse—green and brown on a multicoloured underprint. Hibernia seated in a roundel to the left
Reverse—mainly green on a multicoloured underprint. Illustration of the Queen's University of Belfast

		EF	*UNC*
NI.234	*Signatory: D. J. Harrison (Manager)*		
	Prefix A dated 9.5.1991 to prefix K dated 28.5.1993.	£45	£60
	Prefix Z – replacement note	£70	£100

Obverse—green, brown and purple on a multicoloured underprint. Hibernia seated in a roundel to the left
Reverse—mainly green on a multicoloured underprint. Illustration of the Queen's University of Belfast

		EF	*UNC*
NI.235a	*Signatory: G. McGinn (Chief Executive N. I.)*		
	Prefix L dated 1.7.1995 to prefix BC dated 5.9.2000	----	£40
	Prefix Z – replacement note.		£60
NI.235b	*Signatory: D. McGowan (Chief Executive N. I.)*		
	Prefix BD to prefix BQ dated 1.1.2003 and ongoing	------	£35

FIFTY POUNDS

Size 156 mm x 85 mm approximately

Obverse—green, brown and blue on a multicoloured underprint. Hibernia seated in a roundel to the left
Reverse—mainly brown on a multicoloured underprint. Illustration of the Queen's University of Belfast

		EF	UNC
NI.241a	*Signatory: G. McGinn (Chief Executive N. I.)*................................ Prefix A dated 1.7.1995..	*EF* £75	*UNC* £95
NI.241b	*Signatory: R. Keenan (Chief Executive U.K.)*.................................. Prefix A dated 5.4.2004 (starting from A 200001)	*EF* ----	*UNC* £90

ONE HUNDRED POUNDS

Size 160 mm x 90 mm approximately

First issued in 1974. Value sign at top right and bottom left is shown as "100".
Obverse—red on a multicoloured underprint. Hibernia to the right
Reverse—mainly red; Bank of Ireland building surrounded by images representing industry in Northern Ireland

		VF	EF
NI.251a	*Signatory: H. H. M. Chestnutt (Manager)* Prefix A...	*VF* £450	*EF* ------
NI.251b	*Signatory: A. S. J. O'Neill (Manager)* Prefix A...	£350	-------

"Sterling" added at centre and value sign at top right and bottom left is now shown as "£100". (From 1984)

		EF	UNC
NI.252a	*Signatory: A. S. J. O'Neill (Manager)*		
	Prefix A...	£350	£450
NI.252b	*Signatory: D. J. Harrison (Manager)*		
	Prefix A...	£230	£300

Size 164 mm x 90 mm approximately

Obverse—red and brown on a multicoloured underprint. Hibernia seated in a roundel to the left
Reverse—mainly red on a multicoloured underprint. Illustration of the Queen's University of Belfast

		EF	UNC
NI.253	*Signatory: D. J. Harrison (Manager)*		
	Prefix A dated 28.8.1992...	£200	£250

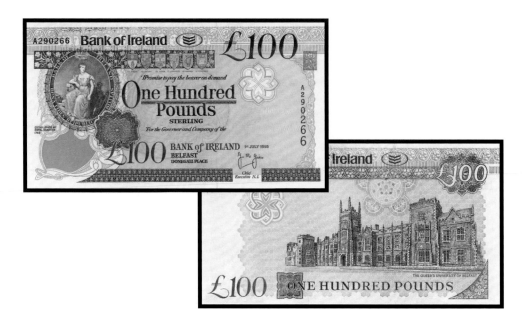

Obverse—red, mauve, brown and blue on a multicoloured underprint. Hibernia seated in a roundel to the left.
Reverse—mainly mauve on a multicoloured underprint. Illustration of the Queen's University of Belfast.

		EF	UNC
NI.254	*Signatory: G. McGinn (Chief Executive N. I.)*		
	Prefix A dated 1.7.1995..	—	£180

BELFAST BANKING COMPANY LIMITED

The Belfast Banking Company was formed in Belfast in 1827, taking over the business of two local private banking partnerships which dated back to 1808 and 1809. In 1917 it was acquired by the London City and Midland Bank, and six years later all of its branches in what was then the Irish Free State were sold off to the Royal Bank of Ireland. This made the Belfast Bank the only Irish note-issuing bank which had no branches outside Northern Ireland.

The Midland Bank made a successful takeover bid for the Northern Bank in 1965, and in July 1970 the Belfast Bank's separate existence ended when the Midland's two Irish subsidiaries were merged in the name of the Northern Bank Limited.

ONE POUND

Size 152 mm x 84 mm approximately
Obverse — black with a blue value panel at the centre
Reverse — blue panel with the name of the bank and value

		F	VF
NI.301a	*Handsigned, with black serial numbers*		
	Prefix A dated 2.1.1922 to prefix E/E dated 8.11.1928	£90	£160

		EF	UNC
NI.301b	*Handsigned, with blue serial numbers*		
	Prefix E/F dated 9.11.1939 to prefix F/G dated 10.8.1940	£35	£50

FIVE POUNDS

Size 185 mm x 90 mm approximately

Obverse—black with the value in red at the centre
Reverse—red panel with the name of the bank and value

		F	VF
NI.302a	*Handsigned, with black serial numbers* Prefix B/G dated 3.1.1923 to prefix B/U dated 7.9.1927		Rare
NI.302b	*Handsigned, with red serial numbers* Prefix B/U dated 8.3.1928 to prefix D/X dated 2.10.1942.......	*VF* £55	*EF* £110
NI.302c	*Handsigned, with red serial numbers* Prefix D/X to prefix E/D dated 6.1.1966	*EF* £60	*UNC* £90

TEN POUNDS

Size 213 mm x 108 mm approximately
Obverse—black with the value in green at the centre
Reverse—green panel with the name of the bank and value

		F	VF
NI.303a	*Handsigned, with black serial numbers* Prefix X to prefix Y dated 3.1.1923...		Rare
NI.303b	*Handsigned, with green serial numbers* Prefix Y dated 9.1.1929 to prefix A/N dated 1.1.1943..............	*VF* £65	*EF* £120
NI.303c	*Handsigned, with green serial numbers* Prefix A/N dated 3.12.1963 to prefix A/O dated 5.6.1965......	*EF* £70	*UNC* £100

TWENTY POUNDS

Size 210 mm x 110 mm approximately

Obverse—black with the value in purple at the centre
Reverse—purple panel with the name of the bank and value

		F	VF
NI.304a	*Handsigned, with black serial numbers* Prefix D dated 3.1.1923..	£180	£320
NI.304b	*Handsigned, with purple serial numbers* Prefix D dated 9.11.1939 to prefix E dated 10.8.1940...............	£150	£280
NI.304c	*Handsigned, with black serial numbers* Prefix E dated 3.2.1943 and 5.6.1965..	£120	£240

FIFTY POUNDS

Size 210 mm x 110 mm approximately

Obverse—black with the value in orange at the centre
Reverse—orange panel with the name of the bank and value

		F	VF
NI.305a	*Handsigned, with black serial numbers* Prefix B dated 3.1.1923 and 3.5.1923	£260	£420
NI.305b	*Handsigned, with orange serial numbers* Prefix B dated 9.11.1939 and 10.8.1940	£220	£380

		VF	EF
NI.305c	*Handsigned, with black serial numbers* Prefix B dated 3.2.1943 and 3.12.1963	£250	£450

ONE HUNDRED POUNDS

Size 210 mm x 110 mm approximately

Obverse — black with the value in red at the centre
Reverse — red panel with the name of the bank and value

		F	VF
NI.306a	*Handsigned, with black serial numbers*		
	Prefix A dated 3.1.1923 and 3.5.1923	£400	£600
NI.306b	*Handsigned, with red serial numbers*		
	Prefix A dated 9.11.1939	£400	£600
NI.306c	*Handsigned, with black serial numbers*		
	Prefix A dated 3.2.1943	£350	£550

		VF	EF
NI306d	*Handsigned, with red serial numbers*		
	Prefix A dated 3.12.1963	£280	£450
NI306e	*Printed signature G. B. Smyth, red serial numbers*		
	Prefix B dated 8.5.1968...	£350	£550

FIRST TRUST BANK

The First Trust Bank was established in the early 1990's as a result of a merger between Allied Irish Banks plc and the Trustee Savings Bank. The new bank did not issue any five Pound notes.

TEN POUNDS

Size 142 mm x 75 mm approximately

Obverse — brown and purple on a multicoloured underprint. Portrait of a young man to the right.
Reverse — brown and multicoloured. Illustration of the Spanish galleass "The Girona" at the centre

		EF	UNC
NI.411a	*Signatory: E. F. McElroy (Group Managing Director)*		
	Prefix AB to prefix HB dated 10.1.1994	£25	£35
	Prefix ZB – replacement note...		Rare
NI.411b	*Signatory: D. E. Harvey (Managing Director)*		
	Prefix JB to prefix NB dated 1.3.1996	£35	£50
	Prefix ZB – replacement note...		Rare

Obverse—brown and purple on a multicoloured underprint. Portrait of a young man to the right. Additional gold security feature at top right.
Reverse—brown and multicoloured. Illustration of the Spanish galleass "The Girona" at the centre

NI.412   *Signatory: D. J. Licence (Managing Director, First Trust Bank)*
Prefix AA to prefix LA dated 1.1.1998, and ongoing ....   ----   £25
Prefix ZA – replacement note. ....   Rare

TWENTY POUNDS

Size 150 mm x 80 mm approximately

Obverse—mauve and brown on a multicoloured underprint; portrait of a mature lady to the right.
Reverse—mauve on a multicoloured underprint. Illustration of rock chimney at Lacada Point, Giant's Causeway.

		EF	UNC
NI.421a	*Signatory: E. F. McElroy (Group Managing Director)*		
	Prefix AC to prefix HC dated 10.1.1994....................................	£40	£60
	Prefix ZC—replacement note..		Rare
NI.421b	*Signatory: D. E. Harvey (Managing Director)*		
	Prefix JC to prefix NC dated 1.1.1996, and	£60	£80
	Prefix PC to prefix RC dated 1.3.1996..	£60	£80
	Prefix ZC—replacement note..		Rare

Obverse—mauve and brown on a multicoloured underprint; portrait of a mature lady to the right. Additional gold security feature at top right
Reverse—mauve on a multicoloured underprint. Illustration of rock chimney at Lacada Point, Giant's Causeway

NI.422   *Signatory: D. J. Licence (Managing Director, First Trust Bank)*

	EF	UNC
Prefix AA to prefix XA dated 1.1.1998, and ongoing..............	----	£40
Prefix ZA—replacement note.		Rare

FIFTY POUNDS

Size 155 mm x 85 mm approximately

Obverse—blue and green on a multicoloured underprint. Portrait of a mature man to the right
Reverse—blue, green and multicoloured. Picture of two cherubs holding a commemorative medal of 1588 depicting the defeat of the Spanish Armada

	EF	UNC
NI.431 *Signatory: E. F. McElroy (Group Managing Director)*		
Prefix AD dated 10.1.1994	£95	£130
Prefix ZD—replacement note.		Rare

Obverse—blue and green on a multicoloured underprint. Portrait of a mature man to the right. Additional silver security feature over value at top right

Reverse—blue, green and multicoloured. Picture of two cherubs holding a commemorative medal of 1588 depicting the defeat of the Spanish Armada

	EF	UNC
NI.432 *Signatory: D. J. Licence (Managing Director, First Trust Bank)*		
Prefix AA dated 1.1.1998..	----	£100
Prefix ZA—replacement note.		Rare

ONE HUNDRED POUNDS

Size 160 mm x 90 mm approximately

Obverse—green, brown and black on a multicoloured underprint. Portraits of a mature man and woman to the right

Reverse—green, brown and black on a multicoloured underprint. Illustration of the Spanish Armada at the centre

		EF	UNC
NI.441a	Signatory: E. F. McElroy (Group Managing Director)		
	Prefix AE dated 10.1.1994..	£180	£220
	Prefix ZE—replacement note......................................		Rare
NI.441b	Signatory: D. E. Harvey (Managing Director)		
	Prefix AE dated 1.3.1996...	£220	£280
	Prefix ZE—replacement note......................................		Rare

Obverse—green, brown and black on a multicoloured underprint. Portraits of a mature man and woman to the right. Additional silver security feature over value at top right

Reverse—green, brown and black on a multicoloured underprint. Illustration of the Spanish Armada at the centre

		EF	UNC
NI.442	Signatory: D. J. Licence (Managing Director, First Trust Bank)		
	Prefix AA dated 1.1.1998...	----	£200
	Prefix ZA—replacement note.......................................		Rare

NATIONAL BANK LIMITED

The Bank was founded in 1835 by Daniel O'Connell. Its Irish branches were acquired by the Bank of Ireland in December 1965, and for a short time thereafter it carried on business as the National Bank of Ireland Limited. A few years later its separate identity disappeared when it was merged into the Bank of Ireland.

Examples of early National Bank notes.

ONE POUND

Size 149 mm x 80 mm approximately

Obverse—black—green panel at centre with "£1"
Reverse—green—Hibernia with harp and wolfhound at the centre flanked by £1 value

		F	VF
NI.501	Signatory: F. H. Green		
	No prefix letters; dated 6.5.1929, 1.11.1931, 1.1.1932 .... 15.8.1932 and 1.8.1933.	£55	£100

Size 152 mm x 84 mm approximately

Obverse—black on a green and yellow underprint. Hibernia with harp and wolfhound at the centre
Reverse—green and lilac. Bank's Coat of Arms flanked by £1 value panels

		VF	EF
NI.502	Signatory: F. H. Green		
	Prefix A dated 1.2.1937, 1.9.1937 and 2.10.1939	£50	£90

FIVE POUNDS

Size 149 mm x 80 mm approximately
Obverse — dark blue — brown panel at centre with "£5"
Reverse — brown — Hibernia with harp and wolfhound at centre flanked by £5 value

		F	VF
NI.503	*Signatory: F. H. Green* No prefix letters; dated 6.5.1929, 1.8.1933 and 1.10.1934		Rare

Size 155 mm x 91 mm approximately

Obverse — blue on a blue and tan underprint. Hibernia at lower left with harp and wolfhound
Reverse — black on a green and tan underprint. Bank's Coat of Arms at centre

		VF	EF
NI.504a	*Signatory: F. H. Green* Prefix A dated 1.2.1937; 1.9.1937 and 2.10.1939	£70	£130
NI.504b	*Signatory: J. J. O'Donnell* Prefix A dated 1.8.1942; 1.1.1949 and 2.5.1949	£60	£120
NI.504c	*Signatory: R. W. Maguire.* Prefix A dated 1.5.1964 – specimens only		Rare

TEN POUNDS

Size 149 mm x 80 mm approximately

Obverse—green – red/brown panel at centre with "£10"
Reverse—brown – Hibernia with harp and wolfhound at centre flanked by £10 value

		F	VF
NI.505	*Signatory: F. H. Green.* No prefix letters; dated 6.5.1929; 2.10.1931 and 1.8.1933		Rare

Size 152 mm x 84 mm approximately

Obverse—green on a pink and yellow underprint. Hibernia seated with harp and wolfhound at the centre
Reverse—brown on a green and yellow underprint. Bank's Coat of Arms at left centre flanked by £10 value panels

		VF	EF
NI.506a	*Signatory: F. H. Green* Prefix A dated 1.2.1937, 1.9.1937 and 2.10.1939	£100	£180
NI.506b	*Signatory: J. J. O'Donnell* Prefix A dated 1.8.1942 and 2.5.1949	£75	£160
NI.506c	*Signatory: R.H.R. Fry* Prefix A dated 1.7.1959	£75	£160

TWENTY POUNDS

Size 149 mm x 80 mm approximately

Obverse—brown—blue panel at centre with "£20"
Reverse—blue—Hibernia with harp and wolfhound at centre flanked by £20 value panels

		F	VF
NI.507	Signatory: F. H. Green		
	No prefix letters; dated 6.5.1929		Rare

Size 160 mm x 90 mm approximately

Obverse—brown on a grey and yellow underprint. Hibernia at lower left with harp and wolfhound
Reverse—blue, green and yellow. Bank's Coat of Arms at the centre

		VF	EF
NI.508a	Signatory: F. H. Green		
	Prefix A dated 1.2.1937 and 2.10.1939	£180	£320
NI.508b	Signatory: J. J. O'Donnell		
	Prefix A dated 1.8.1942 and 1.1.1949	£160	£280
NI.508c	Signatory: R.H.R. Fry		
	Prefix A dated 1.7.1959	£160	£280

NORTHERN BANK LIMITED

The Northern Bank began life as a private partnership in Belfast in 1809, and became the joint stock Northern Banking Company in 1824, at which time it was the only joint stock banking company anywhere in the British Isles apart from Scotland.

Branches outside Belfast were established from 1835 onwards, and in 1888 the bank opened its first office in Dublin by acquiring the business of the private bankers Ball & Co. Five years earlier the Northern had adopted limited liability, thereby becoming the Northern Banking Company Limited, and in 1929 it shortened its name to Northern Bank Limited.

The Midland Bank (which already owned the Belfast Banking Company) acquired the share capital of the Northern Bank in 1965, and in 1970 merged its two Irish banks in the name of the Northern. In order to raise capital following a disastrous investment in the USA, the Midland sold the Northern Bank in 1987 to National Banks Australia Limited, who in turn are now in the process of selling it to Danske Bank, Copenhagen.

SOME EXAMPLES OF EARLY NOTES

ONE POUND

Size 151 mm x 84 mm approximately

Obverse—black with "ONE" in a blue panel at the centre; vignette with sailing ship above
Reverse—blue. "NBL" in round design at centre with value "1" at either side

	F	VF
NI.601a *Signatory: S.W.Knox (on prefix N-I/A and N-I/E)*		
NI.601b *Signatory: H.H.Stewart (on prefix N-I/B and N-I/F)*		
NI.601c *Signatory: W.F.Scott (on prefix N-I/C)*		
NI.601d *Signatory: A.P.Tibbey (on prefix N-I/D)*		

Red serial numbers
Prefix <u>N-I</u> dated 6.5.1929 to prefix <u>N-I</u> dated 1.8.1929 .... £35 £65
      A   F

	EF	UNC

NI.601e   *Signatory: F. W. White*
Black serial numbers
Prefix N-I dated 1.1.1940 .... £40 £50
      H

Size 135 mm x 67 mm approximately

Obverse—green on a multicoloured background; illustrations of agriculture, shipbuilding and weaving
Reverse green on a multicoloured background; Griffin emblem at the centre

		EF	UNC
NI.602a	*Signatory: W. S. Wilson* Prefix C dated 1.7.1970...	£15	£22
NI.602b	*Signatory: H. M. Gabbey* Prefix C dated 1.10.1971..	£15	£22
NI.602c	*Signatory: W. Ervin* Prefix C dated 1.8.1978..	£10	£14

FIVE POUNDS

Size 150 mm x 86 mm approximately

Heading: Northern Bank Ltd. on earlier notes of the Northern Banking Company Limited.
Obverse – black with "FIVE" in a blue panel at the centre. Vignette with sailing ship above
Reverse – blue; "NBC" in a round panel at the centre with "5" in small round panels at either side

		F	VF
NI.611	*Signatories: Handsigned.* Prefix B dated 1.9.1927 (but issued on or after 6th May 1929)		Rare

Heading: Northern Bank Limited

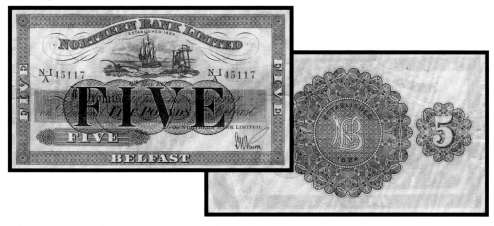

Obverse—black with "FIVE" in a blue panel at the centre. Vignette with sailing ship above
Reverse—blue; "NBL" in a round panel at the centre with "5" in small round panels at either side

		F	VF
NI.612a	*Signatory: S.W.Knox.*		
	Prefix <u>N-I</u> dated 6.5.1929	£60	£110
	A		
NI.612b	Signatory: H. H. Stewart.		
	Prefix <u>N-I</u> dated 6.5.1929	£60	£110
	B		

Size 170 mm x 95 mm approximately

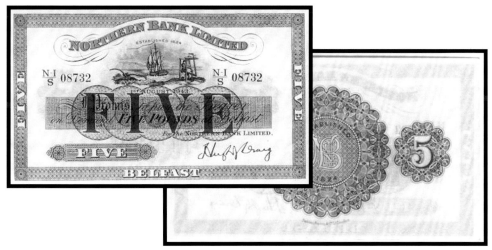

Obverse—black with "FIVE" in a green panel at the centre. Vignette with sailing ship above
Reverse—blue; "NBL" in a round panel at the centre with "5" in small round panels at either side

		VF	EF
NI.613a	*Signatory: F.W.White (on prefix N-I/D, N-I/H, N-I/L, N-I/P)*		
NI.613b	*Signatory: H.J.Craig (on prefix N-I/E, N-I/I, N-I/M, N-I/S)*		
NI.613c	*Signatory: W.F.Scott (on prefix N-I/B, N-I/F, N-I/J, N-I/N, N-I/T)*		
NI.613d	*Signatory: A.P.Tibbey (on prefix N-I/C, N-I/G, N-I/K, N-I/O)*		
NI.613e	*Signatory: J. E. Forde (on prefix N-I/R)*		

Prefix <u>N-I</u> dated 1.9.1937 to prefix <u>N-I</u> dated 1.11.1943............ £50 £100
    B   T

Size 150 mm x 86 mm approximately

Obverse—black with "FIVE" in a green panel at the centre. Vignette with sailing ship above
Reverse—blue; "NBL" in a round panel at the centre with "5" in small round panels at either side

		EF	UNC
NI.614	*Signatory: E.D.Hill.*		
	Prefix <u>N-I</u> dated 1.10.1968 .... U	£45	£65

Size 150 mm x 84 mm approximately

Obverse—blue on a multicoloured background; illustrations of agriculture, shipbuilding and weaving
Reverse—blue on a multicoloured background; Griffin emblem at the centre

		EF	UNC
NI.615a	*Signatory: W. S. Wilson*		
	Prefix D dated 1.7.1970	£60	£80
NI.615b	*Signatory: H. M. Gabbey*		
	Prefix D dated 1.10.1971	£60	£80
NI.615c	*Signatory: J. B. Newland*		
	Prefix D dated 1.7.1974 and 1.1.1976...	£30	£40
NI.615d	*Signatory: W. Ervin*		
	Prefix D dated 1.4.1982	£24	£30
NI.615e	*Signatory: J. Roberts*		
	Prefix D dated 3.2.1986	£24	£30

Size 136 mm x 70 mm approximately

Obverse—blue on a multicoloured background; portrait of W.A.Trail 1844-1933
Reverse—blue on a multicoloured background; images of satellite dish and computer systems

		EF	UNC
NI.616	Signatory: S.H.Torrens (Chief Executive).		
	Prefix A dated 24.8.1988 to 24.8.1990.	£12	£18
	Prefix Z—replacement note	£40	£60

Size 70 mm x 136 mm approximately

Polymer note—vertical format
Obverse—blue with a coloured globe to left and right of centre and a transparent star shape at the bottom
Reverse - blue with a line drawing of a globe and the space shuttle

		EF	UNC
NI.617	Signatory: D.Price (Chief Executive).		
	Prefix MM dated 8.10.1999..	-----	£10
	Prefix Y2K dated 1.1.2000, issued in a presentation pack........	-----	£15
	Prefix N (replacement notes).	£25	£40

TEN POUNDS

Size 200 mm x 112 mm approximately

Heading: Northern Bank Ltd. on earlier notes of the Northern Banking Company Limited.
*Obverse—black with "TEN" in a blue panel at the centre. Vignette with sailing ship above. Listing of
the various branches of the Bank printed across the lower centre*
Reverse—blue; "NBC" in a round panel at the centre with "10" in small round panels at either side

	F	VF
NI.621 *Signatory: handsigned*		
Prefix A dated 1.3.1920 (but issued on or after 6th May 1929)		Rare

Heading: Northern Bank Ltd. on earlier notes of the Northern Banking Company Limited.
*Obverse—black with "TEN" in a blue panel at the centre. Vignette with sailing ship above. Without the
listing of the Bank's branches..*
Reverse—blue; "NBC" in a round panel at the centre with "10" in small round panels at either side.

	F	VF
NI.622 *Signatory: handsigned*		
Prefix B dated 10.10.1921 (but issued on or after 6th May 1929)		Rare

Size 168 mm x 95 mm approximately

Obverse—black with "TEN" in a red panel at the centre. Vignette with sailing ship above
Reverse—blue; "NBL" in a round panel at the centre with "10" in small round panels at either side

		F	VF
NI.623a	*Signatory: handsigned*		
	Prefix <u>N-I</u> dated 1.1.1930 to prefix <u>N-I</u> dated 1.1.1940	£45	£85
	A E		

		VF	EF
NI.623b	*Signatory: W.F.Scott (on prefix N-I/F, N-I/J)*		
NI.623c	*Signatory: A.P.Tibbey (on prefix N-I/G, N-I/K)*		
NI.623d	*Signatory: F.W.White (on prefix N-I/H, N-I/L)*		
NI.623e	*Signatory: H.J.Craig (on prefix N-I/I, N-I/N)*		
NI.623f	*Signatory: J. E. Forde (on prefix N-I/M)*		
	Prefix <u>N-I</u> dated 1.8.1940 to prefix <u>N-I</u> dated 1.11.1943............	£65	£110
	F N		
NI.623g	*Signatory: E.D.Hill.*		
	Prefix <u>N-I</u> dated 1.10.1968	£65	£110
	OO		

Size 151 mm x 85 mm approximately

Obverse—brown on a multicoloured background; illustrations of agriculture, shipbuilding and weaving
Reverse—brown on a multicoloured background; Griffin emblem at the centre

		EF	UNC
NI.624a	*Signatory: W. S. Wilson* Prefix E dated 1.7.1970	£80	£120
NI.624b	*Signatory: H. M. Gabbey* Prefix E dated 1.10.1971	£80	£120
NI.624c	*Signatory: J. B. Newland* Prefix E dated 1.7.1975 to 1.1.1978	£50	£75
NI.624d	*Signatory: W. Ervin* Prefix E dated 1.3.1981 and 1.4.1982	£45	£70
NI.624e	*Signatory: J. Roberts* Prefix E dated 2.1.1985 to 2.3.1987	£40	£60
NI.624f	*Signatory: S. H. Torrens* Prefix E dated 15.6.1988	£35	£55

Size 142 mm x 75 mm approximately

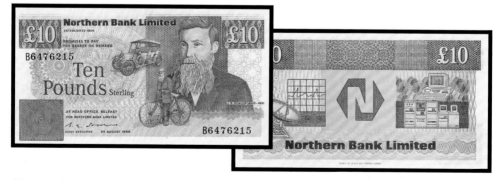

Obverse—brown and red on a multicoloured background; portrait of J.B.Dunlop 1840-1921
Reverse—brown on a multicoloured background; images of satellite dish and computer systems

		EF	UNC
NI.625a	*Signatory: S.H.Torrens (Chief Executive).* Prefix B dated 24.8.1988 to 24.8.1993. .... Prefix Z – replacement note.	£30 £50	£40 £80
NI.625b	*Signatory: J.R.Wright (Chief Executive).* Prefix B dated 30.8.1996. .... Prefix Z – replacement note.	£22 £45	£30 £75

Obverse—brown and red on a multicoloured background; portrait of J.B.Dunlop 1840-1921
Reverse—brown on a multicoloured background; picture of façade of City Hall, Belfast

		EF	UNC
NI.626a	Signatory: G.Savage (Chief Executive).		
	Prefix BA and BB dated 24.2.1997.	---	£22
	Prefix ZZ – replacement note..	£40	£60
NI.626b	Signatory: D.Price (Chief Executive).		
	Prefix BC dated 8.10.1999.	----	£20
	Prefix ZZ – replacement note..	£40	£60

Similar to previous issue but changes to "Northern Bank" typeface and logo.
Obverse—brown and red on a multicoloured background; portrait of J.B.Dunlop 1840-1921
Reverse—brown on a multicoloured background; picture of façade of City Hall, Belfast

		EF	UNC
NI.627	Signatory: D.Price (Chief Executive).		
	Prefix BD dated 29.4.2004..	----	£20
	Prefix ZZ—replacement note..	£40	£60

TWENTY POUNDS

Size 203 mm x 117 mm approximately

Heading: Northern Bank Ltd. on earlier notes of the Northern Banking Company Limited.
Obverse—black with "TWENTY" in a blue panel at the centre. Vignette with sailing ship above
Reverse—blue; "NBC" in a round panel at the centre with "20" in small round panels at either side

		F	VF
NI.631	*Signatory: Handsigned*		
	Prefix A dated 20.10.1921 (but issued on or after 6th May 1929)	£300	£550

Size 159 mm x 90 mm approximately

Obverse—purple on a multicoloured background; illustrations of agriculture, shipbuilding and weaving
Reverse—purple on a multicoloured background; Griffin emblem at the centre

		EF	UNC
NI.632a	*Signatory: W. S. Wilson*		
	Prefix F dated 1.7.1970	£150	----
NI.632b	*Signatory: W. Ervin*		
	Prefix F dated 1.3.1981 and 1.12.1984	£80	£120
NI.632c	*Signatory: J. Roberts*		
	Prefix F dated 2.3.1987	£80	£120
NI632d	*Signatory: S. H. Torrens*		
	Prefix F dated 15.6.1988	£70	£100

Size 150 mm x 80 mm approximately

Obverse — mauve and brown on a multicoloured background; portrait of H.Ferguson 1884–1960
Reverse — mauve on a multicoloured background; images of satellite dish and computer systems

		EF	UNC
NI.633a	*Signatory: S.H.Torrens (Chief Executive).*		
	Prefix C dated 24.8.1988 to 24.8.1993.	£50	£70
	Prefix Z – replacement note.	£90	---
NI.633b	*Signatory: J.R.Wright (Chief Executive).*		
	Prefix C dated 30.8.1996..	£40	£60
	Prefix Z – replacement note.	£80	£120

Obverse — mauve on a multicoloured background; portrait of H.Ferguson 1884–1960
Reverse — mauve on a multicoloured background; picture of façade of City Hall, Belfast

		EF	UNC
NI.634a	*Signatory: G.Savage (Chief Executive).*		
	Prefix CA and CB dated 24.2.1997..	£40	£50
	Prefix ZZ – replacement note..	£70	----
NI.634b	*Signatory: D.Price (Chief Executive).*		
	Prefix CB to CD dated 8.10.1999..	-----	£40
	Prefix ZZ – replacement note..	£65	----

Commemorative issue "175 Years of Banking 1824 – 1999".
Obverse—mauve on a multicoloured background; portrait of H.Ferguson 1884-1960
Reverse—mauve on a multicoloured background; picture of façade of City Hall, Belfast

		EF	UNC
NI.635	*Signatory: D.Price (Chief Executive).*		
	Prefix NB dated 1.9.1999..	-----	£38

FIFTY POUNDS

Size 195 mm x 108 mm approximately

Heading: Northern Bank Ltd. on earlier notes of the Northern Banking Company Limited.
Obverse—black with "FIFTY" in a blue panel at the centre. Vignette with sailing ship above.
Reverse—blue; "NBC" in a round panel at the centre with "50" in small round panels at either side.
These notes were issued on or after 6th May 1929

		F	VF
	....		
NI.641a	*Signatory: Handsigned (usually S. W. Knox)*		
	No prefix letter, red serial numbers—dated 5.8.1914..............	from £400	
NI.641b	*Signatory: Handsigned (usually H. J. Craig)*		
	No prefix letter, black serial numbers – dated 25.4.1918.........	from £400	

Size 185 mm x 110 mm approximately

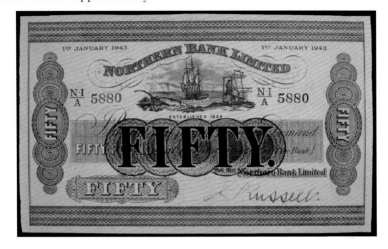

Obverse—black with "FIFTY" in a blue panel at the centre. Vignette with sailing ship above
Reverse—blue; "NBC" in a round panel at the centre with "50" in small round panels at either side

		VF	EF
NI.642a	*Signatory: Handsigned*		
	Prefix <u>N-I</u> dated 1.1.1943	£280	£450
	A		

Letters in central panel on the reverse changed to "NBL"

NI.642b	*Signatory: Handsigned*		
	Prefix <u>N-I</u> dated 1.10.1968	£280	£450
	B		

Size 170 mm x 95 mm approximately

Obverse—orange/brown on a multicoloured background; illustrations of agriculture, shipbuilding and weaving
Reverse—reddish brown; Griffin emblem at the centre

		EF	UNC
NI.643a	*Signatory: W. S. Wilson*		
	Prefix G dated 1.7.1970	£280	----
NI.643b	*Signatory: J. B. Newland*		
	Prefix G dated 1.1.1975	£180	£250
NI.643c	*Signatory: W. Ervin*		
	Prefix G dated 1.3.1981	£140	£200

Size 156 mm x 85 mm approximately

Obverse—green and multicoloured; portrait of Sir F. C. Davidson 1846-1921
Reverse—green and multicoloured; images of satellite dish and computer systems

	EF	UNC
NI.644 Signatory: S. H. Torrens (Chief Executive).		
Prefix D dated 1.11.1990..	£90	£110

Obverse—green, blue and multicolored; portrait of Sir F. C. Davidson 1846–1921
Reverse—green, blue and multicolored; picture of façade of City Hall, Belfast

	EF	UNC
NI.645 Signatory: D.Price (Chief Executive).		
Prefix DA dated 8.10.1999.	----	£100
Prefix ZZ – replacement note.		

ONE HUNDRED POUNDS

Size 210 mm x 110 mm approximately

Heading: Northern Bank Ltd. on earlier notes of the Northern Banking Company Limited.
Obverse—black with "£100" in a blue panel at the centre. Vignette with sailing ship above
Reverse—blue; "NBC" in a round panel at the centre with "100" in small round panels at either side

	F	VF
NI.651 *Signatory: handsigned.*		
No prefix letter – dated 2.6.1919	£500	£750

Size 190 mm x 115 mm approximately

Obverse—black with "£100" in a blue panel at the centre. Vignette with sailing ship above
Reverse—blue; "NBC" in a round panel at the centre with "100" in small round panels at either side

	VF	EF
NI.652a *Signatory: handsigned.*		
Prefix N-I dated 1.1.1943	£550	£750
A		

Letters in central panel on the reverse changed to "NBL"
NI.652b *Signatory: handsigned.*		
Prefix <u>N-I</u> dated 1.10.1968	£450	£650
BB		

Size 170 mm x 95 mm approximately

Obverse—red on a multicoloured background; illustrations of agriculture, shipbuilding and weaving
Reverse—red; Griffin emblem at the centre

		EF	UNC
NI.653a	*Signatory: W. S. Wilson*		
	Prefix H dated 1.7.1970	£350	----
NI.653b	*Signatory: H. M. Gabbey*		
	Prefix H dated 1.10.1971	£350	----
NI.653c	*Signatory: J. B. Newland*		
	Prefix H dated 1.1.1975 to 1.2.1977	£250	£350
NI.653d	*Signatory: W. Ervin*		
	Prefix H dated 1.10.1978 and 1.1.1980	£220	£280

Size 164 mm x 90 mm approximately

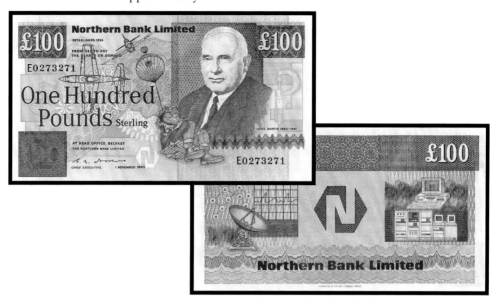

Obverse—red, brown and multicoloured; portrait of Sir James Martin 1893–1981
Reverse—red, brown and multicoloured; images of satellite dish and computer systems

		EF	UNC
NI.654	*Signatory: S. H. Torrens (Chief Executive).*		
	Prefix E dated 1.11.1990.	£180	£230

Obverse—brown and multicoloured; portrait of Sir James Martin 1893-1981
Reverse—mauve and multicoloured; picture of façade of City Hall, Belfast

		EF	UNC
NI.655	*Signatory: D. Price (Chief Executive)*		
	Prefix EA dated 8.10.1999	----	£180

PROVINCIAL BANK OF IRELAND LIMITED

The Provincial Bank of Ireland was formed in 1825 with its head office in London, and the majority of its initial shareholders were resident in England. It gradually took on a more Irish character, and in 1953 the Head Office was moved from London to Dublin. In 1966 the Provincial Bank merged with the Munster & Leinster Bank and the Royal Bank of Ireland to form Allied Irish Banks Limited, and the operations of the three banks were integrated under the Allied Irish name in 1969. Because of legal problems, however, the Provincial Bank retained an office in Royal Avenue, Belfast and continued to issue notes in its own name until 1981. By then the legal difficulties had been overcome and later note issues were in the name of Allied Irish Banks.

SOME EXAMPLES OF EARLY BANKNOTES

ONE POUND

Size 148mm x 85 mm approximately

Obverse—black with "£1" in a green panel at the centre; vignette with Bank building above
Reverse—blue panel with Britannia and Hibernia seated at the centre

		F	VF
NI.701a	*Signatory: Hume Robertson.* Prefix N dated 6.5.1929 and prefix N/A dated 1.8.1930	£50	£90
NI.701b	*Signatory: F. S. Forde.* Prefix N/A dated 1.2.1932 to prefix N/B dated 1.6.1934.........	£45	£80

Obverse—black with "£1" in a green panel at the centre; vignette with Bank building above
Reverse—green panel with Britannia and Hibernia seated at the centre

		VF	EF
NI.702a	*Signatory: F. S. Forde.*		
	Prefix N/C dated 1.8.1935 and 2.11.1936	£70	£120
NI.702b	*Signatory: G. A. Kennedy*		
	Prefix N/D dated 1.9.1937 to prefix N/J dated 1.5.1946..........	£45	£75

Size 150 mm x 85 mm approximately

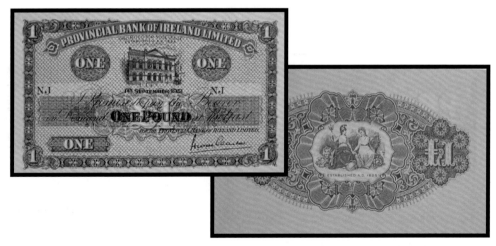

Obverse—black with a mesh background and with "£1" in a green panel at the centre; vignette with Bank building above
Reverse—green panel with Britannia and Hibernia seated at the centre

NI.703a	*Signatory: G. A. Kennedy*	
	Prefix N/J dated 1.5.1946	Rare
	These notes were not issued. A few un-numbered specimen notes are known.	
NI.703b	*Signatory: H. W. M. Clarke.*	
	Prefix NJ and NK dated 1.9.1951...	Rare
	These notes were not issued. A few un-numbered specimen notes are known, as well as a few numbered notes with prefix NJ.	

Obverse—Olive green on a pale green underprint with a cameo at the centre
Reverse—green panel with the Bank's office building in Belfast at the centre

		VF	EF
	Signatory: N. J. Shaw		
NI.704a	Prefix KN dated 1.3.1954 to prefix LN dated 1.10.1954	£60	£110
	(printed by Waterlow & Sons Limited)		
NI.704b	Prefix LN dated 1.12.1965..	£60	£110
	(printed by Thomas de la Rue & Co. Ltd.)		

Size 150 mm x 72 mm approximately

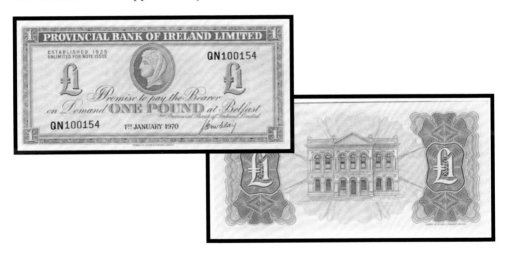

Obverse—Olive green on a pale green underprint with a cameo at the centre
Reverse—green panel with the Bank's office building in Belfast at the centre

		EF	UNC
NI.705	*Signatory: J. G. McClay*		
	Prefix LN dated 1.1.1968 to prefix UN dated 1.1.1972	£25	£35
	Prefix ZZ – replacement note..	£80	----

Size 135 mm x 67 mm approximately

Obverse—green and brown on a multicoloured underprint. Portrait of a boy to the right
Reverse—mainly green. Illustration of the Spanish galleass "The Girona" at the centre

		EF	UNC
NI.706a	*Signatory: J. G. McClay (Manager).*		
	Prefix PN dated 1.1.1977..	£14	£20
	Prefix ZY – replacement note.......................................	£60	---
NI.706b	*Signatory: F.H. Hollway (Manager).*		
	Prefix PN dated 1.1.1979..	£13	£18
	Prefix ZY – replacement note.......................................	£60	---

FIVE POUNDS

Size 148 mm x 86 mm approximately

Obverse—black with "£5" in a blue panel at the centre; vignette with Bank building above
Reverse—green panel with Britannia and Hibernia seated at the centre

		F	VF
NI.711a	*Signatory: Hume Robertson.*		
	Prefix N dated 6.5.1929.	£140	£250
NI.711b	*Signatory: F. S. Forde.*		
	Prefix N dated 5.10.1933	£120	£230

Size 150 mm x 88 mm approximately

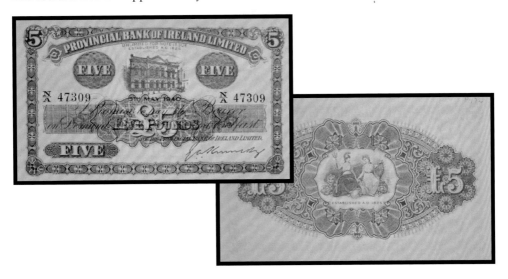

Obverse—blue/grey with "£5" in a brown panel at the centre; vignette with Bank building above
Reverse—brown panel with Britannia and Hibernia seated at the centre

		VF	EF
NI.712a	*Signatory: F. S. Forde.*		
	Prefix N dated 5. 8.1935 and 5.5.1936	£110	£180
NI.712b	*Signatory: G. A. Kennedy*		
	Prefix N/A dated 5.5.1938 to prefix N/B dated 5.4.1946.........	£80	£150

Obverse—grey with a mesh background and with "£5" in a brown panel at the centre; vignette with Bank building above
Reverse—brown panel with Britannia and Hibernia seated at the centre

		VF	EF
NI.713	*Signatory: H. W. M. Clarke*		
	Prefix N/B dated 5.1.1948		Rare
	Prefix NB dated 5.12.1949 to 5.4.1952	£45	£80

Size 166 mm x 93 mm approximately

Obverse—Brown on a pale brown underprint with a cameo at the centre
Reverse—brown panel with the Bank's office building in Belfast at the centre

		VF	EF
	Signatory: N. J. Shaw		
NI.714a	Prefix CN dated from 5.10.1954 to 5.5.1959	£40	£75
	(printed by Waterlow & Sons Limited)		
NI.714b	Prefix DN dated from 5.7.1961 to 6.12.1965.............................	£40	£75
	(printed by Thomas de la Rue & Co. Ltd.)		

Size 140 mm x 85 mm approximately
Obverse—Brown on a pale brown underprint with a cameo at the centre
Reverse—brown panel with the Bank's head office building at the centre

		EF	UNC
NI.715	*Signatory: J. G. McClay*		
	Prefix DN dated 5.1.1968 to prefix ON dated 5.1.1972.............	£30	£45
	Prefix ZZ—replacement note...	£80	----

Size 140 mm x 85 mm approximately

Obverse—blue and purple on a multicoloured underprint. Portrait of a girl to the right
Reverse—mainly blue. Illustration of Dunluce Castle at the centre

		EF	UNC
NI.716a	*Signatory: J. G. McClay (Manager)*		
	Prefix QN dated 1.1.1977	£35	£45
	Prefix ZY—replacement note	£100	---
NI.716b	*Signatory: F.H.Hollway (Manager)*		
	Prefix QN dated 1.1.1979.	£35	£45
	Prefix ZY—replacement note	£100	---

TEN POUNDS

Size 150 mm x 87 mm approximately

Obverse—black with "£10" in a violet panel at the centre; vignette with Bank building above
Reverse—purple panel with Britannia and Hibernia seated at the centre

		F	VF
NI.721a	*Signatory: Hume Robertson.*		
	Prefix N dated 6.5.1929.		Rare
NI.721b	*Signatory: F. S. Forde.*		
	Prefix N dated 10.12.1934		Rare

Obverse—green with "£10" in a red panel at the centre; vignette with Bank building above
Reverse—red panel with Britannia and Hibernia seated at the centre

		VF	EF
NI.722	*Signatory: G. A. Kennedy*		
	Prefix N dated from 10.10.1938 to 10.4.1946	£180	£280

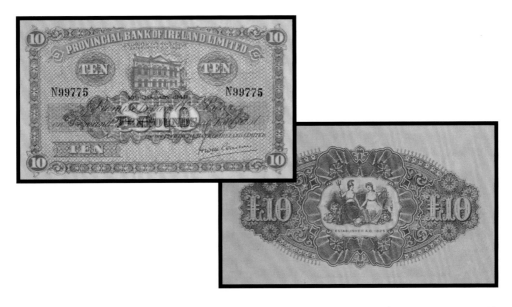

Obverse—green with a mesh background and with "£10" in a red panel at the centre; vignette with Bank building above
Reverse—red panel with Britannia and Hibernia seated at the centre

		VF	EF
NI.723	*Signatory: H. W. M. Clarke*		
	Prefix N dated 10.1.1948	£90	£160

Size 152 mm x 85 mm approximately

Obverse—brown on a multicoloured underprint. Portrait of a young man to the right
Reverse—mainly brown. Illustration of the sinking of the "Girona"

		EF	UNC
NI.724a	*Signatory: J. G. McClay (Manager)*		
	Prefix RN dated 1.1.1977	£55	£75
	Prefix ZY—replacement note...		Rare
NI.724b	*Signatory: F.H.Hollway (Manager)*		
	Prefix RN dated 1.1.1979 and 1.1.1981.......................................	£50	£70
	Prefix ZY—replacement note...		Rare

TWENTY POUNDS

Size 148 mm x 85 mm approximately

Obverse—black with "£20" in a brown panel at the centre; vignette with Bank building above
Reverse—rose-red panel with Britannia and Hibernia seated at the centre

		F	VF
NI.731a	*Signatory: Hume Robertson.*		
	Prefix N dated 6.5.1929.		Rare
NI.731b	*Signatory: G. A. Kennedy*		
	Prefix N dated 20.4.1943 and 20.11.1944	£160	£300

Size 160 mm x 90 mm approximately

Obverse—mauve on a multicoloured underprint; portrait of a mature lady to the right
Reverse—mauve on a multicoloured underprint. Illustration of rock chimney at Lacada Point, Giant's Causeway

		EF	UNC
NI.732	*Signatory: F. H. Hollway (Manager).*		
	Prefix SN dated 1.3.1981	£120	£180
	Prefix ZY—replacement note		probably exists

ONE HUNDRED POUNDS

Size 160 mm x 90 mm approximately

Obverse—green on a multicoloured underprint. Portrait of a mature man to the right
Reverse—green on a multicoloured underprint. Illustration of the Spanish Armada at the centre

	EF	UNC
NI.741 *Signatory: F. H. Hollway (Manager)*		
Prefix TN dated 1.3.1981	£450	----
Prefix ZY—replacement note		probably exists

ULSTER BANK LIMITED

The bank was formed in 1836 by investors who had intended to participate in the establishment of a branch of the National Bank of Ireland in Belfast, but who found the terms offered to them insufficiently inviting. They formed their own bank instead.

The Ulster Bank was acquired by the London County and Westminster Bank Ltd. in 1917, and is now part of the Royal Bank of Scotland group.

EXAMPLES OF EARLY BANKNOTES

ONE POUND

Size 153 mm x 85 mm approximately

Obverse—black with "ONE" in a blue panel at the centre; vignette with sailing ship above Uniface. Multiple rubber stamp overprints reading "ISSUED IN NORTHERN IRELAND AFTER 6TH MAY 1929"

	F	VF

NI.801 *Handsigned.*
No prefix letters—dated 1.3.1926, 1.6.1927, 1.12.1927 .... Rare
(and possibly others).
The rubber stamp was probably applied to any notes dated
prior to 1929 which passed through the Ulster Bank branch
network in Northern Ireland.

Obverse—black with "ONE" in a blue panel at the centre; vignette with sailing ship above. Uniface.

	F	VF

NI.802 *Handsigned.*
No prefix letters – dated from 6.5.1929 to 1.1.1934 .... £60 £100

Obverse—black with "ONE" in a blue panel at the centre; vignette with sailing ship above
Reverse—blue; unframed illustration of the Bank's head office building in Belfast

		F	VF
NI.803	*Handsigned.*		
	No prefix letters—dated from 1.1.1935 to 1.2.1938	£40	£75

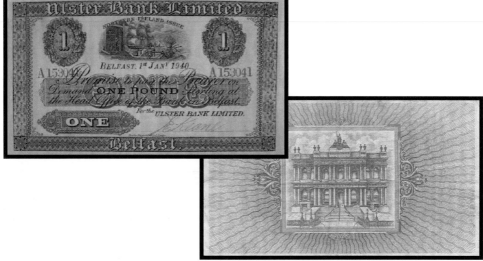

Obverse—black with "ONE" in a blue panel at the centre; vignette with sailing ship above
Reverse—blue; illustration of the Bank's head office building framed in a sunburst pattern

		VF	EF
NI.804a	*Handsigned.*		
	No prefix letters—dated 1.9.1939, and	£45	£80
	Prefix A dated 1.9.1939 and 1.1.1940		
NI.804b	*Signatory: J. R. Williams.*		
	No serial number dated 1.1.1948—specimen only...................		Rare
	Prefix A dated 1.5.1956..	£35	£65

Size 152 mm x 72 mm approximately

Obverse—blue/grey on a multicoloured underprint
Reverse—blue/grey on a red and purple underprint; Coat of Arms at the centre

		EF	UNC
NI.805	*Signatory: J. J. A. Leitch.*		
	No prefix letters—dated 4.10.1966.	£20	£30

Size 135 mm x 67 mm approximately

Obverse—blue/grey on a multicoloured underprint
Reverse—blue/grey on a red and purple underprint; Coat of Arms at the centre

		EF	UNC
NI.806a	*Signatory: A. E. G. Brain (Chief Executive).*		
	Prefix A dated 15.2.1971...	£12	£20
NI.806b	*Signatory: R. W. Hamilton (Chief Executive).*		
	Prefix A dated 1.3.1973 and 1.3.1976..	£6	£9

FIVE POUNDS

Size 205 mm x 115 mm approximately

Obverse—black with "FIVE" in a green panel at the centre; vignette with sailing ship above. Uniface

		F	VF
NI.811	*Handsigned.*		
	No prefix letters – dated 6.5.1929 to 1.1.1934............................	£70	£120

Obverse—black with "FIVE" in a green panel at the centre; vignette with sailing ship above
Reverse—green; unframed illustration of the Bank's head office building in Belfast

		F	VF
NI.812	*Handsigned.*		
	No prefix letters—dated 1.1.1935 to 1.10.1937..........................	£55	£100

Obverse—black with "FIVE" in a green panel at the centre; vignette with sailing ship above.
Reverse—green; illustration of the Bank's head office building framed in a sunburst pattern.

		VF	EF
NI.813a	*Handsigned.* No prefix letters—dated from 1.2.1939 to 1.1.1943	£65	£95
NI.813b	*Signatory: J. R. Williams.* No prefix letters—dated 1.5.1956	£60	£90

Size 141 mm x 85 mm approximately

Obverse—brown on a light multicoloured underprint
Reverse—brown on a multicoloured underprint; Coat of Arms at the centre

		VF	EF
NI.814	*Signatory: J. J. A. Leitch.* No prefix letters—dated 4.10.1966.	£50	£100

Size 145 mm x 78 mm approximately

Obverse—brown on a light multicoloured underprint
Reverse—brown on a multicoloured underprint; Coat of Arms at the centre

		EF	UNC
NI.815a	*Signatory: A. E. G. Brain (Chief Executive)*		
	Prefix B dated 15.2.1971.	£45	£65
NI.815b	*Signatory: R. W. Hamilton (Chief Executive)*		
	Prefix B dated 1.3.1973 to 1.3.1977.	£28	£36
NI.815c	*Signatory: V. Chambers (Chief Executive)*		
	Prefix B dated 1.10.1982 to prefix C dated 1.2.1988	£22	£30

Size 135 mm x 70 mm approximately

Obverse—brown on a multicoloured underprint.
Reverse—brown on a multicoloured underprint; Coat of Arms at the centre

		EF	UNC
NI.816	*Signatory: D. Went (Chief Executive)*		
	Prefix D dated 1.12.1989 to prefix G dated 4.1.1993	£12	£18
	Prefix Z—replacement note		probably exists

Obverse—brown on a multicoloured underprint.
Reverse—brown on a multicoloured underprint; Coat of Arms at the centre

		EF	UNC
NI.817	*Signatory: M. J. Wilson (Group Chief Executive)*		
	Prefix A dated 1.7.1998 to prefix C dated 1.1.2001	---	£10
	Prefix Z—replacement note	---	£25

TEN POUNDS

Size 205 mm x 120 mm approximately

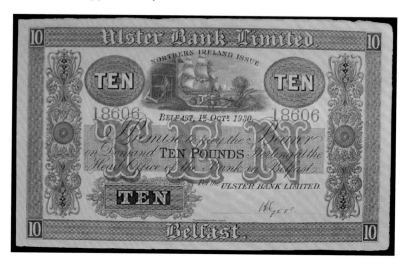

Obverse—black with "TEN" in a red panel at the centre; vignette with sailing ship above
Uniface

		F	VF
NI.821	*Handsigned.*		
	No prefix letters—dated 1.6.1929 to 1.5.1933............................	£90	£180

Obverse—black with "TEN" in a red panel at the centre; vignette with sailing ship above
Reverse—red; unframed illustration of the Bank's head office building

		F	VF
NI.822	*Handsigned.*		
	No prefix letters—dated 1.5.1936..	£90	£180

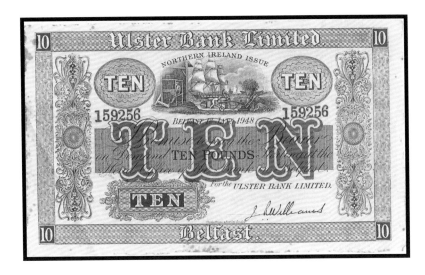

Obverse—black with "TEN" in a red panel at the centre; vignette with sailing ship above
Reverse—red; illustration of the Bank's head office building framed in a sunburst pattern

		VF	EF
NI.823	*Handsigned.* No prefix letters—dated from 1.2.1939 to 1.1.1948	£90	£170

Size 152 mm x 93 mm approximately

Obverse—green on a light multicoloured underprint
Reverse—green on a multicoloured underprint; Coat of Arms at the centre

		VF	EF
NI.824	*Signatory: J. J. A. Leitch.* No prefix letters—dated 4.10.1966.		Rare

Size 151 mm x 85 mm approximately

Obverse—green on a light multicoloured underprint.
Reverse—green on a multicoloured underprint; Coat of Arms at the centre

		EF	UNC
NI.825a	*Signatory: A. E. G. Brain (Chief Executive).* Prefix C dated 15. 2.1971..	£85	£120
NI.825b	*Signatory: R. W. Hamilton (Chief Executive)* Prefix C dated 12.11.1972 to 2.6.1980.	£45	£65
NI.825c	*Signatory: V. Chambers (Chief Executive)* Prefix C dated 1.10.1982 to prefix D dated 1.2.1988..................	£35	£45
NI.825d	*Signatory: D. Went (Chief Executive)* Prefix D and prefix E dated 1.12.1989..	£30	£40

Size 142 mm x 75 mm approximately

Obverse—green on a multicoloured underprint
Reverse—green on a multicoloured underprint; Coat of Arms at the centre

		EF	UNC
NI.826	*Signatory: D. Went (Chief Executive)* Prefix F to prefix H dated 1.12.1990.	£26	£35
	Replacement note—prefix Z	£40	£60

Obverse—green on a multicoloured underprint.
Reverse—green on a multicoloured underprint; Coat of Arms at the centre

		EF	UNC
NI.827a	*Signatory: R. D. Kells (Group Chief Executive).*		
	Prefix A and Prefix B dated 1.1.1997	---	£22
	Prefix Z—replacement note	£25	£40
NI.827b	*Signatory: M. J. Wilson (Group Chief Executive)*		
	Prefix B and prefix C dated 1.7.1999	---	£20
	Prefix Z—replacement note.	£25	£40

TWENTY POUNDS

Size 205 mm x 118 mm approximately

Obverse – black with "TWENTY" in a blue panel at the centre; vignette with sailing ship above
Uniface

	F	VF
NI.831 Handsigned.		
No prefix letters—dated 1.6.1929		Rare

Obverse—black with "TWENTY" in a blue panel at the centre; vignette with sailing ship above
Reverse—blue; illustration of the Bank's head office building framed in a sunburst pattern

	VF	EF
NI.832 Handsigned.		
No prefix letters—dated from 1.3.1941 to 1.1.1948	£180	£350

Size 161 mm x 90 mm approximately

Obverse—purple on a light multicoloured underprint
Reverse—purple on a multicoloured underprint; Coat of Arms at the centre

		EF	UNC
NI.833a	*Signatory: J. J. A. Leitch.* No prefix letter – dated 1.7.1970..		Rare
NI.833b	*Signatory: A. E. G. Brain (Chief Executive).* Prefix D dated 15.2.1971		Rare
NI.833c	*Signatory: R. W. Hamilton (Chief Executive)* Prefix D dated 1.3.1976 and 2.6.1980..	£65	£85
NI.833d	*Signatory: V. Chambers (Chief Executive)* Prefix D dated 1.10.1982 to 1.2.1988..	£50	£70

Size 148 mm x 80 mm approximately

Obverse—purple and blue on a light multicoloured underprint
Reverse—purple on a multicoloured underprint; Coat of Arms at the centre

		EF	UNC
NI.834	*Signatory: D. Went (Chief Executive).* Prefix E and prefix F dated 1.11.1990..	£40	£55

Obverse—purple and mauve on a multicoloured underprint
Reverse—purple on a multicoloured underprint; Coat of Arms at the centre

		EF	UNC
NI.835a	*Signatory: R. D. Kells (Group Chief Executive).*		
	Prefix A and prefix B dated 1.1.1996	£38	£50
NI.835b	*Signatory: M. J. Wilson (Group Chief Executive).*		
	Prefix B dated 1.7.1999 to prefix D dated 1.7.2002	---	£40
	Prefix Z—replacement note.	£45	£65
NI.835b	*Signatory: C. McCarthy (Group Chief Executive).*		
	Prefix D dated 6.1.2004 and ongoing	---	£40
	Prefix Z—replacement note.	£45	£65

FIFTY POUNDS

Size 200 mm x 115 mm approximately

Obverse—black with "FIFTY" in a blue panel at the centre; vignette with sailing ship above
Uniface

	F	VF
NI.841	*Handsigned.*	
	No prefix letters—dated 1.6.1929	Rare

Obverse—black with "FIFTY" in a blue panel at the centre; vignette with sailing ship above
Reverse—blue; illustration of the Bank's head office building framed in a sunburst pattern

	VF	EF
NI.842	*Handsigned.*	
	No prefix letters—dated 1.3.1941 and 1.1.1943	Rare

Size 168 mm x 95 mm approximately

Obverse—green and brown on a light multicoloured underprint
Reverse—green and brown on a multicoloured underprint; Coat of Arms at the centre

		EF	UNC
NI.843	*Signatory: V. Chambers (Chief Executive)*		
	Prefix E dated 1.10.1982.	£150	£220

Size 157 mm x 85 mm approximately

Obverse—green, brown and multicoloured on a light multicoloured underprint
Reverse—mainly green and brown on a multicoloured underprint; Coat of Arms at the centre

		EF	UNC
NI.844	*Signatory: R. D. Kells (Chief Executive).*		
	Prefix D dated 1.1.1997	£85	£100
	Prefix Z—replacement note	£110	£150

ONE HUNDRED POUNDS

Size 203 mm x 120 mm approximately

Obverse—black with "£100" in a blue panel at the centre; vignette with sailing ship above
Uniface

	F	VF
NI.851 *Handsigned.*		
No prefix letters—dated 1.6.1929		Rare

Obverse—black with "£100" in a blue panel at the centre; vignette with sailing ship above
Reverse—blue; illustration of the Bank's head office building framed in a sunburst pattern

	F	VF
NI.852 *Handsigned.*		
No prefix letters—dated 1.3.1941 and 1.1.1943		Rare

Size 157 mm x 100 mm approximately

Obverse—red on a light multicoloured underprint
Reverse—red on a light red and blue underprint; Coat of Arms at the centre

		EF	UNC
NI.853a	*Signatory: R. W. Hamilton (Chief Executive)* Prefix F dated 1.3.1973 and 1.3.1977.	£340	£480
NI.853b	*Signatory: V. Chambers (Chief Executive)* Prefix E dated 1.10.1982.	£280	£400

Size 162 mm x 90 mm approximately
Obverse—purple on a light multicoloured underprint.
Reverse—purple on a light multicoloured underprint; Coat of Arms at the centre

		EF	UNC
NI.854	*Signatory: D. Went (Chief Executive).* Prefix G dated 1.12.1990	£280	£400

The banknotes of Scotland

The first Scottish notes appeared in 1695 in the year of the foundation of the Bank of Scotland and contemporary with the earliest notes of the Bank of England. They were released in values from £5 to £100 sterling; when pound notes appeared in 1704 they were denominated £12 Scots, reflecting the prevailing exchange rate. The Bank's monopoly expired in 1721 and within six years it was faced with a rival with the title of the Royal Bank of Scotland, although the general public referred to them simply as the Old and New Banks.

Both banks originated from a need to put banking on a proper footing and supply paper money for the convenience of the mercantile classes. The third bank, however, appeared in 1746 with the primary objective of stimulating the linen industry, and this was reflected in its name, the British Linen Company which did not change its title to the British Linen Bank until 1906. In the second half of the 18th century smaller banks appeared in various parts of the country, usually confined to a specific locality. Although these banks did much to foster trade and industry in their own areas, the spectacular crash of Douglas Heron & Company in 1772 bankrupted many of the leading families in the south-west of Scotland. Many of the smaller banks, confined to a single town, were fairly ephemeral, remembered by their elusive notes which are now much sought after by collectors of local history as well as notaphilists.

Early in the 19th century, however, there emerged a number of joint-stock banks which were destined to play a major role in the economic development of Scotland. These included the Caledonian Banking Company (1838–1907), the Central Bank (1834–68), the City of Glasgow Bank (1839–79), the Clydesdale Bank (1838), the Commercial Bank (1810–1959), the Eastern Bank (1838–63), the National Bank (1825–1959), the North of Scotland Bank (1836–1950), the Town & County Bank (1825–1908), the Union Bank (1843–1955) and the Western Bank (1832–57). Although the Bank Charter Act of 1844 severely restricted the note-issuing activities of the English provincial banks, the comparable legislation for Scotland a year later enabled the Scottish banks to continue to issue their own notes, although the act banned the foundation of any new note-issuing banks after that date.

Although banking in Scotland was on a sounder footing than in England, the failure of the West of Scotland Bank in 1857 and the City of Glasgow Bank in 1878 both had severe repercussions on the economy of the west of Scotland. The worst effects, so far as the general public possessing notes of these banks was concerned, were mitigated by the undertaking of the National Bank to redeem the notes of the West of Scotland, and by all the other banks acting in concert to redeem the City of Glasgow notes.

As a result of mergers and amalgamations the number of note-issuing banks gradually fell, although by the beginning of the 20th century there were still ten in existence. The Caledonian was absorbed by the Bank of Scotland in 1907 and the Town & County merged with the North of Scotland Bank the following year. In the period after World War II there were further amalgamations. For example, in 1959 the Commercial Bank joined forces with the National Bank to form the National Commercial Bank of Scotland which, in turn, combined with the Royal Bank of Scotland which now acquired the suffix "Limited" inscribed on notes since that date. In the same year the British Linen Bank (acquired by Barclays in 1919) was sold to the Bank of Scotland and the merger was completed the following year.

Of the 19th century joint-stock banks, only the Clydesdale has survived, although it, too, has undergone enormous changes. It was formed in 1838 by the union of the Greenock Union Bank, the Edinburgh & Glasgow Bank, the Eastern Bank and the Dundee Commercial Bank. In 1919 it was acquired by the Midland Bank which four years later also took over the North of Scotland Bank. These banks continued to operate separately until 1950 when they merged to form the Clydesdale & North of Scotland Bank which reverted to the shorter title of the Clydesdale Bank in 1963.

Today, therefore, Scotland enjoys the colourful variety of notes produced by three banks, a far cry from the relatively plain black and white notes of the 18th and early 19th centuries. Although many of the earlier notes were engraved and printed by local firms such as Kirkwood, Lizars and Johnston, later notes were produced by the great English security printers, from Perkins Bacon to De La Rue. Prior to the late 1960s there was no uniformity regarding size or colours but since then both have been brought into line with the notes of the Bank of England. In 1975 James Douglas estimated the total circulation of the three Scottish banks in excess of £250 million, or about 7 per cent of the total for the British Isles. The Royal Bank is now the only Scottish bank to continue issuing pound notes and all three have notes up to £100. Moreover, they have shown a penchant for commemorative notes in recent years, notably the Royal Bank's pounds honouring Alexander Graham Bell, Robert Louis Stevenson and the advent of the Scottish Parliament, and the Clydesdale's £20 notes for the Commonwealth Heads of Government Meeting (1997) and Glasgow and UK City of Architecture and Design (1999), not to mention the series of four £5 notes of 1996 marking the bicentenary of Robert Burns by including verses from his poems.

BANK OF SCOTLAND

Scotland's oldest bank, the Bank of Scotland was founded in 1695 and is thus just a year younger than the Bank of England. During its long history the Bank of Scotland has absorbed the Central Bank of Scotland (1866), the Caledonian Banking Co. Ltd. (1907), and more recently The Union Bank of Scotland Ltd (1955), and the British Linen Bank (1971). Elements of the designs of the banknotes of these two latter Banks can be seen in the contemporary notes of the Bank of Scotland.

ONE POUND

"A" size square notes   (175 mm x 128 mm approximately)

Obverse—brown with a yellow/brown underprint. Royal Arms in a Panel to the left, with the Bank's Coat of Arms towards the top of the note above a grey medallion. Uniface.

		F	VF
SC101a *Signatory: Duncan McNeill (Secretary)*			
Prefix 70/H dated 18.2.1894 to prefix 59/X dated 19.12.1910		£300	£500

		VF	EF
SC101b *Signatory: P. Macdonald (Secretary)*			
Prefix 60/X dated 3.1.1911 to prefix 59/AL dated 24.11.1920.....		£250	£480

SC101c *Signatory: A. J. Rose (Secretary)*			
Prefix 60/AL dated 8.12.1920 to prefix 9/AU dated 16.11.1927.		£230	£420

"B" size notes   (152mm x 84mm approximately)

Obverse—brown and grey with the Royal Coat of Arms in panel at the left; grey and brown medallion at centre.
Reverse—grey; unframed illustration of Head Office building.

SC102 *Signatories: (Lord) Elphinstone (Governor); G.J.Scott* (Treasurer)   *VF*   *EF*
Prefix A dated 1.1.1927 to prefix J dated 17.7.1933 .... £60   £130

Obverse—brown and grey with the Bank's Coat of Arms in panel at the left; grey medallion at centre.
Reverse—grey; framed illustration of Head Office building

SC103a *Signatories: (Lord) Elphinstone (Governor); A. W. M.Beveridge (Treasurer)* *VF*   *EF*
Prefix K dated 15.1.1935 to prefix Q dated 15.9.1937 .... £35   £65

SC103b *Signatories: (Lord) Elphinstone (Governor); J. Macfarlane (Treasurer)*
Prefix R dated 5.1.1939 to prefix Y dated 7.5.1941 .... £25   £50

SC103c *Signatories: (Lord) Elphinstone (Governor); J. B. Crawford (Treasurer)*
Prefix Z dated 2.6.1942 to prefix AA dated 16.10.1943 .... £25   £50

Obverse—brown and grey; no panel at left; larger grey medallion at centre.
Reverse—dark chocolate brown; Bank's Arms at centre.

		VF	EF
SC104	*Signatories: (Lord) Elphinstone (Governor); J.B.Crawford (Treasurer)*		
	Prefix A dated 4.1.1945 to prefix B dated 6.2.1945	£35	£80

Obverse—brown and grey; no panel at left; larger grey medallion at centre.
Reverse—light brown; Bank's Arms at centre.

		EF	UNC
SC105a	*Signatories: (Lord) Elphinstone (Governor); J.B.Crawford (Treasurer)*		
	Prefix B dated 6.2.1945 to prefix R dated 19.11.1952	£25	£40
SC105a	*Signatories: (Lord) Elphinstone (Governor); Sir William Watson (Treasurer)*		
	Prefix R dated 4.9.1953 to prefix T dated 9.11.1953	£30	£45

Obverse—brown with slate blue medallion at centre
Reverse—grey; sailing ship at centre surrounded by thistles.

		EF	UNC
SC106a	*Signatories: (Lord) Elphinstone (Governor); Sir William Watson (Treasurer)*		
	Prefix A dated 1.3.1955 to prefix D dated 4.3.1955	£25	£40
SC106a	*Signatories: Sir John Craig (Governor); Sir William Watson (Treasurer)*		
	Prefix E dated 1.9.1955 to prefix N dated 14.9.1956	£22	£30
SC106a	*Signatories: Lord Bilsland (Governor); Sir William Watson (Treasurer)*		
	Prefix O dated 30.8.1957 to prefix B/A dated 30.11.1960	£22	£30

"C" size notes (150mm x 70mm approximately)

Obverse—brown with slate blue medallion at centre
Reverse—grey; sailing ship at centre surrounded by thistles

SC107a *Signatories: Lord Bilsland (Governor); Sir William Watson (Treasurer)*   *EF*   *UNC*
Prefix A dated 16.11.1961 to prefix N dated 12.12.1962, and......   £20   £28
Prefix A/A dated 3.2.1964 to prefix A/I dated 13.2.1964 (printer's
imprint "LD") £20   £28
Prefix A/J dated 4.5.1965 to prefix A/O dated 11.5.1965 (printers
imprint "LTD" £20   £28

SC107b *Signatories: Lord Polwarth (Governor); J. Letham (Treasurer & General Manager)*
Prefix A/P–A/U dated 1.6.1966 (w/o sorting symbols)............   £18   £28
Prefix A/V–B/C dated 3.3.1967 (with sorting symbols)............   £18   £28

"D" size notes (Size 135mm x 67mm approximately)

Obverse—multicoloured with Bank's Coat of Arms at the centre
Reverse—brown and purple; Shield and thistles flanked by Arms and sailing ship

SC108 *Signatories: Lord Polwarth (Governor); J. Letham (Treasurer & General Manager)*
Prefix A/1 to A/6 dated 17.7.1968; prefix A/7 to A/9 and B/1
to B/4 dated 18.8.1969 ....   £20   £30

Obverse — mainly green; Bank's Arms at the centre, portrait of Sir Walter Scott to the right
Reverse — mainly green; Shield and thistles at centre flanked by sailing ship and Pallas emblem

	EF	UNC
SC109a *Signatories: Lord Polwarth* (Governor); *T.W.Walker* (Treasurer & General Manager)		
Prefix A/1 dated 10.8.1970 to prefix B/20 dated 31.8.1971	£20	£30
Replacement note – prefix Z/1	£50	£80

SC109b *Signatories: Lord Clydesmuir* (Governor); *T.W.Walker* (Treasurer & General Manager)		
Prefix C/1 dated 1.11.1972 to prefix C/27 dated 30.8.1973	£16	£25
Replacement note – prefix Z/1	£50	£80

SC109c *Signatories: Lord Clydesmuir* (Governor); *A. M. Russell* (Treasurer & General Manager)		
Prefix C/28 dated 28.10.1974 to prefix D/1 dated 3.10.1978	£7	£12
Replacement note – prefix Z/1 and Z/2	£30	£55

SC109d *Signatories: Lord Clydesmuir* (Governor); *D. B. Pattullo* (Treasurer & General Manager)		
Prefix D/2 dated 15.10.1979 to prefix D/31 dated 4.11.1980	£7	£10
Replacement note – prefix Z/2 and Z/3	£25	£40

SC109e *Signatories: Sir T. N. Risk* (Governor); *D. B. Pattullo* (Treasurer & General Manager)		
Prefix D/32 to prefix D/42 dated 30.7.1981 (with sorting symbols).	£7	£10
Prefix D/43 dated 7.10.1983 to prefix E/1 dated 18.11.1986 (without symbols)	£5	£9
Replacement note – prefix Z/3	£15	£25

SC109f *Signatories: Sir T. N. Risk* (Governor); *P. Burt* (Treasurer & General Manager)		
Prefix E/1 to prefix E/13 dated 19.8.1988	£3	£5
Replacement note – prefix Z/3	£15	£25

FIVE POUNDS

Size 220mm x 135mm approximately

*Obverse—brown with black value panels. Royal Arms in a panel to the left, with the Bank's Coat of
Arms towards the top of the note above a grey medallion. Uniface.*

	F	*VF*
SC111a *Signatory: D. MacNeill (Secretary)*		
Prefix 17/B dated 5.5.1894 to prefix 8/F dated 17.10.1911		Rare
SC111b *Signatory: P. Macdonald (Secretary)*		
Prefix 9/F dated 18.9.1912 to prefix2/I dated 3.6.1919	£200	£360
SC111c *Signatory: A. J. Rose (Secretary)*		
Prefix 3/I dated 7.10.1920 to prefix 10/L dated 19.5.1931 (approx.)	£180	£330
SC111d *Signatories: Lord Elphinstone (Governor) and G. J. Scott (Treasurer)*		
Prefix 11/L dated 26.6.1931 (approx.) to prefix 4/M dated 25.3.1933	£160	£280
SC111e *Signatories: Lord Elphinstone (Governor) and A. W. M. Beveridge (Treasurer)*		
Prefix 5/M dated17.1.1935 to prefix 8/M dated 23.1.1935	£160	£280

Obverse—brown with black value panels. A Scottish thistle replaces the Royal Shield in the left hand panel. The Bank's Coat of Arms towards the top of the note above a grey medallion. Uniface.

		VF	*EF*
SC112a	*Signatories: Lord Elphinstone* (Governor) *and A. W. M. Beveridge* (Treasurer)		
	Prefix 9/M dated 9.2.1935 to prefix 14/N dated 17.3.1938	£150	£260
SC112b	*Signatories: Lord Elphinstone* (Governor) *and J.Macfarlane* (Treasurer)		
	Prefix 15/N dated 24.4.1939 to prefix 4/P dated 16.10.1941.............	£140	£240
SC112c	*Signatories: Lord Elphinstone* (Governor) *and J. B. Crawford* (Treasurer)		
	Prefix 5/P dated 5.6.1942 to prefix 14/R dated 26.9.1944	£100	£180

Size 178mm x 102mm approximately

Obverse—brown on a light brown underprint. Thistle motif in a panel to the left with the Bank's Arms at the top of the note flanked by brown value panels. Grey medallion lower centre.
Reverse—Dark brown. Bank's Coat of Arms on a lined background with '£5' either side.

SC113	*Signatories: Lord Elphinstone* (Governor) *and J. B. Crawford* (Treasurer)		
	Prefix 1/A dated 3.1.1945 to prefix 10/A dated 2.3.1945	£130	£220

*Obverse—brown on a light brown underprint. Thistle motif in a panel to the left with the Bank's
Arms at the top of the note flanked by brown value panels. Grey medallion lower centre.
Reverse—Light brown. Bank's Coat of Arms on a lined background with '£5' either side.*

VF   EF

SC114   *Signatories: Lord Elphinstone* (Governor) *and J. B. Crawford* (Treasurer) .
Prefix 11/A dated 16.3.1945 to prefix 20/D dated 20.10.1947................   £70   £130

*Obverse—brown on a light brown underprint. Thistle motif in a panel to the left with the Bank's
Arms at the top of the note flanked by black value panels. Grey medallion lower centre.
Reverse—Light brown. Bank's Coat of Arms on a lined background with '£5' either side.*

SC115a   *Signatories: Lord Elphinstone* (Governor) *and J. B. Crawford* (Treasurer)
Prefix 1/E dated 7.11.1947 to prefix 10/M dated 21.11.1952..................   £50   £90

SC115b   *Signatories: Lord Elphinstone* (Governor) *and Sir William Watson* (Treasurer)
Prefix 11/M dated 10.12.1952 to prefix 20/O dated 4.12.1953 ....   £50   £90

*Obverse—brown on a light brown underprint. Thistle motif in a panel to the left with the Bank's
Arms at the top of the note flanked by black value panels. Slate blue medallion lower centre.
Reverse—Light brown. Bank's Coat of Arms on a lined background with '£5' either side.*

SC116a   *Signatories: Lord Elphinstone* (Governor) *and Sir William Watson* (Treasurer)
Prefix 1/A dated 1.3.1955 to prefix 6/D dated 7.4.1955 ....   £40   £70

SC116b   *Signatories: Sir John Craig* (Governor) *and Sir William Watson* (Treasurer)
Prefix 7/D dated 7.4.1955 to prefix 10/G dated 3.9.1955 ....   £40   £70

Obverse—brown on a light brown underprint. Thistle motif in a panel to the left with the Bank's Arms at the top of the note flanked by black value panels. Slate blue medallion lower centre.
Reverse—Dark brown. Redesigned following the merger with the Union Bank. The Bank's Shield at the centre is flanked by two circular panels bearing the Bank's Coat of Arms to the left and the Ship emblem to the right.

	VF	EF
SC117a *Signatories: Sir John Craig* (Governor) *and Sir William Watson* (Treasurer) Prefix 11/G dated 9.4.1956 to prefix 20/L dated 17.4.1956.....................	£30	£60
SC117b *Signatories: Lord Bilsland* (Governor) *and Sir William Watson* (Treasurer) Prefix 1/M dated 1.5.1957 to prefix 20/KA dated 24.5.1960	£25	£45

Size 140mm x 84mm approximately

Obverse—brown on a light brown underprint. Thistle motif in a panel to the left with the Bank's Arms at the top of the note flanked by black value panels. Slate blue medallion lower centre. "£5" values at the bottom of the note are in hollow print.
Reverse—Dark brown. The Bank's shield at the centre is flanked by two circular panels bearing the Bank's Coat of Arms to the left and the ship emblem to the right.

	EF	UNC
SC118 *Signatories: Lord Bilsland* (Governor) *and Sir William Watson* (Treasurer) Prefix 1/A dated 14.9.1961 to prefix 20G dated 22.9.1961	£40	£50

Obverse—brown on a light brown underprint. Thistle motif in a panel to the left with the Bank's Arms at the top of the note flanked by black value panels. Slate blue medallion lower centre. "£5" values at the bottom of the note are in solid print.
Reverse—Dark brown. The Bank's shield at the centre is flanked by two circular panels bearing the Bank's Coat of Arms to the left and the ship emblem to the right.

SC119a *Signatories: Lord Bilsland* (Governor) *and Sir William Watson* (Treasurer) EF UNC
Prefix 1/H dated 25.9.1961 to prefix 15/N dated 14.8.1962................... £30 £40
Prefix A dated 7.10.1963 to prefix D dated 12.1.1965 .... £30 £40

SC119b *Signatories: Lord Polwarth* (Governor) *and Sir William Watson* (Treasurer)
Prefix E dated 7.3.1966 and prefix F dated 8.3.1966 .... £35 £45

SC119c *Signatories: Lord Polwarth* (Governor) *and J. Letham* (Treasurer and General Manager)
Prefix G dated 1.2.1967 and Prefix H dated 2.2.1967 (without symbols) £35 £45
Prefix I dated 1.11.1967 (Sorting symbols added to the reverse)........... £40 £50

Size 146mm x 78mm approximately

Obverse—Multicoloured, blue, brown, green and yellow. Bank's Coat of Arms at the centre.
Reverse—Dark and light green. The Bank's shield at the centre is flanked by two panels bearing the Bank's Coat of Arms to the left and the ship emblem to the right.

EF UNC
SC120 *Signatories: Lord Polwarth* (Governor) *and J. Letham* (Treasurer & General Manager)
Prefix A dated 1.11.1968 to prefix D dated 9.12.1969................................ £70 £90

Obverse—Mainly blue. The Bank's Coat of Arms at the centre with a portrait of Sir Walter Scott to the right

Reverse—Mainly blue. The Bank's shield above thistles at the centre flanked by a sailing ship and Pallas emblem.

		EF	*UNC*
SC121a	*Signatories: Lord Polwarth* (Governor); *T. W. Walker* (Treasurer & General Manager)		
	Prefix A dated 10.8.1970 to prefix K dated 2.9.1971	£45	£70
	Replacement note – prefix ZA	£70	£110
SC121b	*Signatories: Lord Clydesmuir* (Governor); *T. W. Walker* (Treasurer & General Manager)		
	Prefix L dated 4.12.1972 to prefix X dated 5.9.1973	£45	£70
	Replacement note – prefix ZA	£70	£110
SC121c	*Signatories: Lord Clydesmuir* (Governor); *A. M. Russell* (Treasurer & General Manager)		
	Prefix Y and prefix Z dated 4.11.1974, and		
	Prefix AA dated 4.11.1974 to prefix BA dated 19.10.1978	£35	£50
	Replacement note – prefix ZA	£45	£60
SC121d	*Signatories: Lord Clydesmuir* (Governor); *D. B. Pattullo* (Treasurer & General Manager)		
	Prefix BB dated 28.9.1979 to prefix BS dated 28.11.1980	£30	£45
	Replacement note – prefix ZA and ZB	£35	£55
SC121e	*Signatories: Sir T. N. Risk* (Governor); *D. B. Pattullo* (Treasurer & General Manager)		
	Prefix BT dated 27.7.1981 to prefix CK dated 25.6.1982 (with sorting symbols)	£25	£35
	Prefix CL dated 13.10.1983 to prefix DZ dated 29.2.1988 (without symbols)	£18	£25
	Replacement note – prefix ZB	£28	£40

Size 136mm x 70mm approximately

Obverse—Mainly blue. The Bank's Coat of Arms at the centre with a portrait of Sir Walter Scott to the right. The word "STERLING" added
Reverse—Mainly blue. The Bank's shield above thistles at the centre flanked by a sailing ship and Pallas emblem

		EF	*UNC*
SC122a *Signatories: Sir T. N. Risk* (Governer) *and P. Burt* (Treasurer & Chief General Manager)			
Prefix EA to prefix EJ dated 20.6.1990		—	£20
Replacement note – prefix ZB		—	£30
SC122b *Signatories: D. B. Pattullo* (Governor) *and P. Burt* (Treasurer & Chief General Manager)			
Prefix EK dated 6.11.1991 to prefix FB dated 7.1.1994		—	£20
Replacement note – prefix ZB		—	£30

Obverse—Blue and multicoloured. Bank's Arms at the centre of the note with a portrait of Sir Walter Scott to the left.
Reverse—Blue and multicoloured. Illustration entitled "Oil and Energy" at the centre.

		EF	*UNC*
SC123a *Signatories: D. B. Pattullo* (Governor) *and P. Burt* (Treasurer & Chief General Manager)			
Prefix AA to prefix AM dated 4.1.1995		—	£22
Replacement note – prefix ZZ			£25
SC123b *Signatories: D. B. Pattullo* (Governor) *and G. Masterton* (Treasurer & Chief General Manager)			
Prefix AN to prefix AZ dated 13.9.1996		—	£10
Replacement note – prefix ZZ		—	£25
SC123c *Signatories: M. J. Grant* (Governor) *and G. Masterton* (Treasurer & Chief General Manager)			
Prefix BA dated 5.8.1998		—	£10
Replacement note – prefix ZZ		—	£25
SC123d *Signatories: P. Burt* (Governor) *and G. Mitchell* (Treasurer & Managing Director)			
Prefix BS dated 25.6.2002 and ongoing		—	£9
Replacement note – prefix ZZ		—	£25

TEN POUNDS

Size 220mm x 135mm approximately

Obverse—brown with black value panels. Royal Arms in a Panel to the left, with the Bank's Coat of Arms towards the top of the note above a grey medallion. Uniface.

		F	VF
SC131a	*Signatory: D. MacNeill (Secretary)* Prefix 7/A dated 16.10.1894 to prefix 4/B dated 30.9.1909		Rare
SC131b	*Signatory: P. Macdonald (Secretary)* Prefix 5/B dated 20.11.1912 to prefix 8/B dated 5.11.1919	£350	£500
SC131c	*Signatory: A. J. Rose (Secretary)* Prefix 9/B dated 15.8.1921 to prefix 1/C dated 9.3.1929	£350	£500
SC131d	*Signatories: Lord Elphinstone (Governor) and A. W. M. Beveridge (Treasurer)* Prefix 2/C dated 24.1.1935		Rare

Obverse—brown with black value panels. A Scottish thistle replaces the Royal shield in the left hand panel. The Bank's Coat of Arms towards the top of the note above a grey medallion. Uniface.

		VF	EF
SC132a	*Signatories: Lord Elphinstone (Governor) and A. W. M. Beveridge (Treasurer)* Prefix 3/C dated28.1.1938	£280	£450
SC132b	*Signatories: Lord Elphinstone (Governor) and J. B. Crawford (Treasurer)* Prefix 4/C dated 16.7.1942 and prefix 5/C dated 15.10.1942............	£280	£450

Obverse—brown on a light brown underprint. Thistle motif in a panel to the left with the Bank's Arms at the top of the note flanked by black value panels. Slate blue medallion lower centre. Uniface

	VF	EF
SC133 *Signatories: Lord Bilsland* (Governor) *and Sir William Watson* (Treasurer) Prefix 6/C dated 26.9.1963 and prefix 7/C dated 27.9.1963	£180	£280

Size 152mm x 85mm approximately

Obverse—Mainly brown. The Bank's Coat of Arms at the centre with a portrait of Sir Walter Scott to the right
Reverse—Mainly brown. The Bank's shield to the right with the sailing ship and Pallas emblem in round panels.

	EF	UNC
SC134a *Signatories: Lord Clydesmuir* (Governor); *A. M. Russell* (Treasurer & General Manager)		
Prefix A dated 1.5.1974 to prefix N dated 10.10.1979	£50	£65
Replacement note – prefix ZB	£60	£80
SC134b *Signatories: Lord Clydesmuir* (Governor); *D. B. Pattullo* (Treasurer & General Manager)		
Prefix P to prefix W dated 5.2.1981	£50	£65
Replacement note – prefix ZB	£60	£80
SC134c *Signatories: Sir T.N.Risk* (Governor); *D. B. Pattullo* (Treasurer & General Manager)		
Prefix X dated 22.7.1981to prefix CX dated 6.8.1987	£30	£40
Replacement note – prefix ZB	£35	£55
SC134d *Signatories: Sir T. N. Risk* (Governer) *and P. Burt* (Treasurer & Chief General Manager)		
Prefix CX dated 1.9.1989 to prefix EP dated 31.10.1990	£25	£35
Replacement note – prefix ZB	£30	£45

Size 143mm x 75mm approximately

Obverse—Mainly brown. The Bank's Coat of Arms at the centre with a portrait of Sir Walter Scott to the right. The word "STERLING" added
Reverse—Mainly brown. The Bank's shield to the right with the sailing ship and Pallas emblem in round panels

	EF	UNC
SC135 *Signatories: Sir T. N. Risk* (Governer) *and P. Burt* (Treasurer & Chief General Manager)		
Prefix EQ dated 7.5.1992 to prefix GG dated 13.4.1994	£22	£30
Replacement note – prefix ZB and ZC(?)	£40	£55

Obverse—Mainly brown. The Bank's Coat of Arms at the centre with a portrait of Sir Walter Scott to the left
Reverse—Brown and multicoloured. Illustration entitled "Distilling and Brewing" at the centre

	EF	UNC
SC136a *Signatories: D. B. Pattullo* (Governor) *and P. Burt* (Treasurer & Chief General Manager)		
Prefix AA to prefix BM dated 1.2.1995	—	£24
Replacement note – prefix ZZ	£35	£45
SC136b *Signatories: D. B. Pattullo* (Governor) *and G. Masterton* (Treasurer & Chief General Manager)		
Prefix BN to prefix CF dated 5.8.1997	—	£22
Replacement note – prefix ZZ	£35	£45
SC136c *Signatories: M. J. Grant* (Governor) *and G. Masterton* (Treasurer & Chief General Manager)		
Prefix CG to prefix DT dated 18.8.1998	—	£20
Replacement note – prefix ZZ	£35	£45
SC136d *Signatories: Sir John Shaw* (Governor) *and G. Mitchell* (Treasurer & Chief General Manager)		
Prefix DU dated 18.6.2001 and ongoing.	—	£18

TWENTY POUNDS

Size 224mm x 135mm approximately

Obverse—brown with red value panels. Royal Arms in a panel to the left, with the Bank's Coat of Arms towards the top of the note above a grey medallion. Uniface.

		F	VF
SC141a	*Signatory: D. MacNeill (Secretary)* Prefix 5/B dated 26.5.1894 to prefix 6/D dated 2.9.1910..................		Rare
SC141b	*Signatory: P. Macdonald (Secretary)* Prefix 7/D dated 26.10.1911 to prefix 10/E dated 29.12.1920............	£300	£500
SC141c	*Signatory: A. J. Rose (Secretary)* Prefix 1/F date unknown, to prefix 10/F dated 21.6.1932.................	£250	£450
SC141d	*Signatories: Lord Elphinstone (Governor) and G. J. Scott (Treasurer)* Prefix 1/G dated 2.12.1932..	£250	£450
SC141e	*Signatories: Lord Elphinstone (Governor) and A. W. M. Beveridge (Treasurer)* Prefix 2/G dated 11.1.1935 and prefix 3/G dated 16.2.1935..............	£250	£450

Obverse—brown with red value panels. A Scottish thistle replaces the Royal Shield in the left hand panel. The Bank's Coat of Arms towards the top of the note above a grey medallion. Uniface.

		VF	EF
SC142a	*Signatories: Lord Elphinstone (Governor) and A. W. M. Beveridge (Treasurer)* Prefix 4/G dated 28.3.1936 to prefix 7/G dated 22.7.1938................	£350	£550
SC142b	*Signatories: Lord Elphinstone (Governor) and J.Macfarlane (Treasurer)* Prefix 8/G dated 16.5.1939 and prefix 9/G dated 12.9.1939..............	£350	£550
SC142c	*Signatories: Lord Elphinstone (Governor) and J. B. Crawford (Treasurer)* Prefix 10/G dated 5.6.1942 to prefix 5/J dated 11.8.1952..................	£140	£320
SC142d	*Signatories: Lord Elphinstone (Governor) and Sir W. Watson (Treasurer)* Prefix 6/J dated 5.12.1952 to prefix 10/J dated 24.4.1953.................	£120	£280

Obverse—brown with red value panels. Thistle motif in the left hand panel. The Bank's Coat of Arms towards the top of the note above a slate blue medallion. Uniface.

		VF	*EF*
S143a	*Signatories: Sir John Craig* (Governor) *and Sir W. Watson* (Treasurer) Prefix 1/A dated 6.4.1955 to prefix 5/B dated 12.6.1956..................	£80	£140
S143b	*Signatories: Lord Bilsland* (Governor) *and Sir W. Watson* (Treasurer) Prefix 6/B dated 25.3.1958 to prefix 4/H dated 3.10.1963	£70	£120

Size 212mm x 134mm approximately

Obverse—brown with red value panels. Thistle motif in the left hand panel. The Bank's Coat of Arms towards the top of the note above a slate blue medallion. Uniface.

		VF	*EF*
SC144	*Signatories: Lord Polwarth* (Governor) *and J. Letham* (Treasurer) Prefix 5/H to prefix 9/H dated 5.5.1969...	£110	£180

Size 160mm x 90mm approximately

Obverse—Mainly purple. The Bank's Coat of Arms at the centre with a portrait of Sir Walter Scott to the right
Reverse—Purple and red. Illustration of the Bank's head office building at the centre with the shield, sailing ship and Pallas emblem to the left.

		EF	UNC
SC145a	*Signatories: Lord Polwarth* (Governor) *and T. W. Walker* (Treasurer & General Manager)		
	Prefix A dated 1.10.1970..	£100	£180
SC145b	*Signatories: Lord Clydesmuir* (Governor); *T. W. Walker* (Treasurer & General Manager)		
	Prefix A dated 3.1.1973...	£100	£180
SC145c	*Signatories: Lord Clydesmuir* (Governor); *A. M. Russell* (Treasurer & General Manager)		
	Prefix A dated 8.11.1974 and 14.1.1977	£70	£110
SC145d	*Signatories: Lord Clydesmuir* (Governor); *D. B. Pattullo* (Treasurer & General Manager)		
	Prefix A and B dated 16.7.1979, and prefix B dated 2.2.1981	£70	£110
SC145e	*Signatories: Sir T. N. Risk* (Governor); *D. B. Pattullo* (Treasurer & General Manager)		
	Prefix B dated 4.8.1981 to prefix K dated 15.12.1987	£55	£85

Size 150mm x 80mm approximately

Obverse—Mainly purple. The Bank's Coat of Arms at the centre with a portrait of Sir Walter Scott to the right. The word "STERLING" added
Reverse—Purple and red. Illustration of the Bank's head office building at the centre with the shield, sailing ship and Pallas emblem to the left

		EF	UNC
SC146	*Signatories: D. B. Pattullo* (Governor) *and P. Burt* (Treasurer & Chief General Manager)		
	Prefix K dated 1.7.1991 to prefix AU dated 12.1.1993	£40	£60

Obverse—Mainly purple. Bank's Coat of Arms at centre with portrait of Sir Walter Scott to left.
Reverse—Purple, red and brown. Illustration entitled "Education and Research" at the centre.

		EF	UNC

SC147a *Signatories: D. B. Pattullo* (Governor) *and P. Burt* (Treasurer & Chief General Manager)

Prefix AA to prefix AY dated 1.5.1995... — £50
Replacement note – prefix ZZ.. £60 £100

SC147b *Signatories: D. B. Pattullo* (Governor) *and G. Masterton* (Treasurer & Chief General Manager)

Prefix AY dated 25.10.1996 to prefix CE dated 1.4.1998 .... — £40
Replacement note – prefix ZZ.. £60 £100

SC147c *Signatories: M. J. Grant* (Governor) *and G. Masterton* (Treasurer & Chief General Manager)

Prefix CE dated 22.3.1999 .... — £40
Replacement note – prefix ZZ.. £40 £60

SC147d *Signatories:Shaw* (Governor) *and G. Mitchell* (Treasurer & Managing Director)

Prefix CE dated 22.3.1999 .... — £35
Replacement note – prefix ZZ.. £40 £60

FIFTY POUNDS
Size 156mm x 85mm approximately

Obverse—Mainly green. Bank's Coat of Arms at centre with portrait of Sir Walter Scott to left.
Reverse—Green, brown and multicoloured. Illustration entitled "Arts and Culture" at the centre.

SC161a *Signatories: D. B. Pattullo* (Governor) *and P. Burt* (Treasurer & Chief General Manager)

Prefix AA dated 1.5.1995 .... — £95

SC161b *Signatories: M. J. Grant* (Governor) *and G. Masterton* (Treasurer & Chief General Manager)

Prefix AA dated 15.4.1999 and ongoing... — £90

SC161c *Signatories: M. J. Grant* (Governor) *and G. Masterton* (Treasurer & Chief General Manager)

Prefix AA dated 15.4.1999 and ongoing... — £85

ONE HUNDRED POUNDS

Size 220mm x 135mm approximately

Obverse—brown with red value panels. Royal Arms in a panel to the left, with the Bank's Coat of Arms towards the top of the note above a grey medallion. Uniface.

	F	*VF*
SC171a *Signatory: D. MacNeill* (Secretary) Prefix 7/C dated 12.7.1894 to prefix 1/G dated 9.12.1910		rare
SC171b *Signatory: P. Macdonald* (Secretary) Prefix 2/G dated 11.12.1911 to prefix 4/H dated 17.4.1919		Rare
SC171c *Signatory: A. J. Rose* (Secretary) Prefix 5/H dated 7.7.1920, to prefix 8/I dated 8.6.1930.....................		Rare
SC171d *Signatories: Lord Elphinstone* (Governor) *and G. J. Scott* (Treasurer) Prefix 9/I dated 28.5.1932 and prefix 10/I dated 8.11.1932		Rare
SC171e *Signatories: Lord Elphinstone* (Governor) *and A. W. M. Beveridge* (Treasurer) Prefix 1/J dated 8.1.1935 and prefix 2/J dated 31.1.1935		Rare

Obverse—brown with red value panels. A Scottish thistle replaces the Royal Shield in the left hand panel. The Bank's Coat of Arms towards the top of the note above a grey medallion. Uniface.

	VF	*EF*
SC172a *Signatories: Lord Elphinstone* (Governor) *and A. W. M. Beveridge* (Treasurer) Prefix 3/J dated 23.3.1937 and prefix 4/J dated 12.8.1937		Rare
SC172b *Signatories: Lord Elphinstone* (Governor) *and J.Macfarlane* (Treasurer) Prefix 5/J dated 2.4.1940 to prefix 8/J dated 25.9.1942......................		Rare
SC172c *Signatories: Lord Elphinstone* (Governor) *and J. B. Crawford* (Treasurer) Prefix 9/J dated 16.8.1946 to prefix 9/K dated 14.12.1951	£550	£900

Obverse—brown with red value panels. Thistle motif in the left hand panel. The Bank's Coat of Arms towards the top of the note above a slate blue medallion. Uniface.

	VF	*EF*
SC173 *Signatories: Lord Bilsland* (Governor) *and Sir W. Watson* (Treasurer). Prefix 10/K dated 14.9.1956 to prefix 8/N dated 30.11.1962	£400	£700

Size 170mm x 100mm approximately

Obverse—mainly red and orange. Bank's Coat of Arms centre with Sir Walter Scott to right.
Reverse—mainly red. Illustration of the Bank's head office building at the centre with the shield,
sailing ship, Ditat emblem and £100 in the four corners.

	EF	UNC

SC174a *Signatories: Lord Polwarth* (Governor) *and T. W. Walker* (Treasurer & General
Manager)
Prefix A dated 6.12.1971 .... £450 £550

SC174b *Signatories: Lord Clydesmuir* (Governor); *T. W. Walker* (Treasurer & General Manager)
Prefix A dated 6.9.1973 .... £450 £550

SC174c *Signatories: Lord Clydesmuir* (Governor); *A. M. Russell* (Treasurer & General Manager)
Prefix A dated 11.10.1978 .... £400 £500

SC174d *Signatories: Lord Clydesmuir* (Governor); *D. B. Pattullo* (Treasurer & General Manager)
Prefix A dated 26.1.1981 .... £400 £500

SC174e *Signatories: Sir T. N. Risk* (Governor); *D. B. Pattullo* (Treasurer & General Manager)
Prefix A dated 10.6.1982 to prefix A dated 26.11.1986 .... £350 £450

Size 160mm x 90mm approximately

Obverse—mainly red and orange. Bank's Coat of Arms centre with Sir Walter Scott to right. The
word "STERLING" added
Reverse—mainly red. Illustration of the Bank's head office building at the centre with the shield,
sailing ship, Ditat emblem and £100 in the four corners.

	EF	UNC

SC175 *Signatories: D. B. Pattullo* (Governor) *and P. Burt* (Treasurer & Chief General
Manager)
Prefix A dated 24.2.1990 to prefix A dated 9.2.1994 .... £200 £300

Obverse—mainly red. Bank's Coat of Arms centre with Sir Walter Scott to left.
Reverse—red, brown and multicoloured. Illustration entitled "Leisure and Tourism" at the centre.

	EF	*UNC*
SC176a *Signatories: D. B. Pattullo* (Governor) *and P. Burt* (Treasurer & Chief General Manager)		
Prefix AA dated 17.7.1995..	—	£220
Replacement note – prefix ZZ..		Rare
SC176a *Signatories: D. B. Pattullo* (Governor) *and G. Masterton* (Treasurer & Chief General Manager)		
Prefix AA dated 18.8.1997..	—	£190
Replacement note – prefix ZZ..		Rare
SC176a *Signatories: M. J. Grant* (Governor) *and G. Masterton* (Treasurer & Chief General Manager)		
Prefix AA dated 19.5.1999..	—	£190
Replacement note – prefix ZZ..		Rare
SC176a *Signatory: G. Mitchell* (Governor)		
Prefix AA dated 26.11.2003 and ongoing	—	£180
Replacement note – prefix ZZ..		Rare

BRITISH LINEN BANK

Formerly known as The British Linen Company, the Bank was incorporated in 1746 during the reign of George II. The round seal with the figure of Pallas was adopted as the Company's emblem from the outset, and appears on most of the banknotes. In 1906 the name was changed to The British Linen Bank, and the first notes with the new title are dated 1907. Notes of The British Linen Bank were printed initially by Waterlow and Sons Ltd., whose banknote printing business was purchased by Thomas de la Rue in 1961. This change can be seen in the printer's imprint which appears on the notes. The British Linen Bank was merged with the Bank of Scotland in 1970.

ONE POUND

"A" size square notes (150mm x 130mm approximately)

Obverse—Blue with "B.L.B." in large red letters at centre; panel to the left; Royal Coat of Arms at the top. Uniface.

	F	VF
SC201a *Signatories: F. Gordon Brown* (p. Manager) *and handsigned p. Accountant* Prefix T dated 15.1.1907 and prefix U dated 26.12.1907		Rare
SC201b *Signatories: A. S. Aikman* (p. Manager) *and handsigned p. Accountant* Prefix V dated 2.11.1908		Rare
SC201c *Signatories: E. G. Galletley* (p. Manager) *and handsigned p. Accountant* Prefix W dated 15.7.1910 and prefix X dated 11.8.1911	£300	£480
SC201d *Signatories: E. G. Galletley* (p. General Manager) *and handsigned p. Accountant* Prefix Y dated 29.10.1912 and prefix Z dated 17.9.1913	£300	£480

Obverse—Blue with a red sunburst underprint and "B.L.B." in large red letters; panel at left and Royal Arms at top.
Reverse—Blue panel with "DITAT" emblem at centre.

	F	VF

SC201a *Signatories: E. G. Galletley (p. General Manager) and handsigned p. Accountant*
Prefix A dated 23.9.1914 to prefix F dated 5.4.1918 .... £120   £240

SC201a *Signatories: C.J.Grant (p. General Manager) and handsigned p. Accountant*
Prefix H dated 19.8.1919 to prefix L dated 31.7.1924......................... £120   £240

"B" size notes. (150mm x 85mm approximately)

Obverse—Blue with a red sunburst underprint and "B.L.B." in large red letters; panel at left and Royal Arms at top.
Reverse—Blue panel with "DITAT" emblem at centre

	VF	EF

SC203 *Signatory: J. Waugh (Cashier).*
Prefix N dated 1.6.1926 to prefix Z dated 26.1.1933, and £45   £80
Prefix A dated 3.4.1933 to prefix G dated 2.8.1934 .... £45   £80

Obverse—Blue with a red sunburst underprint and "B.L.B." in large red letters; panel at left and the Bank's Coat of Arms at top.
Reverse—Blue panel with "DITAT" emblem at centre.

	VF	EF

SC204 *Signatory: J. Waugh (Cashier).*
Prefix H dated 18. 1.1935 to prefix R dated 26.4.1937 .... £35   £60

Obverse—Blue with a red sunburst underprint and "B.L.B." in large red letters; panel at left and the Bank's Coat of Arms at top. Silk fibres added to paper.
Reverse—Blue panel with "DITAT" emblem at centre.

SC205a *Signatory: J. Waugh (Cashier).*
Prefix S dated 4.7.1937 to prefix Z dated 8.11.1938, and £30   £50
Prefix A dated 12.6.1939 to prefix D dated 13.11.1939, and £30   £50
Prefix E/1 dated 7.3.1940 to prefix U/1 dated 7.4.1944 .... £30   £50

SC205b *Signatory: G.Mackenzie (General Manager)*
Prefix V/1 dated 4.1.1946 to prefix R/2 dated 5.8.1950 .... £25   £40

SC205c *Signatory: A. P. Anderson (General Manager)*
Prefix S/2 dated 4.6.1951 to prefix L/3 dated 12.5.1959 .... £10   £25

Obverse—Blue with a red sunburst underprint and "B.L.B." in large red letters; panel at left and the Bank's Coat of Arms at top. "No." is omitted from the serial number.
Reverse—Blue panel with "DITAT" emblem at centre.

	VF	EF
SC206 *Signatory: A. P. Anderson (General Manager)*		
Prefix M/3 to prefix P/3 dated 15.4.1960.	£14	£28

Obverse—Blue with a red sunburst underprint and "B.L.B." in large red letters; panel at left and the Bank's Coat of Arms at top. Change of printer to Thomas de la Rue & Co. Ltd.
Reverse—Blue panel with "DITAT" emblem at centre.

SC207 *Signatory: A. P. Anderson (General Manager)*
Prefix Q/3 to prefix T/3 dated 30.9.1961 .... £14 £28

"C" size notes. (150mm x 70mm approximately)

Obverse—Blue with a red sunburst underprint and "B.L.B." in large red letters; panel at left and the Bank's Coat of Arms at top.
Reverse—Blue panel with "DITAT" emblem at centre.

	EF	*UNC*
SC208a *Signatory: A. P .Anderson (General Manager)*		
Prefix U/3 to prefix Y/3 dated 31.3.1962..	£25	£35
SC208b *Signatory: T. W. Walker (General Manager)*		
Prefix Z/3 dated 1.7.1963 to prefix P/4 dated 13.6.1967.	£20	£30

Obverse—Blue with a red sunburst underprint and "B.L.B." in large red letters; panel at left and the Bank's Coat of Arms at top—similar to previous issue.
Reverse—Revised blue panel with "ONE" either side of DITAT emblem at centre and sorting symbols added.

SC209 *Signatory: T. W. Walker (General Manager)*		
Prefix Q/4 to prefix T/4 dated 13.6.1967.	£25	£35

"D" size notes. (Size 135mm x 67mm approximately)

Obverse—Blue with multicoloured underprint. Portrait of Sir Walter Scott to the left.
Reverse—Blue panel with "ONE" either side of DITAT emblem at centre.

SC210 *Signatory: T. W. Walker (General Manager)*		
Prefix U/4 dated 29.2.1968 to prefix D/5 dated 20.7.1970.	£20	£30

FIVE POUNDS

Size: 206mm x 130mm approximately

Obverse—Blue with "B.L.B." in large red letters at centre; panel to the left; Royal Coat of Arms at the top. Uniface.

		F	VF
SC211a	*Signatories: handsigned p.Manager and p.Accountant.*		
	Prefix A/3 dated 3.9.1907 to prefix H/3 dated 4.12.1911		Rare
SC211b	*Signatories: handsigned p.General Manager and p.Accountant*		
	Prefix I/3 dated 30.10.1912 to prefix M/3 dated 12.9.1915	£350	£650

Obverse—Blue with a red sunburst underprint and "B.L.B." in large red letters; panel at left and Royal Arms at top.
Reverse—Blue panel with "DITAT" emblem at centre.

		F	VF
SC212	*Signatories: Handsigned p.General Manager and p. Accountant.*		
	Prefix N/3 dated 1.2.1916 to prefix Z/5 dated 3.12.1935	£160	£320

Obverse—Blue with a red sunburst underprint and "B.L.B." in large red letters; panel at left and the Bank's Coat of Arms at top.
Reverse—Blue panel with "DITAT" emblem at centre.

			VF	EF

SC213a *Signatories: A.Dempster (General Manager) and handsigned p. Accountant*
Prefix A/6 dated 20.12.1935 to prefix P/6 dated 30.12.1940 .... £100 £220

SC213b *Signatories: G.Mackenzie (General Manager) and handsigned p. Accountant*
Prefix Q/6 dated 16.7.1941 to prefix B/7 dated 12.1.1943 .... £100 £220

SC213c *Signatories: J.Waugh* (Accountant and Cashier) *and G. Mackenzie* (General Manager)
Prefix C/7 dated 11.2.1943 to prefix O/7 dated 28.1.1944 .... £100 £220

Size 182mm x 100mm approximately

*Obverse—Blue with a red sunburst underprint and "B.L.B." in large red letters; panel at left and the
Bank's Coat of Arms at top.*
Reverse—Blue panel with "DITAT" emblem at centre.

SC214a *Signatories: J. Waugh* (Accountant & Cashier) *and G. Mackenzie* (General Manager)
Prefix P/7 dated 29.5.1944 to prefix U/7 dated 3.11.1944 .... £70 £140

SC214b *Signatory: G. Mackenzie* (General Manager)
Prefix V/7 dated 10.9.1946 to prefix Z/8 dated 2.8.1950 .... £45 £90

SC214c *Signatory: A. P. Anderson* (General Manager)
Prefix A/9 dated 5.12.1950 to prefix Y/11 dated 4.8.1959 .... £35 £70

Size 158mm x 90mm approximately

*Obverse—Blue with a red sunburst underprint and "B.L.B." in large red letters; panel at left and the
Bank's Coat of Arms at top. Printed by De la Rue.*
Reverse—Blue panel with "DITAT" emblem at centre.

SC215 *Signatory: A. P. Anderson* (General Manager)
Prefix Z/11 dated 2.1.1961 and prefix A/12 dated 3.2.1961 .... £60 £130

Size 140mm x 84mm approximately

Obverse—Blue on a red sunburst underprint; portrait of Sir Walter Scott.
Reverse—Revised blue panel with "DITAT" emblem at centre.

	EF	*UNC*
SC216a *Signatory: A. P. Anderson* (General Manager)		
Prefix D/12 dated 21.9.1962 to prefix F/12 dated 19.11.1962..........	£25	£40
SC216b *Signatory: T. W. Walker* (General Manager)		
Prefix G/12 dated 16.6.1964 to prefix I/12 dated 18.8.1964	£25	£40

Size 146mm x 78mm approximately.

Obverse—Blue on a red sunburst underprint; portrait of Sir Walter Scott.
Reverse—Revised blue panel with "DITAT" emblem at centre.

	EF	*UNC*
SC217 *Signatory: T. W. Walker* (General Manager)		
Prefix K/12 dated 22.3.1968 to prefix M/12 dated 24.5.1968..........	£35	£50

TEN POUNDS

Size: 206mm x 130mm approximately

Obverse—Blue with "B.L.B." in large red letters at centre; panel to the left; Royal Coat of Arms at the top. Uniface.

		F	VF
SC221	*Signatories: handsigned p. Manager and p. Accountant.*		
	Prefix S/1 dated 30.1.1907..		Rare

Obverse—Blue with a red sunburst underprint and "B.L.B." in large red letters; panel at left and Royal Arms at top.
Reverse—Blue panel with "DITAT" emblem at centre.

SC222 *Signatories: Handsigned p. General Manager and p. Accountant.*
Prefix T/1 dated 15.2.1916 to prefix V/1 dated 15.3.1920 ....   from £400

TWENTY POUNDS

Size: 206mm x 130mm approximately

Obverse—Blue with "B.L.B." in large red letters at centre; panel to the left; Royal Coat of Arms at the top. Uniface.

		F	VF
SC231	*Signatories: handsigned p. Manager and p. Accountant.*		
	Prefix X/2 dated 2.1.1907 to prefix B/3 dated 31.3.1911		Rare

Obverse—Blue with "B.L.B." in large red letters at centre; panel to the left; Royal Coat of Arms at the top. Uniface.

SC232 *Signatories: handsigned p. General Manager and p. Accountant.*
Prefix C/3 dated 20.10.1912 and prefix D/3 dated 18.11.1912 ....   Rare

Obverse—Blue with a red sunburst underprint and "B.L.B." in large red letters; panel at left and Royal Arms at top.
Reverse—Blue panel with "DITAT" emblem at centre.

SC233 *Signatories: Handsigned p. General Manager and p. Accountant.*
Prefix E/3 dated 3.5.1916 to prefix Z/3 dated 3.10.1935..................   £240   £400

Obverse—Blue with a red sunburst underprint and "B.L.B." in large red letters; panel at left and the Bank's Coat of Arms at top.
Reverse—Blue panel with "DITAT" emblem at centre.

		VF	EF
SC234a	*Signatories: A. Dempster (General Manager) and handsigned p.Accountant.*		
	Prefix A/4 dated 21.7.1939 to prefix D/4 dated 2.8.1940	£200	£350
SC234b	*Signatories: G. Mackenzie (General Manager) and handsigned p. Accountant.*		
	Prefix E/4 dated 25.5.1942 to prefix K/4 dated 24.2.1945	£180	£330

Obverse—Blue with a red sunburst underprint and "B.L.B." in large red letters; panel at left and the Bank's Coat of Arms at top.
Reverse—Blue panel with "DITAT" emblem at centre.

		VF	EF
SC235a	*Signatory: G. Mackenzie (General Manager)*		
	Prefix L/4 dated 2.9.1946 to prefix Q/4 dated 4.8.1949	£170	£280
SC235b	*Signatory: A. P.Anderson (General Manager)*		
	Prefix R/4 dated 12.5.1952 to prefix F/5 dated 11.12.1957	£120	£220

Obverse—Blue with a red sunburst underprint and "B.L.B." in large red letters; panel at left and the Bank's Coat of Arms at top. Printed by De la Rue.
Reverse—Blue panel with "DITAT" emblem at centre.

	VF	EF

SC236 *Signatory: A. P. Anderson* (General Manager)
Prefix G/5 dated 14.2.1962 to prefix I/5 dated 4.4.1962 .... £140   £250

ONE HUNDRED POUNDS

Size: 206mm x 130mm approximately

Obverse—Blue with "B.L.B." in large red letters at centre; panel to the left; Royal Coat of Arms at the top. Uniface.

SC241 *Signatories: handsigned p. Manager and p. Accountant.*
Prefix E/3 dated 3.1.1906 to prefix H/3 dated 15.5.1912 .... Rare

Obverse—Blue with a red sunburst underprint and "B.L.B." in large red letters; panel at left and Royal Arms at top.
Reverse—Blue panel with "DITAT" emblem at centre.

SC242 *Signatories: Handsigned p. General Manager and p. Accountant.*
Prefix I/3 dated 7.1.1916 to prefix N/3 dated 18.7.1933 .... Rare

Obverse—Blue with a red sunburst underprint and "B.L.B." in large red letters; panel at left and the Bank's Coat of Arms at top.
Reverse—Blue panel with "DITAT" emblem at centre.

SC243a *Signatories: A. Dempster (General Manager) and handsigned p.Accountant.*
Prefix O/3 dated 24.6.1935 .... Rare

SC243b *Signatories: G. Mackenzie (General Manager) and handsigned p.Accountant.*
Prefix P/3 dated 4.2.1942 and prefix Q/3 dated 3.3.1943 .... Rare

Obverse—Blue with a red sunburst underprint and "B.L.B." in large red letters; panel at left and the Bank's Coat of Arms at top.
Reverse—Blue panel with "DITAT" emblem at centre.

	VF	EF
SC244 *Signatory: A. P. Anderson (General Manager)* Prefix R/3 dated 6.4.1951 to prefix T/3 dated 27.11.1957	£500	£950

(Actual size 206mm x 130mm)

Obverse—Blue with a red sunburst underprint and "B.L.B." in large red letters; panel at left and the Bank's Coat of Arms at top. Printed by De la Rue.
Reverse—Blue panel with "DITAT" emblem at centre.

SC245 *Signatory: A. P. Anderson (General Manager)* Prefix U/3 dated 9.5.1962 and V/3 dated 1.6.1962..........................	£450	£900

THE CLYDESDALE BANK LIMITED

The Bank was founded in Glasgow in 1838 and expanded rapidly during the 19th century by absorbing a number of other Scottish banks including the Greenock Union Bank, the Edinburgh and Glasgow Bank and the Eastern Bank of Scotland. In 1919 ownership of the Bank passed to the Midland Bank who also purchased the North of Scotland Bank Ltd., but it was not until 1950 that the two Scottish Banks merged to form The Clydesdale & North of Scotland Bank Ltd. In 1987 the Clydesdale Bank was sold by the Midland Bank to the National Australia Bank, and it remains as one the three issuers of paper money in Scotland today.

ONE POUND

"A" size square notes (65mm x 120mm approximately)

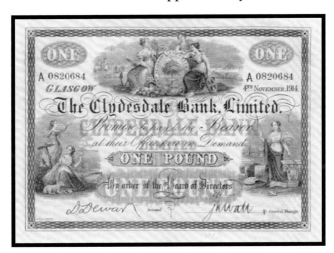

Obverse—black and red. The Arms of Glasgow surrounded by three female figures at the top with further female figure to the left and right; uniface.

		F	VF
SC301	*Signatories: D. Dewar* (Accountant) *and handsigned p. General Manager*		
	From 4.7.1882 to 30.10.1912 without prefix letter, and	£300	£450
	Prefix A dated 8.10.1913 to prefix A dated 9.2.1921.	£160	£270

Obverse—Blue with a red overlay. Similar to previous design with the Arms of Glasgow and female figures
Reverse—Blue. A large panel with the Arms of Glasgow at the centre

SC302a *Signatories: A. Swanson (Cashier) and J. D. Dewar (Accountant)*
Prefix A dated 4.1.1922 and 14.6.1922 ....

	F	VF
	£170	£280

SC302b *Signatories: A. Swanson* (Cashier) *and R. Young* (Accountant)
Prefix A dated 14.3.1923 to prefix A dated 27.10.1926.......................... £150 £240

"B" size notes (152mm x 85mm approximately)

Obverse—Blue with red overlay. Arms of Glasgow with female figures at the top; female figures to the left and right.
Reverse—Blue. A large panel with the Arms of Glasgow at the centre.

SC303a *Signatories: A. Swanson* (Cashier) *and R. Young* (Accountant)
Prefix A dated 3.1.1927 to prefix A dated 7.10.1931...............................

	VF	EF
	£55	£100

SC303b *Signatories: A. Mitchell* (General Manager) *and R. Young* (Accountant & Cashier)
Prefix A dated 2.3.1932 to prefix B dated 24.10.1945............................ £45 £80

SC303c *Signatories: A. Mitchell* (General Manager) *and J. W. Pairmain* (Accountant & Cashier)
Prefix C dated 1.5.1946. .... £65 £120

SC303d *Signatories: J. J. Campbell* (General Manager) *and J. W. Pairmain* (Accountant & Cashier)
Prefix C dated 20.11.1946 to prefix C dated 3.9.1947............................. £35 £60

SC303e *Signatories: J. J. Campbell* (General Manager) *and R. R. Houston* (Accountant & Cashier)
Prefix C dated 7.4.1948 to prefix C dated 14.12.1949 .... £35 £60

FIVE POUNDS

Size 225mm x 125mm approximately

Obverse—black with "Clydesdale Bank Limited" and value panels overlaid in red. Arms of Glasgow at the top of the note; ornate panel to the left. Uniface

F   VF

SC304 *Signatories: D. Dewar (Accountant) and handsigned p. General Manager*
From 4.7.1882 (prefix unknown) to prefix Q_/B dated 9.2.1921.............   Rare

Obverse—blue with "Clydesdale Bank Limited" and value panels overlaid in red. Arms of Glasgow at the top of the note; ornate panel to the left
Reverse—large blue value panel with the Arms of Glasgow at the centre surrounded by "The Clydesdale Bank Limited"

SC305a *Signatories: A. Swanson (Cashier) and J. D. Dewar (Accountant)*   *F   VF*
Prefix Q_/C dated 15.2.1922 to prefix R_/J dated 14.6.1922................   Rare

SC305b *Signatories: A. Swanson (Cashier) and R. Young (Accountant)*
Prefix R_/K dated 31.1.1923 to prefix U_/O dated 9.12.1931..............   £200   £320

SC305c *Signatories: A. Mitchell (General Manager) and R. Young (Accountant & Cashier)* VF   EF
Prefix U_/P dated 16.11.1932 to prefix W_/H dated 27.10.1937, then   £300   £460
printers imprint is added to the bottom left of the note, and
Prefix W_/J dated 25.5.1938 to prefix D_/A dated 24.10.1945 ....   £220   £420

SC305d *Signatories: J. J. Campbell (General Manager) and J. W. Pairmain (Accountant & Cashier).*
Prefix D_/B to prefix D_/R dated 10.7.1946 ....   £220   £420

Obverse—blue with "Clydesdale Bank Limited" and value panels overlaid in red, and with an additional light blue overlay. Arms of Glasgow at the top of the note; ornate panel to the left Reverse—large blue value panel with the Arms of Glasgow at the centre surrounded by "The Clydesdale Bank Limited"

	VF	*EF*
SC306a *Signatories: J. J. Campbell (General Manager) and J. W. Pairmain (Accountant & Cashier)* Prefix AA to prefix AQ dated 3.3.1948..	£250	£450
SC306b *Signatories: J. J. Campbell (General Manager) and R. R. Houston (Accountant & Cashier)* Prefix Prefix AR to prefix BG dated 12.1.1949.	£250	£450

TWENTY POUNDS

Size 225mm x 125mm approximately

Obverse—black with "Clydesdale Bank Limited" and value panels overlaid in red. Arms of Glasgow at the top of the note; ornate panel to the left. Uniface

SC307 *Signatories: D.Dewar (Accountant) and handsigned p. General Manager* From 4.7.1882 (prefix unknown) to prefix P/B dated 9.6.1920	*VF* Rare

Obverse—blue with "Clydesdale Bank Limited" and value panels overlaid in red. Arms of Glasgow at the top of the note; ornate panel to the left
Reverse—large blue value panel with the Arms of Glasgow at the centre surrounded by "The Clydesdale Bank Limited"

SC308a *Signatories: A. Swanson (Cashier) and J. D. Dewar (Accountant).*   *F*   *VF*
       Prefix P/C dated 15.2.1922 to prefix Q/A dated 31.1.1923 ....   Rare

SC308b *Signatories: A. Swanson (Cashier) and R. Young (Accountant).*
       Prefix Q/B dated 2.5.1923 to prefix Q/Z dated 3.6.1931 .... £250   £500

SC308c *Signatories: A. Mitchell (General Manager) and R. Young (Accountant & Cashier). VF*   *EF*
       Prefix R/A dated 16.11.1932 to prefix U/A dated 15.11.1944.................. £320   £550

SC308d *Signatories: J. J. Campbell (General Manager) and J. W. Pairmain (Accountant & Cashier)*
       Prefix U/B to prefix U/J dated 4.6.1947... £320   £550

ONE HUNDRED POUNDS

Size 225mm x 125mm approximately

Obverse—black with "Clydesdale Bank Limited" and value panels overlaid in red. Arms of Glasgow at the top of the note; ornate panel to the left. Uniface

SC309 *Signatories: D. Dewar (Accountant) and handsigned p.General Manager.*   *F*   *VF*
       Final prefix E/V dated 5.8.1914..   Rare

Obverse — blue with "Clydesdale Bank Limited" and value panels overlaid in red. Arms of Glasgow at the top of the note; ornate panel to the left
Reverse — large blue value panel with the Arms of Glasgow at the centre surrounded by "The Clydesdale Bank Limited"

SC310a *Signatories: A. Swanson (Cashier) and J. D. Dewar (Accountant)*   F   VF
    Prefix E/W to prefix F/A dated 15.2.1922..   Rare

SC310b *Signatories: A. Swanson (Cashier) and R. Young (Accountant).*
    Prefix F/B dated 16.12.1925 to prefix F/L dated 3.6.1931 ....   Rare

SC310c *Signatories: A. Mitchell (General Manager) and R. Young (Accountant & Cashier).*
    Prefix F/M dated 19.6.1935 to prefix G/D dated 3.2.1943 ....   Rare

SC310d *Signatories: J. J. Campbell (General Manager) and J. W. Pairmain (Accountant & Cashier).*
    Prefix G/E to prefix G/H dated 26.3.1947 ....   Rare

THE CLYDESDALE & NORTH OF SCOTLAND BANK LIMITED

ONE POUND

"B" size notes (152mm x 85mm approximately)

Obverse—blue/grey with a red/orange underprint. New Coat of Arms at the top of the note; vignettes of shipping and agricultural scenes at the bottom corners.
Reverse—blue with an illustration of a highland river scene.

SC311a *Signatory: J. J. Campbell (General Manager)*..   *VF*   *EF*
     Prefix A dated 1.11.1950 to prefix M dated 1.6.1955, and £15   £35
     Prefix A/N to prefix A/Q dated 1.11.1956...   £15   £35

SC311b *Signatory: R. D. Fairbairn (General Manager)*
     Prefix A/R dated 1.5.1958 to prefix A/U dated 1.11.1960 ....   £15   £35

"C" size notes (152mm x 72mm approximately)

Obverse—mainly green with an orange/brown underprint. Coat of Arms to the right.
Reverse—green; illustration of a ship launching scene.

SC312   *Signatory: R. D. Fairbairn (General Manager)*   *EF*   *UNC*
     Prefix B/A dated 1.3.1961 to prefix B/H dated 1.2.1963..........................   £30   £40

FIVE POUNDS

Size 179mm x 98mm approximately

Obverse—purple on a green and pink underprint. Illustrations of King's College, Aberdeen to the left, and Glasgow Cathedral to the right
Reverse—large purple panel with the new Coat of Arms at the centre with the value to the left and right

		VF	EF
SC313a *Signatory: J. J. Campbell* (General Manager)			
Prefix A dated 2.5.1951 to prefix P dated 1.6.1955, and		£40	£80
Prefix A/Q dated 1.11.1956 to prefix A/X dated 1.2.1958.......................		£40	£80
SC313b *Signatory: R. D. Fairbairn* (General Manager)			
Prefix A/Y, A/Z, A/A and A/B dated 1.3.1960		£40	£80

Size 141mm x 84mm approximately

Obverse—mainly blue with an orange/brown underprint. Coat of Arms to the right.
Reverse—blue; illustration of King's College, Aberdeen.

		VF	EF
SC314 *Signatory: R. D. Fairbairn* (General Manager)			
Prefix B/A dated 20.9.1961 to prefix B/M dated 1.2.1963		£30	£50

TWENTY POUNDS

Size 179mm x 98mm approximately

Obverse—green on a pale yellow underprint. Illustrations of King's College, Aberdeen to the left, and Glasgow Cathedral to the right.
Reverse—large green panel with the new Coat of Arms at the centre with the value to the left and right.

		VF	EF
SC315a *Signatory: J. J. Campbell* (General Manager)			
Prefix A dated 2.5.1951 to prefix B dated 1.2.1958		£70	£120
SC315b *Signatory: R. D. Fairbairn* (General Manager)			
Prefix C dated 1.12.1960 to prefix E dated 1.8.1962		£70	£120

ONE HUNDRED POUNDS

Size 179mm x 98mm approximately

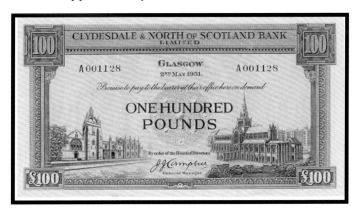

Obverse—blue on a pale yellow/green underprint. Illustrations of King's College, Aberdeen to the left, and Glasgow Cathedral to the right.
Reverse—large blue panel with the new Coat of Arms at the centre with the value to the left and right.

		VF	EF
SC316a *Signatory: J. J. Campbell* (General Manager)			
Prefix A dated 2.5.1951		£350	£650
SC316b *Signatory: R. D. Fairbairn* (General Manager)			
Prefix A dated 1.12.1960		£350	£650

CLYDESDALE BANK LIMITED

ONE POUND

"C" size notes (152mm x 72mm approximately)

Obverse—mainly green with an orange/brown underprint. Coat of Arms to the right.
Reverse—green; illustration of a ship launching scene.

		EF	UNC
SC317a *Signatory: R. D. Fairbairn* (General Manager)			
Prefix C/A dated 2.9.1963 to prefix C/K dated 3.4.1967		£20	£30
SC317b *Sorting symbols added to reverse of the notes*			
Prefix C/L dated 3.4.1967 to prefix C/U dated 1.9.1969		£20	£30

"D" size notes (135mm x 67mm approximately)

Obverse—green with a multicoloured underprint. Portrait of Robert the Bruce to the left.
Reverse—mainly green with an illustration of Robert the Bruce at the battle of Bannockburn.

		EF	UNC
SC318a *Signatory: R. D. Fairbairn* (General Manager)			
Prefix D/A to prefix D/F dated 1.3.1971		£20	£30
SC318a *Signatory: A. R. MacMillan* (General Manager)			
Prefix D/G dated 1.5.1972 to prefix D/Q dated 1.8.1973		£14	£20
SC318a *Signatory: A. R. MacMillan* (Chief General Manager)			
Prefix D/R dated 1.3.1974 to prefix D/BT dated 27.2.1981		£9	£12

FIVE POUNDS

Size 141mm x 84mm approximately

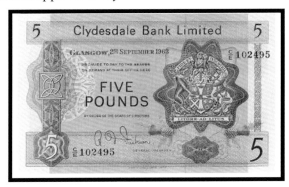

Obverse—mainly blue with an orange/brown underprint. Coat of Arms to the right.
Reverse—blue; illustration of King's College, Aberdeen.

SC319a *Signatory: R. D. Fairbairn (General Manager)*   *EF UNC*
　　　Prefix C/A dated 2.9.1963 to prefix C/R dated 1.5.1967 .... £45　£65

SC319b *Sorting symbols added to reverse of the notes*
　　　Prefix C/S dated 1.5.1967 to prefix C/GG dated 1.9.1969....................... £45　£65

Size 146mm x 78mm approximately

Obverse—blue with a multicoloured underprint. Portrait of Robert Burns to the left.
Reverse—mainly blue. Illustration of a field mouse and wild roses.

SC320a *Signatory: R. D. Fairbairn (General Manager)*   *EF UNC*
　　　Prefix D/A to prefix D/K dated 1.3.1971 .... £45　£65

SC320b *Signatory: A. R. MacMillan (General Manager)*
　　　Prefix D/L dated 1.5.1972 to prefix D/AA dated 1.8.1973............... £45　£65

SC320c *Signatory: A. R. MacMillan (Chief General Manager)*
　　　Prefix D/AB dated 1.3.1974 to prefix D/DX dated 27.2.1981.......... £40　£60

TEN POUNDS

Size 151mm x 93mm approximately

Obverse—mainly brown with a multicoloured underprint. Coat of Arms to the right.
Reverse—brown; illustration of the University of Glasgow.

		EF	UNC
SC321	*Signatory:* R. D. Fairbairn (General Manager)		
	Prefix C/A dated 20.4.1964 to prefix C/D dated 1.12.1967..................	£130	£180

Size 150mm x 85mm approximately

Obverse—brown; portrait of David Livingstone to the left.
Reverse—brown; scene with three African slaves.

		EF	UNC
SC322a	*Signatory:* A. R. MacMillan (General Manager)		
	Prefix D/A dated 1.3.1972 to prefix D/F dated 1.8.1973	£130	£180
SC322b	*Signatory:* A. R. MacMillan (Chief General Manager)		
	Prefix D/G dated 1.3.1974 to prefix D/DZ dated 27.2.1981....................	£120	£160

TWENTY POUNDS

Size 162mm x 93mm approximately

Obverse—mainly red with a multicoloured underprint. Coat of Arms to the right.
Reverse—red; view of George Square, Glasgow.

		EF	UNC
SC323	*Signatory: R. D. Fairbairn* (General Manager)		
	Prefix C/A dated 19.11.1964 to prefix C/H dated 1.12.1967. .... £160		£220

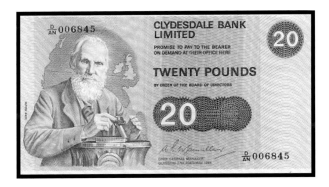

Obverse—purple with a portrait of Lord Kelvin to the left.
Reverse—purple; illustration of Lord Kelvin's lecture room at the University of Glasgow.

		EF	UNC
SC324a	*Signatory: A. R. MacMillan* (General Manager)		
	Prefix D/A to prefix D/J dated 1.3.1972... £180	£180	£280
SC324b	*Signatory: A. R. MacMillan* (Chief General Manager)		
	Prefix D/K dated 2.2.1976 to prefix D/BG dated 27.2.1981............... £160	£160	£240

FIFTY POUNDS

Size 169mm x 95mm approximately

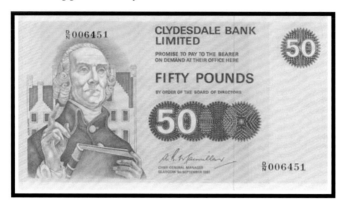

Obverse—olive green with a portrait of Adam Smith to the left.
Reverse—olive green; illustration of a group of old industrial and agricultural tools with sailing ships in the background.

		EF	UNC
SC325	*Signatory: A. R. MacMillan* (Chief General Manager)		
	Prefix D/A to prefix D/Q dated 1.9.1981.	£250	£320

ONE HUNDRED POUNDS

Size 162mm x 93mm approximately

Obverse—mainly purple with a multicoloured underprint. Coat of Arms to the right.
Reverse—purple; river scene with bridge and hills in the background.

		VF	EF
SC326	*Signatory: R. D. Fairbairn* (General Manager)		
	Prefix C/A dated 1.2.1964 to prefix C/B dated 1.2.1968.	£450	£750

Size 169mm x 95mm approximately

Obverse—red with a portrait of Lord Kelvin to the left.
Reverse—mainly red; illustration of Lord Kelvin's lecture room at the University of Glasgow.

SC327a *Signatory: A. R. MacMillan* (General Manager) EF UNC
    Prefix D/A to prefix D/E dated 1.3.1972 .... £450 £650

SC327b *Signatory: A. R. MacMillan* (Chief General Manager)
    Prefix D/F dated 1.2.1976.. £450 £650

CLYDESDALE BANK PLC

ONE POUND

"D" size notes (135mm x 67mm approximately)

Obverse—green with a multicoloured underprint. Portrait of Robert the Bruce to the left.
Reverse—mainly green with an illustration of Robert the Bruce at the battle of Bannockburn.

		EF	UNC
SC328a *Signatory: A. R. MacMillan* (Chief General Manager)			
Prefix D/BU to prefix D/CD dated 29.3.1982...		£9	£12
SC328b *Signatory: A. R. Cole Hamilton* (Chief General Manager)			
Prefix D/CE to prefix D/CR dated 5.1.1983		£7	£10
SC328c *Sorting symbols removed from reverse of the notes*			
Prefix D/CS dated 8.4.1985 to prefix D/DK dated 25.11.1985		£7	£10
Replacement note – prefix D/ZZ...		£25	£35
SC328d *Signatory: A. R. Cole Hamilton* (Chief Executive)			
Prefix D/DL dated 18.9.1987 to prefix D/DW dated 9.11.1988...............		£5	£7
Replacement note – prefix D/ZZ...		£20	£30

FIVE POUNDS

Size 146mm x 78mm approximately

Obverse—blue with a multicoloured underprint. Portrait of Robert Burns to the left.
Reverse—mainly blue. Illustration of a field mouse and wild roses.

		EF	UNC
SC329a *Signatory: A. R. MacMillan* (Chief General Manager)			
Prefix D/DY to prefix D/FP dated 29.3.1982..		£35	£45
SC329b *Signatory: A. R. Cole Hamilton* (Chief General Manager)			
Prefix D/FQ to prefix D/HP dated 5.1.1983.		£35	£45
SC329c *Sorting symbols removed from reverse of the notes*			
Prefix D/HQ to prefix D/JG dated 18.9.1986		£20	£30
SC329d *Signatory: A. R. Cole Hamilton* (Chief Executive)			
Prefix D/JH dated 18.9.1987 to prefix D/LU dated 28.6.1989.................		£20	£30

Size 136mm x 70mm approximately

Obverse—blue with a multicoloured underprint. Revised portrait of Robert Burns to the left.
Reverse—mainly blue. Illustration of a field mouse and wild roses.

		EF	UNC
SC330a *Signatory: A. R. Cole Hamilton* (Chief Executive)			
Prefix E/AA to prefix E/CM dated 2.4.1990..		£14	£20
SC330b *Signatory: F. Cicutto* (Chief Executive)			
Prefix E/CN to prefix E/DN dated 1.9.1994..		£9	£12
Replacement note – prefix D/ZZ..			rare
SC330c *Signatory: F. Goodwin* (Chief Executive)			
Prefix E/DP to prefix E/DY dated 21.7.1996		£9	£12
SC330d *Signatory: G. Savage* (Chief Executive)			
Prefix E/DZ dated 19.6.2002 and ongoing...		—	£10

Obverse—blue with a multicoloured underprint. Portrait of Robert Burns to the left. A set of four notes, to commemorate the 200th anniversary of the poet, Robert Burns. Each note has a different Burns poem printed towards the top left corner.
Reverse—mainly blue. Illustration of a field mouse and wild roses.

These were originally issued as a set with similar serial numbers—
Prefix RB, and with the first digit running sequentially.

		EF	UNC
SC331	*Signatory: F. Goodwin* (Chief Executive)		
	Prefix RB dated 21.7.1996. Set of four notes	—	£60
	Prefix RB dated 21.7.1996. Single note	—	£12

TEN POUNDS

Size 150mm x 85mm approximately

Obverse—brown; portrait of David Livingstone to the left.
Reverse—brown; scene with three african slaves.

		EF	UNC
SC341a	*Signatory: A. R. MacMillan* (Chief General Manager)		
	Prefix D/EA dated 29.3.1982 to prefix D/GV dated 29.3.1982......	£110	£150
SC341b	*Signatory: A. R. Cole Hamilton* (Chief General Manager)		
	Prefix D/GW dated 5.1.1983 to prefix D/PZ dated 18.9.1986.......	£90	£110
	Replacement note – prefix D/ZZ..		Rare
SC341c	*Signatory: A. R. Cole Hamilton* (Chief Executive)		
	Prefix D/QA to prefix D/SW dated 18.9.1987.	£90	£110

Size 150mm x 85mm approximately

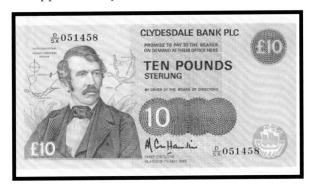

Obverse—brown on a multicoloured underprint. Revised portrait of David Livingstone to the left.
Reverse—mainly brown. Illustration of the birthplace of Livingstone in Blantyre.

		EF	UNC
SC342	*Signatory: A. R. Cole Hamilton* (Chief Executive)		
	Prefix D/SW dated 7.5.1988 to prefix E/GR dated 3.9.1992	£35	£50
	Replacement note – prefix D/ZZ		Rare

Size 143mm x 75mm approximately

Similar to previous issue, but reduced size.

Obverse—brown on a multicoloured underprint. Portrait of David Livingstone to the left.
Reverse—mainly brown. Illustration of the birthplace of Livingstone in Blantyre.

		EF	UNC
SC343a	*Signatory: A. R. Cole Hamilton* (Chief Executive)		
	Prefix E/GR to prefix E/QZ dated 3.9.1992.	£30	£45
	Replacement note – prefix E/ZZ		Rare
SC343b	*Signatory: C. Love* (Chief Executive)		
	Prefix E/QZ to prefix E/VC dated 5.1.1993	£25	£35
	Replacement note – prefix E/ZZ		Rare
SC343c	*Signatory: F. Goodwin* (Chief Executive)		
	Prefix E/VD dated 22.3.1996 to prefix E/WZ dated 27.2.1997	£18	£25
	Replacement note – prefix E/ZZ		Rare

Size 143mm x 75mm approximately

Obverse—brown on a multicoloured underprint. Portrait of Mary Slessor to the left.
Reverse—representation of Mary Slessors missionary work in Africa during the late 19th Century.

SC344a *Signatory: F. Goodwin* (Chief Executive)   *EF UNC*
Prefix A/AA to prefix A/AK dated 1.5.1997..   — £20
Replacement note – prefix E/ZZ.. Rare

SC344b Prefix NAB dated 1.5.1997 .... £60 £85
Notes with prefix NAB were encapsulated in a block of acrylic and issued to
members of the Bank's staff to commemorate 10 years of ownership of the National
Australia Bank. Surplus, un-encapsulated notes were subsequently issued due to a
shortage of new notes, and a few have found their way onto the collectors market.

SC344c *Signatory: J. Wright* (Chief Executive)
Prefix A/AK dated 5.11.1998 to prefix A/CA dated 12.10.1999 .... — £20

SC344d *Signatory: S. Targett* (Chief Executive)
Prefix A/CA to prefix A/CL dated 26.1.2003 .... — £20

SC344e *Signatory: R. Pinney* (Chief Executive)
Prefix A/CL dated 25.4.2003 and ongoing .... — £18

Similar to previous issue with commemorative overprint.

Obverse—brown on a multicoloured underprint. Portrait of Mary Slessor to the left. Overprint to the
right reads "Commemorating the year 2000"
Reverse—representation of Mary Slessors missionary work in Africa during the late 19th Century.

SC345 *Signatory: J. Wright* (Chief Executive)   *EF UNC*
Prefix MM dated 1.1.2000 .... — £18

TWENTY POUNDS

Size 162mm x 93mm approximately

Obverse—purple with a portrait of Lord Kelvin to the left.
Reverse—purple; illustration of Lord Kelvin's lecture room at the University of Glasgow.

		EF	*UNC*
SC351a	*Signatory: A. R. MacMillan* (Chief General Manager) Prefix D/BH to prefix D/BR dated 29.3.1982..	£150	£260
SC351b	*Signatory: A. R. Cole Hamilton* (Chief General Manager) Prefix D/CN dated 5.1.1983 to prefix D/ED dated 8.4.1985.................	£130	£200
SC351c	*Signatory: A. R. Cole Hamilton* (Chief Executive) Prefix D/EE dated 18.9.1987 to prefix D/FV dated 2.8.1990.	£110	£170

Size 162mm x 93mm approximately

Obverse—purple and orange/brown on a multicoloured underprint. Portrait of Robert the Bruce in armour to the left.
Reverse—purple and brown. Illustration of Robert the Bruce in full battle armour on horseback.

		EF	*UNC*
SC352a	*Signatory: A. R. Cole Hamilton* (Chief Executive) Prefix E/AA dated 30.11.1990 to prefix E/NM dated 3.9.1992	£60	£80
	Replacement note – prefix E/ZZ..		Rare
SC352b	*Signatory: C. Love* (Chief Executive) Prefix E/NN to prefix E/SR dated 5.1.1993..	£60	£80
	Replacement note – prefix E/ZZ		Rare

Obverse—purple and orange/brown on a multicoloured underprint. Portrait of Robert the Bruce in armour to the left. Somewhat bolder colours and new design elements added
Reverse—purple and brown. Illustration of Robert the Bruce in full battle armour on horseback. Bolder colours and new design element to the left.

SC353a   *Signatory: F. Ciccutto (Chief Executive)*   *EF*   *UNC*
             Prefix E/SS to prefix F/AX dated 1.9.1994 .... £35   £50
             Replacement note – prefix E/ZZ...   Rare

SC353b   *Signatory: F. Goodwin (Chief Executive)*
             Prefix F/AY to prefix F/BC dated 2.12.1996.................................... ——   £45
             Replacement note – prefix E/ZZ...   Rare

Commemorates the Commonwealth Heads of Government meeting which took place in Edinburgh in October 1997.

Obverse—purple and orange/brown on a multicoloured underprint. Portrait of Robert the Bruce in armour to the left.
Reverse—Illustrations of the Edinburgh International Conference Centre and the new Clydesdale Bank Plaza, with Edinburgh Castle in the background.

SC354   *Signatory: F. Goodwin (Chief Executive)*   *EF UNC*
          Prefix F/BD to F/BF, and prefix C/HG dated 30.9.1997 .... ——   £40

Obverse—purple and orange/brown on a multicoloured underprint. Portrait of Robert the Bruce in armour to the left. Some design elements changed.
Reverse—purple and brown. Illustration of Robert the Bruce in full battle armour on horseback.

		EF	UNC
SC355a	*Signatory: F. Goodwin* (Chief Executive)		
	Prefix A/AA to A/AN dated 1.11.1997.	—	£40
	Replacement note – prefix E/ZZ		Rare
SC355b	*Signatory: J. Wright* (Chief Executive)		
	Prefix A/AR to A/BL dated 12.10.1999	—	£40
SC355c	*Signatory: G. Savage* (Chief Executive)		
	Prefix A/BL to prefix A/BP dated 19.6.2002	—	£35
SC355d	*Signatory: S. Targett* (Chief Executive)		
	Prefix A/BQ to prefix A/BW dated 26.1.2003	—	£35
SC355e	*Signatory: R. Pinney* (Chief Executive)		
	Prefix A/BW dated 25.4.2003 and ongoing	—	£32

Comemorates the 19th Century architect Alexander "Greek" Thomson 1817–75, and Glasgow as the UK City of Architecture and Design, 1999.

Obverse—purple and orange/brown on a multicoloured underprint. Portrait of Alexander "Greek" Thomson to the left.
Reverse—stylised illustration of architecture in Glasgow.

		EF	UNC
SC356	*Signatory: J. Wright* (Chief Executive)		
	Prefix A/AL to A/AQ, and G/AD dated 9.4.1999.	—	£35

Obverse—purple and orange/brown on a multicoloured underprint. Portrait of Robert the Bruce in armour to the left. Similar to the 1999 issue above with additional overprint—"Commemorating the Year 2000".

Reverse—purple and brown. Illustration of Robert the Bruce in full battle armour on horseback.

SC357 *Signatory: J. Wright (Chief Executive)*.. *EF   UNC*
         Prefix MM dated 1.1.2000. .... —   £32

FIFTY POUNDS

Size 169mm x 95mm approximately

Obverse—olive green with a portrait of Adam Smith to the left.
Reverse—olive green; illustration of a group of old industrial and agricultural tools with sailing ships in the background.

SC361 *Signatory: A. R. Cole Hamilton* (Chief Executive).......................................
Prefix D/R dated 3.9.1989 to prefix D/AV dated 20.4.1992.....................

EF   UNC
£120   £200

Size 156mm x 85mm approximately

Obverse—green, brown and multicolour with a portrait of Adam Smith to the left.
Reverse—mainly green and brown; illustration of a group of old Industrial and agricultural tools with sailing ships in the background.

SC362a *Signatory: F. Goodwin* (Chief Executive)
Prefix A/AA and A/CB dated 22.3.1996 ....

EF UNC
— £100

SC362b *Signatory: R. Pinney* (Chief Executive)
Prefix A/CC dated 26.4.2003 and ongoing ....

EF UNC
—   £90

Commemorates 550 years of the University of Glasgow

Obverse—green, brown and multicolour with a portrait of Adam Smith to the left and with an additional overprint—"University of Glasgow 1451 - 2001"
Reverse—mainly green and brown; illustration of a group of old Industrial and agricultural tools with sailing ships in the background.

		EF	UNC
SC363	*Signatory: S. Grimshaw* (Chief Executive)		
	Prefix GU dated 6.1.2001	—	£85

ONE HUNDRED POUNDS

Size 160mm x 90mm approximately

Obverse—mainly red with a portrait of Lord Kelvin to the left.
Reverse—red and yellow; illustration of Lord Kelvin's lecture room at the University of Glasgow.

		EF	UNC
SC371a	*Signatory: A. R. Cole Hamilton* (Chief General Manager)		
	Prefix D/G to prefix D/L dated 8.4.1985	£300	£400
SC371b	*Signatory: A. R. Cole Hamilton* (Chief Executive)		
	Prefix D/M to prefix D/R dated 9.11.1991	£220	£300

Size 162mm x 90mm approximately

Obverse — red, purple and multicolour with a portrait of Lord Kelvin to the left.
Reverse — red, purple and multicolour; illustration of the University of Glasgow.

		EF	UNC
SC372	*Signatory: F. Goodwin* (Chief Executive)		
	Prefix A/AA to prefix A/AD dated 2.10.1996	—	£170

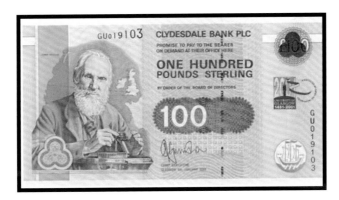

Commemorates 550 years of the University of Glasgow

Obverse — ed, purple and multicolour with a portrait of Lord Kelvin to the left and with an additional
overprint — "University of Glasgow 1451–2001"
Reverse — red, purple and multicolour; illustration of the University of Glasgow.

		EF	UNC
SC373	*Signatory: S. Grimshaw* (Chief Executive)		
	Prefix GU dated 6.1.2001	—	£170

THE COMMERCIAL BANK OF SCOTLAND LIMITED

Founded in 1810 as The Commercial Banking Company of Scotland, the Bank developed during the 19th Century the largest branch system in Scotland. The name was changed to the Commercial Bank of Scotland Limited in 1882 by which time the bank had absorbed the Caithness Bank and the Arbroath Banking Company. In 1959 it amalgamated with the National Bank of Scotland Ltd. to form the National Commercial Bank of Scotland Limited.

ONE POUND

"A" size square notes (160mm x 120mm approximately)

Obverse — mainly black with the value in a yellow and blue underprint. Illustrations of the Bank's principal offices in Edinburgh, Glasgow and London.
Reverse — large blue panel with the Bank's emblem at the centre.

	F	VF
SC401 Signatories: L. M. Mackay (Accountant) and handsigned p. Cashier. Prefix 18/A dated 2.1.1907 to prefix 18/E dated 2.1.1908.		Rare

Obverse — blue on a yellowand light blue underprint. Illustrations of the Bank's principal offices in Edinburgh, Glasgow and London
Reverse — large blue panel with the Bank's emblem at the centre

	F	VF
SC402a Signatories: L. M. Mackay (Accountant) and handsigned p. Cashier. ... Prefix 18/F dated 2.1.1909 to prefix 18/Q dated 3.1.1911.................	£180	£320
SC402b Signatories: L. M. Mackay (Accountant) and G. Riddell (Cashier)		
Prefix 19/A dated 2.1.1912 to prefix 19/Q dated 2.1.1915 (red serial Nos.)	£150	£270
Prefix 20/A dated 2.1.1915 to prefix 20/Q dated 2.1.1917 (black serial Nos.)	£150	£270
Prefix 21/A dated 2.1.1918 (red serial No.).......................................	£160	£290
Prefix 21/B dated 2.1.1918 to prefix 21/I dated 2.1.1923 (black serial Nos.).	£150	£270

Obverse—dark blue on a yellow and red underprint. Portrait of Lord Pitcairn, the first Chairman of the Bank, at lower centre
Reverse—dark blue panel with the Bank's Head Office building at the centre

		F	VF

SC403   *Signatories: R. R. Thomson* (Accountant) *and H. M. Roberts* (Cashier)
Prefix 22/Z dated 31.10.1924 to prefix 22/W dated 1.11.1926........ £180   £280

"B" size notes (150mm x 85mm approximately)

Obverse—dark blue on a yellow and red underprint. Portrait of Lord Pitcairn, the first Chairman of the Bank, at lower centre
Reverse—dark blue panel with the Bank's Head Office building at the centre

	VF	EF

SC404a   *Signatories: R. R. Thomson* (Accountant) *and H. M. Roberts* (Cashier)
Prefix 23A dated 1.12.1927 (Serial letter in Gothic capitals) £70   £160

SC404b   *Signatories: P. Irving* (Accountant) *and R. R. Thomson* (Cashier)
Prefix 23B dated 1.6.1928 to prefix 23C dated 1.12.1928 (Gothic capitals) £45   £90

SC404c   *Signatories: P. Irving* (Accountant) *and R. R. Thomson* (Cashier)
Prefix 23D dated 2.12.1929 to prefix 23Z dated 30.11.1936, ... £25   £60
(Serial letters now in Roman capitals), and
Prefix A/24 dated 2.9.1937 to prefix P/24 dated 4.5.1939.............. £25   £60

SC404d   *Signatories: P. Irving* (Chief Accountant) *and James Thomson* (Cashier)
Prefix Q/24 dated 6.8.1940 to prefix Z/24 dated 4.6.1941, and..... £20   £45
Prefix A/25 dated 4.6.1941, and...................................... £25   £50
Prefix 25B dated 4.6.1941 to prefix 25N dated 2.12.1944 .... £20   £45

Obverse—mainly purple. Portrait of Lord Cockburn in a round panel to the right.
Reverse—purple; large panel with the Bank's Arms at the centre.

		EF	UNC
SC405	*Signatory: Sir J. M. Erskine* (General Manager)		
	Prefix 26A dated 2.1.1947 to prefix 26V dated 2.1.1953	£40	£55

Obverse—mainly blue. Portrait of Lord Cockburn in a round panel to the right
Reverse—blue; large panel with the Bank's Arms at the centre

		EF	UNC
SC405	*Signatory: I. W. Macdonald* (General Manager)		
	Prefix 27A dated 2.1.1954 to prefix 27R dated 2.1.1954	£30	£45

FIVE POUNDS

Size 220mm x 130mm approximately

Obverse—mainly black with the value in a yellow and blue underprint. Illustrations of the Bank's principal offices in Edinburgh, Glasgow and London
Reverse—large blue panel with the Bank's emblem at the centre

	F	VF
SC411 *Signatories: handsigned p. Accountant and handsigned p. Manager*		
Prefix13/A dated 2.1.1908..	Rare	

Obverse—blue on a yellow and light blue underprint. Illustrations of the Bank's principal offices in Edinburgh, Glasgow and London
Reverse—large blue panel with the Bank's emblem at the centre

	F	VF
SC412a *Signatories: handsigned p. Accountant and handsigned p. Manager .....*		
Prefix 13/A dated 2.1.1909 to prefix 13/B dated 2.1.1913	£300	£650
SC412b *Signatories: L. M. Mackay (Accountant) and handsigned p. Manager*		
Prefix 13/C dated 2.1.1913 to prefix 13/M dated 2.1.1923	£280	£550

Size 207mm x 130mm approximately

Obverse—dark blue on a yellow and red underprint. Portrait of Lord Pitcairn, the first Chairman of the Bank, at lower centre
Reverse—dark blue panel with the Bank's head office building at the centre

	F	VF
SC413a *Signatories: R. R. Thomson* (Accountant) *and handsigned p. Manager* Prefix 14/Z dated 31.10.1924 to prefix 14/W dated 1.11.1926.........	£180	£350

	VF	EF
SC413b *Signatories: R. R. Thomson* (Cashier) *and A. Robb* (General Manager) Prefix 14/W dated 1.12.1928 to prefix 14/R dated 1.8.1931.............	£180	£280
SC413c *Signatories: R. R. Thomson* (Cashier) *and Sir J. M. Erskine* (General Manager) Prefix 14/R dated 30.4.1934 to prefix 14/N dated 6.8.1935	£130	£250
SC413d *Signatories: James Thomson* (Cashier) *and Sir J. M. Erskine* (General Manager) Prefix 14/M dated 20.11.1937 to prefix 14/A dated 5.1.1943, and ..	£90	£180
Prefix 15/Z dated 5.1.1943 to prefix 15/M dated 1.12.1944.............	£90	£180

Size 179mm x 102mm approximately

Obverse—mainly purple. Portrait of Lord Cockburn at top flanked by two female figures representing agriculture and shipping.
Reverse—purple. Illustration of an Edinburgh street scene in Victorian times with the Bank's head office building in the background.

		EF	UNC
SC414a	*Signatory: Sir J. M. Erskine* (General Manager)		
	Prefix 16A dated 2.1.1947 to prefix 16Z dated 2.1.1953....................	£60	£85
SC414b	*Signatory: I. W. Macdonald* (General Manager)		
	Prefix 17A dated 2.1.1954 to prefix 17Z dated 2.1.1957, and	£60	£85
	Prefix 18A to prefix 18F dated 2.1.1958	£60	£85

TWENTY POUNDS

Size 220mm x 130mm approximately

Obverse—mainly black with the value in a yellow and blue underprint. Illustrations of the Bank's principal offices in Edinburgh, Glasgow and London
Reverse—large blue panel with the Bank's emblem at the centre

SC421 *Signatories: handsigned p. Accountant and handsigned p. Manager*
Prefix 11/A dated 2.1.1907..   no known examples extant

Obverse—blue on a yellow and light blue underprint. Illustrations of the Bank's principal offices in Edinburgh, Glasgow and London.
Reverse—large blue panel with the Bank's emblem at the centre.

		F	VF
SC422a	*Signatories: handsigned p. Accountant and handsigned p. Manager*		
	Prefix 11/A dated 3.1.1910 to prefix 11/A dated 2.1.1913		Rare
SC422b	*Signatories: L. M. Mackay* (Accountant) *and handsigned p. Manager*		
	Prefix 11/A dated 2.1.1914 to prefix 11/B dated 2.1.1923..................		Rare

Size 207mm x 130mm approximately

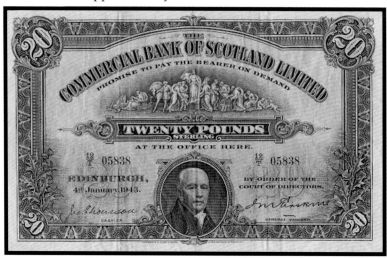

Obverse—dark blue on a yellow and red underprint. Portrait of Lord Pitcairn, the first Chairman of the Bank, at lower centre
Reverse—dark blue panel with the Bank's head office building at the centre

		F	VF
SC423a	*Signatories: R. R. Thomson* (Accountant) *and handsigned p. Manager* Prefix 12/Z dated 31.10.1924 and 1.5.1925...............................		Rare
SC423b	*Signatories: R. R. Thomson* (Cashier) *and A. Robb* (General Manager). Prefix 12/Z dated 1.5.1928 to prefix 12/X dated 1.8.1931.	£250	£450
SC423c	*Signatories: R. R. Thomson* (Cashier) *and Sir J. M. Erskine* (General Manager) Prefix 12/X dated 31.7.1935 to prefix 12/V dated 25.10.1937	£180	£350
SC423d	*Signatories: James Thomson* (Cashier) *and Sir J. M. Erskine* (General Manager) Prefix 12/V dated 2.8.1940 to prefix 12/Q dated 4.1.1943.................	£170	£300

Size 179mm x 102mm approximately

Obverse—mainly blue. Portrait of Lord Cockburn at top flanked by two female figures representing agriculture and shipping
Reverse—blue. Illustration of an Edinburgh street scene in Victorian times with the Bank's head office building in the background

		VF	EF
SC424a	*Signatory: Sir J. M. Erskine* (General Manager) Prefix 13A dated 2.1.1947 to prefix 13KZ dated 2.1.1953.................	£90	£180
SC424b	*Signatory: I. W. Macdonald* (General Manager) Prefix 13K dated 2.1.1954 to prefix 13P dated 2.1.1958.	£80	£160

ONE HUNDRED POUNDS

Size 220mm x 130mm approximately

Obverse—mainly black with the value in a yellow and blue underprint. Illustrations of the Bank's principal offices in Edinburgh, Glasgow and London
Reverse—large blue panel with the Bank's emblem at the centre

SC431   *Signatories: handsigned p. Accountant and handsigned p. Manager*
Prefix 10/A dated 2.1.1907...   no known examples extant

Obverse—blue on a yellow and light blue underprint. Illustrations of the Bank's principal offices in Edinburgh, Glasgow and London.
Reverse—large blue panel with the Bank's emblem at the centre.

SC432a   *Signatories: handsigned p. Accountant and handsigned p. Manager*
Prefix 10/A dated 2.1.1908 to prefix 10/A dated 2.1.1913 ....   Rare

SC432b   *Signatories: L. M. Mackay (Accountant) and handsigned p. Manager*
Prefix 10/A dated 2.1.1914 to prefix 10/A dated 2.1.1923 ....   Rare

Size 207mm x 130mm approximately

Obverse—dark blue on a yellow and red underprint. Portrait of Lord Pitcairn, the first Chairman of the Bank, at lower centre.
Reverse—dark blue panel with the Bank's head office building at the centre.

	F	VF
SC433a *Signatories: R. R. Thomson (Accountant) and handsigned p. Manager.* Prefix 11/Z dated 31.10.1924 and 1.12.1928.		Rare
SC433b *Signatories: R. R. Thomson (Cashier) and A. Robb (General Manager).* Prefix 11/Z dated 30.9.1937..	£500	£900
SC433c *Signatories: James Thomson (Cashier) and Sir J. M. Erskine (General Manager)* Prefix 11/Z dated 1.8.1940 to prefix 11/Y dated 2.1.1943.	£400	£800

Size 179mm x 102mm approximately

Obverse—mainly green. Portrait of Lord Cockburn at top flanked by two female figures representing agriculture and shipping.
Reverse—green. Illustration of an Edinburgh street scene in Victorian times with the Bank's head office building in the background.

	VF	EF
SC434 *Signatory: Sir J. M. Erskine (General Manager)* Prefix 12A dated 2.1.1947 to prefix 12B dated 2.1.1953	£500	£850

TREVOR JONES

THE NATIONAL BANK OF SCOTLAND LIMITED

The National Bank of Scotland was founded in 1825 and rapidly developed a branch system throughout Scotland. It absorbed the Commercial Banking Company of Aberdeen in 1833 and the Perth Union Bank in 1836. The title of the Bank was changed to The National Bank of Scotland Limited in 1882. In 1959 it merged with the Commercial Bank of Scotland Ltd. to form the National Commercial Bank of Scotland Limited.

ONE POUND

"A" size square notes (160mm x 120mm approximately)

Obverse—black lettering on a blue design with a red and yellow sunburst underprint. Royal Coat of Arms at the centre of the note; portrait of the Marquess of Lothian to the left and view of Edinburgh castle to the right.
Reverse—blue Elaborate panel with a view of Edinburgh at the centre.

		F	VF
SC501a	*Signatories: Thomas Shaw* (p. Manager) *and handsigned p. Accountant* Prefix A dated 2.1.1893 to prefix D dated 2.1.1905.		Rare
SC501a	*Signatories: W. Samuel* (p. General Manager) *and handsigned p. Accountant* Prefix F dated 15.5.1908 to prefix L dated 15.5.1919...........................	£140	£280
SC501a	*Signatories: W. Samuel* (p. General Manager) *and A. McKissock* (Accountant) Prefix L dated 11.11.1919 to prefix N dated 15.5.1924	£120	£250
SC501a	*Signatories: W. Lethbridge* (Cashier) *and A. McKissock* (Accountant) Prefix N dated 15.5.1925 to prefix O dated 1.7.1926...........................	£120	£250

"B" size notes (150mm x 85mm approximately)

Obverse—black on a red and yellow sunburst underprint. Royal Arms at the centre; illustrations of Glasgow Cathedral to the left and the Palace of Holyroodhouse to the right.
Reverse—large brown panel on a red and yellow sunburst underprint with a view of Edinburgh at the centre.

		VF	EF
SC502a	*Signatory: W. Lethbridge (Cashier)*		
	Prefix A/A dated 2.11.1927 to prefix A/C dated 1.11.1929................	£60	£100
SC502b	*Signatory: George Drever (Cashier)*		
	Prefix A/D dated 2.2.1931	£60	£100
	Change of printer from Waterlow & Sons Ltd to W. & A.K.Johnston Ltd.		
SC502c	Prefix A/D dated 2.2.1931 to prefix A/F dated 11.11.1933................	£45	£80

Obverse—black on a red and yellow sunburst underprint. Bank's Coat of Arms at the centre; illustrations of Glasgow Cathedral to the left and the Palace of Holyroodhouse to the right.
Reverse—large brown panel on a red and yellow sunburst underprint with a view of Edinburgh at the centre.

		VF	EF
SC503a	*Signatory: George Drever (Cashier)*		
	Prefix A/G dated 12.11.1934 to prefix A/S dated 1.5.1942................	£20	£40
SC503b	*Signatory: J. T. Leggat (General Manager)*		
	Prefix A/T dated 15.3.1943 to prefix A/V dated 15.6.1946	£20	£40
		EF	UNC
SC503c	*Signatory: J. A. Brown (General Manager)*		
	Prefix A/W dated 1.3.1947 to prefix B/G dated 2.1.1953	£30	£45
	Change of printer's imprint to W. & A. K.Johnston & G. W. Bacon Ltd.		
SC503d	Prefix B/H dated 1.6.1953 to prefix B/K dated 1.10.1954.................	£25	£35
SC503e	*Signatory: D. Alexander (General Manager)*		
	Prefix B/L dated 1.3.1955 to prefix B/Z dated 2.2.1959, and	£25	£35
	Prefix C/A dated 1.5.1959		Rare

FIVE POUNDS

Size 210mm x 126mm approximately

Obverse—blue with a red and yellow underprint. Royal Coat of Arms at the centre of the note; portrait of the Marquess of Lothian to the left and view of Edinburgh Castle to the right.
Reverse—blue. Elaborate panel with a view of Edinburgh at the centre.

		F	VF
SC511a	*Signatories: handsigned p.General Manager and handsigned p. Accountant.* Prefix A dated 15.5.1909 to prefix A dated 15.5.1918 .... £200		£380
SC511b	*Signatories: W. Samuel* (p. General Manager) *and handsigned p. Accountant* Prefix A dated 11.11.1919 and prefix A dated 8.7.1920 .... £180		£340
SC511c	*Signatories: W. Lethbridge* (Cashier) *and handsigned p. Accountant* Prefix A dated 1.7.1927 to prefix A dated 11.11.1930........................ £140		£280
SC511d	*Signatories: George Drever* (Cashier) *and handsigned p. Accountant* Prefix A dated 11.11.1932. .... £120		£230

Obverse—blue with a red and yellow underprint. The Bank's Coat of Arms at the centre of the note; portrait of the Marquess of Lothian to the left and view of Edinburgh Castle to the right.
Reverse—blue, elaborate panel with a view of Edinburgh at the centre.

		VF	EF
SC512a	*Signatories: George Drever* (Cashier) *and handsigned p.Accountant* Prefix A and Prefix B dated 1.7.1936	£150	£250
SC512b	*Signatories: George Drever* (Cashier) *and A. A. Bremner* (Accountant) Prefix B dated 1.8.1939 to prefix B dated 1.3.1941	£130	£220
SC512c	*Signatories: George Drever* (Cashier) *and A. A. Bremner* (Chief Accountant) Prefix B dated 6.7.1942	£120	£220
SC512d	*Signatories: George Drever* (Cashier) *and J. T. Leggatt* (General Manager) Prefix B dated 11.1.1943	£110	£200
SC512e	*Signatories: A.S.O.Dandie* (Cashier) *and J. T. Leggatt* (General Manager) Prefix B dated 3.1.1944 to prefix C dated 2.1.1945	£100	£180
SC512f	*Signatories: A.S.O.Dandie* (Cashier) *and J.A.Brown* (General Manager) Prefix C dated 3.6.1947 to prefix D dated 1.5.1954	£60	£120
SC512g	*Signatories: A.S.O.Dandie* (Cashier) *and D.Alexander* (General Manager) Prefix D dated 1.7.1955 to prefix E dated 31.12.1956	£60	£120

Size 178mm x 102mm approximately

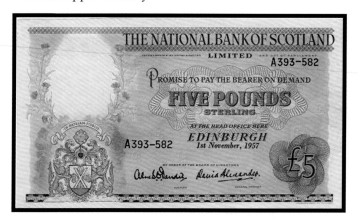

Obverse — green, Bank's Coat of Arms to the bottom left with thistles above.
Reverse — green, illustration of the Forth rail bridge.

		EF	UNC
SC513	*Signatories: A.S.O.Dandie* (Cashier) *and D.Alexander* (General Manager) Prefix A and prefix B dated 1.11.1957	£60	£90

TWENTY POUNDS

Size 210mm x 126mm approximately

Obverse — blue with a red yellow and pink underprint. Royal Coat of Arms at the centre of the note; portrait of the Marquess of Lothian to the left and view of Edinburgh Castle to the right. Reverse — blue. Elaborate panel with a view of Edinburgh at the centre.

		F	VF
SC521a	*Signatories: handsigned p.General Manager and handsigned p. Accountant* Prefix A dated 1.8.1914.		Rare
SC521b	*Signatories: W. Lethbridge* (Cashier) *and handsigned p. Accountant* Prefix A dated 1.3.1928 and 2.1.1930.	£300	£450
SC521c	*Signatories: George Drever* (Cashier) *and handsigned p. Accountant* Prefix A dated 11.11.1932.	£300	£450

Obverse—blue with a red yellow and pink underprint. The Bank's Coat of Arms at the centre of the note; portrait of the Marquess of Lothian to the left and view of Edinburgh Castle to the right. Reverse—blue, elaborate panel with a view of Edinburgh at the centre.

		VF	EF
SC522a	*Signatories: George Drever* (Cashier) *and handsigned p. Accountant* Prefix A dated 16.5.1935 to prefix A dated 1.4.1941	£360	£500
SC522b	*Signatories: A. A. Bremner* (Chief Accountant) *and handsigned p. Cashier* Prefix A dated 8.12.1941 and 6.7.1942	£360	£500
SC522c	*Signatories: George Drever* (Cashier) *and J. T. Leggatt* (General Manager) Prefix A dated 11.1.1943	£360	£500
SC522d	*Signatories: A. S. O. Dandie* (Cashier) *and J. T. Leggatt* (General Manager) Prefix A dated 1.6.1944 and 2.1.1945	£340	£460
SC522e	*Signatories: A. S. O. Dandie* (Cashier) *and J. A. Brown* (General Manager) Prefix A dated 2.6.1947 to prefix A dated 1.5.1954	£300	£450
SC522f	*Signatories: A. S. O. Dandie* (Cashier) *and D. Alexander* (General Manager) Prefix A dated 31.12.1956	£320	£430

Size 178mm x 102mm approximately

Obverse—red, bank's Coat of Arms to the bottom left with thistles above.
Reverse—red, illustration of the Forth rail bridge.

		VF	EF
SC523	*Signatories: A. S. O. Dandie* (Cashier) *and D. Alexander* (General Manager) Prefix A dated 1.11.1957	£90	£170

ONE HUNDRED POUNDS

Size 210mm x 126mm approximately

Obverse—blue with a red yellow and pink underprint. Royal Coat of Arms at the centre of the note; portrait of the Marquess of Lothian to the left and view of Edinburgh Castle to the right. Reverse—blue. Elaborate panel with a view of Edinburgh at the centre.

SC531 *Signatories: handsigned p. General Manager and handsigned p. Accountant.* Prefix A dated 16.5.1935. .... Rare

Obverse—blue with a red yellow and pink underprint. The Bank's Coat of Arms at the centre of the note; portrait of the Marquess of Lothian to the left and view of Edinburgh Castle to the right. Reverse—blue, elaborate panel with a view of Edinburgh at the centre.

SC532a *Signatories: George Drever* (Cashier) *and J. T. Leggat* (General Manager) Prefix A dated 11.1.1943 .... Rare

SC532b *Signatories: A. S. O. Dandie* (Cashier) *and J. A. Brown* (General Manager) Prefix A dated 2.6.1947 to prefix A dated 1.3.1952............................... Rare

SC532c *Signatories: A. S. O. Dandie* (Cashier) *and D. Alexander* (General Manager) Prefix A possibly exists.. Rare

Size 178mm x 102mm approximately

Obverse—green, bank's Coat of Arms to the bottom left with thistles above.
Reverse—green, illustration of the Forth rail bridge.

	VF	EF
Signatories: A. S. O.Dandie (Cashier) *and D. Alexander* (General Manager) Prefix A dated 1.11.1957..	£550	£950

THE NATIONAL COMMERCIAL BANK OF SCOTLAND LTD

The National Commercial Bank of Scotland Limited was formed in 1959 as the result of a merger between The Commercial Bank of Scotland Ltd. and the National Bank of Scotland Ltd. It was the largest bank in Scotland at that time. Its lifespan however was limited as in 1970 it merged with the Royal Bank of Scotland to form the Royal Bank of Scotland Limited.

ONE POUND
"B" size notes (152mm x 84mm approximately)

Obverse—blue; illustration of the Forth rail bridge
Reverse—blue; large panel with the Bank's Coat of Arms at the centre

	EF	UNC

SC601   *Signatory: D. Alexander* (General Manager)
Prefix A to prefix 1F dated 16.9.1959 .... £18   £25

"C" size notes (152mm x 72mm approximately)

Obverse—green; illustration of the Forth rail bridge
Reverse—green; large panel with the Bank's Coat of Arms at the centre

	EF	UNC

SC602a *Signatory: D. Alexander* (General Manager*)*
Prefix A dated 1.11.1961 to prefix 2F dated 4.1.1966 .... £18   £25
SC602b Electronic sorting symbols added to the reverse.
Prefix 2G to prefix 2T dated 4.1.1967 .... £20   £30

"D" size notes (136mm x 68mm approximately)

Obverse—green; illustration of the Forth rail bridge with the new Forth road bridge in the background
Reverse—green; large panel with the Bank's Coat of Arms at the centre

		EF	UNC
SC603	*Signatory: J. B. Burke* (General Manager)		
	Prefix A to prefix K dated 4.1.1968..	£20	£30

FIVE POUNDS

Size 178mm x 102mm approximately

Obverse—mainly green; Bank's Coat of Arms at lower right
Reverse—green; illustration of the Forth rail bridge

		EF	UNC
SC611	*Signatory: D. Alexander* (General Manager)		
	Prefix A to prefix G dated 16.9.1959..	£30	£45

Size 159mm x 90mm approximately

Similar to previous issue but smaller size
Obverse—mainly green; Bank's Coat of Arms at lower right
Reverse—green; illustration of the Forth rail bridge

		EF	UNC
SC612	*Signatory: D. Alexander (General Manager)*		
	Prefix G to prefix J dated 3.1.1961...	£70	£90

Size 140mm x 85mm approximately

Obverse—blue on a multicoloured underprint. Bank's coat of Arms at lower centre
Reverse—blue; view of Edinburgh with the Castle in the background

		EF	UNC
SC613a	*Signatory: D. Alexander (General Manager)*		
	Prefix A dated 2.1.1963 to prefix N dated 1.8.1966.............................	£30	£40
SC613b	*Signatory: J. B. Burke (General Manager)*		
	Electronic sorting symbols added to the reverse.		
	Prefix N to prefix R dated 4.1.1968...	£40	£55

TEN POUNDS

Size 150mm x 90mm approximately

Obverse—brown on a multicoloured underprint. Bank's coat of Arms at bottom centre
Reverse—illustration of the Tay road bridge with Dundee in the background

		EF	UNC
SC621	*Signatory: D. Alexander (General Manager)*		
	Prefix A dated 18.8.1966..	£650	£850

TWENTY POUNDS

Size 178mm x 102mm approximately

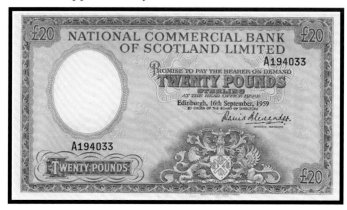

Obverse — mainly green; Bank's Coat of Arms at lower right
Reverse — green; illustration of the Forth rail bridge

	EF	*UNC*
SC631 *Signatory: D. Alexander* (General Manager)		
Prefix A dated 16.9.1959	£140	£190

A second printing, also prefix A and dated 1.6.1967 was prepared but not issued. One or two have come on to the market in the intervening years but they remain very rare.

ONE HUNDRED POUNDS

Size 178mm x 102mm approximately

Obverse — mainly purple; Bank's Coat of Arms at lower right
Reverse — purple; illustration of the Forth rail bridge

	VF	*EF*
SC641 *Signatory: D. Alexander* (General Manager)		
Prefix A dated 16.9.1959	£650	£900

THE NORTH OF SCOTLAND &
TOWN & COUNTRY BANK LIMITED

The North of Scotland Banking company was founded in Aberdeen in 1836. In 1907 the Bank merged with the Town & County Bank Limited, and from 1910 issued notes under the heading The North of Scotland & Town & County Bank Limited. In 1923 the name reverted to The North of Scotland Bank Ltd. which remained until 1950 when the Bank merged with the Clydesdale bank Ltd. to form The Clydesdale & North of Scotland Bank Limited.

ONE POUND

"A" size square notes (174mm x 130mm approximately)

Obverse—black printing on a blue design with a yellow underprint. Illustration of the Marischal College in Aberdeen at top centre with three Coats of Arm in a panel to the left
Reverse—blue and yellow; Bank's Coat of Arms at the centre

	F	VF
SC701a *Signatories: handsigned p. Accountant and p. General Manager.* Prefix A dated 1.3.1910 to prefix B dated 1.3.1916	£280	£420
SC701b *Signatories: handsigned p. Accountant and Mitchell Stuart (p. General Manager).* Prefix C dated 1.3.1918	£280	£420

		F	VF
SC701c	*Prefix C dated 1.3.1918 with rubber stamp overprint in red, reading "Now the North of Scotland Bank Limited" (This rubber stamp overprint may exist on earlier dates)*	£280	£420

		F	VF
SC701c	*Prefix C dated 1.3.1918 with printed overprint in black, reading "Now the North of Scotland Bank Limited"*..............................	£280	£450

FIVE POUNDS

Size 217mm x 135mm approximately

Obverse—black printing on a blue design with a yellow underprint. Illustration of the Marischal College in Aberdeen at top centre with three Coats of Arm in a panel to the left
Reverse—blue and yellow; Bank's Coat of Arms at the centre. Later notes have the denomination "£5" printed six times on the reverse

	F	VF
SC702a *Signatories: handsigned p.Accountant and p.General Manager* Prefix A dated 1.3.1910 to prefix A dated 1.3.1918....................................	£320	£480
SC702b *Prefix A dated 1.3.1918 with rubber stamp overprint in red, reading "Now the North of Scotland Bank Limited"* .... (*This rubber stamp overprint may exist on earlier dates*)	£320	£480
SC702c *Prefix A dated 1.3.1918 and 1.3.1921 with printed overprint in black, reading "Now the North of Scotland Bank Limited"*	£350	£500

TWENTY POUNDS

Size 217mm x 135mm approximately

Obverse—black printing on a blue design with a yellow underprint. Illustration of the Marischal College in Aberdeen at top centre with three Coats of Arm in a panel to the left
Reverse—blue and yellow; Bank's Coat of Arms at the centre

	F	VF
SC703a *Signatories: handsigned p.Accountant and p.General Manager.* Prefix A dated 1.3.1910 to prefix A dated 1.3.1918...	£480	£850
SC703b *Prefix A dated 1.3.1918 with rubber stamp overprint in red,* .... *reading "Now the North of Scotland Bank Limited"* (*This rubber stamp overprint may exist on earlier dates*)	£480	£850
SC703c *Prefix A dated 1.3.1918 and 1.3.1921with printed overprint in black, reading "Now the North of Scotland Bank Limited"*	£480	£850

ONE HUNDRED POUNDS

Whilst £100 notes in this series were almost certainly printed and issued, no issued example has ever been seen. Specimens dated 1910 and 1921 exist.

THE NORTH OF SCOTLAND BANK LIMITED

ONE POUND

"B" size notes (155mm x 85mm approximately)

Obverse—black printing on a blue design with a yellow underprint. Illustration of the Marischal College in Aberdeen at top centre with three Coats of Arm in a panel to the left. Value panels with "£1"
Reverse—blue and yellow; Bank's Coat of Arms at the centre

	F	VF
SC710a *Signatories: handsigned p. Accountant and Mitchell Stuart* (p. General Manager)		
Prefix D dated 1.3.1924 to prefix E dated 1.3.1926..............................	£130	£220
SC710b *Signatories R.W.W. (Accountant) and Mitchell Stuart* (p. General Manager)		
Prefix E and prefix F dated 1.3.1926	£130	£220

Obverse—black printing on a blue design with a yellow underprint. Illustration of the Marischal College in Aberdeen at top centre with three Coats of Arm in a panel to the left. Value panels with "1"
Reverse—blue and yellow; Bank's Coat of Arms at the centre

	VF	EF
SC711a *Signatories R.W.W. (Accountant) and Mitchell Stuart* (p. General Manager)		
Prefix F dated 1.3.1928 to prefix H dated 1.3.1932.	£60	£90
SC711b *Signatories: J.D.P. (Accountant) and R.W.Wath* (p. General Manager).		
Prefix J dated 1.3.1935	£60	£90

Obverse—blue on a pale yellow underprint. Illustration of King's College, Aberdeen at the centre.
Reverse—blue on a pale yellow underprint. Bank's Coat of Arms at the centre

		VF	EF
SC712a	*Signatory: Harvey Smith (General Manager)*		
	Prefix A dated 1.7.1938 to prefix C dated 1.7.1940............................	£25	£50
SC712b	*Signatory: G. L. Webster (General Manager)*		
	Prefix D dated 1.7.1945 to prefix F dated 1.7.1949............................	£25	£50

FIVE POUNDS

Size 215mm x 135mm approximately

Obverse—black printing on a blue design with a yellow underprint. Illustration of the Marischal College in Aberdeen at top centre with three Coats of Arm in a panel to the left
Reverse—blue and yellow; Bank's Coat of Arms at the centre with the denomination "£5" printed six times around it

		F	VF
SC713	*Signatory: handsigned p. Accountant and Harvey Smith (General Manager)*		
	Prefix A dated 2.3.1925...	£380	£500

Size 191mm x 130mm approximately

Obverse—black printing on a blue design with a yellow underprint. Illustration of the Marischal Col-lege in Aberdeen at top centre with three Coats of Arm in a panel to the left
Reverse—blue and yellow; Bank's Coat of Arms at the centre with the denomination "5" printed five times around it

		VF	EF
SC714a	*Signatory: handsigned p. Accountant and Harvey Smith* (General Manager) Prefix A dated 1.3.1928 to prefix A dated 1.3.1932............................ £90		£180
SC714b	*Signatory: Thomas Brown* (Accountant) *and Harvey Smith* (General Manager) Prefix A dated 1.3.1934 .... £90		£180

Size 180mm x 98mm approximately

Obverse—red; illustration of King's College, Aberdeen at the centre
Reverse—red; Bank's Coat of Arms at the centre

		VF	EF
SC715a	*Signatory: Harvey Smith* (General Manager) Prefix AE dated 1.7.1940 to prefix AC dated 1.7.1944 .... £70		£150
SC715b	*Signatory: G. L. Webster* (General Manager) Prefix DE dated 1.7.1947 to prefix EE dated 1.7.1949 .... £70		£150

TWENTY POUNDS

Size 190mm x 130mm approximately

Obverse—black printing on a purple design with an olive underprint. Illustration of the Marischal College in Aberdeen at top centre with three Coats of Arm in a panel to the left
Reverse—purple and olive; Bank's Coat of Arms at the centre with the denomination "20" printed five times around it

		F	VF
SC716	*Signatory: handsigned p.Accountant and Harvey Smith* (General Manager)		
	Prefix A dated 1.3.1930 and 1.3.1934 .... £200		£360

Size 181mm x 98mm approximately

Obverse—green on a light mauve underprint; illustration of King's College, Aberdeen at the centre
Reverse—green on a light mauve underprint; Bank's Coat of Arms at the centre

		VF	EF
SC717a	*Signatory: Harvey Smith* (General Manager)		
	Prefix AT to ET dated 1.7.1940. .... £100		£170
SC717b	*Signatory: G.L.Webster* (General Manager)		
	Prefix FT dated 1.7.1943 to prefix PT dated 1.7.1949 .... £100		£170

ONE HUNDRED POUNDS

Size 190mm x 130mm approximately

Obverse—black printing on a brown design with a green and brown underprint. Illustration of the Marischal College in Aberdeen at top centre with three Coats of Arms in a panel to the left
Reverse—brown and green; Bank's Coat of Arms at the centre with the denomination "100" printed five times around it

		F	VF
SC718	*Signatory: handsigned p. Accountant and Harvey Smith* (General Manager)		
	Prefix A dated 1.3.1930 and 1.3.1934..	£800	£1400

Size 181mm x 98mm approximately

Obverse—dark purple on a light purple underprint; illustration of King's College, Aberdeen at the centre
Reverse—dark purple on a light purple underprint; Bank's Coat of Arms at the centre

		F	VF
SC719	*Signatory: Harvey Smith* (General Manager)		
	Prefix AC to EC dated 1.7.1940...	£500	£800

THE ROYAL BANK OF SCOTLAND

The Royal Bank of Scotland was founded in 1727 and immediately competed strongly with the already well established Bank of Scotland. It took over the Dundee Banking Company in 1864, and then in the 1920's and 1930's acquired several English Banks—namely Drummonds Bank in 1924, Williams Deacons Bank as well as the Western Branch of the Bank of England in 1930, and Glyn Mills & Co. in 1939. More recently, it merged with the National Commercial Bank of Scotland Ltd. in 1969 when it became The Royal Bank of Scotland Limited.

ONE POUND

"A" size square notes (65mm x 120mm approximately)

Obverse—blue on a yellow background with R.B.S. in brown/red letters at the centre. Portrait of George I flanked by Lion and Unicorn at the top. Female figures in the bottom corners. Uniface

		F	EF
SC801a	*Signatories: W. Templeton* (Accountant) *and handsigned p. Cashier*		
	Prefix P dated 2.2.1888 (and perhaps earlier) to prefix Z dated ?		
	Prefix A dated 1.11.1900 to prefix H dated 3.1.1908	£220	£380
SC801b	*Signatories: D. S. Lunan* (Accountant) *and handsigned p. Cashier*		
	Prefix H dated 5.5.1908 to prefix Z dated 29.6.1919, and		
	Prefix A dated 24.3.1920	£160	£300
SC801c	*Signatories: D. Speed* (Accountant) *and handsigned p. Cashier*		
	Prefix A dated 14.5.1920 to prefix M dated 14.5.1926	£130	£250

"B" size notes (152mm x 85mm approximately)

Obverse—blue on a yellow background with a red/brown underprint. Portrait of George I flanked by Lion and Unicorn at the top. Female figures in the bottom corners
Reverse—blue panel with illustrations of the Bank's head office buildings in Edinburgh and Glasgow

		VF	EF
	Signatories: D. Speed (Accountant) and handsigned p. Cashier		
SC802a	Suffix A dated 2.2.1927 (just over 100,000 notes issued, then		Rare
SC802b	Prefix A dated 2.2.1927 to prefix L dated 24.12.1936	£45	£80
SC802c	*Signatory: D. Speed* (Chief Accountant)		
	Prefix A/1 dated 2.1.1937 to prefix G/1 dated 1.7.1942, also	£35	£70
	Prefix D/1 with suffix A dated 1.9.1939 .... only one known		
SC802d	*Signatory: T. Brown* (Chief Accountant).		
	Prefix H/1 dated 1.3.1943 to prefix T/1 dated 1.7.1951....................	£25	£55
SC802e	*Signatory: J. D. C. Dick* (Chief Accountant).		
	Prefix U/1 dated 16.7.1951 to prefix X/1 dated 1.11.1952, then		
	change of printer's imprint to "W. and A. K. Johnston and G. W. Bacon Ltd., Edinburgh".		
SC802f	Prefix Y/1 dated 1.4.1953 and Z/1 dated 1.8.1953, and		
	Prefix AA dated 1.12.1953 to prefix AE dated 3.1.1955....................	£25	£45

Obverse—blue/black on a darker yellow background with a red/brown underprint. Portrait of George I flanked by Lion and Unicorn at the top. Female figures in the bottom corners
Reverse—blue/black panel with illustrations of the Bank's head office buildings in Edinburgh and Glasgow

		EF	UNC
SC803	*Signatory: W. R. Ballantyne* (General Manager)		
	Prefix AF dated 1.4.1955 to prefix BS dated 1.7.1964......................	£20	£28

"C" size notes (152mm x 72mm approximately)

Obverse—blue/black on a yellow background with a red/brown underprint. Portrait of George I flanked by Lion and Unicorn at the top. Female figures in the bottom corners
Reverse—blue/black panel with illustrations of the Bank's head office buildings in Edinburgh and Glasgow

		EF	UNC
SC804a	*Signatory: W. R. Ballantyne* (General Manager) Prefix CA dated 1.8.1964 to prefix CG dated 1.6.1965........................	£18	£25
SC804b	*Signatory: G. P. Robertson* (General Manager) Prefix CH dated 2.8.1965 to prefix CX dated 1.11.1967......................	£18	£25

"D" size notes (135mm x 67mm approximately)

Obverse—mainly green on a multicoloured underprint. Portrait of David Dale to the left
Reverse—mainly green with illustrations of the Bank's head offices in Edinburgh and Glasgow

		EF	UNC
SC805	*Signatory: G. P. Robertson* (General Manager) Prefix A/1 to prefix A/24 dated 1.9.1967.	£18	£25

FIVE POUNDS

Size 228mm x 128mm approximately

Obverse—blue on a yellow background with red/brown overprint. Blue panel to the left; portrait of George I flanked by Lion and Unicorn at the top. Uniface

	F	EF
SC806a *Signatories: handsigned p. Accountant and p. Cashier.*		
Various handwritten dates:		
Prefix D to 26.12.1907		Rare
Prefix E from 23.12.1909 to 3.1.1922	£200	£350
SC806b *Signatories: D. Speed* (Accountant) *and handsigned p. Cashier*	*VF*	*EF*
Prefix E dated 29.6.1923 to 10.1.1942	£180	£300
SC806c *Signatories: W. Whyte* (Cashier & General Manager) *and D. Speed* (Chief Accountant)		
Signatories: I. M. Thomson (Cashier & General Manager) *and T. Brown* (Chief Accountant)		
Prefix F dated 1.7.1942 to 16.10.1950	£100	£260

Size 178mm x 104mm approximately

Obverse—blue on a yellow background with red/brown overprint. Blue panel to the left; portrait of George I flanked by Lion and Unicorn at the top. Uniface. Similar to previous issue

	EF	UNC
SC807a *Signatories: I. M. Thomson* (Cashier & General Manager) *and J. D. C.Dick* (Chief Accountant)		
Prefix G dated 2.1.1952 to 1.7.1953	£90	£130
SC807b *Signatories: W. A. Watt and W. R. Ballantyne* (joint Chief Cashiers and General Managers) *and J. D. C. Dick* (Chief Accountant)		
Prefix G dated 1.7.1953 and 1.3.1955	£100	£150
SC807c *Signatories: W. R. Ballantyne* (Cashier & General Manager) *and A. G. Campbell* (Chief Accountant)		
Prefix G dated 1.4.1955 to 3.1.1963	£90	£130

Size 146mm x 78mm approximately

Obverse—blue on a yellow background with red/brown overprint. Blue panel to the left; portrait of George I flanked by Lion and Unicorn at the top. Uniface. Similar to previous issue

	EF	UNC
SC808a *Signatories: W. R. Ballantyne* (Cashier & General Manager) *and A. G. Campbell* (Chief Accountant)		
Prefix H dated 2.11.1964	£80	£120
SC808b *Signatories: G. P. Robertson* (Cashier & General Manager) *and A. G. Campbell* (Chief Accountant)		
Prefix H dated 2.8.1965 and 1.10.1965.	£80	£120

Obverse—mainly blue on a multicoloured underprint. Portrait of David Dale to the left
Reverse—blue. Illustration on the Bank's head office in Edinburgh

	EF	UNC
SC809 Signatories: G. P. Robertson (General Manager) and A. G. Campbell (Chief Accountant)		
Prefix J/1 dated 1.11.1966 to prefix J/5 dated 1.3.1967 .... £55		£80

TEN POUNDS

Size 228mm x 128mm approximately

Obverse—blue on a yellow background with red/brown overprint. Blue panel to the left; portrait of
George I flanked by Lion and Unicorn at the top. Uniface

	F	VF
SC810 Signatories: handsigned p. Accountant and p. Cashier		
Various hand written dated, including:		
Prefix C dated 3.3.1914 to 10.4.1917, and		Rare
Prefix D dated 5.4.1921 to 1.8.1940	£450	£700

TWENTY POUNDS

Size 228mm x 128mm approximately

Obverse—blue on a yellow background with red/brown overprint. Blue panel to the left; portrait of George I flanked by Lion and Unicorn at the top. Uniface

		F	VF
SC811a	*Signatories: handsigned p. Accountant and p. Cashier*		

SC811a   *Signatories: handsigned p. Accountant and p. Cashier*
Various hand written dated, including:
Prefix C to 1912 ....   Rare
Prefix D from 1912 to 3.1.1947 (the earlier notes have higher
values) ....*from £150*   £340

SC811b   *Signatories: I.M.Thomson (Cashier & General Manager) and T.Brown*
(Chief Accountant)   *VF*   *EF*
Prefix E dated 1.7.1947 to 2.7.1951 ....   £180   £320

SC811c   *Signatories: I. M. Thomson (Cashier & General Manager) and J. D. C. Dick*
(Chief Accountant)
Prefix F dated 1.12.1952 ....   £150   £280

SC811d   *Signatories: W. R. Ballantyne (General Manager) and A. G. Campbell*
(Chief Accountant)
Prefix G dated 1.5.1957 ....   £150   £280

SC811e   *Signatories: G. P. Robertson (General Manager) and A. G. Campbell*
(Chief Accountant)
Prefix H ....   possibly exists

ONE HUNDRED POUNDS

Size 228mm x 128mm approximately

Obverse—blue on a yellow background with red/brown overprint. Blue panel to the left; portrait of George I flanked by Lion and Unicorn at the top. Uniface

	F	VF
SC812a *Signatories: handsigned p. Accountant and p. Cashier*		
Various hand written dated, including:		
Prefix C to 1912		Rare
Prefix D from 1912 to 1.8.1940 (perhaps later).................................. from £500		£750
SC812b *Signatories: I. M. Thomson* (Cashier & General Manager) *and T. Brown* (Chief Accountant)		
Prefix E dated 1.10.1949	£450	£750
	VF	EF
SC812c *Signatories: W. R. Ballantyne* (General Manager) *and A. G. Campbell* (Chief Accountant)		
Prefix F dated 1.10.1960	£550	£950

SC813 *Signatories: G. P. Robertson* (General Manager) *and A. G. Campbell* (Chief Accountant)		
Prefix G dated 3.2.1966..	£450	£850

THE ROYAL BANK
OF SCOTLAND LIMITED

ONE POUND

"D" size notes (135mm x 67mm approximately)

Obverse—mainly green. Illustration of the Forth road and rail bridges
Reverse—green, Bank's Coat of Arms at the centre

		EF	UNC
SC814a	*Signatories: A. P. Robertson and J. B. Burke* (General Managers) Prefix A/1 to prefix A/45 dated 19.3.1969..	£14	£20
SC814b	*Signatory: J. B. Burke* (Managing Director) Prefix A/46 to prefix A/68 dated 15.7.1970......................................	£14	£20

Obverse—green on a multicoloured underprint. Bank's Arms to the right
Reverse—green, illustration of Edinburgh Castle

		EF	UNC
SC815	*Signatory: J. B. Burke* (Managing Director) Prefix A/1 dated 5.1.1972 to prefix C/57 dated 1.5.1981..................	£10	£15

FIVE POUNDS

Size 146mm x 79mm approximately

Obverse—blue on a multicoloured underprint. Bank's Arms to the left
Reverse—blue, view over Edinburgh with the Castle at the centre

		EF	UNC
SC816a	*Signatories: A. P. Robertson and J. B. Burke* (General Managers) Prefix A/1 to prefix A/14 dated 19.3.1969	£40	£60
SC816b	*Signatory: J. B. Burke* (Managing Director) Prefix A/15 to prefix A/19 dated 15.7.1970.	£40	£60

Obverse—blue on a multicoloured underprint. Bank's Arms to the right
Reverse—blue, illustration of Culzean Castle

		EF	UNC
SC817	*Signatory: J. B. Burke* (Managing Director) Prefix A/1 dated 5.1.1972 to prefix B/13 dated 1.5.1981	£35	£50

TEN POUNDS

Size 151mm x 84mm approximately

Obverse—brown on a multicoloured underprint. Bank's Coat of Arms at bottom centre
Reverse—brown, illustration of the Tay bridge

	EF	UNC

SC818   *Signatories: A. P. Robertson and J. B. Burke* (General Managers)
Prefix A/1 dated 19.3.1969 .... £120   £180

Obverse—brown on a multicoloured underprint. Bank's Coat of Arms to the right
Reverse—brown, illustration of Glamis Castle

	EF	UNC

SC819   *Signatory: J. B. Burke* (Managing Director)
Prefix A/1 dated 5.1.1972 to prefix A/49 dated 1.12.1981................. £75   £95

TWENTY POUNDS

Size 160mm x 90mm approximately

Obverse—purple on a multicoloured underprint. Bank's Coat of Arms at bottom centre
Reverse—purple, illustration of the Forth road and rail bridges

		EF	UNC
SC820	*Signatories: A. P. Robertson and J. B. Burke* (General Managers)		
	Prefix A/1 dated 19.3.1969	£150	£220

Obverse—purple on a multicoloured underprint. Bank's Coat of Arms to the right.
Reverse – purple. Illustration of Brodick Castle

		EF	UNC
SC821	*Signatory: J. B. Burke* (Managing Director)		
	Prefix A/1 dated 5.1.1972 to prefix A/6 dated 1.5.1981	£120	£180

ONE HUNDRED POUNDS

Size 160mm x 90mm approximately

Obverse — red on a multicoloured underprint. Bank's coat of Arms at bottom centre
Reverse — red, illustration of the Forth road and rail bridges

	EF	UNC
SC822 *Signatories: A. P. Robertson and J. B. Burke* (General Managers)		
Prefix A/1 dated 19.3.1969		Rare

Obverse — red on a multicoloured underprint. Bank's coat of Arms to the right
Reverse — red, illustration of Balmoral Castle

	EF	UNC
SC823 *Signatory: J. B. Burke* (Managing Director)		
Prefix A/1 dated 5.1.1972 to 1.5.1981	£600	£850

THE ROYAL BANK
OF SCOTLAND PLC

ONE POUND

"D" size notes (135mm x 67mm approximately)

Obverse—green on a multicoloured underprint. Bank's Arms to the right
Reverse—green, illustration of Edinburgh Castle

		EF	UNC
SC831a	*Signatory: C. R. Winter* (Managing Director)		
	Prefix C/58 to prefix C/66 dated 3.5.1982	£14	£20
	Sorting symbols removed from reverse.		
SC831b	Prefix C/67 dated 1.10.1983 to prefix D/32 dated 3.1.1985	£7	£10
SC831c	*Signatory: C. R. Winter* (Chief Executive)		
	Prefix D/33 to prefix D/67 dated 1.5.1986	£4	£7
SC831d	*Signatory: R. M. Maiden* (Managing Director)		
	Prefix D/68 to prefix D/81 (maybe higher) dated 17.12.1986	£5	£8
	Replacement note – prefix Z/1	£40	£60

Obverse—green on a multicoloured underprint. Portrait of Lord Ilay, first Governor of the Bank, to the right
Reverse—green on a multicoloured underprint. Illustration of Edinburgh Castle

		EF	UNC
SC832	*Signatory: R. M. Maiden* (Managing Director)		
	Prefix A/1 to prefix A/40 dated 25.3.1987	£4	£6
	Replacement note – prefix Z/1	£16	£25

"E" size notes (129mm x 65mm approximately)

Similar to previous issue.

Obverse—green on a multicoloured underprint. Portrait of Lord Ilay, first Governor of the Bank, to the right.
Reverse—green on a multicoloured underprint. Illustration of Edinburgh Castle.

		EF	UNC
SC833a	*Signatory: R. M. Maiden* (Managing Director)		
	Prefix A/41 dated 13.12.1988 to prefix B/21 dated 19.12.1990	—	£5
	Replacement note – prefix Z/1	£16	£25
SC833b	*Signatory: C. M. Winter* (Chief Executive)		
	Prefix B/22 to prefix B/51 dated 24.7.1991	—	£4
	Replacement note – prefix Z/1	£16	£25
SC833c	*Signatory: G. R. Matthewson* (Chief Executive)		
	Prefix B/52 dated 24.3.1992 to prefix C/72 dated 1.10.1997	—	£3
	Replacement note – prefix Z/1	£14	£20
SC833d	Notes printed on un-watermarked paper, sometimes known as the "headless" notes.		
	Prefix C/28 to prefix C/31 dated 23.3.1994	£15	£25
SC833e	*Signatory: G. R. Matthewson* (Group Chief Executive)		
	Prefix C/73 to prefix C/82 dated 30.3.1999	—	£2
	Replacement note – prefix Z/1	£10	£15
SC833f	*Signatory: F. Goodwin* (Group Chief Executive)		
	Prefix C/83 to prefix C/97 dated 1.10.2001	—-	£2
	Replacement note – prefix Z/1	£10	£15

Obverse—mainly Green with portrait of Lord Ilay. Similar to regular issue but with overprint to the left to commemorate the European Summit in Edinburgh, December 1992
Reverse—green on a multicoloured underprint. Illustration of Edinburgh Castle

		EF	UNC
SC834	*Signatory: G. R. Matthewson* (Chief Executive)		
	Prefix EC dated 8.12.1992	—	£4

Obverse—mainly Green with portrait of Lord Ilay. Similar to regular issue but with overprint to the left to commemorate the death of Robert Louis Stevenson 1850–94
Reverse—portrait of robert Louis Stevenson.

		EF	UNC
SC835	*Signatory: G. R. Matthewson* (Chief Executive)		
	Prefix RLS dated 3.12.1994	—	£3

Obverse—mainly Green with portrait of Lord Ilay. Similar to regular issue but with overprint to the left to commemorate the 150th anniversary of the birth of Alexander Graham Bell 1847–1922
Reverse—portrait of Alexander Graham Bell and a representation of his work

		EF	UNC
SC836	*Signatory: G. R. Matthewson* (Chief Executive)..................................		
	Prefix AGB dated 3.3.1997	—	£3

Obverse—mainly Green with portrait of Lord Ilay. Similar to regular issue but with overprint to the left to commemorate the first meeting of the Scottish Parliament
Reverse—illustration of the Scottish Parliament building

	EF	UNC
SC837 *Signatory: G. R. Matthewson* (Group Chief Executive)		
Prefix SP dated 12.5.1999	—	£2

FIVE POUNDS

Size 145mm x 78mm approximately

Obverse—blue on a multicoloured underprint. Bank's Arms to the right
Reverse—blue, illustration of Culzean Castle

	EF	UNC
SC841a *Signatory: C. R. Winter* (Managing Director)		
Prefix B/13 dated 3.5.1982 to prefix B/36 dated 5.1.1983................	£35	£50
Sorting symbols removed from reverse.		
SC841b Prefix B/37 dated 4.1.1984 to prefix B/58 dated 3.1.1985................	£35	£50
SC841c *Signatory: R. M. Maiden* (Managing Director)		
Prefix B/59 to prefix B/82 (possibly higher) dated 17.12.1986.......	£35	£50
Replacement note – prefix Z/1..		Rare

Obverse—blue on a multicoloured underprint. Portrait of Lord Ilay to the right
Reverse—blue on a multocoloured underprint. Illustration of Culzean Castle

		EF	UNC
SC842	*Signatory: R. M. Maiden* (Managing Director)		
	Prefix A/1 dated 25.3.1987 to prefix A54 dated 22.6.1988	£18	£25
	Replacement note – prefix Z/1	£35	£50

Size 135mm x 70mm approximately

Similar to previous issue but reduced size

Obverse—blue on a multicoloured underprint. Portrait of Lord Ilay to the right
Reverse—blue on a multocoloured underprint. Illustration of Culzean Castle

		EF	UNC
SC843a	*Signatory: R. M. Maiden* (Managing Director)		
	Prefix A/55 dated 13.12.1988 to prefix B/5 dated 24.1.1990...........	£10	£16
	Replacement note – prefix Z/1	£35	£50
SC843b	*Signatory: G. R. Matthewson* (Chief Executive)		
	Prefix B/6 dated 23.3.1994 to prefix B/57 dated 29.4.1998	—	£10
	Replacement note – prefix Z/1	£35	£50
SC843c	*Signatory: G. R. Matthewson* (Group Chief Executive)		
	Prefix B/58 to prefix B/67 dated 30.3.1999	—	£9
	Replacement note – prefix Z/1	£25	£40
SC843d	*Signatory: F. Goodwin* (Group Chief Executive)		
	Prefix B/68 to prefix B/72 dated 27.6.2000	—	£8
	Replacement note – prefix Z/1	£25	£40

Commemorates the Queen's Golden Jubilee.

Obverse—similar to regular issue. Mainly blue; portrait of Lord Ilay to the right. Gold overprint "The Queen's Golden Jubilee 2002" to the left.
Reverse—blue and multicolour. Portrait of the Queen with an earlier portrait from 1952.

	EF	UNC
SC844 Signatory: *F. Goodwin* (Group Chief Executive) Prefix TQGJ dated 6.2.2002	—	£10

Issued to commemorate the 250th anniversary of the Royal and Ancient Golf Club of St. Andrews, established 1754.

	EF	UNC
SC845 Signatory: *F. Goodwin* (Group Chief Executive) Prefix R&A dated 14.5.2004	—	£10

TEN POUNDS

Size 153mm x 85mm approximately

Obverse—brown on a multicoloured underprint. Bank's coat of Arms to the right
Reverse—brown, illustration of Glamis Castle

		EF	UNC
SC851a	*Signatory: C. R. Winter* (Managing Director)		
	Prefix A/49 dated 3.5.1982 to prefix A/88 dated 3.1.1985	£55	£80
SC851b	*Signatory: R. M. Maiden* (Managing Director)		
	Prefix A/89 to prefix A/98 (possibly higher) dated 17.12.1986......	£80	£100
	Replacement note – prefix Z/1..		Rare

Obverse—brown on a multicoloured underprint. Portrait of Lord Ilay to the right
Reverse—brown on a multicoloured underprint. Illustration of Glamis Castle

		EF	UNC
SC852	*Signatory: R. M. Maiden* (Managing Director)		
	Prefix A/1 dated 25.3.1987 to prefix B/31 dated 24.1.1990...............	£30	£40
	Replacement note – prefix Z/1	£50	£70

Size 142mm x 75mm approximately

Similar to previous issue but reduced size.

Obverse—brown on a multicoloured underprint. Portrait of Lord Ilay to the right.
Reverse—brown on a multicoloured underprint. Illustration of Glamis Castle.

		EF	UNC
SC853a	*Signatory: G. R. Matthewson* (Chief Executive).................................		
	Prefix B/32 dated 28.1.1992 to prefix D/3 dated 23.3.1994	—	£22
	Replacement note – prefix Z/1	£40	£60
SC853b	*Signatory: F. Goodwin* (Group Chief Executive)		
	Prefix D/4 dated 27.6.2000 to prefix D/5 dated 1.10.2001................	—	£18
	Replacement note – prefix Z/1	£35	£50

TWENTY POUNDS

Size 160mm x 90mm approximately

Obverse—purple on a multicoloured underprint. Bank's Coat of Arms to the right.
Reverse—purple, illustration of Brodick Castle

		EF	UNC
SC861	*Signatory: C. R. Winter* (Managing Director)		
	Prefix A/6 dated 3.5.1982 to prefix ? dated 3.1.1985........................	£80	£110

Obverse—purple on a multicoloured underprint. Portrait of Lord Ilay to the right
Reverse—purple on a multicoloured underprint. Illustration of Brodick Castle

		EF	UNC
SC862	*Signatory: R. M. Maiden* (Managing Director)		
	Prefix A/1 dated 25.3.1987 to prefix A/3 dated 24.1.1990...............	£55	£70
	Replacement note – prefix Z/1...	£90	£140

Size 150mm x 80mm approximately

Similar to previous issue but reduced size

Obverse—purple on a multicoloured underprint. Portrait of Lord Ilay to the right.
Reverse—purple on a multicoloured underprint. Illustration of Brodick Castle.

		EF	UNC
SC863a	*Signatory: C. M. Winter* (Chief Executive)		
	Prefix A/4 to prefix A/8 dated 27.3.1991	£35	£50
	Replacement note – prefix Z/1..	£70	£100
SC863b	*Signatory: G. R. Matthewson* (Chief Executive)		
	Prefix A/9 dated 28.1.1992 to prefix B/3 dated 29.4.1998...............	—	£40
	Replacement note – prefix Z/1..	£45	£70
SC863c	*Signatory: G. R. Matthewson* (Group Chief Executive)		
	Prefix B/4 to prefix B/27 dated 30.3.1999	—	£38
	Replacement note – prefix Z/1..	£35	£60
SC863d	*Signatory: F. Goodwin* (Group Chief Executive)		
	Prefix B/29 to prefix B/56 dated 27.6.2000	—	£32
	Replacement note – prefix Z/1..	£35	£60

Commemorative issue for the 100th birthday of Her Majesty the Queen Mother.

Obverse—similar to regular issue . Portrait of Lord Ilay to the right. Gold Crown and Commemorative text to the left.
Reverse—purple and multicolour. Portrait of the Queen Mother with Glamis Castle in the background.

		EF	UNC
SC864	*Signatory: F. Goodwin* (Group Chief Executive)		
	Prefix QETQM dated 4.8.2000	—	£40

ONE HUNDRED POUNDS

Size 160mm x 90mm approximately

Obverse—red on a multicoloured underprint. Bank's coat of Arms to the right.
Reverse—red, illustration of Balmoral Castle

		EF	UNC
SC881	*Signatory: C. R. Winter* (Managing Director) Prefix A/1 dated 3.5.1982 and 3.1.1985	£280	£450

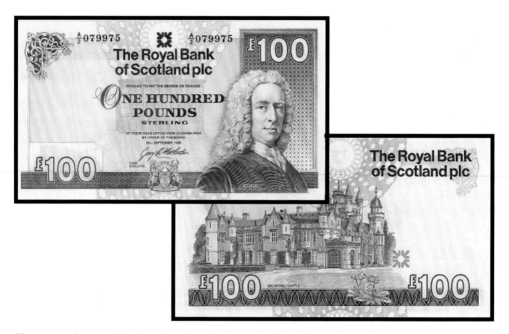

Obverse—red on a multicoloured underprint. Portrait of Lord Ilay to the right
Reverse—red on a multicoloured underprint. Illustration of Balmoral Castle

		EF	UNC
SC882a	*Signatory: R. M. Maiden* (Managing Director) Prefix A/1 dated 25.3.1987 and 24.1.1990...	£200	£280
SC882b	*Signatory: G. R. Matthewson* (Chief Executive) Prefix A/1 dated 28.1.1992 to prefix A/2 dated 30.9.1998	——	£180
SC882c	*Signatory: G. R. Matthewson* (Group Chief Executive) Prefix A/2 dated 30.3.1999..	——	£160
SC882d	*Signatory: F. Goodwin* (Group Chief Executive) Prefix A/2 dated 27.6.2000..	——	£160

THE UNION BANK OF SCOTLAND LIMITED

The title of The Union Bank of Scotland was adopted by the former Glasgow Union Banknig Company in 1843. In 1905 the contract for printing the Bank's notes was secured by Waterlow & Sons Limited; earlier notes had been printed by Perkins Bacon. The banknotes of the Uniob Bank of Scotland changed relatively little over the years with the most significant design change

ONE POUND

"A" size square notes (150mm x 130mm approximately)

Obverse—Blue with a large red "ONE" overlaid in red at the centre. The Bank's Coat of Arms is at the top of the note with twin equestrian statues in the lower corners.
Reverse—Large blue panel with the figure '1' circled by "The Union Bank of Scotland Limited"

		F	VF
SC901a	*Signatories: J. R. Wood* (Accountant) *and handsigned p. Cashier*......... Prefix A dated 6.4.1905 to prefix A dated 1.5.1907.		rare
SC901b	*Signatories: G. H. Moritz* (Accountant) *and handsigned p. Cashier* Prefix B dated 2.1.1908 and 28.9.1909		rare
SC901c	*Signatories: John Alexander* (Accountant) *and handsigned p. Cashier* Prefix B dated 12.2.1910 to prefix D dated 20.8.1913.	£250	£420
SC901d	*Signatories: J. F. McCrindle* (Accountant) *and handsigned p. Cashier* Prefix D dated 3.8.1914 to prefix H dated 10.12.1920	£200	£380

Obverse—Blue with a large red "ONE" overlaid in red at the centre and with additional red and yellow sunburst overlay. The Bank's Coat of Arms is at the top of the note with twin equestrian statues in the lower corners.
Reverse—Large blue panel with the figure "1" circled by "The Union Bank of Scotland Limited".

	F	VF

SC902 *Signatories: N. L. Hird* (General Manager) *and J. F. McCrindle* (Cashier)
Prefix A dated 1.10.1921 and prefix B dated 2.10.1923. .... £280 £450

"B" size notes (150mm x 85mm approximately)

Obverse—Blue with a large red "ONE" overlaid in red at the centre and red and yellow sunburst overlay. The Bank's Coat of Arms is at the top with twin equestrian statues in the lower corners.
Reverse—Blue panel with the figure "1" circled by "The Union Bank of Scotland Limited".

	VF	EF

SC903a *Signatories: N. L. Hird* (General Manager) *and J. F. McCrindle* (Cashier)
Prefix A dated 2.6.1924 to prefix C dated 3.10.1927 .... £70 £120

SC903b *Signatories: N. L. Hird* (General Manager) *and J. F. McCrindle* (Chief Accountant)
Prefix D dated 2.1.1929 to prefix F dated 5.12.1931 .... £50 £100

SC903c *Signatories: N. L. Hird* (General Manager) *and J. D. Wink* (Chief Accountant)
Prefix G dated 1.6.1933 to prefix I dated 31.3.1936 .... £25 £50

SC903d *Signatories: N. L. Hird* (General Manager) *and M. J. Wilson* (Cashier)
Prefix K dated 12.2.1937 to prefix V dated 28.9.1945 .... £25 £45

SC903e *Signatories: J. A. Morrison* (General Manager) *and M. J. Wilson* (Cashier)
Prefix V dated 20.3.1946 to prefix X dated 1.6.1948 .... £25 £45

Obverse—blue with a large red "ONE" at the centre and with a red and yellow sunburst overlay. Redesigned Coat of Arms to the left and sailing ship emblem to the right.
Reverse—mainly blue with an illustration of an industrial scene on the river Clyde.

		VF	EF
SC904a	*Signatory: J. A. Morrison* (General Manager)		
	Prefix A dated 1.3.1949 to prefix G dated 1.9.1953............................	£28	£45
SC904b	*Signatory: Sir William Watson* (General Manager)		
	Prefix H dated 1.6.1954	£60	£120

FIVE POUNDS

Size 196mm x 130mm approximately

Obverse—Blue with a large red "FIVE" overlaid in red at the centre. The Bank's Coat of Arms is at the top of the note with twin equestrian statues in the lower corners.
Reverse—Large blue panel with the figure "5" circled by "The Union Bank of Scotland Limited".

		F	VF
SC911	*Signatories: handsigned p. Accountant and handsigned p. Cashier*		
	Prefix A dated 25.2.1905 to prefix C dated 18.8.1920.........................	£360	£650

Obverse—Blue with large red 'FIVE' at the centre and red and yellow sunburst overlay.
The Bank's Coat of Arms is at the top of the note with twin equestrian statues in the lower corners.
Reverse—Large blue panel with the figure "5" circled by "The Union Bank of Scotland Limited".

		F	VF
SC912a	*Signatories: N. L. Hird* (General Manager) *and handsigned p. Cashier*		
	Prefix A dated 5.4.1921 and 4.5.1923	£220	£420
SC912b	*Signatories: N. L. Hird* (General Manager) *and J. F. McCrindle* (Cashier)		
	Prefix A dated 4.8.1923 to prefix B dated 15.1.1927...........................	£200	£350
SC912c	*Signatories: N. L. Hird* (General Manager) *and J. F. McCrindle* (Chief Accountant)		
	Prefix B dated 6.7.1928 to 4.5.1932..	£160	£320
SC912d	*Signatories: N. L. Hird* (General Manager) *and J. D. Wink* (Chief Accountant)		
	Prefix C dated 2.2.1933 to 18.5.1936	£100	£180
SC912e	*Signatories: N. L. Hird* (General Manager) *and M. J. Wilson* (Cashier)	*VF*	*EF*
	Prefix C dated 18.8.1937 to prefix G dated 31.8.1944........................	£140	£280
SC912f	*Signatories: J. A. Morrison* (General Manager) *and M. J. Wilson* (Cashier)		
	Prefix G dated 12.9.1946 to prefix H dated 3.5.1949	£110	£230

Size 182mm x 100mm approximately

Obverse—blue with a large red "FIVE" at the centre and with a red and yellow sunburst overlay.
Redesigned Coat of Arms to the left and sailing ship emblem to the right.
Reverse—mainly blue with an illustration of an industrial scene on the river Clyde.

		VF	EF
SC913a	*Signatory: J. A. Morrison* (General Manager)		
	Prefix A dated 17.7.1950 to prefix C dated 1.10.1953	£60	£100
SC913b	*Signatory: Sir William Watson* (General Manager)		
	Prefix D dated 2.4.1954	£150	£350

TEN POUNDS

Size 196mm x 130mm approximately

Obverse—Blue with a large red "TEN" overlaid in red at the centre. The Bank's Coat of Arms is at the top of the note with twin equestrian statues in the lower corners.
Reverse—Large blue panel with the figure "10" circled by "The Union Bank of Scotland Limited".

		F	VF
SC921	*Signatories: handsigned p. Accountant and handsigned p. Cashier*		
	Prefix A dated 4.4.1905 to prefix A dated 6.8.1920.		Rare

Obverse—Blue with large red "TEN" at the centre and red and yellow sunburst overlay. The Bank's Coat of Arms is at the top of the note with twin equestrian statues in the lower corners.
Reverse—Large blue panel with the figure "10" circled by "The Union Bank of Scotland Limited".

SC922a	*Signatories: N. L. Hird* (General Manager) *and J. F. McCrindle* (Cashier)	
	Prefix A dated 3.8.1923	Rare
SC922b	*Signatories: N. L. Hird* (General Manager) *and J. F. McCrindle* (Chief Accountant)	
	Prefix A dated 4.7.1928	Rare
SC922c	*Signatories: N. L. Hird* (General Manager) *and J. D. Wink* (Chief Accountant)	
	Prefix A dated 8.12.1933 and 8.7.1935	from £400

TWENTY POUNDS

Size 196mm x 130mm approximately

Obverse—Blue with a large red "TWENTY" overlaid in red at the centre. The Bank's Coat of Arms is at the top of the note with twin equestrian statues in the lower corners.
Reverse—Large blue panel with the figure "20" circled by "The Union Bank of Scotland Limited".

	F	VF

SC931 *Signatories: handsigned p. Accountant and handsigned p. Cashier*
Prefix A dated 31.3.1905 to prefix A dated 4.6.1920............................ Rare

Obverse—Blue with large red 'TWENTY' at the centre and red and yellow sunburst overlay. The Bank's Coat of Arms is at the top of the note with twin equestrian statues in the lower corners.
Reverse—Large blue panel with the figure "20" circled by "The Union Bank of Scotland Limited".

	F	VF
SC932a *Signatories: handsigned p. General Manager and p. Cashier*		
Prefix A dated 2.8.1923 to prefix A dated 14.8.1935	£280	£400
SC932a *Signatories: handsigned p. General Manager and p. Chief Accountant*	*VF*	*EF*
Prefix A dated 31.5.1937 to prefix B dated 2.1.1942...........................	£280	£420
SC932a *Signatories: N. L. Hird (General Manager) and M. J. Wilson (Cashier)*		
Prefix B dated 30.4.1942 to prefixB dated 10.7.1944.........................	£220	£360
SC932a *Signatories: J. A. Morrison (General Manager) and M. J. Wilson (Cashier)*		
Prefix B dated 2.12.1946 and 1.9.1947	£200	£340

Size 182mm x 100mm approximately

Obverse—Blue with a large red "TWENTY" at the centre and with a red and yellow sunburst overlay.
Redesigned Coat of Arms to the left and sailing ship emblem to the right.
Reverse—Mainly blue with an illustration of an industrial scene on the river Clyde.

		F	VF
SC933	*Signatory: J. A. Morrison* (General Manager)		
	Prefix A dated 1.9.1950 to prefix A dated 1.5.1953............................	£160	£280

ONE HUNDRED POUNDS

Size 196mm x 130mm approximately

Obverse—Blue with a large red "£100" overlaid in red at the centre, flanked by twin equestrian statues. The Bank's Coat of Arms is at the top of the note.
Reverse—Large blue panel with the figure "100" circled by "The Union Bank of Scotland Limited".

SC941 *Signatories: handsigned by the Accountant and Cashier*
Prefix A dated 7.4.1905 to prefix A dated 2.4.1919............................. Rare

Obverse—Blue with a large red "£100" overlaid in red at the centre, flanked by twin equestrian statues. Red and yellow sunburst overlay. The Bank's Coat of Arms is at the top of the note.
Reverse—Large blue panel with the figure "100" circled by "The Union Bank of Scotland Limited".

SC942a *Signatories: handsigned p. General Manager and p. Cashier*
Prefix A dated 1.8.1923 to prefix A dated 20.5.1936............................ Rare

SC942b *Signatories: handsigned p. General Manager and p. Chief Accountant.*
Prefix A dated 1.3.1939 to prefix A dated 2.1.1942............................. Rare

SC942c *Signatories: J. A. Morrison* (General Manager) *and M. J. Wilson* (Cashier) VF   EF
Prefix A dated 18.2.1947 .... £800   £1200

Size 185mm x 105mm approximately

Obverse—Blue with a large red "ONE HUNDRED" at the centre and with a red and yellow sunburst overlay. Redesigned Coat of Arms to the left and sailing ship emblem to the right.
Reverse—Mainly blue with an illustration of an industrial scene on the river Clyde.

		VF	EF
SC943a *Signatory: J. A. Morrison* (General Manager)			
Prefix A dated 9.10.1950 and 10.3.1952...		£700	£1200
SC943b *Signatory: Sir William Watson* (General Manager)			
Prefix A dated 1.10.1954. Only 100 printed			Rare

Provincial private banks

PROVINCIAL PRIVATE BANKS have a poor historical reputation, which is to a great extent quite undeserved. Many banking histories originate from or were commissioned by the later joint stock banking companies. It may be the case that they had a vested interest in emphasising their own illustrious contribution and then minimising the innovations and achievements of the private banks. In this short article ROGER OUTING looks at their note issues.

Provincial private banks performed an invaluable function in supporting the commencement of the English industrial revolution. They did so at a time when the Bank of England never stirred itself from the confines of Threadneedle Street and when London private Banks were completely focused on London.

Provincial private banks developed banking practices and procedures and familiarised the emerging business community with what we would today refer to as "financial services". The subsequent failures of private banks, of which there were plenty, was a consequence of the fact that they were operating at the very edge of economic and commercial innovation and their size was limited to six partners in order to protect the Bank of England from competition. The provincial private banks were inventing and creating the business of banking and doing so under artificial constraints. Failures in these circumstances should not be a surprise.

Whilst there were plenty of failures it can be easily overlooked that a great many private banks did prosper for long periods. They often went on to provide the foundation upon which joint stock banks could subsequently build and become successful. Private banks were the essential precursors to joint stock banks. Private banks and joint stock banks should be regarded as sequential developments within a single system of banking that developed over a 200-year period.

The Original "Big Five"

The term "Big Five" normally refers to Barclays, Lloyds, Midland, National Provincial, and Westminster Banks who, after 1900, came to collectively dominate English banking. The table opposite lists an "Original Big Five"—namely the first five provincial private banks to establish themselves.

The table tells a quite remarkable story in that none of these five innovators failed. They all maintained their commercial viability and independence for at least 100 years, sometimes longer. These private banks then became part of the joint stock movement in the latter half of the nineteenth century and so established themselves within the modern banking institutions with which we are familiar. The table illustrates that these private banks were an essential part of the origins of the modern banking system and should not be regarded merely as a failed relic of past economic

development. Each of the "Original Big Five" issued their own banknotes and provided account facilities serviced by the use of cheques. Their early banknotes or cheques rarely become available to collectors although 19th century examples can be located.

The subsequent growth in provincial private banks can be summarised as follows:

1750—12 provincial banks established.
1797—230 provincial banks established.
1810—721 provincial banks established.

Clearly there was an explosive expansion in the provision of banking facilities throughout provincial England and Wales. By 1820 every town of substance had its own local bank with its own local banknote issues. It is from this period that material becomes available to present day collectors.

Newcastle Exchange Bank

Illustrated above is a £5 note, dated 3rd March 1803, from the firm of Surtees, Burdon & Brandling of the Newcastle Exchange Bank. This Bank was established by Aubone Surtees and Rowland Burdon in 1768 and progressed through 35 years of successful trading before failing in 1803. Notes of £1, £5 and £10 are known for the whole trading period although it is the later issues, as illustrated, which are more readily available.

This £5 note has a vignette of The Exchange Building, Newcastle and the intertwined counterfoil printing at the extreme left margin is printed in blue. Handwritten elements, date etc., are also in blue ink. This makes it a two-colour banknote, which was unusual at the time. It is hand signed by the principal partner, "John Surtees". It will be noted that the name of the bank, the Newcastle Exchange Bank, is not printed on the banknote. However it will be found in the watermark that

The Original Big Five			
Year Link	Town	Name	*M o d e r n*
1685	Derby	Crompton, Newton & Co.	Nat. West.
1688	Nottingham	Thomas Smith	Nat. West.
1700	Dover	Fector & Minet	Nat. West.
1716	Gloucester	James Wood	Lloyds
1737	Stafford	John Stevenson	Lloyds

reads, "The Newcastle Exchange Bank, Surtees B & B". This combined use of high quality vignette, two colours and watermarking makes this note a more technically sophisticated product that Bank of England notes of the same period.

The banks demise illustrates an inherent weakness of private banks based upon a family partnership. In 1800 Aubone Surtees, original founder of the bank had died in his ninetieth year. His two sons, Aubone and John, carried on the partnership and were joined by John Brandling. When the original founder of a bank departs it often seems that the experience and wisdom that made the bank successful is also lost. This seems to the case here for 3 years later the Exchange Bank failed. Debts of £234,000 were announced in 1811 and total repayments were just 8/1d in the pound. The final 8d was not paid until 1832.

An interesting footnote is that notes of the Exchange Bank, to a face value of over £200,000, were auctioned off in Durham in 1807. This auction was a matter of business speculation and not an indication of collector interest. There is no record of the prices realised.

Whilst competently managed by the original founder the Newcastle Exchange Bank did successfully provide a banking service to local businesses. The subsequent partners were entirely honourable but apparently did not have the expertise necessary to maintain the trading viability of the business.

Faversham Bank

Shown opposite is a £5 note dated 1st October 1887, from the firm of Hilton, Rigden & Rigden of the Faversham Bank (also known as Faversham Commercial Bank). This note has an additional feature that became standard during the 19th century namely a reference to a London banker, which in this case was, "Prescott, Cave, Buxton & Co.". Most private banks had a London banker acting as agent and this was usually indicated on the banknote issues. Also this note is "cut cancelled" with the signature being cut out of the note as a form of cancellation. Many notes can be found with this form of cancellation.

In Victorian England when banknotes passed through a commercial or retail firm they were often hand stamped with that firm's name. Consequently this Faversham £5 note carries two faint hand stamps (not visible in illustration) of "Bartlett, Baker & Confectioner, Market Place, Faversham" and "London County Banking Co, Knightsbridge". This gives some indication of the both local and the more distant travels that this individual note has actually made. Many banknotes of the period carry such hand stamps. Other banknotes can be found which carry bankruptcy hand stamps that record the final travails of a failed bank.

Provincial banknotes that are "cut cancelled" carry retail or bankruptcy hand stamps are all quite collectable. Collectors who insist on "uncirculated" notes may be missing the point that collecting English Provincial banknotes is rather more about preserving social history than accumulating a complete "set" of something or other.

The Faversham Bank was taken over by Prescott's in 1892, which then passed to the Union of London & Smiths in 1903, which then passed to the National Provincial in 1918, and so to National Westminster in 1968. An example of a private bank being independently successful for almost 100 years before becoming part of the national banking structure that is with us today.

The provincial private banks also began to develop and spread the habit of using cheques. Provincial Clearing Houses were often established to support the efficient exchange of cheques in a manner duplicating the London experience.

Ipswich Cheque

Illustrated below is a cheque on the firm of Alexanders, Maw & Co. of the Ipswich & Needham Market Bank and dated "Oct 7th 1873". There is no mention of the name of the bank on the cheque—a mildly irritating feature of some private bank cheques. The cheque is wholly printed in red on special security paper designed to resist alteration to the cheque values, as cheque forgery was a significant problem at the time. As a further security device the cheque is watermarked with "East Malling, Kent" which is the mark of Waterlow & Sons, Security Printers, who printed this cheque.

The Ipswich & Needham Market Bank was established in 1744, and enjoyed over 150 years of independent and successful trading before becoming a founder member of the banking institution now known as Barclays Bank.

End of the Road

The demise of private banks was achieved in stages that encompassed almost 100 years. Firstly, legislation in 1826 allowed joint stock banks, other than the Bank of England, for the first time. Secondly, the Bank Charter Act 1844 placed restrictive prohibitions on the issue of banknotes. Finally, company law in 1858 allowed limited liability to be applied to banks. The accumulative effect of this legislation, and the amalgamation process which it triggered off, will be considered in more detail next month when the history of joint stock banking is dealt with.

By 1900 the banknote issues of the private banks were a minor amount of the total money supply. The very last private bank of issue was the firm of Fox, Fowler and Co. who had conducted a banking business at Wellington, Somerset, since 1787. This longstanding private bank finally relinquished its independent existence and its banknote issue when it amalgamated with Lloyds Bank in 1921. These final banknote issues are highly prized by collectors today.

During the 19th century in Great Britain many towns and cities and even villages had banks which issued their own notes. These are known as "Provincial" notes and are eagerly sought after, especially by local historians. The notes illustrated here are a selection which appeared at a Spink auction and are illustrated here with their kind permission.

Books
for the banknote collector

On the following pages is a list of books of interest to the banknote collector. They are listed under their area of main interest and by author alphabetically. Many of the titles are out of print but can often be acquired from your favourite numismatic bookseller.

General

IAN ANGUS, *Paper Money*, London, 1974.

COURTNEY L. COLLING Guide & checklist of World Notgeld 1914–1947, 2000.

JOE CRIBB, *Money: From Cowrie Shells to Credit Cards*, London 1986.

LESLIE DUNKLING and ADRIAN ROOM, *The Guinness Book of Money*, Enfield, 1990.

W. KRANISTER, The *Moneymakers International*, Cambridge, 1989.

BARRY KRAUSE, *Collecting Paper Money for Pleasure and Profit*.

MONETARY RESEARCH INSTITUTE *Bankers Guide to Foreign currency*, Housten TX, 2001.

COLIN NARBETH, ROBIN HENDY AND CHRISTOPHER STOCKER, *Collecting Paper Money and Bonds*, London, 1979.

COLIN NARBETH, *Encyclopedia of Paper Money*, London, 1967.

JOHN ORNA-ORNSTEIN, *The Story of Money*, London, 1997.

ALBERT PICK, *Briefmarkengeld*, Brunswick, 1970. *Papiergeld*, Brunswick, 1967. *Papiergeldkatalog Europa seit 1900*, Munich, 1973. *Paper Money Catalogue of the Americas*, Munich, 1973. *Standard Catalog of World Paper Money*, 3 vols., Krause Publications, Iola, 1998.

FRED REINFELD, *The Story of Paper Money*.

JOHN E. SANDROCK, *World Paper Money Collection*, New York, various editions.

FRED SCHWANN, *Collecting Paper Money*, New York, 1996.

NEIL SHAFER, *The Wonderful World of Paper Money*, 1972. *Let's Collect Paper Money*, 1976.

GEORGE J. STEN, *Banknotes of the World*, 2 vols, Menlo Park, 1967. *Encyclopedia of World Paper Money*, New York, 1965.

Military Invasion and Occupation Notes

JAMES MACKAY, *Banknotes at War*, London, 1977.

CARLTON F. SCHWAN, *Military Payment Certificates World War II Allied Military Currency*, Ohio, 1974.

CARLTON F. SCHWAN AND JOSEPH E. BOLING, *World War II Military Currency*, Ohio, 1978.

JAMES RUTLANDER, *Allied Military Currency*, New York, 1968.

NEIL SHAFER, *Philippine Emergency and Guerrilla Currency of World War II*, Racine, 1974.

ARLIE SLABAUGH, *Japanese Invasion Money*, Chicago, 1977.

GASTONE SOLLNER, *Moneta d'Occupazione e di Liberazione della Iia Guerra Mondiale*, Mantua, 1965.

ZVI STAHL, *Jewish Ghettos' and Concentration Camps' Money (1933-45)*, Israel, 1990.

RAYMOND TOY, *World War II Allied Military Currency*, San Diego, 1969.

RAYMOND TOY AND BOB MEYER, *World War II Axis Military Currency*, Tucson, 1967.

BENJAMIN WHITE, *The Currency of the Great War*, London, 1921.

JOHN F. YARWOOD, *A Guide to British Military Tokens*, Horsham, Australia, 1998.

Algeria

PAUL DUGENDRE, *Catalogue des Billets de la Banque de l'Algerie et de la Tunisie*, Paris, 1953.

Angola

LUIS M.R. DE SOUSA, *O Papel-Moeda em Angola*, Luanda, 1969.

Argentina

JOSE MARIA MUNARI, *Papel Moneda Argentina 1935-1967*, Buenos Aires, 1967.

Australia

GREG MCDONALD, *Australian Coins and Banknotes*, Umina Beach, 1985.

ALAN NICHOLSON, *Australian Banknote Catalogue*, Melbourne, 1979.

DION H. SKINNER, *Rennick's Australian Coins and Banknotes Guide*, Adelaide, 1980.

P. STEELE, *Collect Australian Coins and Banknotes*, Dubbo NSW, 1988.

G. W. TOMLINSON, *Australian Bank Notes 1817–1963*, Melbourne, 1963.

MICHAEL VORT-RONALD, *Collect Australian Banknotes*, Dubbo NSW, 1998.

Austria

ALBERT PICK AND R. RICHTER, *Oesterreich Banknoten und Staatspapiergeld ab 1759*, Berlin, 1972.

Baltic States

A. PLATBARZDIS, *Coins and Notes of Estonia, Latvia, Lithuania*, Stockholm, 1968.

M. TITUS, *Paper Currencies of Estonia*, Menlo Park, 1971.

Belgium

J. DE MEY, *Le Papier-Monnaie Belge d'Outremer, 1896-1963*, Brussels, 1976.
Le Papier-Monnaie Belge, 1814–1976, Brussels, 1976.
IBNS, *Paper Money of the 20th Century: Belgium and Colonies*, St. Louis, 1975.
FRANCOIS MORIN, *Catalogue des Billets de Banque Belge 1900 a 1974*, Brussels, 1974.
Cataloge des Billets de Banque de Congo etc, Boom, 1974.

Bolivia

LUIS A. ASBUN-KARMY, *Monedas de Bolvia*, La Paz, 1977.

Brazil

BANCO DO BRASIL, *Cedulas Brasileiras*, Rio de Janeiro, 1965.
ALVARO GONCALVES, *Catalogo de Cedulas e Moedas Brasileiras*, Sao Paulo, 1969.
DALE A. SEPPA, *The Paper Money of Brazil*, Chicago, 1976.
VIOLO LISSA, *Catalogo do Papel-Moeda do Brasil*, Brasilia, 1981.
DOS SANTOS TRINGUEIROS, *Dinhero do Brasil*, Rio de Janeiro, 1966.
A. TODISCO, *Catalogue of Brazilian Banknotes*, IBNS, 1961.

British West Africa

RICHARD J. FORD, *British West African Currency Board Bank Notes*, Walton-on-the-Naze, 1970.

Burma

M. ROBINSON AND L.A. SHAW, *The Coins and Banknotes of Burma*, Manchester, 1980.

Canada

BANK OF CANADA, *The Story of Canada's Currency*, Ottawa, 1981.
The National Currency Collection and the Bank of Canada Currency Museum, n.d.
J.E. CHARLTON, *Standard Catalogue of Canadian Paper Money*, Toronto, 1980.
HANS ZOELL, *Simplified Catalog of Canadian-Newfoundland Coins and Paper Money*, 1961.

Chile

JOSE M. GALETOVIC AND HECTOR BENAVIDES, *El Billete Chileno*, Santiago, 1973.

China

W.H. LU, *Paper Money Catalogue of the People's Republic of China and Macau*, Kuala Lumpur, 1998.
KING-ON MAO, *History of Chinese Paper Currency*, Hong Kong, 1968-77.
History of Paper Currency of the People's Republic of China, Hong Kong, 1972.
WARD D. SMITH AND BRIAN MATRAVERS, *Chinese Banknotes*, Menlo Park, USA, 1970.
HSU YIH TZON, *The Illustrated Encyclopedia of the Chinese Banknotes*, Taipei, 1981.

Colombia

YASHA BERESINER AND EDOUARDO DARGENT, *Catalogue of the Paper Money of Colombia and Peru*, London 1973.
ERNESTO CALLEJOS, *Catalogo de Billetes Emitidos...de Colombia*, Medellin, 1978.

Cuba

NEIL SHAFER, *Cuban Paper Money 1857-1968*, St. Louis, 1970.

Cyprus

MAJOR F. PRIDMORE, *Modern Coins and Notes of Cyprus*, London, 1974.

Denmark

AXEL RUBOW, *Nationalbankens Historie 1878-1908*, Copenhagen, 1920.
FROVIN SIEG, *Seddelkatalog 1874-1976*, Ulbjerg, 1977.

El Salvador

ALCEDO F. ALMANZAR AND BRIAN R. STICKNEY, *The Coins and Paper Money of El Salvador*, San Antonio, 1973.
ENRIQUE FRANKE, *The Banknotes of the Republic of El Salvador*, San Salvador, 1974.

England

W. MARSTON ACRES, *The Bank of England from Within*, Oxford, 1931.
DAVID BEVAN, *A Guide to Collecting English Banknotes*, New Malden, 1970.
BRYAN BURKE, *Nazi Counterfeiting of British Currency in World War II*, San Bernardino, 198.7
G. CHANDLER, *Four Centuries of Banking*, 2 vols, 1964–68.
SIR JOHN CLAPHAM, *The Bank of England: A History*, Cambridge, 1944.
W. CRICK AND J. WADSWORTH, *A Hundred Years of Joint-Stock Banking*, London, 1958.
VINCENT DUGGLEBY, *English Paper Money*, London, 2002.
PHILIP GEDDES, *Inside the Bank of England*, London, 1987.
G. L. GRANT, *Standard Catalogue of Provincial Banks and Banknotes*, London, 1977.
T. GREGORY, *The Westminster Bank Through a Century*, London, 1936.
VIRGINIA HEWITT AND J. M. KEYWORTH, *As Good as Gold*, London, 1987.
C. R. JOSSET, *Money in Britain*, Newton Abbott, 1971.
JAMES MACBURNIE, *The Story of the Yorkshire and Lancashire Bank*, Manchester, 1922.
A.D. MACKENZIE, *The Bank of England Note*, Cambridge, 1953.
P. W. MATTHEWS AND A. W. TUKE, *The History of Barclays Bank*, London, 1926.
DAVID M. MILLER, *Bank of England and Treasury Notes 1694-1970*, Newcastle, 1970.
COLIN NARBETH, *Collect British Banknotes*, London, 1970.
R. S. SAYERS, *The Bank of England, 1891-1944*, Cambridge, 1976.
H. WITHERS, *National Provincial Bank, 1833-1933*, London, 1933.

Finland

ERKKI BORG, *Suomessa Kaytetet Raha*t, Helsinki, 1976
FINLANDS BANK, *Inhemska Sedeltyper in Finland, 1809-1951*, Helsinki, 1952.
HANNU PAATELA, *Research Collection of Bank Notes Used in Finland 1662-1978*, Helsinki, 1978.
KURT PETTERSON, *Suomen Rahojen Hinnasta 1811-1979*, Helsinki., 1979.
TUKKO TOLVIO, *The Coins and Banknotes of Finland*.

France

JEAN LAFAURIE AND RAYMOND HABREKORN, *Catalogue des Emissions Officielles Francaises de Papier-Monnaie 1797-1952*, Auxerre, 1953-4.
M. MUSZYNSKI, *Les Billets de la Banque de France*, Villiers sur Marne, 1975 .
ARGUS THIMONIER, *Monnaies et Billets Francxe depuis 1774*, Paris, 1960.

Germany

KURT JAEGER AND ULLRICH HAEVECKER, *Die Deutschen Banknoten seit 1871*, Cologne, 1979.
ARNOLD KELLER. *Das Papiergeld des Ersten Weltkrieges*, Berlin, 1957.
Das Papiergeld des Zweiten Weltkrieges, Berlin, 1953.
Das Papiergeld der Deutschen Kolonien, Munster, 1967.
KAI LINDMAN, serienscheine, Sassenburg, 2000.
MANFRED MULLER AND ANTON GEIGER, *Das papiergeld der Deutschen Eisenbahnen und der Reichspost*, Frankenthal, 2000
ALBERT PICK AND J. RIXEN, *Papiergeld Spezialkatalog Deutschland 1874-1980*, Berlin, 1982.

Gibraltar

D.C. DEVENISH, *Currency Notes of Gibraltar*, London, 1969.

Greece

PAUL G. PYLARINOS, *Greek Paper Money*, Athens, 1976.
A. TARASSOULEAS, *Paper Money of Greece*, Athens, 1982.

Greenland

PETER FLENSBORG, *Gronlandske Pengesedler, 1803-1967*, Copenhagen, 1970.

Guatemala

ODIS H. CLARK, *Paper Money of Guatemala, 1834-1946*, San Antonio, 1971.
DWIGHT MUSSER, *The Paper Money of Guatemala*, USA, 1959.

Hawaii

MAURICE M. GOULD AND KENNETH BRESSETT, *Hawaiian Coins, Tokens and Paper Money*, Racine, 1961.
GORDON MEDCALF AND ROBERT FONG, *Hawaiian Money and Medals*, Kailua, 1967.
Paper Money of the Kingdom of Hawaii 1859-1905, Honolulu, 1966.
AND RONALD RUSSELL, *Hawaiian Money Standard Catalog*, Honolulu., 1978.

Hungary

RICHARD A. BANYAI, *The Legal and Monetary Aspects of the Hungarian Hyper-inflation*, Tucson, 1971.

MIHALY KUPA AND BELA AMBRUS, *Magyarorszag Papirpenzei*, Budapest, 1964.
Paper Money of Hungary 1803-1918, Budapest, 1963.

Iceland

FINNUR KOLBEINSSON, *Islenzkar Myntir*, Reykjavik, 1978.

India

KISHORE JHUNJHUNWALA, *Indian Paper Money Since 1950*, Mumbai, 1998.

Indonesia

DONALD L. FOLTZ, *Paper Money of the Republic of Indonesia*, Indianapolis, 1970.

Ireland

G. BARROW, *The Emergence of the Irish Banking System*, Dublin, 1975.
MÁRTAN MAC DEVITT, *Irish Banknotes, Irish Government Paper Money from 1928*, Dublin, 1999.
Irish Banknotes, Irish Paper Money 1783-2001, Dublin, 2004.
DEREK YOUNG, *Guide to the Currency of Ireland, Legal tender Notes 1928-1972*, Dublin, 1972.
Guide to the Currency of Ireland, Consolidated Bank Notes, 1929-1941, Dublin, 1977.

Isle of Man

ISLE OF MAN BANK, *100 Years of Banking*, Douglas, 1965.
ERNEST QUARMBY, *Banknotes & Banking in the Isle of Man 1788-1970*, London, 1971.
PILCHER RALFE, *Sixty Years of Banking, 1865-1925*, Douglas, 1926.

Israel

SYLVIA HAFFNER, *The History of Modern Israel's Money from 1917-1967*, San Diego, 1968.
A.H. KAHAN, *Israel's Money and Medals*, New York, 1976.

Italy

CESARE BOBBA, *Carta Moneta Italiane, Asti*, 1974.
Catalogo della Carta-Moneta d'Occupazione, Asti, 1975.
MARIO DE FANTI, *Carta-Moneta Italiana, 1866-1961*, Casciano, 1966   .
LUIGI DE ROSA, *Il Banco di Napoli Istituto di Emissione*, Naples, 1976.
LIBERO MANCINI, *Catalogo Italiano della Cartamoneta 1746-1966*, Bologna, 1966.
ADOLFO MINI, *La Carta Moneta italiana 1746-1960*, Palermo, 1967.
GASTONE SOLLNER, *Catalogo della Carta-Moneta Italiana dal 1866 ad Oggi*, Milan, 1964.

Jamaica

JEROME REMICK, *Jamaican Banknotes*, St. Louis, 1968.

Japan

BANKOKU KAHEI KENKYUKAI, *Government and Bank of Japan Issues and Military Issues*, Tokyo, 1970.
IBNS, *Paper Money of the 20th Century: Japan*, St. Louis, 1981.
Y. OHASHI, *Nippon Shihei Taikei Zukan*, Tokyo, 1957.

Katanga

PETER SYMES, *The Bank Notes of Katanga*, Kirkcaldy, 1998.

Korea

BANK OF KOREA, *The History of Korean Money*, Seoul, 1969.
KIM IN SIK, *Illustrated Catalog of Korean Currency*, Seoul, 1978.

Luxembourg

FERN WICTOR, *Monnaies et Essais-Monnaies du Grand-Duche de Luxembourg 1796-1965*, Luxembourg, 1965.

Malaysia

IBNS, *Paper Money of the 20th Century*: Malaysia, Dallas, 1973.
K. C. BOON, *Standard Price Guide of Malaysian Banknotes and Coins 1939-2002*, Kuala Lumpur, 2003.
C.C. LOW, *Malaya Banknote Catalog*, Racine, 1967.
WILLIAM SHAW AND ALI KASSIM HAJI, *Paper Currency of Malaysia*, etc, Kuala Lumpur, 1971.
SARON SINGH, KASSIM HAJI, C.C. LOW AND TONY LYE FONG, *Standard Catalogue of Coins and Banknotes of Malaysia*, etc, Kuala Lumpur, 1976.
STEPHEN TAN, *Standard Catalogue of Malaysia, Singapore, Brunei Coins and Paper Money*, 1998.

Maldive Islands

TIM J. BROWDER, *Maldive Islands Money*, Santa Monica, 1969.

Malta

EMMANUEL SAID, *Malta Coin, Banknote and Medal Catalogue*, Valletta, 1982.

Mexico

DOUGLAS AND DUANE, *The Complete Encyclopedia of Mexican Paper Money*, Iola, 1982.
CARLOS GAYTAN, *Billetes de Mexico*, Mexico City, 1965.
Paper Curency of Mexico, California, 1975.

Monaco

RAYMOND DE VOS, *History of the Monies, Medals and Tokens of Monaco*, New York, 1977.

Mongolia

E.D. GRIBANOV, *The Currency of the Mongolian People's Republic*, St. Louis, 1965.

Morocco

M. MUSZYNSKI AND H. SCHWEIKERT, *Le Papier-Monnaie du Maroc*, Paris, 1974.

Mozambique

BANCO NACIONAL ULTRAMARINO, *Papel-Moeda Para Mocambique*, 1877-1973, Lisbon, 1978.
COLIN R. OWEN, *The Banknotes of Mozambique*, Benoni, 1976.

Netherlands

J. MEVIUS AND F.G. LELIVELT, *De Nederlandse Bankbiljetten van 1814 tot Heden*, Amsterdam, 1981.

New Zealand

P. G. ECCLES, *The Premier Catalogue of New Zealand Coins and Banknotes*, Auckland, 1980.
ALISTAIR F. ROBB, *Coins, Tokens and Banknotes of New Zealand*, Wellington, 1976.

Nicaragua

BRIAN STICKNEY AND ALCEDO ALMANZAR, *The Coins and Paper Money of Nicaragua*, USA, 1974.

Norway

KARL SAETHRE AND HANS GUNNAR ELDORSEN, *Norske Pengeselder*, Loddefjord, Norway, 2003.

Papua New Guinea

DR WILLIAM J.D. MIRA, *From Cowrie to Kina*, Sydney, 1986.

Paraguay

DALE A. SEPPA, *Paraguayan Paper Money*, Chicago, 1974.

Peru

EDUARDO DARGENT, *El Billete en el Peru*, Lima, 1979.

Philippines

NEIL SHAFER, *A Guide Book of Philippines Paper Money*, Racine, 1964.

Poland

TADEUSZ JABLONSKI, *Polski Pieniadz Papierowny*, 1794-1948, Warsaw, 1964.
MARIAN KOWLSKI, *Katalog Banknotow Polskich 1916-1972*, Warsaw, 1973.

Portugal

FRANCISCO MALAFAYA, *Catalogo de Notafilia Portugal*, Porto, 1977.

Romania

V. COMAN, *Katalog der Rumanischen Banknoten*, Munster, 1967.
COL. R. IOAN DOGARU, *Catalogul Monedelor si Bancnotelar Romanesti*, Bucharest, 1978.
OCTAVIAN LUCHIAN, *Monede si Bancnote Romanesti*, Bucharest, 1977.

Russia

C. DENIS, *Catalogue des Monnaies Russes*, Paris, 1927.
N. KARDAKOFF, *Katalog der Geldscheine von Russland und der Baltischen Staaten*, Berlin, 1953.
LEONID Z. KATS and VALERY P. MALYSHEV, *Encyclopedia of Russian Paper Money 1769-1995*, St Petersburg, 1998.
DMITRI KHARITONOV, *Jewish Paper Money in Russia*, Prague, 2004.
PENTII LAURILA, *Soviet Paper Money and Bonds Used as Currency 1895-1990*, Tornio, Finland, 1990.
N. NAVOLOCHKIN, *Soviet Numismatics*, Moscow, 1970.

Scotland

JAMES L. ANDERSON, *The Story of the Commercial Bank of Scotland*, Edinburgh, 1910.

BANKING MEMORABILIA, *Registers of the National Bank of Scotland*, Carlisle, 2004.

C. W. BOASE, A Century of Banking in Dundee, Edinburgh, 1867.

JOHN BUCHANAN, *Glasgow Banking in Olden Times*, Glasgow, 1884.

S.G. CHECKLAND, *Scottish Banking: A History 1695-1973*, Glasgow, 1975.

DENNET *Scottish banknote catalogue*, Norwich, 2001

JAMES DOUGLAS, *Scottish Banknotes*, London, 1975. *20th Century Scottish Banknotes, Vols. 1 & 2*, Carlisle, 1984. Revised 2002.

SIR WILLIAM FORBES, *Memoirs of a Banking-House*, Edinburgh, 1859.

WILLIAM GRAHAM, *The One Pound Note in Scotland*, Edinburgh, 1911. *The Bank Note Circulation of Scotland*, Edinburgh, 1926.

TREVOR JONES, *20th Century Scottish Banknotes: Clydesdale Bank*, Carlisle, 1998.

ALEXANDER KEITH, *The North of Scotland Bank 1836-1936*, Aberdeen, 1936.

ANDREW W. KERR, *A History of Banking in Scotland*, London, 1884.

CHARLES A. MALCOLM, *The Bank of Scotland 1695-1945*, Edinburgh, 1945. *The History of the British Linen Bank*, Edinburgh, 1950.

C. MUNN, *The Scottish Provincial Banking Companies, 1747-1864*, Edinburgh, 1981.

NEIL MUNRO, *The History of the Royal Bank of Scotland 1727-1927*, Edinburgh, 1928.

ROBERT | PRINGLE, *20th Century Scottish Banknotes: Royal Bank*, Carlisle, 1986.

ROBERT S. RAIT, *The History of the Union Bank of Scotland*, Glasgow, 1930.

J.M. REID, *The History of the Clydesdale Bank*, Glasgow, 1938.

South Africa

W. BERGMAN, *A History of the Regular and Emergency Paper Money Issues of South Africa*, Cape Town, 1971.

HAROLD P. LEVIUS, *Catalogue of South African Paper Money since 1900*, Johannesburg, 1972.

South East Asia

COLIN BRUCE, *Standard Guide to South Asian Coins and Paper Money Since 1556*, Iola, 1982.

HOWARD A. DANIEL, *The Catalogue and Guidebook of Southeast Asian Coins and Currency*, Ohio, 1978.

Spain

IBNS, *Paper Money of the 20th Century: Spanish Civil War*, St. Louis, 1978.

FLORIAN R. VELEZ-FRIAS AND JORGE A. VILA, *Catalogo del papel Moeda Espanol*, Madrid, 1975.

JOSE A. VICENTE, *Catalogo de Billetes Espanoles 1783-1977*, Madrid, 1977. *Catalogo Basico Monedas y Billetes 1869-1977*, Madrid, 1978.

Sri Lanka

H.W. CODRINGTON, *Ceylon Coins and Currency, 1924*, reprinted London 1999.

Surinam

THEO VAN ELMPT, *Surinam Paper Currency, 1760-1957*, London, 1998.

Sweden

SVEN FLODBERG, *Katalog over Sveriges Sedlar, 1858-1971*, Lund, 1972.

A. PLATBARZDIS, *Sveriges Sedlar 1661-1961*, Lund, 1963. *Sveriges Sedlar Enskilda Bankernas Sedlar 1831-1902*, Lund, 1965.

LENNART WALLEN AND BJARNE AHLSTROM, *Sveriges Sedlar*, Stockholm, 1978.

Switzerland

URS GRAF, *Das Papiergeld der Schwiz, 1881-1068*, Munser, 1970 .

Thailand

BANK OF THAILAND, *Banknotes of Thailand*, Bangkok, 1972.

SILAS LITTLE, *Banknotes of Thailand*, Falls Church, USA, 1973.

Turkey

DR MINE EROL, *Osmanli Imparatorlugunda Kagit Para*, Ankara, 1970.

CUNEYT OLCER, *50 Yilin Turk Kagit Paralari*, Istanbul, 1973.

USA

FREDERICK BART, *Comprehensive Catalog of United States Paper Money Errors.*

ELVIRA and VLADIMIR CLAIN-STEFANELLI, *American Banking*, Washington, 1975.

GROVER CRISWELL, *Confederate States of America Paper Money*, Florida, 1976.

W. P. DONLON, *United States Large Size Paper Money*, Utica, 1970.

RICHARD DOTY, *America's Money, America's Story*, Iola, 1998.

ROBERT FRIEDBERG, *Paper Money of the United States*, New York, various editions.

GENE HESSLER, *Comprehensive Catalog of US Paper Money US Essay, Proof and Specimen Notes, 1979. the Engraver's Line*

RON HORSTMAN, *Collecting National Bank Notes.*

CHESTER L. KRAUSE AND ROBERT F. LEMKE, *United States Paper Money*, Iola, 1999.

ERIC P. NEWMAN, *The Early Paper Money of America*, Iola, 1998.

ARLIE R. SLABAUGH *Confederate States Paper Money*, Iola, 2000.

Uruguay

DALE A. SEPPA, *Uruguayan Paper Moneh*, Chicago, 1974.

Wales

IVOR WYNNE JONES, *Money Galore—the Story of the Welsh Pound*, Landmark, 2004.

Yemen

PETER SYMES, MURRAY HANEWICH AND KEITH STREET, *The Bank Notes of the Yemen*, Chester, 1998.

Yugoslavia

VOJISLAV MIHAILOVIC AND DRAGSOLAV GLOGONJAC, *Katalog Novca Srbije I Crne Gore 1868-1918*, Belgrade, 1973.

DIMITRI SPAJIC, *Paper Money of the Yugoslavian States*, USA, 1969.

Cheques and Postal Orders

STEPHEN CRIBB, *The Standard Catalogue of Postal Orders*, Ruislip, 1984.

JAMES DOUGLAS, *Collect British Cheques*, London, n.d. (c. 1981) *A Collector's Guide to Cheques and Bills of Exchange*, Carlisle, n.d.

HOWARD LUNN, *Promotional Postal Orders*, Nottingham,. N.d. [1990].

ROGER OUTING, *The Cheques of Barclays Bank, Huddersfield*, 2004.

DAVID SHAW, *A Collector's Guide to British Cheques*, Shrewsbury, 1986.

Museums and Libraries

Listed below are the Museums and Libraries in the UK which have coin collections and many also have banknotes or items of notaphilic interest on display or available to the general public. However, before setting off on a long journey it is advisable to contact the museum you wish to visit to check that any notes they have are available for viewing.

A

Anthropological Museum, University of Aberdeen, Broad Street, **Aberdeen,** AB9 1AS (01224 272014).

Curtis Museum (1855), High Street, **Alton,** Hants (01420 2802).

Ashburton Museum, 1 West Street, **Ashburton,** Devon.

Ashwell Village Museum (1930), Swan Street, **Ashwell,** Baldock, Herts.

Buckinghamshire County Museum (1862), Church Street, **Aylesbury,** Bucks (01296 88849).

B

Public Library and Museum (1948), Marlborough Road, **Banbury,** Oxon (01295 259855).

Museum of North Devon (1931), The Square, **Barnstaple,** EX32 8LN (01271 46747).

Roman Baths Museum, Pump Room, **Bath,** Avon (01225 461111 ext 2785).

Bagshaw Museum and Art Gallery (1911), Wilton Park, **Batley,** West Yorkshire (01924 472514).

Bedford Museum (1961), Castle Lane, **Bedford** (01234 353323).

Ulster Museum (1928), Botanic Gardens, **Belfast** BT9 5AB (01232 381251).

Berwick Borough Museum (1867), The Clock Block, Berwick Barracks, Ravensdowne, **Berwick.** TD15 1DQ (01289 330044).

Public Library, Art Gallery and Museum (1910), Champney Road, **Beverley,** Humberside (01482 882255).

City Museum and Art Gallery (1861), Chamberlain Square, **Birmingham** B3 3DH (0121 235 2834).

Blackburn Museum, Museum Street, **Blackburn,** Lancs (01254 667130).

Museum Collection, Town Hall, **Bognor Regis,** West Sussex.

Museum and Art Gallery,(1893), Civic Centre, **Bolton,** Lancashire (01204 22311 ext 2191).

Art Gallery and Museum, Central Library, Oriel Road, **Bootle,** Lancs.

Roman Town and Museum (1949) Main Street, **Boroughbridge,** N. Yorks. YO2 3PH (01423 322768).

The Museum (1929), The Guildhall, **Boston,** Lincs (01205 365954).

Natural Science Society Museum (1903), 39 Christchurch Road, **Bournemouth,** Dorset (01202 553525).

Bolling Hall Museum (1915), Bolling Hall Road, **Bradford,** West Yorkshire BD4 7LP (01274 723057).

Cartwright Hall Museum and Art Gallery (1904), Lister Park, **Bradford,** West Yorkshire BD9 4NS (01274 493313).

Museum and Art Gallery (1932), South Street, **Bridport,** Dorset (01308 22116).

The City Museum (1820), Queen's Road, **Bristol** BS8 1RL (0117 9 27256).

District Library and Museum (1891), Terrace Road, **Buxton,** Derbyshire SK17 6DU (01298 24658).

C

Fitzwilliam Museum (1816), Department of Coins and Medals, Trumpington Street, **Cambridge** (01223 332900).

National Museum & Galleries of Wales, Cathays Park, **Cardiff** (029 20397951).

Guildhall Museum (1979), Greenmarket, **Carlisle,** Cumbria (01228 819925).

Tullie House (1877), Castle Street, **Carlisle,** Cumbria (01228 34781).

Chelmsford and Essex Museum (1835), Oaklands Park, Moulsham Street, **Cheltenham,** Glos CM2 9AQ (01245 353066).

Town Gate Museum (1949), **Chepstow,** Gwent.

Grosvenor Museum (1886), Grosvenor Street, **Chester** (01244 21616).

Public Library (1879), Corporation Street, **Chesterfield,** Derbyshire (01246 2047).

Red House Museum (1919), Quay Road, **Christchurch,** Dorset (01202 482860).

Colchester and Essex Museum (1860), The Castle, **Colchester,** Essex (01206 712931/2).

D

Public Library, Museum and Art Gallery (1921), Crown Street, **Darlington,** Co Durham (01325 463795).

439

Borough Museum (1908), Central Park, **Dartford,** Kent (01322 343555).

Dartmouth Museum (1953), The Butterknowle, **Dartmouth,** Devon (01803 832923).

Museum and Art Gallery (1878), The Strand, **Derby** (01332 255586).

Museum and Art Gallery (1909), Chequer Road, **Doncaster,** South Yorkshire (01302 734293).

Dorset County Museum(1846), **Dorchester,** Dorset (01305 262735).

Central Museum (1884), Central Library, St James's Road, **Dudley,** West Midlands (01384 453576).

Burgh Museum (1835), The Observatory, Corberry Hill, **Dumfries** (01387 53374)**.**

Dundee Art Galleries and Museums (1873). Albert Square, **Dundee** DD1 1DA (01382 23141).

The Cathedral Treasury (995 AD), The College, **Durham** (0191-384 4854).

Durham Heritage Centre, St Mary le Bow, North Bailey, **Durham** (0191-384 2214).

E

Royal Museum of Scotland (1781), Queen Street, **Edinburgh** EH1 (0131 225 7534).

Royal Albert Memorial Museum (1868), Queen St, **Exeter** EX4 3RX (01392 265858).

G

Hunterian Museum (1807), Glasgow University, University Avenue, **Glasgow** G12 8QQ (041 339 8855).

Art Gallery and Museum (1888), Kelvingrove, **Glasgow** G3 (0141 357 3929).

Museum of Transport (1974), Kelvin Hall, Bunhouse Road, **Glasgow** G3 (0141 357 3929).

City Museum and Art Gallery (1859), Brunswick Road, **Gloucester** (01452 524131).

Guernsey Museum and Art Gallery, St Peter Port, **Guernsey** (01481 726518).

Guildford Museum (1898), Castle Arch, **Guildford,** Surrey GU1 3SX (01483 444750).

H

Gray Museum and Art Gallery, Clarence Road, **Hartlepool,** Cleveland (01429 268916).

Public Museum and Art Gallery (1890), John's Place, Cambridge Road, **Hastings,** East Sussex (01424 721952).

City Museum (1874), Broad Street, **Hereford** (01432 268121 ext 207).

Hertford Museum (1902), 18 Bull Plain, **Hertford** (01992 582686).

Honiton and Allhallows Public Museum (1946), High Street, **Honiton,** Devon (01404 44966).

Museum and Art Gallery (1891), 19 New Church Road, **Hove,** East Sussex (01273 779410).

Tolson Memorial Museum (1920), Ravensknowle Park, **Huddersfield,** West Yorkshire (01484 541455).

Hull and East Riding Museum (1928), 36 High Street, **Hull** (01482 593902). *Celtic, Roman and medieval coins and artifacts from local finds. Some later coins including tradesmen's tokens.*

I

The Manx Museum, Douglas, **Isle of Man** (01624 675522).

J

Jersey Museum, Weighbridge, St Helier, **Jersey** (01534 30511).

K

Dick Institute Museum and Art Gallery (1893), Elmbank Avenue, **Kilmarnock,** Ayrshire (01563 26401).

L

City Museum (1923), Old Town Hall, Market Square, **Lancaster** (01524 64637).

City Museum (1820), Municipal Buildings, The Headrow, **Leeds,** West Yorkshire (01532 478279).

Leicester Museum and Art Gallery (1849), New Walk, **Leicester** (01533 554100).

Pennington Hall Museum and Art Gallery, **Leigh,** Lancashire.

Museum and Art Gallery (1914), Broadway, **Letchworth,** Herts (01462 65647). *Ancient British coins minted at Camulodunum, Roman, me*

City Library, Art Gallery and Museum (1859), Bird Street, **Lichfield,** Staffs (01543 2177).

Liverpool Museum(1851), William Brown Street, **Liverpool** L3 8EN (0151 207 0001).

Bank of England Museum, Threadneedle Street, **London** EC2 (020-7601 5545).

British Museum(1752), HSBC Coin Gallery, Great Russell Street, **London** WC1 (020-7636 1555).

British Numismatic Society (1903), Warburg Institute, Woburn Square, **London** WC1.

Cuming Museum (1906), Walworth Road, **London** SE17 (020-7703 3324/5529).

Gunnersbury Park Museum (1927), Acton, **London** W3.

Horniman Museum and Library (1890), **London** Road, Forest Hill, London SE23 (020-7699 2339).

Imperial War Museum, Lambeth Road, **London** SE1 6HZ (020-7416 5000).

Sir John Soane's Museum (1833), 13 Lincoln's Inn Fields, **London** WC2 (020-7405 2107).

National Maritime Museum, Romney Road, Greenwich, **London** SE10 (020-8858 4422).

Victoria and Albert Museum (1852), South Kensington, **London** SW7 (020-7938 8441).

Ludlow Museum (1833). The Assembly Rooms. Castle Square, **Ludlow** (01584 873857).

Luton Museum and Art Gallery (1927), Wardown Park, **Luton,** Beds (01582 36941).

M

Museum and Art Gallery (1858), **Maidstone**, Kent (01622 754497).

The Manchester Museum (1868), The University, **Manchester** M13 (0161-275 2634).

Margate Museum (1923), The Old Town Hall, Market Place, **Margate**, Kent (01843 225511 ext 2520).

Montrose Museum and Art Gallery (1836). Panmure Place, **Montrose**, Angus DD10 8HE (01674 73232).

N

Newark-on-Trent Museum (1912), Appleton Gate, **Newark**, Notts (01636 702358).

Newbury District Museum, The Wharf, **Newbury**, Berkshire (01635 30511).

O

Heberden Coin Room, Ashmolean Museum (1683), **Oxford** (01865 278000).

P

Peterborough Museum (1881), Priestgate, **Peterborough**, Cambs (01733 340 3329).

City Museum and Art Gallery (1897), Drake Circus, **Plymouth**, Devon (01752 264878).

Waterfront Museum, 4 High Street, **Poole**, Dorset (01202 683138). *(view by appointment).*

City Museum (1972), Museum Road, Old **Portsmouth** PO1 (023 80827261).

Harris Museum and Art Gallery (1893), Market Square, **Preston**, Lancashire (01772 58248).

R

Reading Museum and Art Gallery, (1883) Blagrave Street, **Reading**, Berks (01734 399809).

Rochdale Museum (1905), Sparrow Hill, **Rochdale**, Lancs (01706 41085).

Municipal Museum and Art Gallery (1893), Clifton Park, **Rotherham** (01709382121).

S

Saffron Walden Museum (1832) (1939), Museum Street, **Saffron** Walden, Essex (01799 522494).

Salisbury and South Wiltshire Museum (1861), The Cathedral Close, **Salisbury,** Wilts (01722 332151).

Scarborough Museum (1829), The Rotunda, Vernon Road, **Scarborough**, North Yorkshire (01723 374839).

Shaftesbury and Dorset Local History Museum (1946), 1 Gold Hill, **Shaftesbury**, Dorset (01747 52157).

City Museum (1875), Weston Park, **Sheffield** (0114 2 768588).

Rowley's House Museum, Barker Street, **Shrewsbury**, Salop (01743 361196).

Museum of Archaeology (1951), God's House Tower, Town Quay, **Southampton**, Hants (023 8022 0007).

Botanic Gardens Museum, Churchtown, **Southport,** Lancs (01704 87547).

Southwold Museum (1933), St Bartholomew's Green, **Southwold**, Suffolk (01502 722375).

Stamford Museum (1961), Broad Street, **Stamford**, Lincs (01780 66317).

Municipal Museum (1860), Vernon Park, Turncroft Lane, **Stockport**, Cheshire (0161 474 4460)

Stroud Museum (1899), Lansdown, **Stroud**, Glos (01453 376394).

Museum and Art Gallery (1846), Borough Road, **Sunderland,** Tyne & Wear (0191 514 1235).

Swansea Museum (1835), Victoria Road, **Swansea**, W. Glamorgan, SA1 1SN (0792 653765).

T

Tamworth Castle and Museum (1899), The Holloway, **Tamworth**, Staffs (01827 63563).

Somerset County Museum, Taunton Castle, **Taunton**, Somerset (01823 255510/320200). *C*

Thurrock Local History Museum (1956), Civic Square, **Tilbury**, Essex (01375 390000 ext 2414).

Royal Cornwall Museum (1818), River Street, **Truro,** Cornwall (01872 72205).

W

Wakefield Museum (1919), Wood Street, **Wakefield,** West Yorkshire (01924 295351).

Epping Forest District Museum, 39/41 Sun Street, **Waltham Abbey**, Essex EN 9.

Warrington Museum and Art Gallery (1848). Bold Street, **Warrington**, Cheshire, WA1 1JG (01925 30550).

Worcester City Museum (1833), Foregate Street, **Worcester** (01905 25371).

Wells Museum (18903), 8 Cathedral Green, **Wells,** Somerset (01749 3477).

Municipal Museum and Art Gallery (1878), Station Road, **Wigan**, Lancashire.

City Museum (1851), The Square, **Winchester**, Hants (01962 848269).

Wisbech and Fenland Museum (1835), Museum Square, **Wisbech,** Cambridgeshire (01945 583817).

Y

The Museum of South Somerset (1928), Hendford, **Yeovil**, Somerset (01935 24774).

Castle Museum (1938), **York** (01904 653611).

The Yorkshire Museum (1823), **York** (01904 629745).

Club
directory

Most numismatic societies encompass banknotes in their agenda and many have regular speakers on the subject. Details given here are the names of the Numismatic Clubs or Societies, their dates of foundation, venue, days and times of meetings. Meetings are usually monthly unless otherwise stated. Finally, the telephone number of the club secretary is given; the names and addresses of club secretaries are withheld for security reasons, but full details may be obtained by writing to the Secretary of the British Association of Numismatic Societies, Philip Mernick, c/o Bush Boake Allen Ltd, Blackhorse Lane, London E17 5QP.

Banbury & District Numismatic Society (1967). Banbury British Rail Working Mens Club. 2nd Mon (exc Jul & Aug), 19.45. (01295 254451).

Bath & Bristol Numismatic Society (1950). Fry's Club, Keynsham, Bristol. 2nd Thu, 19.30. (0117 9039010).

Bedford Numismatic Society (1966). RAF Association Club, 93 Ashburnham Road, Bedford MK40 1EA. 3rd Mon, 19.30. (01234 228833 / 358369).

Bexley Coin Club (1968). St Martin's Church Hall, Erith Road, Barnehurst, Bexleyheath, Kent. 1st Mon (exc Jan & Aug), 20.00. (0208 303 0510).

Birmingham Numismatic Society (1964). Friend's Meeting House, Linden Lane, Bourneville,Birmingham. 1st Wed, 19.45. (0121 308 1616).

Matthew Boulton Society (1994). PO Box 395, Birmingham B31 2TB (0121 781 6558 fax 0121 781 6574).

Bradford & District Numismatic Society (1967). East Bowling Unity Club, Leicester Street, Bradford, West Yorkshire. 3rd Mon, 19.00. (01532 677151).

Brighton & Hove Coin Club (1971). Methodist Church Hall, St Patrick's Road, Hove, East Sussex. Last Wed (exc Dec), 20.00. (01273 419303).

British Cheque Collectors' Society (1980). John Purser, 71 Mile Lane, Cheylesmore, Coventry, West Midlands CV3 5GB.

British Numismatic Society (1903). Warburg Institute, Woburn Square, London WC1H 0AB. Monthly (exc Jul, Aug & Dec), 18.00. (01329 284661)

Cambridgeshire Numismatic Society (1946). Friends' Meeting House, 12 Jesus Lane (entrance in Park Street), Cambridge, CB5 8BA. 3rd Mon, Sept–June, 19.30. (01767 312112).

Chester & North Wales Coin & Banknote Society (1996). Liver Hotel, 110 Brook Street, Chester. 1st Tue, 20.00. (0151 478 4293)

Cheltenham Numismatic Society, The Reddings & District Community Association, North Road, The Reddings, Cheltenham. 3rd Mon, 19.45 (01242 673263)

Coin Correspondence Club (1988). Postal only. A.H. Chubb, 49 White Hart Lane, Barnes, London SW13 0PP. (0181-878 0472).

Crawley Coin Club (1969). Furnace Green Community Centre, Ashburnham Road, Furnace Green, Crawley, West Sussex. 1st Tue, 20.00. (01293 548671).

Crewe & District Coin & Medal Club (1968). Memorial Hall, Church Lane, Wistaston, Crewe, 2nd Tue (exc Jan & July), 19.30. (01270 69836).

Darlington & District Numismatic Society (1968). Darlington Arts Centre, Vane Terrace, Darlington, Co Durhm. 3rd Wed, 19.30. (01609 772976).

Derbyshire Numismatic Society (1964). The Friends' Meeting House, St Helens Street, Derby. 3rd Mon (exc August), 19.45. (01283 211623).

Devon & Exeter Numismatic Society (1965). Red Cross Centre, Butts Road, Heavitree, Exeter, Devon. 3rd Tue, 19.30. (01392 461013).

Edinburgh Numismatic Society (1996). Department of History and Applied Arts, Royal Museum of Scotland, Chambers Street, Edinburgh EH1 1JF. 3rd Mon, 19.30. (0131 225 7534).

Enfield & District Numismatic Society (1969). Millfield House Arts Centre, Silver Street, Edmonton, London N18 1PJ. 3rd Mon, 20.00. (0181-340 0767).

Essex Numismatic Society (1966). Chelmsford & Essex Museum, Moulsham Street, Chelmsford, Essex. 4th Fri (exc Dec), 20.00. (01277 656627).

Glasgow & West of Scotland Numismatic Society (1947). The College Club, University of Glasgow, University Avenue, Glasgow G12. 2nd Thu, Oct–May, 19.30. (0141 633 2564).

Harrow & North West Middlesex Numismatic Society (1968). Harrow Arts Centre, Hatch End Harrow, Middlesex. 2nd and 4th Mon, 20.00. (020 8952 8765).

Havering Numismatic Society (1967). Fairkytes Arts Centre, Billet Lane, Hornchurch, Essex. 1st Tue, 19.30. (01708 704201).

Hayes & District Coin Club. The United Reformed Church Hall, Swakeleys Road, Ickenham, Middlesex. 3rd Thu, 19.45. (0181-422 9178).

Horncastle & District Coin Club (1963). Bull Hotel, Bull Ring, Horncastle, Lincs. 2nd Thu (exc Aug), 19.30. (01754 2706).

Huddersfield Numismatic Society (1947). Huddersfield Library, Princess Alexandra Walk, Huddersfield, West Yorkshire. 1st Mon (exc Jul & Aug), 19.30. (01484 226300).

Hull & District Numismatic Society (1967). The Young People's Institute, George Street, Hull. Monthly (exc Aug & Dec), 19.30. (01482 441933).

International Bank Note Society (1961). General Secretary Clive Rice, 25 Copse Side, Binscombe, Godalming, Surrey GU7 3RU (ibnsuk@onetel.com).

International Bank Note Society, London Branch (1961). Victory Services Club, 63–79 Seymour Street, London W1. Last Thu (exc Dec), 18.00. (020-8360 2759).

International Bank Note Society, East Midlands Chapter (1995). Wollaton Park Community Association, Harrow Road, Wollaton Park. Last Sat (exc Dec). (0115 928 9729).

International Bank Note Society, Scottish Chapter (1995). West End Hotel, Palmerston Place, Edinburgh. Last Sat (exc Dec), 14.30 (0141 642 0132).

International Bank Note Society, North West Chapter (1974). Burnley. Last Sat (exc Dec), 14.30.

Ipswich Numismatic Society (1966). Ipswich Citizens Advice Bureau, 19 Tower Street, Ipswich, Suffolk. 3rd Wed, 19.30. (01473 711158).

Kent Towns Numismatic Society (1913). Adult Education Centre, 9 Sittingbourne Road (Maidstone) and King's School Preparatory School, King Edward Road (Rochester). 1st Fri of month, 19.30 alternately at Maidstone and Rochester. (01622 843881).

Kingston Numismatic Society (1966). King Athel-stan's School, Villiers Road, Kingston-upon-Thames, Surrey. 3rd Thu (exc Jan), 19.30. (020-8397 6944).

Lancashire & Cheshire Numismatic Society (1933). Manchester Central Library, St Peter's Square, Manchester M2 5PD. Monthly, Sep-June, Wed (18.30) or Sat (14.30). (0161 445 2042).

Lincolnshire Numismatic Society (1932). Grimsby Bridge Club, Bargate, Grimsby, South Humberside. 4th Wed (exc Aug), 19.30.

London Numismatic Club (1947). Institute of Archaeology, 31–34 Gordon Square, London WC1H 0PY. Monthly, 18.30.

Loughborough Coin & Search Society (1964). Wallace Humphry Room, Shelthorpe Community Centre, Loughborough, Leics. 1st Thu, 19.30. (01509 261352).

Merseyside Numismatic Society (1947). The Lecture Theatre, Liverpool Museum, William Brown Street, Liverpool L3 8EN. Monthly (exc July & Aug), 19.00. (0151-929 2143).

Mid Lanark Coin Circle (1969). Hospitality Room, The Civic Centre, Motherwell, Lanarkshire. 4th Thu, Sep–Apr (exc Dec), 19.30. (0141-552 2083).

Monmouthshire Numismatic Society. W. R. Lysaght Institute, Corporation Road, Newport. 2nd Wed, 19.30. (029 20 561564)

Morecambe & Lancaster Numismatic Society. Monthly, 19.30. (01524 411036).

Newbury Coin & Medal Club (1971). Monthly, 20.00. (01635 41233).

Northampton Numismatic Society (1969). Old Scouts RFC, Rushmere Road, Northampton. 3rd Mon, 20.00.

Norwich Numismatic Society (1967). Assembly House, Theatre Street, Norwich, Norfolk. 3rd Mon, 19.30. (01493 651577).

Nottinghamshire Numismatic Society (1948). The Meeting Room, County Library, Angel Row, Nottingham NG1 6HP. 2nd Tue (Sep-Apr), 19.30. (0115 9257674).

Nuneaton & District Coin Club (1968). United Reformed Church Room, Coton Road, , Nuneaton, Warwickshire. 2nd Tue, 19.30. (01203 371556).

Orders & Medals Research Society (1942). National Army Museum, Royal Hospital Road, Chelsea, London SW3. Monthly, 14.30. (020-8680 2701).

Ormskirk & West Lancashire Numismatic Society (1970). Eagle & Child, Ormskirk. Lancs. 1st Thu, 20.15. (01704 531266).

Peterborough Coin & Medal Club (1967). The Club Room, APV-Baker Social Club, Alma Road, Peterborough, Cambs. Last Tue (exc July & Aug), 19.30.

Plymouth Coin & Medal Club (1970). RAFA Club, 5 Ermington Terrace, Mutley Plain, Plymouth, Devon. 4th Wed (exc Dec), 19.30. (01752 362859).

Postal Order Society, Mal Tedds, 1 Fairham Court, Wilford, Nottingham, NG11 7EN (0115 981 5639).

Preston & District Numismatic Society (1965). Eldon Hotel, Eldon Street, Preston, Lancs. 1st and 3rd Tue, 20.00. (012572 66869).

Reading Coin Club (1964). Reading Library, Abbey Square, Reading. 1st Tue, 20.00. (0118 9332843).

Redbridge Numismatic Society (1968). Gants Hill Library, Cranbrook Road, Ilford, Essex. 4th Wed, 19.30. (020-8554 5486).

Rochford Hundred Numismatic Society. Civic Suite, Rayleigh Town Hall, Rayleigh, Essex. 2nd Thu, 20.00. (01702 230950).

Romsey Numismatic Society (1969). Romsey WM Conservative Club, Market Place, Romsey, Hants SO5 8NA. 4th Fri (exc Dec), 19.30. (01703 253921).

Rotherham & District Coin Club (1982). Rotherham Art Centre, Rotherham, South Yorkshire. 1st Wed, 19.00. (01709 528179).

Royal Mint Coin Club, PO Box 500, Cardiff CF1 1HA (01443 222111).

Royal Numismatic Society (1836). Society of Antiquaries, Piccadilly, London W1. Monthly (Oct-June), 17.30. Joe Cribb, Coins and Medals, British Museum, London WC1B 3DG (020-7323 8585).

Rye Coin Club (1955). Rye Further Education Centre, Lion Street, Rye, East Sussex. 2nd Thu (Oct-Dec, Feb-May), 19.30. (01424 422974).

St Albans & Hertfordshire Numismatic Society (1948). St Michael's Parish Centre, Museum Entrance, Verulamium Park, St Albans, Herts AL3 4SL. 2nd Tue (exc Aug), 19.30. (01727 862060).

Sheffield Numismatic Society. Telephone for venue. 2nd Wed, 19.00. (0114 2817129)

South East Hants Numismatic Society. Havant Conservative Club, East Street, Havant. 1st Fri. (01329 389419).

South Manchester Numismatic Society (1967). Nursery Inn, Green Lane, Heaton Mersey, Stockport. Fortnightly Mon, 20.00. (0161-485 7017).

S. Wales & Monmouthshire Numismatic Society (1958). The W. R. Lysaght Institute, Corporation Road, Newport. 2nd Wed, 19.30. (029 20561564).

Torbay & District Coin Club (1967). British Rail Social Club, Brunel Road, Newton Abbott, Devon TQ12 4PB. 1st Tue, 1945. (01803 326497).

Tyneside Numismatic Society (1954). RAFA Club, Eric Nelson House, 16 Berwick Road, Gateshead, Tyne & Wear. 2nd Wed, 19.30. (0191 3719700).

Wessex NS (1948). Hotel Bristowe, Grange Road, Southbourne, Bournemouth, Dorset. 2nd Thurs (exc Aug), 19.45. (020 7731 1702).

Wiltshire Numismatic Society (1965). Raven Inn, Poulshot, Nr Devizes, Wiltshire. 3rd Mon, Mar-Dec, 20.00. (01225 703143).

Worthing & District Numismatic Society (1967). Kingsway Hotel, Marine Parade, Worthing, West Sussex BN11 3QQ. 3rd Thu, 19.30. (01634 260114).

Yorkshire Numismatic Society (1909). Swarthmore College, Woodhouse Square, Leeds. 1st Sat (exc Jan, Aug & Dec) (01943 463049).

Many Society meetings are featured in the "What's On" Calendar in COIN NEWS every month.

directory of
Auctioneers

Listed here are the major UK auction houses which handle coins, medals, banknotes and other items of numismatic interest. Many of them hold regular public auctions, whilst others handle numismatic material infrequently.

Baldwin's Auctions Ltd

11 Adelphi Terrace, London WC2N 6BJ (020-7930 6879 fax 020-7930 9450). Website: www.baldwin.sh.

Banking Memorabilia

PO Box 14, Carlisle CA3 8DZ (0169 7476465).

Bloomsbury Auctions

Bloomsbury House, 24 Maddox Street, London W1S 1PP. (020 7495 9494 fax: 020 7495 9499). e-mail: info@bloomsburyauctions.com www.bloomsbury.com

Bonhams/Glendining's

Montpelier Street, Knightsbridge, London SW7 1HH. (020 7393 3914). www.bonhams.com.

A. F. Brock & Company

269 London Road, Hazel Grove, Stockport, Cheshire SK7 4PL (0161-456 5050/5112). Website: www.afbrock.co.uk

Corbitts

5 Moseley Sreet, Newcastle upon Tyne NE1 1YE (0191-232 7268 fax 0191-261 4130).

Croydon Coin Auctions

272 Melfort Road, Thornton Heath, Surrey CR7 7RR (020-8656 4583/020-8684 6515 fax 020-8656 4583). www.croydoncoinauctions.co.uk.

Dix Noonan Webb

16 Bolton Street, Piccadilly, London W1J 8BQ (020 7499 5022 fax 020 7499 5023) Website www.dnw.co.uk.

Dundee Philatelic Auctions

15 King Street, Dundee DD1 1JD. (01382 224946).

Edinburgh Coin Shop

11 West Crosscauseway, Edinburgh EH8 9JW (0131 668 2928 fax 0131 668 2926).

B. Frank & Son

3 South Avenue, Ryton, Tyne & Wear NE40 3LD (0191 413 8749 fax 0191 413 2957). e-mail: bfrankandson@aol.com

Hoods Postal Coin Auctions

23 High Street, Kilbirnie, Ayrshire KA25 7EX (fax/tel 01505 682157). Postal only

Kleeford Coin Auctions

19 Craythorns Crescent, Dishforth, Thirsk YO7 3LY. (tel/fax 01845 577977).

Lockdale Coins

37 Upper Orwell Street, Ipswich IP4 1BR. (01473 218588). www.lockdales.co.uk.

London Coins Auction

12 Redhill Wood, New Ash Green, Kent DA3 8QH. (020 8 688 5297) www.londoncoins.co.uk.

Morton and Eden

45 Maddox Street, London, W1S 2PE. (020 7493 5344 fax: 020 7495 6325). www.mortonandeden.com

Neales

192–194 Mansfield Road, Nottingham NG1 3HU (0115 9624141 fax 0115 9856890).

Noble Numismatics Pty Ltd

169 Macquarie Street, Sydney 2000, Australia. (+61 2 9233 6009) e-mail: info@noble.net.au

Sheffield Coin Auctions

7 Beacon Close, Sheffield S9 1AA (0114 2490442).

Spink & Son Ltd

69 Southampton Row, Bloomsbury, London WC1B 4ET (020 7563 4000 fax 20 7563 4066). www.spink-online.com

Warwick & Warwick

Chalon House, Scarbank, Millers Road, Warwick CV34 5DB (01926 499031 fax 01926 491906) email info@warwickandwarwick.com

directory of
Dealers

The dealers listed below have comprehensive stocks of papermoney, unless otherwise stated. Specialities, where known, are noted. Many of those listed are postal dealers only, so to avoid disappointment always make contact by telephone or mail in the first instance, particularly before travelling any distance.

Abbreviations:
ADA—Antiquities Dealers Association
ANA—American Numismatic Association
BADA—British Antique Dealers Association
BNTA—British Numismatic Trade Association
IAPN—International Association of Professional
  Numismatists
IBNS—International Bank Note Society
P—Postal only
L—Publishes regular lists
F—Fairs

A. Ackroyd (IBNS)
  62 Albert Road, Parkstone, Poole, Dorset BH12 2DB (tel/fax 01202 739039). *P. L. Banknotes, cheques etc.*

David Allen Coins and Collectables
  PO Box 125, Pinner, Middlesex HA5 2TX (020 866 6796). *P. L. British and world coins, tokens, banknotes.*

Keith Austin/KABC (IBNS)
  PO Box 89, Carlisle, Cumbria CA3 0GH (01228 819149). L. *Banknotes.* E-mail: kaustin@kabc.freeserve.co.uk

Banking Memorabilia (IBNS)
  PO Box 14, Carlisle, Cumbria (0169 747 6465). 09.00– 18.00 (not Sun). *Cheques, banknotes, related ephemera. auctions.*

Banknotes 4U
  P.O Box 123, Huddersfield HD8 9WY (01484 860415). *British & World Banknotes, Cheques & banking memorabilia.*

Bath Stamp and Coin Shop (BNTA)
  Pulteney Bridge, Bath, Avon BA2 4AY (01225 463073). Mon-Sat 09.30–17.30. *British, world coins and banknotes.*

R. P. & P. J. Beckett
  Maesyderw, Capel Dewi, Llandyssul, Dyfed SA44 4PJ. E-mail: orders@rppjbeckett.com Fax 01559 395631 *P. World crowns, coin sets and banknotes.*

Berkshire Coin Centre
  35 Castle Street, Reading, Berkshire RG1 7SB (01734 575593). 10.00–16.00 weekdays, half-day Sat. *British and world coins and banknotes.*

Barry Boswell (IBNS)
  24 Townsend Lane, Upper Boddington, Daventry, Northants NN11 6DR (01327 261877). *P. L. British and world banknotes.* E-mail: Barry.Boswell@btinternet.com.

A. F. Brock & Company
  269 London Road, Hazel Grove, Stockport, Cheshire SK7 4PL (0161 456 5050/5112). Mon-Sat 09.30–17.30. Website: www.afbrock.co.uk

E. J. & C. A. Brooks (BNTA, IBNS)
  44 Kiln Road, Thundersley, Essex SS7 1TB (01268 753835). *Any time up to 23.00. L. British coins and banknotes.*

Iain Burn (IBNS)
  2 Compton Gardens, 53 Park Road, Camberley, Surrey GU15 2SP (01276 23304). *England and Treasury notes.*

Cambridge Stamp Centre Ltd
  9 Sussex Street, Cambridge CB4 4HU (01223 63980). Mon-Sat 09.00–17.30. *British coins and banknotes.*

M. Coeshaw
  PO Box 115, Leicester LE3 8JJ (0116 2873808). *P.*

Coin & Collectors Centre
  PO Box 22, Pontefract, West Yorkshire WR8 1YT (01977 704112). *P. British coins and banknotes.*

Coincraft (ANA, IBNS)
  44/45 Great Russell Street, London WC1B 3LU (020 7636 1188 and 020 7637 8785 fax 020 7323 2860). Mon-Fri 09.30–17.00, Sat 10.00–14.30. *L (newspaper format). Coins and banknotes.* www.coincraft.com.

Coinote Services Ltd
  74 Elwick Road, Hartlepool TS26 NYL (01429 273044). *P. L. Coins and banknotes 1615 todate. Accessories and books.*

The Collector
  242 High Street, Orpington, Kent BR6 0LZ (01689 890045). Mon-Sat 09.30–17.00 (closed Tue). *Coins, medals, banknotes, badges, militaria, cigarette cards etc*

Collectors' Forum
  237 South Street, Romford, Essex RM1 2BE (01708 723357). Mon-Sat 09.30-18.00 Thu 09.30-14.00. *British coins, medals and banknotes.*

Collectors Gallery (BNTA, IBNS)
  24 The Parade, St Marys Place, Shrewsbury SY1 1DL (01743 272140 fax 01743 366041). Mon-Fri 09.00– 18.00, half-day Sat. *Coins and banknotes. Accessories and related books. Stockist of Abafil Coin Cases.* www.collectors-gallery.co.uk.

Corbitts (BNTA)
  5 Mosley Street, Newcastle Upon Tyne NE1 1YE (0191 232 7268 fax: 0191 261 4130). *Dealers and auctioneers of all coins, medals and banknotes.*

G. D. Courtenay
  58 New Peachey Lane, Uxbridge, Middlesex UB8 3SX. *P. L. Coins, medals, tokens and banknotes.*

Davidson Monk Fairs
  PO Box 201, Croydon, Surrey CR9 7AQ (020 8656 4583). *Organiser of bi-monthly fairs at Jurys Hotel, 16-22 Great Russell Street, London WC1.*

Paul Davies Ltd (ANA, BNTA, IAPN)
  PO Box 17, Ilkley, West Yorkshire LS29 8TZ (01943 603116). *P. World coins and banknotes.*

Dei Gratia
PO Box 3568, Buckingham MK18 4ZS (01280 848000).
P. L. Pre-Roman to modern coins, antiquities, banknotes.

Clive Dennett (BNTA, IBNS)
66 St Benedicts Street, Norwich, Norfolk NR2 4AR
(01603 624315). Mon-Fri 09.00–17.30, Sat 09.00–16.00
(closed Thu). *L. World paper money.*

C. J. Denton (ANA, BNTA, FRNS)
PO Box 25, Orpington, Kent BR6 8PU (01689 873690).
P. World coins.

Dolphin Coins (ANA)
22 High Street, Leighton Buzzard, Bedfordshire, LU7
7EB. (01525 383822 Fax: 01525 383872). Mon-Fri
09.30– 17.00. Sat appt only. *L. British and world coins
and banknotes.* Website: www.dolphincoins.com.

Dorset Coin Co Ltd (BNTA)
193 Ashley Road, Parkstone, Poole, Dorset BH14 9DL
(01202 739606, fax 01202 739230). *P. L. Separate coin
and banknote lists.*

Duncannon Partnership
4 Beaufort Road, Reigate, RH2 9DJ (01737 244222 fax:
01737 224743) *Suppliers of albums, coin products and
accessories.*

Edinburgh Coin Shop (ANA) (BNTA)
11 West Crosscauseway, Edinburgh EH8 9JW (0131
668 2928 fax 0131 668 2926). Mon-Sat 10.00–17.30. *L.
World coins, medals and banknotes. Postal auctions.*

Ely Stamp & Coin Shop
27 Fore Hill, Ely, Cambs CB7 1AA (01353 663919).
Mon, Wed-Sat 09.30–17.30. *World coins, medals and
banknotes.*

Jos Eijermans (Maastricht Fair)
P.O.Box 3240, NL-5930 AE (31-77-477-4047 Fax:
31-77-477-4027) E-mail: APnC.Eijermans@wxs.
nl *Organisers of Papermoney, Bond and Share fair–
Maastricht.*

Evesham Stamp & Coin Centre
Magpie Antiques, Paris House, 61 High Street,
Evesham, Worcs WR11 4DA (01386 41631). Mon-Sat
09.00–17.30. *British coins and banknotes.*

Richard N. Flashman
54 Ebbsfleet Walk, Gravesend, Kent, DA11 9EW. *L. P.
British banknotes.*

Format of Birmingham Ltd (ANA, BNTA, IAPN,
IBNS)
18-19 Bennetts Hill, Birmingham B2 5QJ (0121 643
2058). Mon-Fri 09.30-7.00. *L. Coins, tokens and medals.*

B. Frank & Son (ANA, IBNS)
3 South Avenue, Ryton, Tyne & Wear NE40 3LD
(0191 413 8749). *P. L. Banknotes and cheques, coins
of the world. Organiser of the North of England Coin &
Banknote fair.* E-mail: bfrankandson@aol.com

John Gaunt
21 Harvey Road, Bedford MK41 9LF (01234 217685).
By appointment. *Numismatic books.*

Alistair Gibb (IBNS)
5 West Albert Road, Kirkcaldy, Fife KY1 1DL (01592
269045). *P. L. Banknotes and books on banking.*

Kate Gibson (IBNS)
P.O. Box 819 Camberly, GU16 6ZU (01276 24954. *L
World banknotes.* www.katespapermoney.co.uk.

Glance Back Books
17 Upper Street, Chepstow, Gwent NP6 5EX (01291
626562). 10.30–17.30. *World coins, medals, banknotes.*

K. Goulborn
Rhyl Coin Shop, 12 Sussex Street, Rhyl, Clwyd
(01745 338112 or 01745 344856). *P. L. British coins and
banknotes.*

Ian Gradon (IBNS)
PO Box 359, Durham, DH7 6WZ. (0191 3719 700).
www.worldnotes.co.uk. *P. L. World bank notes.*

Granta Stamp & Coin Shop
28 Magdalene Street, Cambridge CB3 0AF (01223
315044) Mon-Sat 10.30-18.30. *English coins and
banknotes.*

Grantham Coins (BNTA)
PO Box 60, Grantham, Lincs (01476 870565). *P. L.
English coins and banknotes.*

Eric Green—Agent in UK for Ronald J. Gillio Inc,
1013 State Street, Santa Barbara, California, USA (020
8907 0015, Mobile 0468 454948). *Gold coins, banknotes*

Ian Haines
PO Box 45, Hereford, HR2 7YP (01432 268178). *P. L.
British and foreign coins and banknotes.*

A. D. Hamilton & Co (ANA, BNTA)
7 St Vincent Place, Glasgow G1 5JA (0141 221 5423,
fax 0141 248 6019). Mon-Sat 09.00-17.30. *British
and World coins and banknotes.* Website: www.
adhamiltons.com

John Harvey (IBNS)
PO Box 118, Bury St. Edmunds, IP33 2NE (01284
761894). *British Isles, Scotland, Channel Islands.*

Craig Holmes
6 Marlborough Drive, Bangor, Co Down BT19 1HB.
P. L. Low cost banknotes of the world.

R. G. Holmes
11 Cross Park, Ilfracombe, Devon EX34 8BJ (01271
864474). *P. L. Coins, modern world crowns and foreign
banknotes.*

Homeland Holding Ltd (IBNS)
Homeland, St John, Jersey, Channel Islands JE3 4AB
(01534 65339). Mon-Fri 09.00-2.00. *World coins.*

HTSM Coins
26 Dosk Avenue, Glasgow G13 4LQ. *P. L. British and
foreign coins and banknotes.*

Intercol London (ANA, BNTA, IBNS)
43 Templars Crescent, London N3 3QR (020 8349 2207
or 020 7354 2599). *P. Paper money of the world.*

Peter Ireland Ltd (BNTA, IBNS)
31 Clifton Street, Blackpool, Lancs FY1 1JQ (01253
21588 fax 0253 300232). Mon-Sat 09.00-17.30.*British
and world coins, medals and tokens (some banknotes).*

JAK (J. R. Leonard Ltd) (IBNS)
31 Vapron Road, Mannamead, Plymouth, Devon
PL3 5NJ (01752 665405). *P. L. GB and Commonwealth
banknotes.*

Richard W. Jeffery
Trebehor, Porthcurno, Penzance, Cornwall TR19
6LS (01736 871263). *P. British and world coins and
banknotes.*

KB Coins (BNTA)
50 Lingfield Road, Martins Wood, Stevenage, Herts
SG1 5SL (01438 312661). 09.00–18.00 by appointment
only. *L. Mainly British coins and banknotes.*

Peter Licence
31 Reigate Way, Wallington, Surrey SM6 8NU (020
8688 5297). *P. British and World coins.*

Lighthouse Publications (UK)
4 Beaufort Road, Reigate, Surrey RH2 9DJ (01737
244222 Fax 01737 24743). *L. Manufacturers and
stockists of albums, cabinets and accessories.*

Lindner Publications Ltd
3a Hayle Industrial Park, Hayle, Cornwall TR27
4DX. Mon–Fri 09.00–13.00. *L. Manufacturers of
albums, cabinets and accessories.* Website: www.
stampaccessories.net.

Lockdale Coins
36 Upper Orwell Street, Ipswich IP4 1HP, (01473
218588), 23 Magdalene Street, Cambridge CB3 0AF,
(01223 361163), 168 London Road South, Lowestoft
NR33 0BB, (01502 568468). *L. (Shop's open 9.30–4.30
Mon–Sat). World coins, medals, banknotes and
accessories.* Website: www.lockdales.co.uk.

London Coins
12 Redhill Wood, New Ash Green, Kent DA3
8QH. (01474 871464) www.londoncoins.co.uk.. *British
and world coins.*

Clive Maxwell-Yates

21 Nicolas Road, Chorlton Manchester, M21 1LG (0161 881 7015). *P. L. World banknotes.*

Michael Coins

6 Hillgate Street, London W8 7SR (020 7727 1518). Mon-Fri 10.00-17.00. *World coins and banknotes.*

Graeme & Linda Monk (ANA, BNTA)

PO Box 201, Croydon, Surrey, CR9 7AQ (020 8656 4583 fax 020 8656 4583). *P. Fair organisers.*

Peter Morris

1 Station Concourse, Bromley North Station, Bromley, BR1 1NN or PO Box 223, Bromley, BR1 4EQ (020 8313 3410 Fax: 020 8466 8502). Mon-Fri 10.00–18.00, Sat 0900-14.00 or by appointment. *L. British and world coins and banknotes, numismatic books.* Website: www. petermorris.co.uk.

Colin Narbeth & Son Ltd (ANA, IBNS)

20 Cecil Court, Leicester Square, London WC2N 4HE (020 7379 6975). Mon-Sat 10.30-17.00. *World banknotes.* Website: www.colin-narbeth.com.

New Forest Leaves

Bisterne Close, Burley, Ringwood, Hants BH24 4BA (014253 3315). *Publishers of numismatic books.*

Notability (IBNS)

'Mallards', Chirton, Devizes, Wilts SN10 3QX (01380 723961). *P. L. Banknotes of the world.* Website: www. notability.org.uk.

Michael O'Grady (IBNS)

PO Box 307, Pinner, Middlesex HA5 4XT (020 8428 4002). *P. British and world paper money.* E-mail: mike@ogrady.clara.co.uk

Penrith Coin & Stamp Centre

37 King Street, Penrith, Cumbria CA11 7AY (01768 64185). Mon-Sat 09.00–17.30. *World coins and notes.*

Pentland Coins (IBNS)

Pentland House, 92 High Street, Wick, Caithness KW14 5L. *P. British, world coins and world banknotes.*

John Pettit Pty Ltd

GPO Box 4593, Sydney 2001, Australia. (00612 9235 0888) www.johnpettit.com. *P. L. Rare banknote specialist*

Phil Phipps (IBNS)

PO Box 31, Emsworth, Hants PO10 7WE (tel/fax 01243 376086). *P. L. World and German banknotes.* E-mail: phillip@worldcurrency.cc.

David Pratchett

Trafalgar Square Collectors Centre, 7 Whitcomb Street, London WC2H 7HA. (020 7930 1979). Mon-Fri 10.00–7.30. *Specialist in world coins and banknotes.* Website: www.coinsonline.co.uk.

Pomexport (No. One Money Man)

P.O Box, Ridgefield Park, New Jersey, 07660 (1 201 641 6641 fax: 1 201 641 1700) *Wholesale Paper Money, Stocks , Bonds Coins, Medals & Tokens.*

Quentin Freres

18 Rue Saint Gilles, 75003 Paris, France (33 1 42 713794, fax 33 1 42 713754). email quentin@worldnet. fr. *Specialists in world banknotes.*

George Rankin Coin Co Ltd (ANA, BNTA)

325 Bethnal Green Road, London E2 6AH (020 7729 1280 fax 020 7729 5023). Mon-Sat 10.00-18.00 (half-day Thu). *World coins and banknotes.*

Mark T. Ray (formerly MTR Coins)

22a Kingsnorth Close, Newark, Notts NG24 1PS. (01636 703152). *P. British coins and banknotes.*

Scottish Banknotes

Sconser, Isle of Skye, IV48 8TD (01478 650450) E-mail: johnaunc@aol.com. *Scottish Banknotes*

Scot Mint

5 Main Street, Ayr, Scotland, KA8 8BU. (01292 268244 Fax: 01292 268626). e-mail: rob@scotmint.com *Medals, Badges, Militaria, Banknotes Coins, Collectables & Accessories*

Safe Albums (UK) Ltd

Freepost (RG 1792), Wokingham, Berks RG11 1BR (01734 328976 fax 01734 328612). *P. Banknote albums, coin holders, etc.*

Simmons Gallery (ANA, BNTA, IBNS)

P.O Box 104, Leystone, London E11 IND (0207 8989 8097 fax 020 7831 2090). *Organisers of the London Coin Fair, Cumberland Hotel, Marble Arch, London W1. L. Coins, tokens and medals.* Website: simmonsgallery. co.uk.

E. Smith (ANA, IBNS)

PO Box 348, Lincoln LN6 0TX (01522 684681 fax 01522 689528). *P. Organiser of the Morley, Leeds, monthly coin fair. World coins and paper money.*

Spink & Son Ltd (ANA, BNTA, IAPN, IBNS)

69 Southampton Row, Bloomsbury, London WC1B 4ET (020 7563 4000 Fax: 020 7563 4066). Mon-Sat 09.30–17.30. *Ancient, medieval and modern world coins, orders, medals and decorations, banknotes and numismatic books—new and secondhand.* Website: www.spink.com.

Stamp & Collectors Centre

404 York Town Road, College Town, Camberley, Surrey GU15 4PR (01276 32587 fax 01276 32505). Mon, Tue, Thu, Sat 09.00–17.00, Wed, Fri 09.00–1900. *World coins, medals and banknotes.*

Mel Steinberg & Son

P.O Box 752, San Anselmo, CA94979 (415 897 1654) E-mail: melsteinberg@mindspring.com. *World Banknotes*

Sterling Coins & Medals

2 Somerset Road, Boscombe, Bournemouth, Dorset BH7 6JH (01202 423881). Mon-Sat 09.30–16.30 (closed Wed). *World coins and banknotes.*

Vera Trinder Ltd

38 Bedford Street, Strand, London WC2E 9EU (020 7836 2365/6). Mon-Fri 08.30-17.30. *L. Catalogues and books, albums, envelopes, cases and accessories.*

Vista World Banknotes

5 Greenfields Way, Burley-in-Wharfdale, Ilkley, W.Yorks, LS29 7RB. *World Notes list.* E-mail: vistabanknotes@barclays.net.

Pam West, British Notes (IBNS, ANA, PCDA)

PO Box 257, Sutton, Surrey SM3 9WW (020 8641 3224). *P. L. English banknotes, British banknotes accessories.* Website: west-banknotes.co.uk.

West Cornwall Stamp Centre

13 Fore Street, Hayle, Cornwall TR27 4DX (01736 751910 fax: 01736 751911. *L. Coin Accessories.*

West Essex Coin Investments (BNTA, IBNS)

Croft Cottage, Station Road, Alderholt, Fordingbridge, Hants SP6 3AZ (01425 656 459). *P. L. British and World coins and paper money.*

R & J White (IBNS)

29 Shortacre, Basildon, Essex SS14 2LR (01268 522923). *P. L. Banknotes and world ephemera.*

Trevor Wilkin

PO Box 182, Cammeray, NSW, Australia (0061 2 9438 5040. <trevorsnotes@bigpond.com>. *P. L. World banknotes. Specialist in polymer notes.*

wrb-banknotes

P.O Box 52, Downham Market, PE38 0WX. E-mail: rdennettnotes@aol.com

Barry Wright

54 Dooley Drive, Bootle, Merseyside. L30 8RT. *P. L. World banknotes.*

www.antiquestall.com

Online market place for banknotes and collectables.

Banks, Mints and numismatic
Bureaux
of the world

Many national banks and mints operate numismatic bureaux and sales agencies from which coins, notes and other numismatic products may be obtained direct. The conditions under which purchases may be made vary considerably. In many cases at the present time bureaux will accept orders from overseas customers quoting their credit card number and its expiry date; but in others payment can only be made by certified bank cheque, or international money order, or by girobank. Cash is seldom, if ever, acceptable. It is best to write in the first instance to enquire about methods of payment.

A

National Mint, Baghe Arg, Kabul, Afghanistan

Bank Mille Afghan, Kabul, Afghanistan

Banque d'Algerie, Sucursale d'Alger, 8 Boulevard Carnot, Alger, Algeria

Banco de Angola, Luanda, Daroal, Angola

Casa de Moneda de la Nacion, Avenida Antartica, Buenos Aires, BA, Argentina

Royal Australian Mint, Department of the Treasury, Canberra, ACT, Australia

GoldCorp Australia, Perth Mint Buildings, GPO Box M924, Perth, Western Australia 6001

Oesterreichsiches Hauptmunzamt, Am Heumarkt 1, A-1031 Wien, Postfach 225, Austria

Oesterreichische Nationalbank, A-1090 Wien, Otto Wagner-platz 3, Austria

B

Treasury Department, PO Box 557, Nassau, Bahamas (*coins*)

Ministry of Finance, PO Box 300, Nassau, Bahamas (*banknotes*)

Bank of Bahrain, PO Box 106, Manama, Bahrain

Eastern Bank, PO Box 29, Manama, Bahrain

Monnaie Royale de Belgique, Avenue de Pacheco 32, B-1000 Bruxelles, Belgium

Banque Nationale de Belgique SA, Caisse Centrale, Bruxelles, Belgium

Banque de Bruxelles SA, 2 Rue de la Regence, Bruxelles 1, Belgium

Casa de la Moneda, Potosi, Bolivia

Banco Central de Bolivia, La Paz, Bolivia

Casa da Moeda, Praca da Republica 173, Rio de Janeiro, Brazil

Hemus FTO, 7 Vasil Levski Street, Sofia C-1, Bulgaria

Banque de la Republique, Bujumbura, Burundi

C

Banque Centrale, Douala, Boite Postale 5.445, Cameroun

Royal Canadian Mint, 320 Sussex Drive, Ottawa 2, Ontario, Canada K1A 0G8

Casa de Moneda, Quinta Normal, Santiago, Chile

Casa de Moneda, Calle 11 no 4-93, Bogota, Colombia

Numismatic Section, The Treasury, Avarua, Rarotonga, Cook Islands

Banco Centrale de Costa Rica, Departamento de Contabilidad, San Jose, Costa Rica, CA

Central Bank of Cyprus, PO Box 1087, Nicosia, Cyprus

Artia, Ve Smekach 30, PO Box 790, Praha 1, Czech Republic

D

Den Kongelige Mønt, Amager Boulevard 115, København S, Denmark

Danmarks Nationalbank, Holmens Kanal 17, 1060 København K, Denmark

Banco Central de Santo Domingo, Santo Domingo, Dominican Republic

E

Banco Central, Quito, Ecuador

Mint House, Abbassia, Cairo, Egyptian Arab Republic

Exchange Control Department, National Bank of Egypt, Cairo, Egyptian Arab Republic

Banco Central de la Republica, Santa Isabel, Equatorial Guinea

Commercial Bank of Ethiopia, Foreign Branch, PO Box 255, Addis Ababa, Ethiopia

F

Currency Board, Victoria Parade, Suva, Fiji

Suomen Rahapaja, Katajanokanlaituri 3, Helsinki 16, Finland

Suomen Pankki, PO Box 10160, Helsinki 10, Finland

Hotel de Monnaie, 11 Quai de Conti, 75-Paris 6e, France

G

Banque Centrale Libreville, Boite Postale 112, Gabon

Verkaufstelle fur Sammlermunzen, D-638 Bad Homburg vdH, Bahnhofstrasse 16–18, Germany

Staatliche Munze Karlsruhe, Stephanienstrasse 28a, 75 Karlsruhe, Germany

Staatliche Munze Cannstatt, Taubenheimerstrasse 77, 7 Stuttgart-Bad, Germany

Bayerisches Hauptmunzamt, Hofgraben 4, 8 Munich, Germany

Hamburgische Munze, Norderstrasse 66, 2 Hamburg 1, Germany

Bank of Ghana, PO Box 2674, Accra, Ghana

Pobjoy Mint, Mint House, 92 Oldfields Road, Sutton, Surrey SM1 2NW

Royal Mint, Llantrisant, Mid Glamorgan, Wales, CF7 8YT

Royal Mint Coin Club, PO Box 500, Cardiff, CF1 1HA

Bank of Greece, Treasury Department, Cash, Delivery & Despatch Division, PO Box 105, Athens, Greece

Casa Nacional de Moneda, 6a Calle 4-28, Zona 1, Ciudad Guatemala, Republica de Guatemala CA

States Treasury, St Peter Port, Guernsey, Channel Islands

Bank of Guyana, PO Box 658, Georgetown, Guyana

H

Banque Nationale de la Republique d'Haiti, Rue Americaine et Rue Fereu, Port-au-Prince, Haiti

Banco Central de Honduras, Tegucigalpa DC, Honduras CA

State Mint, Ulloi utca 102, Budapest VIII, Hungary

Artex, PO Box 167, Budapest 62, Hungary

Magyar Nemzeti Bank, Board of Exchange, Budapest 54, Hungary

I

Sedlabanki Islands, Reykjavik, Iceland

Indian Government Mint, Bombay 1, India

Arthie Vasa, Keabajoran Baru, Djakarta, Indonesia

Perum Peruri, Djakarta, Indonesia

National Mint, Tehran, Iran

Bank Markazi Iran, Tehran, IranCentral Bank of Iraq, PO Box 64, Baghdad, Iraq

Central Bank of Ireland, Dublin 2, Republic of Ireland

The Treasury, Government Buildings, Prospect Hill, Douglas, Isle of Man

Israel Stamp and Coin Gallery, 4 Maze Street, Tel Aviv, Israel

Istituto Poligraphico e Zecca dello Stato, Via Principe Umberto, Roma, Italy

J

Decimal Currency Board, PO Box 8000, Kingston, Jamaica

Mint Bureau, 1 Shinkawasakicho, Kita-ku, Osaka 530, Japan

Numismatic Section, Treasury Department, St Helier, Jersey

Central Bank of Jordan, Amman, Jordan

Banque Nationale du Liban, Rue Masraf Loubnan, Beirut, Lebanon

K

Central Bank, PO Box 526, Kuwait

L

Bank of Lithuania, Cash Department, Gedimino av. 6, 2001 Vilius, Lithuania

Caisse Generale de l'Etat, 5 Rue Goethe, Luxembourg-Ville, Grande Duche de Luxembourg

M

Institut d'Emission Malgache, Boite Postale 205, Tananarive, Madagascar

Central Bank of Malta, Valletta 1, Malta

Casa de Moneda, Calle del Apartado no 13, Mexico 1, DF, Mexico

Le Tresorier General des Finances, Monte Carlo, Principaute de Monaco

Banque de l'Etat du Maroc, Rabat, Morocco

Banco Nacional Ultramarino, Maputo, Republica de Mocambique

British Bank of the Middle East, Muscat

N

Royal Mint, Dharahara, Katmandu, Nepal

Nepal Rastra Bank, Katmandu, Nepal

Rijks Munt, Leidseweg 90, Utrecht, Netherlands

Hollandsche Bank-Unie NV, Willemstad, Breedestraat 1, Curacao, Netherlands Antilles

Central Bank of Curacao, Willemstad, Curacao, Netherlands Antilles

The Treasury, Private Bag, Lambton Quay, Wellington, New Zealand

Banco de Nicaragua, Departamento de Emison, La Tresoria, Apartada 2252, Managua, Nicaragua

Nigerian Security Printing and Minting Corporation, Ahmadu Bello Road, Victoria Island, Lagos, Nigeria

Central Bank of Nigeria, Tinubu Square LB, Lagos, Nigeria

Norges Bank, Oslo, Norway

Den Kongelige Mynt, Hyttegaten, Konigsberg, Norway

P

Pakistan State Mint, Baghban Pura, Lahore 9, Pakistan

National Development Bank, Asuncion, Paraguay

Casa Nacional de Moneda, Calle Junin 791, Lima, Peru

Central Bank of the Philippines, Manila, Philippines

Bank Handlowy w Warszawie, Ul. Romuald Traugutta 7, Warsaw, Poland

Desa Foreign Trade Department, Al. Jerozolimskie 2, Warszawa, Poland

Casa da Moeda, Avenida Dr Antonio Jose de Almeida, Lisbon 1, Portugal

R

Cartimex, 14-18 Aristide Briand St, PO Box 134-135, Bucharest, Roumania

Bank of Foreign Trade, Commercial Department, Moscow K 16, Neglinnaja 12, Russian Federation

Banque Nationale du Rwanda, Boite Postale 351, Kigali, Republique Rwandaise

S

Numismatic Section, Box 194, GPO, Apia, Samoa

Azienda Autonoma di Stato Filatelica-Numismatica, Casalla Postale 1, 47031 Repubblica di San Marino

Banque Internationale pour le Commerce, 2 Avenue Roume, Dakar, Senegal

Bank of Yugoslavia, PO Box 1010, Belgrade, Serbia

The Treasury, PO Box 59, Victoria, Seychelles

Bank of Sierra Leone, PO Box 30, Freetown, Sierra Leone

The Singapore Mint, 249 Jalan Boon Lay, Jurong, Singapore

South African Mint, PO Box 464, Pretoria, South Africa

Government Printing Agency, 93 Bukchang Dong, Chungku, Seoul, Republic of South Korea

Fabrica Nacional de Moneda y Timbre, Jorge Juan 106, Madrid 9, Spain

Bank of Sri Lanka, PO Box 241, Colombo, Sri Lanka

Hong Kong and Shanghai Banking Corporation, PO Box 73, Colombo 1, Sri Lanka

Sudan Mint, PO Box 43, Khartoum, Sudan

Bank of Sudan, PO Box 313, Khartoum, Sudan

Bank of Paramaribo, Paramaribo, Suriname

Kungelige Mynt och Justeringsverket, Box 22055, Stockholm 22, Sweden

Eidgenossische Staatskasse, Bundesgasse 14, CH-3003, Berne, Switzerland

Central Bank of Syria, Damascus, Syrian Arab Republic

T

Central Mint of China, 44 Chiu Chuan Street, Taipei, Taiwan, ROC

Royal Thai Mint, 4 Chao Fah Road, Bangkok, Thailand

Numismatic Section, The Treasury, Nuku'alofa, Tonga

Central Bank of Trinidad and Tobago, PO Box 1250, Port of Spain, Trinidad

Banque Centrale de Tunisie, Tunis, Tunisia

State Mint, Maliye Bakanligi Darphane Mudurlugu, Istanbul, Turkey

U

Bank of Uganda, PO Box 7120, Kampala, Uganda

Numismatic Service, US Assay Office, 350 Duboce Avenue, San Francisco, CA, 94102, USA

Office of the Director of the Mint, Treasury Department, Washington, DC, 20220, USA

Philadelphia Mint, 16th and Spring Garden Streets, Philadelphia, PA, 19130, USA

Franklin Mint, Franklin Center, Pennsylvania, 19063, USA

Banco Central del Uruguay, Cerrito 351, Montevideo, RO del Uruguay

V

Ufficio Numismatico, Governatorato dello Stato della Citta de Vaticano, Italy

Banco Central de Venezuela, Caracas, Venezuela

Y

Yemen Bank, Sana'a, Yemen.

Z

Bank of Zambia, PO Box 80, Lusaka, Zambia

Chief Cashier, Reserve Bank, PO Box 1283, Harare, Zimbabwe

Bank of England, 1845—the Five Pound Bank Note Office.

Banknotes and
The law

Counterfeit Currency

A counterfeit is a forgery or imitation of a coin or banknote produced with the intention of defrauding the revenue of the State or deceiving members of the public. By the Coinage Offences Act (1861) it was a felony to counterfeit gold or silver coins. Lesser offences included the gilding of farthings and sixpences to pass them off as half-sovereigns, the possession of moulds, machines or tools clandestinely removed from the Royal Mint, the impairment or diminution of gold or silver coins by filing or clipping (or even the possession of such filings and clippings).

The Coinage Act of 1870 made provision for the counterfeiting of base-metal coins, or the stamping of letters or words on coins of any kind, or the forging of colonial coinage. The most celebrated prosecution under this Act occurred in 1930 when Martin Coles Harman was convicted and fined £5 for issuing bronze coins resembling the British penny and halfpenny for the island of Lundy of which he was then the proprietor. Interestingly, no attempt was made to prosecute the Birmingham Mint which actually struck the coins (prudently omitting the H mintmark).

The making of medals or coins resembling current coin became a misdemeanour under the Counterfeit Medal Act of 1883.This Act is invoked from time to time against manufacturers or distributors of medallic pieces or coin jewellery. Such pieces, often struck in 9 carat gold, are deemed to infringe the Act if, for example, they have a figure even vaguely resembling St George and the Dragon on one side. The use of the royal effigy, however, without due authorisation, is regarded as a misdemeanour punishable by an unlimited fine and the confiscation of tools, dies and instruments. At the present time it is a serious offence to make a counterfeit of a currency note or coin with the intention of passing it off or tendering it as genuine. This offence carries a maximum penalty of ten years' imprisonment or an unlimited fine, or both. Making a counterfeit of a currency note or coin without lawful authority incurs a penalty up to two years' imprisonment or an unlimited fine, or both.

Passing or tendering as genuine anything which is known or believed to be a counterfeit of a currency note or coin renders the criminal on conviction to a term of ten years' imprisonment or an unlimited fine, or both. The mere possession of any forged note or coin is itself a criminal offence. Possessing countertfeits without authority or permission so to do, and doing so knowingly, renders the possessor liable to two years' imprisonment or an unlimited fine, or both. The Act also stipulates that the reproduction of a current banknote—of the Bank of England or of the Scottish and Northern Irish banks is a serious offence. This clause covers even such apparently innocent acts as making a photocopy (whether in black and white or full colour) of a current banknote, the photography of such a note or the illustration of such a note in any book, magazine or newspaper. Strict regulations are laid down concerning the legitimate illustration of notes, whether current or not, in books and periodicals; such illustrations must be either greatly reduced or enlarged *and* must bear a prominent defacement, such as SPECIMEN or CANCELLED. It is also a serious offence to utilise a reproduction of a current British banknote in any medium. Theoretically this includes such things as tea-towels, T-shirts, mugs, plates and other souvenirs in glass or ceramics, but in practice the law seems to turn a blind eye to such practices. Imitations and parodies of notes and coins are also regarded as infringements of the law, but in these instances prosecution of the offender seldom proceeds; a warning is generally regarded as sufficient, provided that the offending article or articles are withdrawn and suppressed.

The advent of high-definition colour photo-copying in recent years has brought the offence of reproduction into prominence once more. The regulations have been tightened considerably and there have been several cases of successful prosecution. In each case, however, the intent deliberately to deceive the public by passing a colour photocopy as a genuine note was proved. Technically the offence takes places as soon as the photocopy is made, for whatever purpose, but as a rule only those cases in which an element of fraudulent deception subsequently arose were pursued with the full rigour of the law. The law is quite clear, however, and it is a criminal offence to make a colour photocopy or photograph of any current British note unless permission to do so has been obtained from the Treasury. The maximum penalty on conviction is an unlimited fine.

The note-issuing banks have, of course, taken steps in recent years to incorporate further security devices into their notes, notably the use of latent images and underprints in colours which are difficult, if not impossible to photocopy accurately. At the same time, the adoption of metal strips and more complex watermark devices has theoretically made the task of the forger much more difficult. If, by some unlucky chance, someone passes a dud note on to you, you must make no attempt to pass it in turn. To do so renders you liable to prosecution for uttering a forgery. Forged notes must be handed over to the police as soon as possible. If you receive a forged note in payment for goods or services you are entitled to claim its face value from the person who gave it to you. Even if the person giving you the note did not realise that it was counterfeit, it is assumed in law that he or she represented to you that the note was worth its face value at the time the note was passed. If the tenderer knew that the note was forged, he can be prosecuted; but at the end of the day he is still liable to you for the fraud and can be sued in the civil courts for the recovery of the sum involved. If, on the other hand, you received the money as a gift, you have no legal claim against the person who gave it to you. If you pay someone with a counterfeit note or coin unknowingly, you have committed no offence, but you must pay again. The degree of culpability is often difficult to prove or disprove, but it is unlikely that a prosecution would be initiated on the basis of a single note.

Legal Tender

The dictionary defines this as currency which a creditor is bound by law to accept as payment of a money debt. Debts and purchases must be paid for in cash of legal tender unless the creditor or seller is willing to accept payment in another form, such as a postal order, money order, cheque or, nowadays, credit card. Bank of England notes of any denomination are legal tender in England and Wales. Formerly Bank of England pound notes (but no other) were legal tender in Scotland. Technically, since the demise of the pound note, no Bank of England notes are legal tender in Scotland, although in practice they circulate freely north of the Border. Even more surprisingly, Scottish banknotes are not legal tender anywhere, not even in Scotland! The subtle difference is reflected in the actual wording of the promise on English and Scottish banknotes. Thus English notes are inscribed "*I promise to pay the bearer on demand the sum of . . .*" without stipulating any specific place, the promise being made by the Chief Cashier. Scottish notes, on the other hand, have the promise in the third person. It is the bank itself which makes the promise "*to pay the bearer on demand . . . pounds sterling at their head office here in Edinburgh, by order of the Board*". In practice, however, Scottish banknotes are accepted without question, not only throughout Scotland but also in parts of England, and

are generally accepted in London, although there is no obligation on the part of a creditor so to do.

Apart from gold coins, the base-metal pound coin is legal tender for payment of any amounts. So, too, presumably, are the various two-pound and five-pound base-metal coins of recent years, even though they have been struck as commemoratives and not intended for general circulation in the ordinary sense. Smaller denominations are only legal tender up to a maximum value in each case. In the case of 50p coins, 25p crowns and 20p coins, they may be used alone, or in combination with each other, in payment of amounts up to £10. 10p and 5p coins, alone or in combination, may be used for sums up to £5. Bronze 1p and 2p coins, however, can only be used for payment of amounts up to 20p. In practice, of course, you can probably get away with making payment in larger quantities (within reason!) although strictly speaking there is no obligation on the part of your creditor to accept them.

Value Added Tax

This is a matter which primarily concerns dealers, but it also applies to those who dabble in coins on a part-time basis, and has implications for collectors at all levels. Briefly, anyone conducting a business, or in self-employment, who has a turnover in excess of £43,000 per annum, must register with HM Customs and Excise for the collection and payment of Value Added Tax. Anyone whose turnover is less than £43,000 is exempt from the obligation to register, but is at liberty to register if he or she feels that this would be advantageous. It is nice to think that there is an element of choice in this, although one would be hard pressed to think why anyone would voluntarily register for VAT unless they absolutely had to! Incidentally, the government raised the VAT registration level by 40 per cent to £35,000 in March 1991 with the avowed intention of relieving a large number of businesses from this burden, at a time when the rate of tax was increased from 15 per cent to 17.5 per cent. Assuming that you are a dealer with a turnover above the magic limit, then you are committing a serious offence if you fail to register. Registration then lays you open to the full machinery of the system. You have to charge VAT on all goods and services, issuing VAT invoices and receipts and keeping detailed accounts which are liable to snap inspection at any time. You have to make quarterly returns to Customs and Excise of the amount of tax you have collected. From this you are allowed to deduct the VAT which you yourself have paid out in the course of your business, and you then have to remit the difference to the VAT collector. Of course, should the amount you have paid exceed the tax you have collected, you receive a repayment in due course. This arises in businesses which handle zero-rated goods and services, but coins and medals do not come within that category.

From January 1, 1995 the special margin scheme of accounting for VAT currently available for certain second-hand goods, such as cars, was extended to almost all second-hand goods. The scheme allows businesses buying and selling eligible goods to account for VAT only on the difference between the buying and selling prices of these items.

A special system of accounting has recently been introduced which enables some dealers to account for VAT without the need to keep a detailed record of every transaction. Certain works of art, antiques and collector's items, including "secondhand" coins, defined in Notice 712 *Second-hand goods*, were exempt from VAT at import. From January 1, 1996 these items became subject to VAT at import at an effective rate of 2.5 per cent.

Importing Coins by Mail

Elsewhere in this volume will be found the names and addresses of mints, banks and numismatic bureaux around the world from whom it may be possible to obtain currency direct. It is a wise precaution to write to these bodies in the first instance for details of their sales and distribution. In some cases they appoint a dealer in Britain as an agent and this is a method of purchase that removes a great deal of the hassle and red tape. Nowadays, however, many mints and banks are quite happy to use the credit card system to make it easy to part you from your money. The problem arises, however, when the notes are despatched. As a rule, banks and mints stipulate quite clearly that they will not accept orders prepaid in cash, and it is an offence to send coins or banknotes out of the country as payment, except through banks authorised for this purpose. Cheques drawn on British banks should not be used. Indeed, this may be actively discouraged by the imposition of heavy clearance and handling charges at the other end. The converse is also true, although Americans seem to think that dollar cheques drawn on some obscure mid-West bank will be eagerly accepted here, and are consequently aggrieved when it is tactfully pointed out to them that this creates enormous problems—to say nothing of the swingeing bank charges incurred in converting such cheques to sterling. Other than credit cards, the Girobank system is probably the best method of remitting currency from one country to another; full details may be obtained from any post office. Details on the preferred method of sending remittances, or transferring cash to another country, as well as the transmission of coins by post to different countries, will be found in the *Royal Mail International Service Guide*.

The receipt of postal packets containing banknotes from abroad makes you liable for Value Added Tax on their importation. As a rule, the despatching mint or bank will have affixed a Customs declaration to the packet, listing the contents, their weight and value, and it is on that basis that VAT will be calculated. The position regarding the import and export of coins by post is more complicated, and applies also to goods sent on approval. In such cases you must consult your Customs and Excise office who will advise you on the correct procedure and what your liabilities will be to tax in either case. This also applies to dealers taking stock out of the country to a show and then re-importing the unsold stock afterwards, or importing material purchased at the show.

Buying and Selling

When goods are sold, the seller and the buyer enter into a contract which confers rights and imposes obligations on both parties. The contract need not be in writing. There is no law governing the quality of goods sold by a private individual. If you purchase a coin from a fellow-collector as a result of an informal meeting at the local numismatic society it is incumbent on you to ensure that what you buy is what you think you are buying. If you purchase something from a dealer or shopkeeper, however, you are entitled under the Sale of Goods Act to goods of "merchantable quality" which means that they must be reasonably fit for their purpose. Items sold under a specific description, on the other hand, must correspond exactly with that description. If they do not, the seller *even a private individual* can be sued under the Sale of Goods Act. This is an important distinction because there is an erroneous notion that the Act does not apply to transactions between private individuals. If A sells a coin to B, purporting it to be a rare date, and B subsequently discovers that the date has been deliberately altered, then B can sue A. Even if A claims that he made the sale in good faith, believing the coin to be a genuine rare date, he will still be liable for restitution (giving B his money back) and may also face a claim for damages. The Sale of Goods Act thus overturns the traditional adage *caveat emptor* which, in its full formula, translates as "let the buyer beware for he ought not to be ignorant of the nature of the property which he is buying from another party". Traditionally this was the maxim applicable at auctions. Once the auctioneer's gavel had dropped, the successful bidder had, in effect, made a contract with the vendor and was bound to pay for the lot, even if he subsequently discovered that what he had purchased was not what he had imagined. The view was that it was up to the purchaser to ensure beforehand that what he purchased was genuine and answered the description in the sale catalogue.

Because of vexatious disputes arising from questions of authenticity, and with the Sale of Goods Act breathing down their necks, many auctioneers now have a safety net, in the form of extensions. These enable successful bidders to delay payment for two or three weeks while they seek expertisation of doubtful material. In other words, the law allows a cooling-off period, but only for the legitimate purpose of verifying the authenticity of items over which there may be some doubt. This is only operative in cases where a coin or medal is sold as genuine, and described and estimated in value accordingly. In many doubtful cases, however, an auctioneer will cover himself by adding the crucial words "as is" to the description of a lot. Then, indeed, it is a case of *caveat emptor*. The auctioneer has done everything humanly possible to draw attention to the controversial nature of the item, and it must then rest on the judgment of the purchaser.

On the subject of auctions there are legal aspects which are not always apparent, as well as subtle differences in law and practice between England and Scotland. These tend to arise in cases where coins and medals come up for sale at provincial general mixed auctions, rather than in the sales conducted by numismatic auctioneers. Goods up for auction may be subject to an upset price which is made public as the price at which the bidding will start. A reserve price, on the other hand, is known only to the auctioneer, and if it is not reached, the goods will not be sold. Upset prices are common in Scotland, reserve prices in England. If no upset price is specified and the goods are not subject to a reserve price then the highest bid secures them, even though it may not be as high as the vendor hoped for. If a seller notifies other bidders that he is bidding for his own goods, or that he has employed an agent to bid for him, the bidding is legal. If he does not give notice and bids himself, or gets someone to bid for him, thus forcing up the price, the sale is fraudulent, and the buyer can purchase the goods for the amount of the last bid he made before fraudulent bidding started.

One frequently hears dark, but usually apocryphal, tales of "the ring" in action to depress the bidding and secure items below the price commensurate with their actual value. This is a fraudulent practice and in law is regarded as a criminal conspiracy. In practice, however, it would be very difficult for a group of dealers or other individuals to keep the bidding down merely by sitting on their hands. This practice could only operate successfully in sales which were largely, if not entirely, frequented by dealers. But coin sales, like other specialist collector-orientated auctions, are characterised by a high proportion of private bidders in attendance. Any conspiracy by a ring would merely allow some private bidder to step in and secure the lot at a bargain price. Rings are illegal, but in practice prosecutions are very rare as it is extremely difficult to obtain proof of their operations. What is more likely to happen is that dealers have been known to act in concert to force up the bidding to frighten off some unwelcome interloper. Here again, such tales are legion, but astonishingly lacking in specific details. The golden rule in attending auctions is to know what you are going after, and to have a pretty precise idea of how much you are prepared to pay. Do not be stampeded in the heat of the moment into going way beyond your limit.

Taxation of Profits on Disposal

The Inland Revenue define an asset as "any form of property (other than sterling) wherever situated". A disposal includes a sale, exchange or gift of an asset, or the receipt of a capital sum in respect of them. In layman's terms you dispose of an asset when you sell it, give it away, exchange it or lose it. A transfer of assets between husband and wife doesn't count (unless they are legally separated), nor does the transfer of an asset you leave when you die. If a disposal results in a profit you could be liable to tax. Any profit made on the sale of certain assets, including coins, medals and other collectables, constitutes a capital gain and is subject to Capital Gains Tax (CGT) which is now charged at the same 25% and 40% rates as income tax. However the government allows you to make a total capital gain

in the current tax year of £5,500 before tax becomes chargeable. If this is the case, and the total proceeds from disposal do not exceed £10,000, then a simple declaration to this effect is all you need to make in the relevant section of your annual tax return.

Computing the actual capital gain is a complicated matter. Suppose you purchased a banknote in 1960 for £5,000 and sold it in 1993 for £12,000. On the face of it, you've made a capital gain of £7,000 and you might think that you were liable to CGT because the gain was over £5,500. However, the *length of time* you've held the asset also has to be taken into consideration. From April 6, 1988 the law was altered so that only gains made after March 31, 1982 are now taxable. In effect, you are taxed as if you acquired the coin on March 31, 1982. The initial value of the coin is deemed to be its market value at that date. If the gain from March 1982 to the time of disposal is greater than the overall gain from acquisition in 1960 to disposal in 1993, you take the lesser of the two figures. If this produces a gain, whereas the old method of working it out would have produced a loss, you will be regarded, for tax purposes, as having made neither a gain nor a loss on disposal. You have a choice of opting for computing from the time of actual acquisition or from March 1982, whichever seems the more advantageous; but once you've made your choice you cannot subsequently change your mind.

How do you establish what the coin was worth in March 1982? The Inland Revenue tend to regard Seaby, Krause or other relevant catalogues as their yardstick. The difference between the nominal or catalogue value in 1982 and what you eventually got for the coin *assuming that the latter was greater,* might be regarded as the capital gain, but even then the position is complicated by inflation in the intervening years eroding the real value of the coin.

At this stage things get really complicated as you have to work out the indexation allowance. This is determined by the Retail Prices Index (RPI), and you need to know the RPI for (a) the month of disposal, and (b) the month in which you acquired the asset, or March 1982, if later. The RPI is announced each month by the Departmenrt of Employment and is published in its *Employment Gazette* which ought to be available in your local public library. Take the RPI for the month of the disposal and subtract the RPI for the month when indexation commenced. Then divide the result by the RPI for the month when indexation began, and work out this figure to the nearest third decimal place. This is known as the indexation factor, which you then multiply by the initial value of your coin. Simple isn't it? In most cases, however, I expect you will have made a capital loss in real terms, so these sums, though necessary to satisfy the Inland Revenue, are largely academic.

If you have enjoyed this publication why not visit our secure website to view our other titles as well as a sample download of our monthly magazine Coin News (12-page Banknote Section featured every month).

A hard copy catalogue is also available—for your free copy of our Collector's Choice catalogue write to

Token Publishing Ltd, Orchard House, Duchy Road, Heathpark, Honiton, Devon EX14 1YD Tel: 01404 46972 email:info@tokenpublishing.com

For all your collecting needs. . .

visit tokenpublishing.com

INDEX TO ADVERTISERS